Reputational Risk Management Financial Institutions

Reputational Risk Management in Financial Institutions

Edited by Thomas Kaiser and Petra Merl

Published by Risk Books, a Division of Incisive Media Investments Ltd

Incisive Media
32–34 Broadwick Street
London W1A 2HG
Tel: +44(0) 20 7316 9000
E-mail: books@incisivemedia.com
Sites: www.riskbooks.com
www.incisivemedia.com

© 2014 Incisive Media

ISBN 978 1 78272 101 7

British Library Cataloguing in Publication Data
A catalogue record for this book is available from the British Library

Publisher: Nick Carver
Commissioning Editor: Sarah Hastings
Managing Editor: Lewis O'Sullivan
Editorial Development: Alice Levick
Designer: Lisa Ling
Copyeditor: Laurie Donaldson

Typeset by Mark Heslington Ltd, Scarborough, North Yorkshire
Printed and bound in the UK by PrintonDemand-Worldwide

Conditions of sale
All rights reserved. No part of this publication may be reproduced in any material form whether by photocopying or storing in any medium by electronic means whether or not transiently or incidentally to some other use for this publication without the prior written consent of the copyright owner except in accordance with the provisions of the Copyright, Designs and Patents Act 1988 or under the terms of a licence issued by the Copyright Licensing Agency Limited of Saffron House, 6–10 Kirby Street, London EC1N 8TS, UK.

Warning: the doing of any unauthorised act in relation to this work may result in both civil and criminal liability.

Every effort has been made to ensure the accuracy of the text at the time of publication, this includes efforts to contact each author to ensure the accuracy of their details at publication is correct. However, no responsibility for loss occasioned to any person acting or refraining from acting as a result of the material contained in this publication will be accepted by the copyright owner, the editor, the authors or Incisive Media.

Many of the product names contained in this publication are registered trade marks, and Risk Books has made every effort to print them with the capitalisation and punctuation used by the trademark owner. For reasons of textual clarity, it is not our house style to use symbols such as TM, ®, etc. However, the absence of such symbols should not be taken to indicate absence of trademark protection; anyone wishing to use product names in the public domain should first clear such use with the product owner.

While best efforts have been intended for the preparation of this book, neither the publisher, the editor nor any of the potentially implicitly affiliated organisations accept responsibility for any errors, mistakes and or omissions it may provide or for any losses howsoever arising from or in reliance upon its information, meanings and interpretations by any parties.

Contents

About the Editors ix
About the Authors xi
Introduction xix

PART 1: REPUTATION AND REPUTATIONAL RISK MANAGEMENT

1 Reputational Risk: A Short Introduction 3
  David Shirreff

2 What History Teaches Bankers about Reputation Management 11
  Richard J. Parsons

3 An Asset–Liability View of Banks' Reputation 21
  Sergio Scandizzo
  European Investment Bank, Luxembourg

4 Reputational Risk in the Universe of Risks: Boundary Issues 37
  Hema Parekh

5 Corporate Governance Changes Following Reputational Damage in the Financial Industry 49
  Ahmed Barakat
  Nottingham University
  Business School, UK

PART 2: METHODOLOGIES AND PROCESSES FOR MANAGING REPUTATIONAL RISK

6 Reputational Risk and Prudential Regulation 73
  Mattia L. Rattaggi
  UBS

7	Managing Stakeholder Expectations *Sandra Dow* Middlebury College	85
8	Environmental and Social Risks from the Perspective of Reputational Risk *Nina Roth and Olivier Jaeggi* UBS and ECOFACT	111
9	The Relationship between Reputational Risk Management and Business Continuity *Alexander Klotz, Tibor Konya; Abtin Maghrour* UniCredit Bank AG; Transfer of Innovative and Integrative Management Solutions (tiim)	129
10	Tracking Reputation and the Management of Perception at UniCredit *Armin Herla* UniCredit	145

PART 3: BEST-PRACTICE EXAMPLES

11	Successful Recovery from Reputational Crises: Legitimate versus Illegitimate Risk Case Studies *Steffen Bunnenberg* Bunnenberg Bertram Rechtsanwaelte	157
12	Reputational Risk Management Across the World: A Survey of Current Practices *Thomas Kaiser* KPMG in Germany and Goethe University, Frankfurt	185
13	Governance as the Starting Point for a Reputational Risk-Management Process *Carsten Steinhoff and Rainer Sprengel* Norddeutsche Landesbank and Portigon Financial Services	205

14	**Managing Reputational Risk in a Major European Banking Group** *Davide Bazzarello* UniCredit	**227**
15	**The Implementation of the UniCredit Group Approach** *Thomas Beil* UniCredit Bank AG	**245**
16	**Promotional Banks: An Introduction to Reputational Risk Management** *Heidi Rudolph* KfW Bankengruppe	**269**
17	**Reputational Risk Management in a Global Insurance Company** *Claudia Meyer and Maurice LeBlanc* Allianz SE	**281**
18	**Reputational Consequence Management: The Future** *Mike Finlay* RiskBusiness International Limited	**299**
	Index	**313**

About the Editors

Thomas Kaiser has been working in the risk-management profession for more than 15 years. Through membership in several international and German banking organisations, he has been closely involved in the creation of the operational risk rules of the Basel II accord and their interpretation. Kaiser is a director with the financial risk-management practice at KPMG, and is responsible for operational and reputational risk-management consulting projects across the globe. Kaiser is also honorary professor at Goethe University in Frankfurt, teaching risk management at graduate and executive level. He holds a master's degree in business administration from Saarbrücken University and a PhD in financial econometrics from Tübingen University. Kaiser is also a professional member of the Institute of Operational Risk and a member of its German chapter's inner circle.

Petra Merl has been working in the risk-management profession for more than 15 years. Her career includes various roles in risk control, most of which were focused on counterparty and market risk control. She worked for Commerzbank AG and was head of market risk in HypoVereinsbank AG, Milan. She joined the OpRisk community in 2011 and implemented the Reputational Risk Framework in HypoVereinsbank AG in 2012. Merl is a first vice president with HypoVereinsbank AG, is responsible for operational and reputational risk control in Unicredit Bank AG and has functional authority over all divisional operational risk managers in the AMA subgroup. Here responsibility encompasses governance, qualitative and quantitative aspects of those risk types. Together with Thomas Kaiser, she has started a regular exchange of reputational risk management professionals of major German banks and insurance companies, which has also resulted in publications and conference presentations. Petra holds a Diploma in mathematics and business administration from University of Regensburg. She is a professional member of the Institute of Operational Risk and a member of the German chapter's inner circle. Petra is a subject matter expert in PRIMIA's advisory group for reputational risk.

About the Authors

Ahmed Barakat works as an assistant professor in risk management and is a member of the Centre for Risk, Banking and Financial Services at Nottingham University Business School. He has written several research papers on risk management, corporate governance, banking, insurance and financial reporting quality. He previously worked as a postdoctoral research associate in accounting and finance at Lancaster University, a research assistant in banking and finance at Goethe University, Frankfurt, where he obtained his doctoral degree, and assistant lecturer in accounting and auditing at Ain Shams University, where he received his master's and bachelor's degrees.

Davide Bazzarello works in the Group Risk Management at Unicredit, and is responsible for group operational and reputational risk. He joined Unicredit in September 2000, working on financial risks on trading as well as banking books. Bazzarello began his career as an analyst in the Treasury Department at Banca Popolare Commercio e Industria. He holds an MSc in financial markets from Bocconi University in Milan.

Thomas Beil works in the UniCredit Bank AG, Munich, and is responsible for reputational risk control. He completed a banking apprenticeship in 1978, began studying economics in Munich in 1982 and joined UniCredit in 1987 as a business graduate. Since then, he has held responsibilities in various executive positions, mainly in credit risk management.

Steffen Bunnenberg is a founding partner of the law firm Bunnenberg Bertram in Berlin. He has advised companies on reputational crises for many years, calling on a long consulting practice in personal rights. He received a doctorate from the University of Freiburg in Breisgau, Germany. Bunnenberg worked previously with the press chamber of the regional court of Berlin and the press and information office of the German government, as well as in an internationally known law firm, which specialised in press and entertainment law. He is one of the authors of the Handbook for personal rights.

Sandra Dow is professor of finance and chair of the Fisher MBA Program at the Monterey Institute of International Studies, a graduate school of Middlebury College. Her research and teaching interests lie in the management of extra-financial risk. She has published extensively in these areas and has presented her work at major scholarly conferences worldwide. Dow has been active in executive education in North America and Europe. She holds a PhD in finance from Concordia University in Montreal.

Mike Finlay is chief executive of RiskBusiness International Limited, a global risk advisory business founded in 2003 and staffed by ex-market practitioners. He previously held positions in banking operations, global payments and derivative trading. Finlay is a frequent lecturer for the Bank of International Settlements and a visiting lecturer at Judge Business School, Cambridge. He is also the vice-chair of the Institute of Operational Risk.

Armin Herla is head of service and stakeholder intelligence (S&SI) at UniCredit. His team's mission is to deliver a comprehensive view on the perception of HVB with all relevant stakeholder groups by measuring analysing and reporting. Furthermore, S&SI is the main complaint office of Unicredit Bank and has the task of developing and running initiatives in order to improve customer satisfaction as well as to support the network to work efficiently on customer-satisfaction improvements.

Olivier Jaeggi, prior to founding ECOFACT in 1998, worked in credit risk control at UBS, where he was in charge of managing environmental risks. He graduated in environmental engineering from the Swiss Federal Institute of Technology, Zurich, and has completed executive education programmes at Harvard Business School and at the University of Oxford. He is a member of PRMIA's subject-matter expert advisory group on reputational risk and, since 2012, has contributed to the annual sustainability report produced by the MIT

Sloan Management Review in collaboration with the Boston Consulting Group. He is also a regular contributor to the sustainability blog of the MIT Sloan Management Review.

Alexander Klotz has more than 25 years' operative and strategic experience in protecting people, assets and information – leveraging on a widespread international network of security professionals and law-enforcement contacts. Since 1997, Klotz has worked for several international companies in corporate security management, covering the fields of physical security, business continuity and crisis management, information security and security intelligence. Since 2011 he has been chief security officer at the UniCredit Bank AG, and is also a board member of the German Competence Centre against Cybercrime and a Member of the International Security Management Association. He holds a master's degree in educational sciences and sociology.

Tibor Konya joined the private sector in 2007 after working in the armed forces, beginning at Daimler AG in security management with the focus on international security management, enabling business in high-risk countries. He has wide experience in business continuity and crisis management, information security, security intelligence and international security management. Konya joined the UniCredit Bank AG in 2012 as head of business continuity/crisis management and strategic security. He is a founding member of the German Competence Centre against Cybercrime. Konya holds a master's degree in economics.

Maurice LeBlanc is a senior risk manager and works in the operational and reputational risk management team of Allianz Group. Previously, he spent seven years working in Boston and Munich for KPMG, with a focus on insurance and asset management clients. LeBlanc holds degrees in economics and accounting.

Abtin Maghrour has more than 10 years' experience in international trading with the focus on pharmaceuticals and commodities. He joined the financial sector in 2010 as a management consultant, and has supported his clients since then within several diverse international projects. Maghrour has expert knowledge in business continuity and crisis management, risk management and process management. He holds a master's degree in strategy and marketing and an MSc in science and technology, policy and management from the University of Edinburgh.

Claudia Meyer is global head of operational and reputational risk management at Allianz Group. Before that, she worked as global head of enterprise risk management in Allianz Asset Management AG (AGI and PIMCO). In 15 years of working for HypoVereinsbank/Unicredit she was, besides being a branch manager, working as a project manager for the implementation of new processes and systems in the retail and wealth-management business. She was also leading the operational risk project for Basel II AMA approval. Meyer holds a master's degree in business administration and economics.

Hema Parekh is a risk specialist in the Risk Advisory Division of the Federal Reserve Bank of Richmond. Her focus areas include Basel II AMA as co-lead for the Basel II qualification team, as well as operational risk management, including model risk, third-party risk, governance and new-product risk. Her other areas of focus include resolution planning and model risk management. As co-chair of the qualification team, Parekh co-leads the FR system and interagency subject-matter experts in supervising the work of Basel II mandatory firms. Before joining Richmond Fed in 2011, Parekh worked as a consultant. She also worked at a G-SIFI firm for many years. She gained an MBA from Emory University, USA, and a master's in economics and finance from Bombay University.

Richard J. Parsons is the author of *Broke: America's Banking System*, published in 2013 by the Risk Management Association. Prior to writing and speaking about the banking industry, Parsons spent more than 31 years at Bank of America/Merrill Lynch, where he was an executive vice president and member of the Management Operating Committee. He is a frequent contributor to the *RMA Journal* and the *American Banker*. In October 2013, the *Wall Street Journal* published his op-ed, "Sending a Bad Message to Big Banks". Parsons has a BA in history from Ohio Wesleyan University and an MBA from the University of Virginia Darden School of Business.

Mattia L. Rattaggi holds a PhD in economic theory from the University of Fribourg, where he also worked for several years as a teaching assistant in economic history, history of economic thought and political economy. He pursued postdoctoral research at the University of Cambridge (UK), specialising in economic methodology and in Keynes's writings. Before joining UBS in 1999, he headed asset and liability management in the treasury of Zürcher Kantonalbank, and worked as a senior economist with the Swiss Bankers' Association. He is currently managing director and head of regulatory relations at UBS. Prior to his current role, he occupied senior positions within Risk Control and Compliance at UBS.

Nina Roth is an environmental and social risk (ESR) manager. With a background in political science, she started her career in Deutsche Bank's Corporate Social Responsibility Department, where she was responsible for reporting and the bank's sustainability ratings. She developed the bank's first ESR and reputational risk framework, which focused on controversial weapons, nuclear power and agribusiness, as well as engaging with non-governmental organisations. Roth is the global ESR programme manager for UBS, where she is in charge of ESR assessments for the investment bank. She is also developing the bank's ESR client-engagement strategy. In addition, Roth represents UBS in the Roundtable for Sustainable Palm Oil, where she co-chairs the Financial Institutions Task Force and is a member of the Complaints Panel.

Heidi Rudolph works for KfW Group in Germany, and is head of operational risk controlling and business continuity management. In addition, she is responsible for reputational risk management at KfW. Rudolph joined KfW in October 2012, having spent three years at Deutsche Börse Group working in operational risk and BCM. She began her career as an audit consultant at Mazars Group.

Sergio Scandiszo is the author of *Risk and Governance: A Framework for Banking Organisations*; *The Operational Risk Manager's Guide*, now in its second edition; and *Validation and Use Test in AMA*. All were published by Risk Books. He was also a contributing author to the award-winning Risk Books title *Advanced Measurement Approach to Operational Risk*. Scandiszo is also associate editor of the *Journal of*

Operational Risk and the author of several journal papers on fuzzy logic, genetic algorithms and risk management. He is currently head of model validation at the European Investment Bank in Luxembourg, before which he was a principal in the London office of PricewaterhouseCoopers and, before that, a senior manager of the Operational Risk Group at the Canadian Imperial Bank of Commerce in Toronto. He holds degrees in computer science and finance.

David Shirreff has written on business and finance for various international publications for several decades, most recently for *The Economist* (2001–14). He published *Dealing with Financial Risk* (Profile Books) in 2004 and, as an antidote to reporting on recent financial crises, he has written three musicals, *Broke Britannia!* (2009), *EuroCrash!* (2011) and *Barack and the Beanstalk* (2013). A more serious work, *Don't Start from Here*, calling for more radical bank reform, was published in 2014.

Rainer Sprengel is head of operational risk management and risk reporting/policies at Portigon Financial Services (formerly WestLB AG), having 20 years' experience in both risk management and project management globally. He studied business administration at the University of Göttingen. As project head for the AMA implementation, he contributed to WestLB's successful AMA approval in 2008. Sprengel is member of the OpRisk working groups of both BaFin/Bundesbank and the VöB (German Association of Public Banks). Within ORX (Operational Riskdata Exchange Association), he was a member in the Scenario Working Group. Further to this, he is a lecturer for the Frankfurt School of Finance and a member (professional) of the Institute of Operational Risk.

Carsten Steinhoff is head of the Operational Risk Control Department at NORD/LB, Hanover. He studied bank management and controlling at the University of Göttingen in Germany. After working with a bank in Italy, he moved to NORD/LB, where he followed an on-the-job PhD programme. His thesis was on Operational Risk Quantification, with a focus on scenarios within LDA models. Before taking charge of the Operational Risk Control Department, Steinhoff created NORD/LB's internal OpRisk model and was engaged in the foundation of the German loss data bases DakOR and ÖffSchOR. His current research interest focuses on the development of holistic OpRisk management frameworks, stress-testing environments and reputational risk topics.

Introduction
Thomas Kaiser and Petra Merl

Reputational risk – or RepRisk – is an emerging topic in the universe of risks. On the one hand, reputation is a key asset for every institution, every corporation and every bank. It is the basis for trust, customer and employee loyalty, business partnerships, transaction volume and ultimately earnings. On the other hand, during the financial crises the reputation of all banks suffered across the whole industry. That is why reputation seems to be regarded as an ever more important and fragile asset. Financial institutions have governance structures, methods and processes in place that deal with improving reputation and at least some aspects of keeping reputation, such as public-relations departments, marketing departments, issue-management processes, crisis communication processes and so forth. While those approaches have their merits, managing reputation without systematically identifying, assessing, reporting, managing and monitoring the risks threatening it generally does not lead to an efficient institutional set-up.

Thus some of the major financial institutions have started to implement methods and processes for dealing with the issue of reputation as a risk discipline with a dedicated management process around it. According to the editors' experience, this was often facilitated by senior management's keen interest in the management of reputational risk. Additionally, regulators have begun to develop an interest in reputational risk. While global regulation (such as the publications of the Basel Committee on Banking Supervision and the Financial Stability Board) touch upon that topic in only a high-level and/or fragmented manner, single regulators have begun to establish more comprehensive rules (see the Reputation Risk

Guidelines issued by the Hong Kong Monetary Authority in 2009 as well as the draft guidelines CP 14 on the supervisory review and evaluation process issued by the European Banking Authority in July 2014). Even in the absence of dedicated rules for reputational risk management, regulators have started to investigate how banks deal with that topic under the umbrella of Pillar II audits. Such audits increasingly result in observations and findings that in turn trigger additional investment into the management and mitigation of this risk.

Taking into consideration the specific situation of the financial services industry as well as the regulatory framework described above, the following goals for reputational risk management can be established. The primary objective of reputational risk management naturally is to prevent damaging events from happening and to mitigate the impact of events that have already occurred. The set-up of the framework to accommodate those two dimensions has to take into account regulatory requirements as a constraint. It turns out that, when designing such a reputational risk-management framework, even the most fundamental methodological questions such as "Is it a risk type in its own right or just a consequential risk?" and "Is it risk management, communication, compliance or some other department that is responsible for coordinating activities around reputational risk?" are being answered fairly differently by different banks.

The editors of this book started an initiative to foster an exchange of ideas on these and related topics among major German banks and insurance companies (the RepRisk-Forum) in early 2012. A number of contributors to this book were recruited from that group. In the majority of cases, operational risk-management departments are already, or are on their way to becoming, in charge of reputational risk management. The RepRisk Forum has been linked to the Institute of Operational Risk (IOR) in order to facilitate the further development of the topic.

It appears that reputational risk is an even more difficult topic to deal with than operational risk, which in turn most practitioners find more difficult than market and credit risk to contend with. This view is based on a number of factors. Besides the fact that reputational risk management is a fairly new discipline (with a maturity level similar to that of operational risk management in the late 1990s), the abundance of cause–effect relationships with other risk types, as well as the difficulty to identify and quantify reputational risk in a comprehensive manner, contribute to this sense of difficulty.

This book is a contribution to the evolution of reputational risk management as a new risk discipline, providing answers and solutions to the questions and quandaries raised above. It is organised as follows.

The section titled "Reputation and Reputational Risk Management" establishes the context and background to the topic. "Reputational Risk: A Short Introduction" by David Shirreff provides evidence of major reputational risk events in the past and present. Rick Parsons has a look at "What History Teaches Bankers about Reputation Management", comparing the importance of reputation throughout two millennia and reflecting on the banking situation as it stands in 2014. "An Asset–Liability View of Banks' Reputation" is then taken by Sergio Scandizzo, who examines the development of the reputation of a bank during the post-crisis years via the creation of a reputational balance sheet. Hema Parekh's chapter deals with "Reputational Risk in the Universe of Risks: Boundary Issues". She demonstrates the various interconnections between RepRisk and other risk types. Finally Ahmed Barakat has a look at "Corporate Governance Changes Following Reputational Damage", which is an empirical study of the way in which companies deal with reputational crises by changing governance structures.

The next section looks at the "Methodologies and Processes for Managing Reputational Risk", investigating the key elements of a reputational risk process. Mattia Rattagi lays the groundwork by looking at "Reputational Risk and Prudential Regulation". He describes and analyses global and European regulatory approaches to reputational risk. "Managing Stakeholder Expectations" is the topic of Sandra Dow's contribution. She presents the results of her examination into the performance of financial services firms by looking at observable factors relevant for the various stakeholders involved. Nina Roth and Olivier Jaeggi look at "Environmental and Social Risks from the Perspective of Reputational Risk". They establish these risks as important components of a sound reputational risk-management framework. "The Relationship between Reputational Risk Management and Business Continuity" is discussed by Alexander Klotz, Tibor Konya and Abtin Maghrour. They demonstrate why business continuity is an important factor for the reputation of banks, as it requires a comprehensive management process. Armin Herla's topic is "Reputation and Management of Perception at UniCredit ". He outlines UniCredit Bank's approach to assessing its reputation through the polling of various stakeholder groups. The section concludes with the chapter titled "Successful Recovery from Reputational Crises: Legitimate versus Illegitimate Risk Case Studies" by Steffen Bunnenberg, in which the author provides insights into the various forms of claims made and the subsequent response of the banks involved.

Thomas Kaiser kicks off the final section titled "Best-Practice Examples" with "Reputational Risk Management across the World: A Survey of Current Practices", in which he compares the results of a global study on the status of reputational risk management in banks with the results of a similar study of German banks. Carsten Steinhoff and Rainer Sprengel establish "Governance as the Starting Point for a Reputational Risk-Management Process", demonstrating which governance structures are required for an efficient reputational risk framework. "Managing Reputational Risk in a Major European Banking Group" is the title of the contribution by Davide Bazzarello. He outlines how UniCredit Group contends with reputational risk at group level and how this is rolled out in various subsidiaries. "The Implementation of the Unicredit Group Approach", written by Thomas Beil, outlines the implementation methodology undertaken by UniCredit Bank at a local level. Heidi Rudolph's chapter – "Reputational Risk in Promotional Banks" – demonstrates why reputational risk is somewhat different for promotional banks and the way in which they are managed. As an example of a non-bank approach, Claudia Meyer provides insight into "Managing Reputational Risk in a Global Insurance Company", in which she outlines the reputational risk framework of an international insurance organisation. Mike Finlay concludes the book with his view on "Reputational Consequence Management: The Future".

Reputational Risk Management in Financial Institutions aims at further developing the discipline of reputational risk management. After digesting the book, readers will find it (even more) evident that there is no unique solution to establishing such a framework. No matter what the framework looks like in detail, it requires a solid risk culture, close links to the business model in question, cooperation between various divisions of the company, the specific, dedicated consideration of the expectations and concerns of individual stakeholders, and many more aspects. A continued, open exchange of ideas between interested parties will help shape governance structures, methods and processes that not only allow financial services firms to cope with regulatory requirements, but actually add value to the company.

Part 1

Reputation and Reputational Risk Management

1

Reputational Risk: A Short Introduction

David Shirreff

Loss of reputation can kill a bank. It may not happen overnight, but, unless prompt and comprehensive action is taken, the damage takes hold and is soon irreversible. Let us look at two examples from ancient history.

NatWest Markets was the investment-banking arm of NatWest (now part of the Royal Bank of Scotland – RBS). In 1997 the investment bankers suffered severe losses in long-term interest-rate derivatives because of poor risk management. The way the news came out, and the poor response of senior managers to a clear loss of reputation, resulted in the closure of the investment bank, and, within three years, the sale of NatWest to RBS.

Union Bank of Switzerland (not to be confused with today's UBS) prided itself on being one of the top global investment banks. Also in 1997, it misjudged the risk on long-term equity derivatives and ran up losses of around US$1 billion. The entire risk-management culture of the firm was below standard and failed to adjust sufficiently and convincingly following the loss. Within months the bank was taken over by its smaller rival, Swiss Bank Corporation. The merged bank was renamed UBS.

These are extreme cases. Usually banks that take a hit to their reputation can carry on their business. The loss in terms of forgone revenue is hard to quantify. But the risk to its reputation is ignored at a bank's peril. Several global banks today are experiencing the impact on their bottom line of having persistently ignored the potential danger of years of putting profits first, reputation second.

The value of reputation is not a new concept in banking.

Prestigious buildings, smart suits and polite behaviour were all designed to distinguish members of the banking profession from less trustworthy businesses. But the concept of risk management, which grew up in the trading room, particularly in derivatives, rather than in bank boardrooms and client suites, concentrated more on calculating the risks that were quantifiable, such as market and credit risk, than on emphasising the softer behavioural issues that can have a much longer-term impact on the profitability and even survival of a bank.

A book on risk management (Goldman Sachs and SBC Warburg Dillon Read 1998), written by two of the firms reckoned at the time to be among the smartest in the business, identified six risks that threatened financial institutions, including operational risk and legal risk. It added a possible seventh, "reputational risk", noting that this risk was not among the categories identified in 1994 by the Basel Committee on Banking Supervision, the global arbiter of capital requirements for banks.

Reputational risk, says the book, "is the risk that any action taken by a firm or its employees creates a negative perception in the external market place. Companies increasingly recognise the overriding significance of this risk, which can arise as a result of problems in almost any part of a business, and as a result of any number of risk factors, but can have an impact on a company's standing and its business far in excess of the initial problem."

In fact, a joint group of banks, securities and insurance regulators did mention reputational risk in a paper on the supervision of conglomerates (Tripartite Group of Bank, Securities and Insurance Regulators 1995). But its assumption was that the risk would arise by contagion through ownership by another commercial or industrial group, not within the hallowed institution itself.

Unfortunately, the notion of a severe and insidious risk to its reputation, which lurks at the heart of every financial institution, mostly received only lip service during the following decade. Risk management, until very recently, was regarded as a skill that helps a bank to profits and gives it an edge over the competition.

The idea that a financial institution can aspire be world-class, yet still seek to rationalise the dodgy behaviour of a few rogues in its ranks, is still not truly dead. Witness the defence of his bank by Brady Dougan, chief executive of Credit Suisse, before a hearing of the US Senate Subcommittee on Investigations in February 2014. Mr Dougan complained that "Swiss-based private bankers went to great lengths to disguise their bad conduct from Credit Suisse executive management." Or, similarly, the ill-judged performance of Bob Diamond, former chief executive of Barclays, before a British parliamentary select committee in July 2012: he blamed the bank's manipulation of Libor interest rates on a handful of people, yet still insisted that Barclays itself was a fantastic institution. "I worry that the world looks at Barclays and a small group of traders, or a group of traders, who had reprehensible behaviour, and that that is being put on Barclays in a way that is not representative of the firm that I love so much," he said.

Reputation cannot, or should not, be compartmentalised in this way. Unfortunately, the devolution of banks, particularly investment banks, into a collection of fiefs or even individuals with their own profit centre and risk–reward profile has fuelled the dangerous notion that the parts matter as much as the institution.

That culture has infected at least one generation of high-flying bankers. Correcting the error, if it is correctable, will take at least another generation.

It seems almost incredible now that a global investment bank would risk jeopardising its reputation for the sake of a few million in profits. But that is what happened consistently during the past decade.

Take Deutsche Bank, one of the top ten in many capital-market disciplines. In the middle of last decade it sold dozens of financial products to unsophisticated customers, which were far too complex and risky to be understood properly either by the customer or even by the bank's own salesman. Chief of these products was an interest-rate swap known as a CMS ladder swap, which obliged the customer, usually a municipality or small company, to make payments according to a deceptively harmless-looking formula. If the prevailing interest rate moved outside a narrow band, the customer faced a steeply increasing rate of repayment. If the prevailing interest rate stayed inside the band Deutsche Bank had the option to terminate the contract. It was an instrument horribly loaded in Deutsche Bank's favour, as several court cases in Germany revealed.

Such was the culture at Deutsche Bank at the time that it preferred to face each court action as it came, rather than settle out of court with the customer or a whole group of customers. It knew that new claims could not be brought after three years had elapsed since the transaction was signed. Of course it is true that the customers were also to blame for entering a contract that they didn't fully understand. But in most cases Deutsche Bank had an implicit, in some cases explicit, duty of care to sell an appropriate instrument to its not fully sophisticated customer.

It took the financial crisis, changes at the top of the bank, threats of widespread litigation and a steep fall in profits to make Deutsche Bank more careful of its reputation. In February 2014 Deutsche Bank decided to settle a 12-year running battle with the descendants of Leo Kirch, for a reported €900 million. The dispute centred on whether ill-judged remarks in 2002 by Rolf Breuer, the bank's chief executive, had helped to push Mr Kirch's media empire into bankruptcy.

Blaming a reputational blow on an individual, especially a rogue trader, doesn't cut much ice these days. Nick Leeson took the rap for the crash of Barings in 1995, but investigations showed that the British merchant bank's risk managers were unable or unwilling to dig too deeply into a futures-trading operation in Singapore that seemed so profitable. Similarly, Société Générale gave Jerome Kerviel star-trader status, but failed to question the system that was supporting his trades. The list of rogue traders is long. The reputation of those banks that harboured them has seldom bounced back.

There is a wonderful German phrase, *"kriminelle Energie"* which is often used by companies to explain fraud committed within their ranks. How could fraud possibly be detected when it was a matter of "criminal energy"? Criminal energy can truly thrive only in an institution that is careless about its reputation.

But very often not even criminal energy is required. Take Britain's home-grown embarrassment, the collapse of Northern Rock in August 2007, which turned out to be a failure not only of risk managers and the bank's leadership, but of supervision – with not a rogue trader in sight. The bank had been piling on mortgage assets with apparently no upper limit, because it was securitising and selling the loans as fast as it was making them. In June that year, a couple of months ahead of Northern Rock's crash, its supervisor, the Financial Services Authority (FSA), was so content with its business model that it actually encouraged expanded use of its capital base. So who was to blame when the balloon went up? The salesmen on the front line? Their management? The supervisor? Or was it the Bank of England's obstinate refusal to provide the bank with liquidity? That triggered a classic bank run, with depositors queuing outside branches for their money. The FSA managed to salvage some of its reputation by launching an unflinching internal inquiry and striving strenuously to ensure it was not caught napping again. Ironically, this hard-hitting report came out only months before the next hammer blow, when RBS and a bevy of other banks had to be bailed out. Mervyn King, the Bank of England governor, survived for another six years – probably because of fears that his resignation would have damaged confidence further.

The scandal of payment protection insurance (PPI), which pervaded the British high street banking scene for more than a decade, shows that reputational damage can afflict an entire sector. It turned out that customers of many high street banks were often involuntarily charged a premium to insure them against inability to pay their bills. In many cases the insurance was completely superfluous; in many others it did not actually offer watertight protection. Redressing the wrong has cost the banks many billions of pounds. But even more costly has been the loss of trust in the banking system. It seems that skewed incentives, encouraging staff to add PPI charges by stealth, were at the root of the trouble.

So, when RBS was accused in 2013 of driving some of its still-solvent corporate customers into expensive debt restructuring in order to make more money out of them, the accusation, and the suspicion of skewed incentives, seemed to fit with the culture we already knew about. It is a sad reality that banks, especially the big global variety, are no longer trusted to do the best job for their customer. There is a recognition that the bank's employees face a conflict of interest between serving the customer and feeding funds into their own profit centre, and perhaps their personal bonus package. This may be closer to the real world than the illusion of perfect customer service. But customer service is what these banks still emphasise in their advertising.

Only a handful of internal studies by banks themselves have opened the window on some deep cultural problems, which ultimately led to a loss of reputation. The Salz review of Barclays, published in April 2013, must have made excruciating reading for those responsible for damage done to the bank. The report noted that reputational risk was not prioritised at board level until 2011. It recorded the cavalier attitude of many employees, which led the bank to follow the letter, but not the spirit, of rules designed to clean it up. "We believe a culture developed within Barclays, quite possibly derived originally from the investment bank," the report said, "which came across to some as being 'clever' or what some people have termed 'too clever by half' ..."

Similarly, UBS did an analysis of how it screwed up so badly in 2008 and 2009, both in terms of losses on structured derivatives and in running foul of the US authorities for helping US citizens to avoid tax. The underlying reason for its getting into such deep water was a cavalier attitude to its reputation, despite warnings from the Federal Swiss Banking Commission. There is a suggestion that UBS employees decided that continuing to solicit funds from the US that were not tax-compliant was a gamble worth taking. The report's rather predictable conclusion is that "the bank's reputation is to be treated uncompromisingly as its most valuable asset. This implies honest, law-abiding and responsible behaviour on the part of every individual."

The UBS report also considers the conundrum of whether to take legal action against executives responsible for the failure. One of the reasons the bank gives for not going ahead with prosecutions is the risk of damage to the bank's reputation. Paradoxically, transparency may not always, in the judgement of its stakeholders, be seen as the best way to limit damage to a bank's reputation.

That level of pragmatism is probably wrong, and not in the long-term interests of the bank, or in this case the Swiss financial sector. Former UBS officers, who should have been shamed by public prosecution or litigation, headed it off by volunteering to forgo some of their previous earnings. Some of these officers have popped up again in prominent financial positions.

But perhaps the broader lesson is that the reputation of a big and complex institution is not black or white: it is always grey. Things go wrong; traders step out of line; rules and even laws are stretched to the limit. The more important goal, even more important than a spotless reputation, is arguably to keep the bank alive and show that it is under control. Take the case of JPMorgan Chase and "the London Whale". By all standards it was a fiasco: it took press accounts of City gossip in early 2012 to alert the bank's own senior management to the possibility that there might be a problem. One of the most revered banks in the world was running enormous unhedged positions in synthetic credit derivatives in a unit that was supposed to be reducing the entire bank's interest-rate risk. Eventually, the bank had to recognise losses of around US$6 billion on the trades. A report by the US Senate Permanent Subcommittee on Investigations concluded,

> In contrast to JPMorgan Chase's reputation for best-in-class risk management, the whale trades exposed a bank culture in which risk limit breaches were routinely disregarded, risk metrics were frequently criticized or downplayed, and risk evaluation models were targeted by bank personnel seeking to produce artificially lower capital requirements.

Surprisingly, however, the episode did not kill the bank, nor was it fatal for Jamie Dimon, who survived as chairman and chief executive. This was despite the fact that Mr Dimon played down first market reports of the losses as a "tempest in a teapot".

The report reveals that there was fierce internal debate about the valuation of the trades. It seems JPMorgan was able to persuade the market that it had the situation under control, despite the enormity of the positions. There was no suggestion that customers might lose money. Even the shareholders, who in the end had to eat the losses, remained largely loyal to the bank. Temporary damage to the share price began to recover within two months.

There are probably lessons to be learned from how JPMorgan dealt with the crisis, internally and externally, once it was acknowledged. But there is also the strength of the JPMorgan brand built over the past decades, and indeed its culture. The revelations about Barclays and UBS laid bare a cynical attitude within these banks to clients and the authorities. That does not come across in the JPMorgan report, despite the bank's initial attempts to play down the losses.

In this book on reputational risk there are plenty of lists of dos and don'ts. But the overarching message for guardians of a bank's reputation is the need for simplicity and transparency in presenting the bank, and in dealing with reputational threats as they arise.

Ideally, the interests of each employee should be aligned with the long-term prosperity of the bank. There should be no incentives that focus employee interests more narrowly or shorter-term than that.

There should be transparency in dealing with all stakeholders and customers, especially when things go wrong. Cases of fraud, poor risk management or other actions that risk the bank's reputation should be aired and dealt with promptly, not swept under the carpet.

Finally, there must be constant awareness that one's first instinct, even that of the well-trained and motivated team player, is to pretend that a bad thing just didn't happen.

REFERENCES

Goldman Sachs and SBC Warburg Dillon Read, 1998, *The Practice of Risk Management* (London: Euromoney Books).

Tripartite Group of Bank, Securities and Insurance Regulators, 1995, "The Supervision of Financial Conglomerates", available at www.iosco.org/library/pubdocs/pdf/IOSCOPD47.pdf.

2

What History Teaches Bankers about Reputation Management

Richard J. Parsons

"Perhaps a man's character is like a tree, and his reputation like its shadow: The shadow is what we think of it, the tree is the real thing."
                                                    Abraham Lincoln

WHAT DOES HISTORY TEACH BANKERS ABOUT REPUTATION?
In this chapter the subject of reputation development and management will be examined through a look back in history. Three topics will be explored:

❏ taking a historical perspective on the reputation of bankers, the case will be made that bankers today would be wise to understand why society does not trust the institution of banking, and specifically its practitioners, the bankers;
❏ from there the chapter will examine how one of history's great managers of reputation – Julius Caesar – approached the building and maintenance of his own reputation and that of the Roman Empire; and
❏ reflecting on the writings of Karl von Clausewitz, Niccolò Machiavelli and Thomas Paine, the chapter will close with a discussion of the link between reputation and the motivation behind building a certain reputation.

ADAM SMITH AND THE BANKERS' 'CONTEMPT OF RISK'
The father of capitalism, Adam Smith, has long been associated with his advocacy of the efficacy of free markets. In *Wealth of Nations*,

written in the 18th century, Smith introduces the concepts of "perfect liberty" and "natural price" to his readers. Left undisturbed by unnatural impulses such as government controls, Smith argues (Smith 1909, p. 59) that the price of an object will adjust over time aligned to demand and supply of such object.

> The market price of every particular commodity is regulated by the proportion between the quantity which is actually brought to market, and the demand of those who are willing to pay the natural price of the commodity ... When the quantify of any commodity which is brought to market falls short of the effectual demand, all those who are willing to pay the whole value of the rent, wages and profit, which must be paid in order to bring thither, cannot be supplied with the quantity which they want. Rather than want it altogether, some of them will be willing to give more. A competition will immediately begin among them, and the market price will rise more or less above the natural price ...

This much of Smith's philosophy about capitalism is well known and accepted as the foundation of his system of free markets at work.

What may surprise the casual reader of Smith's *Wealth of Nations* is his view that bankers should not be allowed to operate in a free market. He finds bankers especially vulnerable to "the contempt of risk and the presumptuous hope of success" (Smith 1909, p. 115). In short, for Smith, bankers cannot be trusted. Their reputation for greed and excessive risk taking, therefore, requires the state to impose "a violation" of the bankers' "natural liberty" (Smith 1909, p. 263).

> ... to restrain a banker from issuing such notes, when all his neighbors are willing to accept of them, is a manifest violation of that natural liberty which it is the proper business of law, not to infringe, but to support. Such regulations may, no doubt, be considered as in some respect a violation of natural liberty. But those exertions of the natural liberty of a few individuals, which might endanger the security of the whole society, are, and ought to be, restrained by the laws of government ... The obligation of building party walls, in order to prevent the communication of fire, is a violation of the natural liberty, exactly of the same kind with the regulations of the banking trade which here proposed.

Adam Smith was from Scotland. *Wealth of Nations* was published in 1776. Within two years of the work's release, the City of Glasgow Bank failed. Racked by massive fraud, the bank until that time had enjoyed a solid reputation for safety and stability. Its six directors and two officers were arrested. The City of Glasgow Bank failure was just one bank failure in a long line of failures before and after the publication of Smith's book.

Sadly, the history of banking in free markets is a parallel history of bank failures. Nineteenth-century England suffered through no fewer than four bank crises while the US witnessed six crises during the same century. Adam Smith would not have been surprised given his low regard for the memories and skills of bankers.

Fast-forward to the 1920s in the United States. The National City Bank of New York – the precursor to Citibank – had celebrated its 100th anniversary in 1912. It was recognised as the largest bank in the world by the mid-1920s, and no one questioned the strength of Citibank. As the bank's assets grew, at least for a while, so too did its reputation. However, by the decade's end, Citibank's reputation seemed to evaporate, as did management's *über*-confidence in its business model and acumen.

From 1925 to 1929, Citibank's loan portfolio ballooned at the remarkable pace of 18.7% annual compounded growth rate.[1] During those boom years Citibank's management fashioned a reputation for innovation. At the centre of their business model was the development of what they called "the financial department store", a phrase that gained wide usage in the US beginning in the early 1990s.

By the mid-1920s Citibank comprised three different lines of business: Local Bank, International Bank and Domestic Wholesale Bank. In addition to the bank, Citibank also controlled City Company, a securities firm engaged in underwriting, municipal and foreign government financing, and trust administration. Citibank's organisational blueprint would become, by the end of the 20th century, the model adopted by megabanks in Europe and the US, further evidence that the Citibank of the 1920s was well ahead of its time.

The rapid growth combined with a far-flung geographic footprint set the stage for trouble at Citibank in October 1929, when the Stock Market Crash inflicted catastrophic losses on investors. Because of its aggressive tolerance for risk and return – especially margin loans – Citibank found itself keenly vulnerable to falling stock market prices.

Throughout Citibank's rapid growth of the 1920s, the bank was led by its chief executive officer, Charles E. Mitchell, a high-profile New York career banker. When the Crisis hit full force in late 1929 and into 1930, Mitchell attempted to position himself and Citibank as industry leaders prepared to guide the country through a time of financial peril. Mitchell made frequent trips to Washington, DC, where politicians initially welcomed his presumed expert counsel and impressive position of authority.

However, by the early 1930s the reputation of bankers had sunk to all-time lows in the US. Looking for scapegoats, Washington politicians blamed the "banksters" for the Great Depression. In January 1933 Mitchell was called to testify in front of the Senate Banking Committee. Headed by its new chief counsel, the pugnacious Ferdinand Pecora, the Senate Banking Committee was determined to prove that irresponsible bankers triggered the Great Depression by fostering wide-scale speculation in their blind pursuit of profits. As the leader of the biggest bank, Mitchell was Pecora's first target.

In the kind of inflammatory language common 80 years later during the financial crisis, one senator remarked in 1933 that "the best way to restore confidence is to take these crooked presidents out of banks and treat them the same way as they treated Al Capone when Capone avoided payment of his tax" (Cleveland and Huertas 1985, p. 185). Like politicians, the newspapers found the banking community an easy target for wrath: "We regret to announce the loss of a handsome set of iridescent halos. Finder will kindly return to the officers of National City Bank" (Cleveland and Huertas 1985, p. 160, quoting *New Yorker* 1933). We also read (Cleveland and Huertas 1985, pp. 184–5, quoting *American Mercury* 1932),

> The title of banker, formerly regarded as a mark of esteem in the United States, is now almost a term of opprobrium. There seems some danger, in fact, that in forthcoming editions of the dictionary, it may be synonymous with rascal ... and we may see a day when to be called a son-of-banker will be regarded as justifiable ground for the commission of assault and mayhem.

Mitchell, it was discovered by Pecora during questioning, had earned over US$1 million in income in 1929, but paid no taxes owing to a capital loss he incurred when he sold Citibank stock to his wife. Clearly, Mitchell's fishy transaction was suspicious, if not illegal. Though the revelation of not paying taxes resulted in his arrest and indictment for tax evasion, eventually Mitchell would be cleared of criminal charges yet forced in a civil settlement to pay over millions to the federal government.

> "The way to gain a good reputation is to endeavor to be what you desire to appear."
>
> Socrates

CEASAR AND CITIBANK

Whether Charles Mitchell ever studied *The Works of Julius Caesar* is unknown.[2] However, if Mitchell had, he would have been exposed to one of the few people in history who made reputation management a full-time job. Julius Caesar lived from 100 BC to 44 BC.

For Caesar, reputation was a tool for enforcing his will and the will of Rome on adversaries. He nurtured his reputation with diligence, edifying it through his writing, and spreading it across the Roman Empire through what today would be called a word-of-mouth marketing campaign.

To begin to understand Julius Caesar's reputation, it would be helpful to first describe it. Caesar and Rome had a vision to control their known world. Believing their political and military systems far superior to the practices of any other nation, Caesar understood that Rome's vision faced practical limitations. The chief limitation was the simple fact that Roman interests, like those of Citibank in the 1920s, were far-flung and so wide that successful administration was impossible without the active cooperation and self-management of indigenous people.

People conquered by Rome – both militarily or through fear of military takeover – were vital to the long-term wellbeing of the Roman Empire. Caesar sought to impose on those he conquered a desire to adopt Roman culture and customs. Evidence of Rome's enduring success in this endeavour can best be seen today in the Roman-based language common to much of Europe. Julius Caesar crafted a reputational strategy that embraced expressions of loyalty, patience and the power to enforce his will by force if left with no other alternative.

> Caesar is better than his promise ... It was the settled principle of the Roman people that their allies and friends should not only suffer no loss but be enhanced in influence and dignity and honor ... Friendship with the Roman people should be a distinction and a safeguard, not a liability [Julius Caesar 1957, p. 32].

In 58 BC, not unlike the times depicted in the movie *Gladiator*, the conquered people of Gaul (present-day France) were under frequent threat of attack by the Germans (a word in Latin for "barbarians") as well as the Helvetians (Swiss). In Caesar's *Works*, he writes of his encounter with Ariovistus, a leader of a confederation of Germanic tribes.

A clever leader, Ariovistus attempts to beguile Caesar with assurances that his entry into Gaul was at the request of the local Gallic people. Though there was some semblance of truth to this statement, Caesar knew that the Gallic people had not issued Ariovistus an open-ended invitation to occupy their lands.

Determined to show himself the reluctant warrior, Caesar listens, and then challenges the German chief's claims in a nonthreatening manner. Unpersuaded, Ariovistus ultimately rushes into war against Caesar, having overestimated Caesar's temperament and underestimated Rome's military might. When the two armies do battle, despite the advantage of both numbers and fearsome stature, the German intruders quickly fall to Caesar's crack troops.

Bankers can learn three things from Caesar.

First, for Caesar, reputation was an end in itself. Since his objective, as well as that of Rome, was to influence the behaviours of other nations, Caesar recognised the efficiency gained by overinvesting in reputation management. By doing so, Rome engendered trust from allies without having to spend precious government resources occupying conquered people. The point here for bankers is that a reputation that promotes trust is of enormous value during difficult times. In the case of Citibank and Charles Mitchell in the booming 1920s, little effort had been made to cultivate trust with the politicians who acted as judge and jury in 1933.

Second, Caesar's willingness to fight acted as a deterrent against potential disrupters to the Roman Empire. Bankers need to protect critical client relationships. Competitors target these relationships, knowing that often to win the client it will be necessary to compromise either pricing (eg, interest rate or fees) or credit standards (eg, reducing covenants or removing personal guarantees or sufficient collateral). When this occurs, a good banker must know when it is time to stop the competitor dead in their tracks and match the pricing and terms so that the client is not lost. If the competitor recognises that a bank will not be bullied into losing business, over time this competitor will redirect their efforts.

Third, however, the discerning banker must learn from the full landscape of the history of Rome. As described in Edward Gibbon's trilogy of *The Decline and Fall of the Roman Empire* (Gibbon 1946), over the course of hundreds of years, Rome learned that there limits to its ability to defend all its empire. At some point the marginal cost of maintaining control over the frontier was greater than the marginal benefit.

As Rome eventually learned, bankers need to know there are certain limits to how far a bank can and should go to protect market share and client relationships. Returning to Charles Mitchell of Citibank, in December 1931 Mitchell offered this self-incriminating comment to the Senate Commission of Manufactures: "National City [now Citibank] was forced by competitive pressures to join this trend [ie, broker-margin loans] or face the loss of business" (Cleveland 1985, p. 175).

Perhaps no greater damage is done to the reputation of bankers than it is when "competitive pressures" create a contagion of wide-scale imprudent banking practices.

> "War is thus an act of force to compel our adversary to do our will."
> Clausewitz (1962)

REPUTATION MANAGEMENT: IT'S ALL ABOUT THE TREE

Is it possible that bankers are too fast to "go to war" with competitors in an effort to protect or expand market share? And, as a result, is it possible bankers place their pride before their reputations?

Bankers who can suffer the indignity of slow growth, even negative growth, when other banks are growing like wildfire, are rare. Only patient bankers who understand the vicious cycles of banking have the fortitude and emotional DNA to build a bank that that can survive for generations.

For bankers determined to build strong banks that last, they may wish to turn to Niccolò Machiavelli, an Italian who lived from 1469 to 1527. The term "Machiavellian" has gained a pejorative, sinister, even diabolical quality more than 500 years after Machiavelli wrote *The Prince*; in truth the book offers a constructive framework for bankers to think about building and sustaining reputation.

From Machiavelli we learn three things helpful to bankers.

First, in the chapter "How a Prince Must Act in Order to Gain Reputation", Machiavelli warns Princes that "nothing makes a Prince so well thought of as to undertake great enterprises to prove his capacity."[3] Though the term "public relations" likely did not exist around the year 1500, the concept was certainly one familiar to Machiavelli. He adjures his reader to maintain "the dignity of the station, which under no circumstances be compromised".

Herein lies the challenge for bankers: to "undertake great enterprises" often brings a measure of risk not aligned to the long-term health of banks. Rare is the banker who is not over time brought down to earth by a zeal for fast growth or hungry for glorious acquisitions that push the bank beyond its ability to control and manage the new organisation. And, when controls prove inadequate, "the dignity of the station" of bankers – which is reputation – is put at risk.

Second, in Chapter XXIII, "Of Flatterers",[4] Machiavelli warns the Prince to be prudent in selecting colleagues. In this chapter he gives special attention to the peril of "flatterers" whose dissembling lips prevent the Prince from hearing truth. Like Princes, some bankers, especially as they gain stature and position, become swallowed up with notions of self-importance and fall prey to conniving sweet-talkers. Bankers must hear the unvarnished truth. Leaders who surround themselves with flatterers are sure to fall victim eventually to the warnings of Machiavelli to the Prince.

Third, in the chapter "How the Princes Should Keep the Faith",[5] Machiavelli reminds his Prince that "he must therefore keep his mind ready to shift as the winds and tides of Fortune turn ..." By this statement the author presages the words of Charles Darwin, who wrote in the 19th century, "Though Nature grants long periods of time for the work of natural selection, she does not grant an indefinite period; for as all organic beings are striving to seize on each place in the economy of nature, if any one species does not become modified and improved in a corresponding degree with its competitors, it will be exterminated" (Darwin 1909).

To the informed reader, it is possible that the inclusion of the ideas of Charles Darwin and Niccolò Machiavelli in this chapter suggests that reputation building is an amoral exercise. Darwin inadvertently shaped the development of Social Darwinism as espoused most notably by his brilliant cousin, Herbert Spencer, the 19th-century English philosopher credited with coining the term "survival of the fittest". And Machiavelli is long associated with a philosophy that states that "the end justifies the means".

Quite certainly, the pages of history are packed full of people whose reputations are built on the promotion and promulgation of evil. So the question arises, how is a "good" reputation engendered?

To answer this question, it is possible to consider a myriad examples from history. But, for the purpose of this chapter, the writings of Thomas Paine, a Brit who emigrated to the United States just a few years before the American Revolution, will be considered.

Few people in the world recognise the inflammatory role Paine played to fan the fires of liberty and democracy. His first publication was little more than a pamphlet. Entitled *Common Sense*, it became so popular by 1774 that one in three Americans owned a copy. It is said that George Washington read it to his troops to pep them up at a time when his army faced starvation and bitter cold (Nelson 2006).

In addition to writing *Common Sense*, Paine also wrote two other treatises of historic importance, *The American Crisis* and *Rights of Man*. It is in the latter where Paine writes,

> The duty of man is not a wilderness of turnpike gates, through which he is to pass by tickets form one to the other. It is plain and simple, and consists but of two points. His duty to God, which every must feel; and with respect to his neighbor, to do as he would be done by. If those to whom power is delegated do well, they will be respected.

Paine raises the bar of reputation building. He suggests that "respect" is the anchor of reputation, and that respect is earned by leaders aspiring to act with a sense of duty that goes beyond caring for oneself. Paine would most surely challenge bankers to strive to move beyond reputation to respect. For him reputation devoid of respect is no reputation at all.

What is the banker's duty? Do bankers ask themselves this question?

Abraham Lincoln once said that "a man's character is like a tree, and his reputation like its shadow". If history teaches bankers anything, it is that virtuous character is the antecedent to a sterling reputation.

Bankers would best serve society by thinking first about the tree.

And the shadow will take care of itself.

---

1 The discussion of First National Bank/Citibank is from Cleveland and Huertas (1985), Chapters 7–9, pp. 113–87.
2 Commentary in this part of the chapter is drawn from Caesar's writings about the Gallic War (Julius Caesar 1957).
3 Commentary for this paragraph is drawn from Machiavelli (1954), pp. 157–62.
4 Commentary for this paragraph is drawn from Machiavelli (1954), pp. 166–9.
5 Commentary for this paragraph is drawn from Machiavelli (1954), pp. 128–31.

REFERENCES

Julius Caesar, 1957, *The Works of Julius Caesar* (New York: Black's Readers Service Company).

Cleveland, Harold van B, and Thomas F. Huertas, 1985, *Citibank 1812–1970* (Cambridge, MS: Harvard University Press).

Clausewitz, Karl von, 1962, *War, Politics, and Power* (Washington, DC: Regnery Gateway), p. 65.

Gibbon, Edward, 1946, *The Decline and Fall of the Roman Empire* (New York: The Heritage Press).

Machiavelli, Niccolò, 1954, *The Prince* (New York: The Heritage Press).

Nelson, Craig, 2006, *Thomas Paine* (New York: Penguin Books).

Smith, Adam, 1909, *An Inquiry into the Nature and Causes of the Wealth of Nations* (New York: P. F. Collier & Son).

Van Doren, Carl (ed.), 1922, *Selections from the Writings of Thomas Paine* (New York: The Modern Library).

3

An Asset–Liability View of Banks' Reputation

Sergio Scandizzo

European Investment Bank, Luxembourg

"If the confidence of the public in the integrity of accountants' reports is shaken, their value is gone."

Arthur Andersen, 1932

In this chapter we examine the role played by reputation during and after the financial crisis, as a fundamental factor in some high-profile demises – therefore not only, as it is usually discussed, as a consequence of other risks, but as a primary cause – as well as a driver in the shaping of the governance of the financial system of today and tomorrow, at a time when many of the current and future legislative and regulatory developments are being and will be influenced by the reputation of the most high-profile institutions and of the financial industry as a whole.

BANKS' REPUTATION AFTER THE CRISIS

How important is reputation for a bank today? If you ask any practitioner, if you survey the academic literature, if you read trade magazines or listen to consultants' presentations, the answer seems univocal and straightforward: it's not just important, it is critical. Banking is an industry based on confidence and trust; reputation is fundamental for building a franchise, retaining customers, and attracting employees. When reputation gets harmed, the business suffers and if, for some reason, it collapses, so does the business. And yet ... is it really so simple?

The last years have tested the resilience of individual institutions and of the industry as a whole almost to a breaking point. Volatility, liquidity, leverage, operational failures and fraud have reached unprecedented levels and, as a consequence, so have legal disputes, regulatory fines and even, in a few cases, civil and criminal prosecutions. The impact on the reputation of the most high-profile financial institutions, not to mention supervisors and the financial system as a whole, has been severe and, one would have expected, shattering. But, in fact, the relation between reputation and performance, both during and after the 2008–9 financial crisis, seems to have worked in very different ways from one bank to the other. For one thing, some banks seem to be able to bounce back from setbacks much more nimbly and quickly while others suffer negative consequences for longer periods of time. A striking example of this difference is provided by the cases of JPMorgan and Barclays, the former having agreed to pay almost US$15 billion in fines and settlements related to the marketing of residential mortgage-backed securities (RMBSs), not to mention US$6 billion trading losses (plus around another US$1 billion in fines) related to the infamous "London Whale" scandal, the latter having been fined a "mere" £450 million for its involvement in the Libor rigging scandal. And yet, as one commentator described it (Meek 2014),

> From loss in share price to the resignations of key senior staff members, Barclays clearly suffered, and continues to suffer, from the significant reputational damage of Libor. Meanwhile JP Morgan suffered a short dip in share price after the London Whale incident, but has since seen a steady increase in share price.

One might similarly wonder, if reputation plays such a simple and straightforward role as it is usually described, how Goldman Sachs – which, aside from its involvement in regulatory and legal disputes not unlike those of JP Morgan, was once portrayed in *Rolling Stone* magazine as a giant vampire squid wrapped on the surface of the planet – could have managed to hold on to its position as the pre-eminent American investment bank. Clearly, there is more there than meets the eye.

First of all, banking is not a monolithic business. Banking services are very diverse, and so are the public and the stakeholders' perceptions and expectations towards those services. The customers, shareholders, creditors and employees of companies such as JPMorgan and Goldman Sachs seem to have a fairly tolerant attitude towards those companies' missteps. One reason for this may be linked to the nature of the services those banks provide and to the way that nature has evolved over recent years.

Secondly, the importance of reputation is linked to the information asymmetry between a company and its various stakeholders. The larger this gap, the more relevant the role that reputation plays in the company's success. Such a gap is notoriously important in financial institutions, but its relevance varies across the different banking products and as the nature of some of those products evolves.

Also, if it is true that, post-crisis, we are facing a fundamental reshaping of the financial system and of its governing priorities and relationships, then perhaps a change of comparable proportions is to be found in the role that reputation plays in the perceived and actual performance of its players.

And, finally, the financial crisis has seen the collective perception of the banking sector as a whole deteriorate dramatically and, as a consequence, the public's ability to distinguish among the various industry players to equally drastically diminish, making the role of reputation potentially less important and certainly different.

REPUTATION IN BANKING: ASSET OR LIABILITY?

Most academic literature and corporate policies tend to treat reputation along the same lines as brand, that is, as an intangible asset that can be impaired by operational mistakes or inappropriate behaviour. Within this framework, reputation risk is a derivative risk, a risk that always arises as a result of something else and that potentially magnifies the consequences of other exposures. Along these lines, the Basel Committee on Banking Supervision (BCBS) defines reputational risk as the "risk arising from negative perception on the part of customers, counterparties, shareholders, investors, debt-holders, market analysts, other relevant parties or regulators that can adversely affect a bank's ability to maintain existing, or establish new, business relationships and continued access to sources of funding" (BCBS 2009).

Several cases are routinely mentioned to show evidence of how reputational fallout can harm shareholders' value. For instance, JPMorgan's many years of partnership with Banesto turned into a liability in 1993 when the Bank of Spain took control of Banesto, alleging mismanagement and reckless lending. Two months later JPMorgan's market capitalisation had lost US$1.5 billion.

In 2004 a foreign-exchange scandal engulfed National Australia Bank and did not spare its auditors (PwC), whose independence in their investigation was questioned. There was a public split in the bank's board of directors, who also failed to address regulators' observations. Between January and September 2004 the share price dropped 19% for an overall impact on shareholder return of US$2 billion.

In September of the same year the Financial Services Agency (the Japanese regulator) closed Citigroup's private banking business in Japan for "serious violations" of banking laws, after Citigroup had failed to address similar 2001 findings. Notwithstanding a precipitous visit to Japan of Citi's CEO in October of the same year in an attempt to repair the company's image, French retailer Carrefour fired Citi as adviser on the sale of its Japanese operations.

We will call this perspective the "asset-side view" of reputation, where reputation is, like brand, an asset that can be impaired as a consequence of improper management and as such can negatively affect the value of the firm when such impairment is recognised by investors.

It is not our intention to prove or disprove this perspective, although some scholars have indeed argued along that line, but rather to show that there is more to reputation than meets the eye, and that by just looking at the impact on reputation of banks' actions we are missing some fundamental aspects of the issue at hand.

A different way to look at reputation is to consider it the same way risk managers look at capital, that is, as a cushion against losses. Jones, Jones and Little (2000) have studied whether companies with better reputations, as measured by *Fortune*'s annual ratings of America's largest corporations, suffered less severe declines in market value in the stock market crashes of 1987 and 1989. They have found that, although reputation did not seem to have mattered much during the 1987 crash, it did make a difference in 1989, when the stock prices of companies with better reputations dropped significantly less than the others.

If reputation works like capital, then, like capital, it may have an impact on the risk profile just by being reduced and by consequently becoming less of a cushion against failures and consequent (reputational) losses. As a lower amount of financial capital translates into a higher risk of bankruptcy, similarly, an already tarnished reputation may not survive a further blow, thereby putting a company in what we may call a "reputational bankruptcy". Unlike normal capital, which is reduced in proportion to the financial loss suffered, reputational capital is unaccounted for and needs to be measured separately. It follows that, when assessing reputation risk, it is not enough to estimate likelihood and impact of harmful events. The corresponding loss of reputation (reputational capital) needs to be estimated in order to highlight the consequent weakening of the company's resilience in the face of future events.

While in some cases a good reputation seems to soften the impact of major failures, allowing the institution to recover relatively unscathed, in others the reliance of the business on other parties' trust appears like a weakness that can make otherwise objective strengths, such as capital and liquidity, become irrelevant. Garry Honey (2009) argues that different stakeholders will have different expectations of the company's behaviour and that measurement of reputation and of the related risk should be based on the gap between such expectations and the company's performance.

If, however, we recognise that reputation is the sum of stakeholders' expectations and that reputation risk is the difference between these expectations and the actual performance a bank delivers, it is difficult not to wonder whether a liability-side view of reputation is also possible.

Rather than just as an asset that would yield a stream of benefits, or as a kind of equity capital that could absorb the impact of failures and losses, reputation can also be seen as tied to a set of obligations, arising from the bank's dealings with its stakeholders, which place on it duties and responsibilities to be fulfilled over time. These obligations may go well beyond what a bank is legally obliged to do and may encompass a very wide spectrum of domains, from customer service to corporate citizenship all the way to outright macroeconomic responsibility. This last responsibility may have become prominent in recent years, but has somehow always been there. Every society since the Neolithic has engaged in the production of surplus, and the ability to save and transfer this surplus (wealth) has ever since been fundamental to their success. In Western societies

Table 3.1 The reputational balance sheet

Reputation as asset	Reputation as liability
Customers' (and other stakeholders') goodwill	Stakeholders' expectations
	Reputation as capital
	Buffer against failures: helps maintaining goodwill when failing to meet expectations

banks have played this fundamental role for centuries (Caldararo 2011), hence their status and consequent obligations.

We can therefore look at reputation as having a threefold nature: asset, liability and capital. The impact of reputation on the performance, and possibly on the survival, of a financial institution is a direct consequence of the interplay of these three avatars.

Albeit not a case from the banking industry, Arthur Andersen provides an interesting example of this multiple nature of reputation at work (Markham 2006). On March 15, 2002, the Department of Justice indicted Arthur Andersen on charges of obstruction of justice for shredding paperwork related to ongoing SEC investigations on the Enron scandal. On June 15, after ten days of deliberation, a jury found Arthur Andersen guilty. The firm agreed to cease auditing public corporations by the end of August 2002, after which all its international offices were bought by the remaining, by then, "big four".

On the liability side, Arthur Andersen had failed to meet expectations on several occasions before the period leading up to the Enron scandal. The Waste Management and Sunbeam accounting scandals at the end of the 1990s had already tarnished the firm's image, while on March 4, 2002, Andersen lawyers agreed to pay US$217 million to settle pending litigation with the Baptist Foundation of Arizona, at that time the largest non-profit bankruptcy when it filed for Chapter 11 in 1999, at a cost of US$600 million to investors.

On the asset side, confidence in Arthur Andersen had been shaken so badly that customers began to flee the firm in earnest, including long-term Fortune 500 clients such as Colgate-Palmolive and Merck, after its criminal indictment for obstruction of justice, while the overseas offices quickly moved to sever ties with their US parent with entire country groups leaving Andersen to join other large accounting firms.

As equity, Andersen's reputational capital had therefore been essentially depleted by the time the firm was indicted and there was little it could do to salvage its business, even as it appealed the verdict and had it eventually remitted by the US Supreme Court in 2005.

A quip would have probably applied to the reputational balance sheet of Arthur Andersen, which was to be coined several years later:[1] "On the left side there is nothing right and on the right side there is nothing left."

One might take a step forward in this interpretation and wonder if reputation can behave as both an asset and a liability, whether a gap can emerge between these two roles, not unlike what happens with traditional assets and liabilities. In other words, given the fact that reputation is both a source of goodwill and an obligation to deliver along certain key dimensions, does any unbalance between these two unwritten kinds of contracts create a special set of risks to the financial institution?

The well-known adage that it takes a long time to build a reputation but very little to lose it suggests that, indeed, a good reputation delivers its economic benefits in the long run – similarly to, say, a mortgage contract – but that at the same time it creates short-term expectations in a bank's stakeholders – not unlike depositors' expectation of continuous availability of their funds – which need to be promptly fulfilled and defaulting on which can be very expensive. Fulfilling stakeholders' expectations fuels (one might say "funds") a bank's reputation, but, while this is a day-to-day endeavour, the build-up of the reputation asset takes time. As an asset, reputation has long maturity; as a liability, it comes due quickly and regularly. A "gap" therefore emerges between the time it takes to build and reap the benefits of a good reputation and the exposure that this reputation creates should the bank's performance fall short of the expectations.

With traditional assets and liability, short-term funds may become more expensive, and even dry up completely in times of crisis, while long-term assets continue to yield the same return and may become even more illiquid during a crisis. On the reputational side, short-term commitments may become more and more demanding over time and, especially in extreme circumstances, more difficult to fulfil, while the reputational stock builds slowly over the years, but can become very hard to leverage upon in a crisis, when the whole industry suffers a drop in credibility and stakeholders have a hard time distinguishing among institutions.

The case of Bear Sterns, the US investment bank that was eventually taken over by JPMorgan in a rescue sponsored by the Federal Reserve, is perhaps the clearest example of how this mechanism may almost inexorably play out. In June 2007, following heavy losses at two of its hedge funds specialising in mortgage backed-securities, Bear Sterns agreed to bail out those funds by buying out several Wall Street banks that had lent the funds money and to provide a US$1.6 billion credit line. These actions aimed at containing the overall financial fallout from the funds collapse were unprecedented, as bear Sterns had always resisted putting too much of its capital at risk and was motivated precisely by its executives' concern for the reputational consequence of letting the funds fail. Yet, these attempts at fulfilling expectations notwithstanding, Bear Sterns's reputational capital was nonetheless depleted. David Weidner observed in his column for MarketWatch that "the real damage is how the firm and its management are perceived on the Street" and that the hedge funds' collapse "may be a bigger blow to the firm's and the industry's reputation".

This became painfully clear less than one year later, when clients and counterparts started to abandon the once thriving Wall Street firm. By the end of business on March 13, 2008, so many clients had pulled their money from Bear Stearns that the firm had run through US$15 billion in cash reserves. Assurances that the firm had still a solid cash reserve did little to stop the slide, and on March 16 Bear Sterns signed a merger agreement with JPMorgan. Later, the Securities and Exchange Commission Chairman Christopher Cox wrote, "Notwithstanding that Bear Stearns continued to have high quality collateral to provide as security for borrowings, market counterparties became less willing to enter into collateralized funding arrangements with Bear Stearns" and "The market rumors about Bear Stearns liquidity problems became self-fulfilling."[2]

THE ROOTS OF THE FINANCIAL CRISIS AND THE CHANGING ROLE OF REPUTATION

At the root of the financial crisis lies a fundamental failure in understanding and managing the risks undertaken by financial institutions across a wide spectrum of geographies and activities. Such failure had two components: one related to technique, the other to governance. The former has been the main object of analysis from insiders and practitioners, focusing on excessive reliance on historical data, lack of stress testing, neglect of correlation effects, fat tails and so on. The last of these has chiefly attracted the attention of regulators, politicians and the general public, who have, in various ways, pointed out how financial institutions spread their risks out to their various stakeholders while retaining the profits exclusively for their shareholders (Scandizzo 2013). This behaviour is exemplified in the now infamous "originate and distribute" model, where subprime mortgages, given to customers without virtually any credit check and as such extremely risky, would be subsequently "dumped" into asset-backed securities issued by special-purpose vehicles and sold to unsuspecting investors around the globe. However, irresponsible as this particular behaviour might be, it is only the tip of the iceberg. Even institutions not directly involved in the subprime mess have made every effort to ensure their losses were as much as possible absorbed by depositors, bondholders, employees and taxpayers, while at the same time trying to protect the value of their shares (and the bonuses of their executives).

A generalised result of these explanations is the conclusion that the financial industry as a whole has failed the communities it was supposed to support and that its reputation has been severely tarnished as a consequence. This conclusion, however, prompts the question of how this has happened in an industry where reputation is supposed to be such a critical asset, and also a fundamental barrier to entry. Why, in other words, have institutions that for many decades have prided themselves on their reputation for integrity and client services failed so spectacularly to live up to it?

Morrison and Wilhelm (2013) have an interesting take on the evolution of reputation's role in the investment banking industry. They argue that in our economic system there is a hierarchy of contractual commitments that goes from the most reliant on standardisation, laws and regulation to the most extra-legal, which rely mainly on tacit information, personal networks and reputation. Investment banking activities traditionally used to be on the latter end of the scale, but, due to a combination of technological change and regulatory intervention, it has lately moved steadily towards the former. One key consequence of this dislocation is that, for firms providing services that are based more and more on standardised contracts and codified legal frameworks, reputation is of lesser importance.

One further consequence of this contractualisation of financial services is that certain banking services become more and more like commodities in the eyes of customers. Just as we do not really care which brand of petrol gets into the tank – so long as the pump is accessible and the price is in line with the market – current accounts, credit cards, consumer loans and mortgages are chosen on the basis of price and little else. This implies that it is very hard for banks to differentiate their offer, but also that it is equally hard for the public to distinguish among institutions offering more or less the same services at comparable prices. Marketing efforts can go only so far, and there is very little difference – and, as technology progresses, there will be less and less – in the quality of a current account, a cash machine or an Internet banking website whether it is from Citi, HSBC or UBS. The "asset value" of the reputation linked to these services will be more and more difficult to exploit, while the "liability potential" will become actually higher as any problem at a particular institution may reflect badly on the whole industry. This is already largely the case and the most popular interpretations of the 2008–9 financial crisis offer ample evidence of it. From the generalised belief that highly paid investment bankers were to blame (when in fact the advisory and M&A were among the least involved in the whole subprime/collateralised mortgage obligation frenzy) to the widespread idea that all banks were saved at the taxpayer's expenses (whereas most of the EU governments did not put any hard cash into the banking industry and the US government even made a profit on the Troubled Asset Relief Program investment), it appears that trying to differentiate between the behaviours of different institutions was, at least as far as the general public was concerned, a hopeless exercise. We should also add that this held not just for the general public, but also by and large for concerned politicians and even to some extent for regulators.

As mentioned earlier in the chapter, reputation is a relevant asset when there is an information gap to be filled. It matters less when you are selling something that is well known and standardised, as customers have a hard time – and little incentive – to try differentiating among individual industry players. One of the consequences of this commoditisation is that reputation becomes more of an industry than a company issue, which makes its potential as a liability grow larger.

As observed in *American Banker* magazine (Landy 2012),

> Consumers appear to have less patience now for distinguishing between big bank brands, except when it comes to differentiating between large banks and the very largest banks (since the inception of our ranking three years ago, the giants have consistently populated the bottom tier). Reputation scores for most regional banks, meanwhile, landed within a tight range of one another. With so few points separating the best from the rest, it looks as though reputation isn't the differentiator that some banks might have hoped.

Without attempting to provide a cross-industry analysis of the issue, we might briefly observe that the same combined wave of technological and regulatory evolution that has brought investment banking towards a more legally and informationally standardised framework has impacted on other banking business lines. It is perhaps unsurprising that retail banking services are nowadays not just commoditised, but seamlessly integrated in our day-to-day information infrastructure (think mobile banking, computerised credit checks, online trading and so on). The development and harmonisation of regulation has also ensured that asset management and retail brokerage firms can also be judged more objectively and through standardised performance criteria, hence reducing the relevance of informal knowledge in the process of customer choice. For the companies operating in these sectors the reputation of the financial industry (and of the specific business category) as a whole is likely to be more relevant as a potential liability than their individual good name. For private bankers and wealth managers – as well as for the more advisory-oriented investment bankers – informal networks, implicit knowledge and individual reputation will probably continue to exercise a relevant role, at least for the near future.

Macey (2013) provides reasoning and evidence that contradict both the theoretical and the empirical/anecdotic arguments on the relevance of reputation discussed earlier in this chapter. He argues that the traditional reputational model, whereby the cost of a bad reputation exceeds any financial gain a company might obtain through reprehensible behaviour, is wrong. The fact that it is difficult to distinguish whether a given failure has been caused by dishonesty, or other factors that the company could not control, contributes to explaining why the reputation of financial firms such as JPMorgan, Morgan Stanley and Goldman Sachs does not seem to have suffered from some of the scandals mentioned above. He further argues that manufacturing companies can signal their quality through the provision of warranties and money-back guarantees, an option that is not available to financial institutions whose products may cause losses for complex reasons that may be out of the institution's control. However, this is one more feature that distinguishes the distribution of information – and hence the role of reputation – across the basic classes of goods and services and in particular so-called credence goods from experience goods and commodities.[3]

From this discussion we can broadly conclude that the nature of reputation changes, while going from one extreme of the product spectrum to the other, from being an asset to becoming an outright liability. When quality is difficult to judge *ex ante*, reputation acts as a differentiator, as a source of goodwill and as a cushion against losses. In these cases reputation is an asset and actually softens the impact of operational failures and consequent bad news on shareholders' value.

On the other hand, when quality is transparent, when products tend to become standardised and differentiation becomes more difficult, reputation tends to be perceived more as an indicator of collective quality, and behaves as a liability, actually amplifying the impact of failures and even contributing to the propagation of the damage throughout the industry.

Eisenegger and Künstle (2012) observe not only a highly significant correlation between reputational indicators and share price, but also that, within reputational indicators, those referring to the social dimension (as opposed to the economic one) show a much more pronounced worsening of, as well as a strong correlation with, financial (under-) performance during and after the 2008–9 financial crisis. These findings highlight the importance of understanding how stakeholders' expectations have evolved and have become more differentiated after the crisis, but also show how the uniqueness of the banking business is reflected in its difficulty to perform so long as a fundamental part of its collective reputation remains in tatters.

Regulation is also influencing the relevance of reputation in the financial industry, but its role too is twofold. On one hand, regulation contributes to filling the information gap between the firm and the market. It can of course be more or less effective, and the financial crisis has provided ample evidence of the latter, but the increasing breadth and depth of regulatory requirements and their progressive standardisation across jurisdiction, where the Basel Committee on Banking Supervision has played a central role, undoubtedly contributes to reducing the relevance of reputation in customers' choices by ensuring a standard minimum level in the services provided, not unlike what happens in the utilities market. On the other hand, after the financial crisis, the actions of regulators and legislators have been strongly influenced by the generalised drop in the public confidence towards both financial institutions and their supervisors. So, while regulation tends to reduce the relevance of reputation, it is at the same time shaped by it.

Historically, stricter regulation and more invasive supervisory powers usually follow times of crisis and contraction while a lighter touch, in both rule making and enforcement, is adopted in times of economic expansion. This approach mirrors financial institutions' own perception and rationalisation of risk, which in turn translates into lobbying and political pressure for easing of legislation and regulation when times look good. But the more pervasive role of regulation has an impact on market participants' perception of the stability and reliability of the system and of who is responsible for it. We may be initially reassured of a more relevant regulatory role in the financial industry, but this reassurance comes with a progressively heavier reliance on the supervisors' reputation. When the latter suffers a blow, not only the initial confidence evaporates, but the whole industry appears unsafe, as so much of its perceived stability had been relying on the expectation of good supervisory performance.

CONCLUSION

From the arguments discussed in this chapter we can draw three main conclusions.

First, the nature of corporate reputation is multifaceted and considering it just as an asset to protect misses a fundamental component of the dynamics at play in today's financial industry.

Besides the classical role of reputation as an intangible asset, there is another, perhaps more subtle and harder to grasp, that relates to the fulfilment of stakeholders' expectations and to the ability to withstand failures in the public eye. Any attempt at managing the reputation of a financial institution should not neglect its potential to cause its downfall precisely because of the very expectations it implies in the minds of the stakeholders.

Second, the nature of reputation in the financial industry evolves, and analyses of the way financial institutions have emerged from the financial crisis shows that, especially in certain areas of the business, reputation is not any more the differentiating factor it used to be, while at the same time remaining, at least for the moment, a potential liability for the whole sector. As a consequence of the crisis, the expectations placed on financial institutions have become more demanding and complex due in equal part to the renewed awareness of their importance to the economy and to the perception that they have survived relatively unscathed from their failure to live up to their pre-crisis reputation.

Third, reputation is a major factor in regulators' and legislators' decision about the future supervisory framework of the financial industry. This is both because how their constituencies' perceive the financial industry will inevitably reflect in regulatory and political decisions, and because a heavier and higher-profile role for the regulatory framework will create heightened expectations in both market players and the public at large. Fulfilling those expectations and preventing them from becoming an industry-wide liability will be a major challenge for the financial system as a whole.

> The views expressed in this article are those of the author and they do not necessarily represent those of the European Investment Bank.

---

1 "The left side of the balance sheet has nothing right and the right side of the balance sheet has nothing left. But they are equal to each other. So accounting-wise we are fine" – AIG vice chairman Jacob Frenkel at a bankers' gathering, available at www.seekingalpha.com, October 11, 2008.

2 Chairman Cox letter to Basel Committee in support of new guidance on liquidity management, March 20, 2008.

3 The following description from Emons (1997) seems especially well suited to financial services: "With a credence good, consumers are never sure about the extent of the good they actually need. Therefore, sellers act as experts determining the customers' requirements. This information asymmetry between buyers and sellers obviously creates strong incentives for sellers to cheat on services."

REFERENCES

Basel Committee on Banking Supervision, 2009, "Enhancements to the Basel II Framework", July.

Caldararo N. L., 2011, "The Theory of Banking: Why Banks Exist and Why We Fear Them", August 11, available at http://ssrn.com/abstract=1908310 or http://dx.doi.org/10.2139/ssrn.1908310.

Eden, C., and F. Ackermann, 1998, *Making Strategy: The Journey of Strategic Management* (London: Sage Publications).

Eisenegger, M., and D. Künstle, 2012, "Long-Term Reputation Effects in the Global Financial Industry: How the Financial Crisis Has Fundamentally Changed Reputation Dynamics"

Emons, W., 1997, "Credence Goods and Fraudulent Experts", *Rand Journal of Economics*.

Jones, G. H., B. H. Jones and P. Little, 2000, "Reputation as Reservoir: Buffering Against Loss in Times of Economic Crisis", *Corporate Reputation Review* 3, pp. 21–9.

Honey G., 2009, *A Short Guide to Reputation Risk* (Farnham: Gower).

Landy, H., 2012, "The Fragile State of Bank Reputations: Results from Our 2012 Study", *American Banker*, July.

Macey, J. R., 2013, *The Death of Corporate Reputation: How Integrity Has Been Destroyed on Wall Street* (Upper Saddle River, NJ: Financial Times Press).

Markham, J. W., 2006, *A Financial History of Modern U.S. Corporate Scandals: From Enron to Reform* (Armonk, NY: M. E. Sharpe).

Meek, J., 2014, "Reputation Damage and Modelling Reputation Risk", *Operational Risk & Regulation* 15, January.

Morrison, A., and L. White, 2013, "Reputational Contagion and Optimal Regulatory Forbearance", *Journal of Financial Economics* 110(3), pp. 642–58.

Morrison, A. D., and W. J. Wilhelm Jr, 2013, "Trust, Reputation and Law: the Evolution of Commitment in Investment Banking", mimeo, February.

Scandizzo, S., 2011, "A Framework for the Analysis of Reputational Risk", *Journal of Operational Risk* 6(3), pp. 1–23, Fall.

Scandizzo, S., 2013, *Risk and Governance: A Framework for Banking Organizations* (London: Risk Books).

4

Reputational Risk in the Universe of Risks: Boundary Issues

Hema Parekh

INTRODUCTION

This chapter highlights the interconnection between various risk types, such as credit, market, operational and reputational. Its purpose is to explain these interconnections and how various business operations impact reputational risk. By providing specific examples of commonly observed losses and events, the author has sought to increase awareness about reputational risk among risk managers. Whether you are in the camp that believes that reputational risk is a distinct risk category or in the camp that believes it is an impact of failure to manage one or more risks, there is no argument that it is something that all risk and business managers have to consider in everything they do.

Reputational risk is integrated into every aspect of banking and therefore highly correlated to other types of risk. The interconnection between reputational risk and the universe of other risks has become complex due to the quickly evolving technological revolution and globalisation in banking. This is an appropriate moment for a closer look at the issues emerging from this revolution to help increase understanding and management of reputational risk.

THE UNIVERSE OF RISKS

Risk-management programmes often focus on each area of risk as a distinct risk category. How a bank defines its universe of risks varies by type of bank and country of its domicile, as well as jurisdictional regulatory mandates. Risks such as credit, market, liquidity, interest-rate, operational, legal, strategic, compliance, reputational and business are found in most banks' risk libraries. It has been noted by many that one of the root causes of the financial crisis of 2008 was failure on the part of bank management and risk managers to connect the dots between risk categories. There was significant focus on managing each individual risk category and not adequate focus on risks between and across different risk categories, also known as boundary issues. It is extremely important to understand these boundary issues because the barriers between these categories are eroding, and persuading risk specialists entrenched in the individual silos to take a broader view is a difficult task. Banks now find themselves in a complex world of instantaneous access to information and execution of transactions. To respond to evolving business models, banks' risk-management programmes are growing more complex and sophisticated as professional risk managers utilise more data and more modelling to identify, monitor and mitigate risk in the banks.

In order to understand reputational risk and related boundary issues, we need first to understand what reputational risk is. Unlike with more matured risk disciplines such as credit risk, there is not a generally agreed-upon definition of reputational risk. Opinion is divided as to whether reputational risk is a category of risk in its own right, or merely the consequence of a failure to manage other risks. The latter view predominates where there is a tradition of well-structured risk measurement and management. In a bank where risk managers feel they have identified the traditional key risks (eg, credit, market) facing their business, they may be more inclined to consider reputational damage as simply a failure to manage these risks properly. In contrast, where traditional risks are less quantifiable, they are more likely to see reputational threat as a risk class in its own right. There is a truth in both views, as shown in Figure 4.1.

In the US the Federal Reserve System's *Commercial Bank Examination Manual* defines reputational risk as "the potential that negative publicity regarding an institution's business practices, whether true or not, will cause a decline in the customer base, costly litigation or revenue reductions (Federal Reserve 2006). Reputational risk can also be defined as the current and potential risk of an

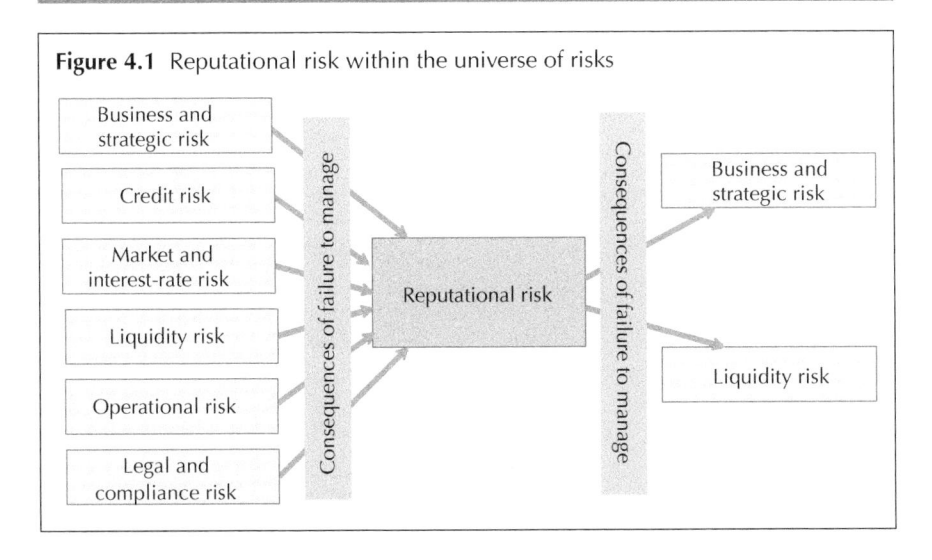

Figure 4.1 Reputational risk within the universe of risks

- Business and strategic risk
- Credit risk
- Market and interest-rate risk
- Liquidity risk
- Operational risk
- Legal and compliance risk

→ Consequences of failure to manage → Reputational risk → Consequences of failure to manage →

- Business and strategic risk
- Liquidity risk

economic loss due to a negative perception of the bank's image by its main stakeholder groups. Whatever position banks take on this, many in the banking industry agree that reputation is an extremely important intangible corporate asset, and one of the most difficult to protect. It is also clear that serious reputational damage can occur simply as a result of perceived failures, even if those perceptions are not grounded in fact. Perception, therefore, is the biggest threat to reputation. Changes in the business environment have also made companies more vulnerable to reputational damage. The development of global media and communication channels, increased scrutiny from regulators and reduced customer loyalty are commonly cited as three issues that expose banks to increased reputational risk.

If reputation is such an important asset, then a question is, how does a bank acquire this asset? Two key elements to understanding the interconnection between reputational risk and other risks is to know what factors impact a bank's reputation and who makes up the stakeholder group. Commonly observed factors contributing to good reputation are service/product quality, ethics/corporate governance, employee relations, customer service, intellectual capital, financial performance, environmental and social issues, philanthropy/charity and capital. This is by no means an exhaustive list. Looking at these factors it is obvious that understanding how different aspects of an organisation's activities impinge on

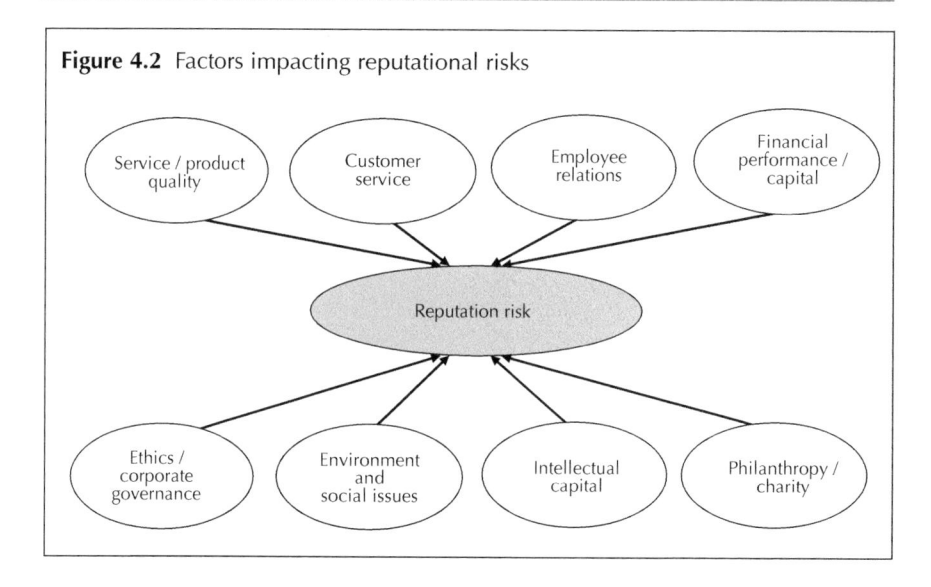

Figure 4.2 Factors impacting reputational risks

Factors (top): Service/product quality; Customer service; Employee relations; Financial performance/capital

Center: Reputation risk

Factors (bottom): Ethics/corporate governance; Environment and social issues; Intellectual capital; Philanthropy/charity

stakeholder perceptions is a vital aspect of protecting a bank's reputation.

Generally, a bank would consider investors, customers, employees, suppliers, counterparties, financial/investment analysts, regulators, legislators, the community in which it operates and non-governmental organisations as its stakeholders. Any negative change in a bank's image could influence their relationship with the bank. So, on one side, a bank has these stakeholder groups and on the other there are contributory factors such as service/product quality, ethics/corporate governance, employee relations, customer service, intellectual capital, financial performance, environmental and social issues, philanthropy/charity and capital. For example, while a failure to comply with a rule could generate fines and penalties considered as operational losses (operational risk), it would certainly have a reputational impact on investors, customers and the community where the bank operates.

REPUTATIONAL RISK AND OPERATIONAL RISK

Interaction between the stakeholder groups and impact factors creates unlimited permutations and combinations of actions and interactions that could create situations for something to go wrong, impacting a bank's reputation in a negative way. Reputational risk is interwoven with every activity undertaken by a bank, its manage-

Figure 4.3 Reputation risk: key stakeholders

Stakeholders: Investors, Customers, Employees, Suppliers, Community, Non-governmental agencies, Counter parties, Financial / investment analysts, Regulators, Legislators — all connected to Reputation Risk.

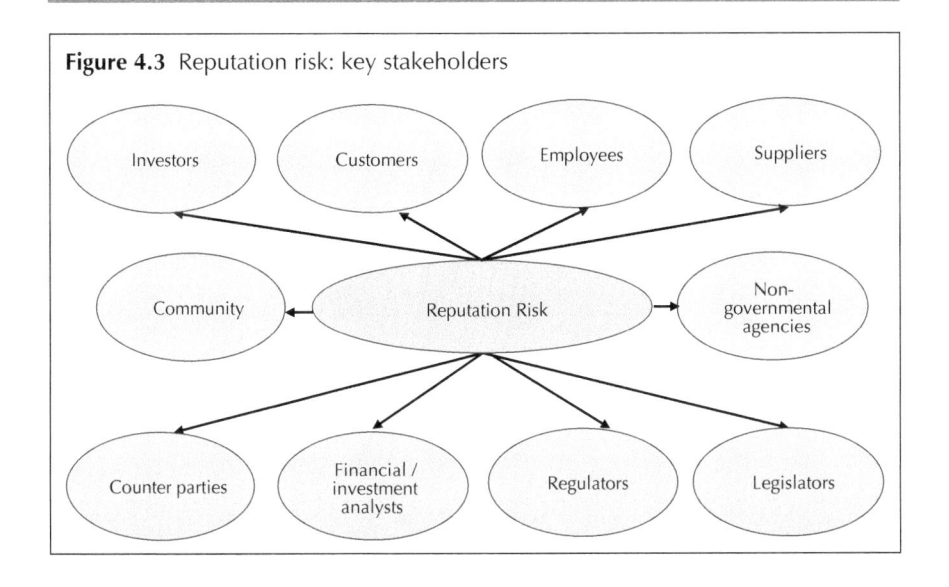

ment, its employees, its suppliers, etc. Let us look at how reputational risk could arise as a consequence of any of the traditional risk categories. We will start with operational risk. The Bank of International Settlement (BIS) defines operational risk as: "the risk of loss resulting from inadequate or failed internal processes, people, and systems or from external events. This definition of operational risk includes legal risk – which is the risk of loss (including litigation costs, settlements, and regulatory fines) resulting from the failure of the bank to comply with laws, regulations, prudent ethical standards, and contractual obligations in any aspect of the bank's business – but excludes strategic and reputational risks."[1] Operational risk is embedded directly and/or indirectly in every activity of a bank, from teller transactions to trading activities, and this risk is increasing with the rise in complexity of markets, products and systems. Recent events have shown that banks of all sizes struggle with risks that arise from people, processes, systems and external events. More fundamentally, it is the evolution of information technology and of the nature of financial services – what those services are, how they are managed, how they are delivered – that has really shifted the nature and sources of operational risk.

You do not have to go far back in history to find an example of how an operational risk event could have significant impact on a bank's reputation. Let us start with the 2008 crisis. In the wake of the crisis there have been high-profile events that resulted from breakdowns in internal controls and operational processes, and lapses of oversight and control functions – events involving inappropriate sales of products, non-compliance with anti-money-laundering laws, and losses from complex hedging and investment strategies. An example of inappropriate product or service was strong-arm collection practices used by third parties engaged in collecting on defaulted auto and credit-card loans, which led to litigation losses and reputational risk to JPMorgan. The impact on reputational risk was so significant that some banks chose to divest from certain businesses or change their business practices and business models.

One headline-grabbing example from 2012 involves the IPO event for Facebook. Operational glitches at the Nasdaq exchange resulted in multiple errors, many unhappy investors and significant losses to Nasdaq, expensive litigations and significant damage to its reputation. It is important for a bank to understand when a failure in managing operational risk could threaten reputation.

Additionally, market conditions and earnings pressure contributed to institutions engaging in non-traditional business activities and engaging with commercial customers that are third-party payment processors (TPPPs). These bank customers provide services to merchants, including credit-card and loan payment processing via automated clearing houses or remotely created checks. Operational, legal, BSA compliance, reputational and even credit risks can result from these relationships. Operational failures relating to such firms can have significant consequences. For example, in 2008 Wachovia bank (which was acquired by Wells Fargo in October of that year) was ordered to pay US$150 million to victims of a telemarketing fraud perpetrated by one of its business customers. The bank's failed internal operational processes for conducting adequate due-diligence reviews and properly managing its relationship with the TPPP were cited as the underlying causes. This event resulted in significant damage to Wachovia's reputation with its customers, regulators, industry and the communities where it operated. This event highlights the close tie between strategic risk (new-product approval), operational risk (due diligence), financial risk and reputational risk.

Such highly publicised events led most large banks to refrain from doing business with certain TPPPs and strengthened their due diligence processes. These TPPPs have now turned to smaller banks. In January 2014, Four Oaks FinCorp (FOFN) in North Carolina, USA (a US$809 million-asset bank), agreed to pay US$1.2 million to settle claims for ignoring warning signs of a scheme to defraud customers. This example demonstrates that a bank's size does not matter. No matter the size, a bank has to understand boundaries between traditional risks and reputational risk.

Ensuring ethical practices throughout the supply chain makes controlling risks to reputation from third-party partnerships hard to manage. This is a particularly elusive area of risk management. Damage to the reputation of a business partner, adviser or auditor can be transferred to a bank by simple association, and is less easily repaired than the cost of an unpaid bill or an unmet contract.

Traditionally, activities such as IT, payment/settlement, information access and vendor management were pigeon-holed or placed in silos and dealt with individually. This approach creates barriers to understanding operational risks as well as its boundary with reputational risk and needs to be revisited and given a new operating environment, which has become a complex world of instantaneous access to information and execution of transactions. Effective risk identification requires that risk managers and bank management understand various types of risks inherent in the banking products or processes, including impact of failure to manage reputational risk.

REPUTATIONAL RISK AND CREDIT RISK

Credit risk is most simply defined as the potential that a bank borrower or counterparty will fail to meet its obligations in accordance with agreed terms.[2] A bank makes credit decisions considering a borrower's ability to make payments. Once the credit is given a bank has to monitor the borrower to ensure that the borrower meets all the commitment per the contract. The entire life cycle, beginning with making a credit decision, then executing the required agreement and monitoring the borrower's commitment until the entire obligation is paid-off, involves multiple processes. These processes are associated with activities related to the origination, underwriting, monitoring, and management of loan agreements. Management of the loan agreements broadly refers to such things as regulatory compliance and compliance with the contractual terms of the loan agreement, servicing, loss mitigation, financial reporting, warehouse lending, structuring and oversight, MIS and loan data management. Post-credit decisioning activities involve people, processes and systems, and failure at any point could lead to financial loss as well as damage to reputation.

The history of banking has plenty of examples of bank failures due to mismanagement of credit risk. When a bank experiences significant credit losses, it threatens its profitability and damages its reputation. It's depositors as well as counterparties lose trust in its viability and there is a run on its deposits, further intensifying liquidity pressures. Counterparties are not willing to extend credit lines or provide liquidity.

Everyone was impacted directly or indirectly by the mortgage crisis of 2008. Many believe that the crisis was caused by the banks' failure to manage credit risk. In addition to the financial losses, the banks involved in the mortgage business – either as originators of loans or investors in mortgage-backed securities – as well as those who packaged these loans and sold them, suffered significant reputational risk. Many banks entered into securitisation agreements. When markets froze due to the liquidity crunch, these banks bought back securitised loans simply to protect their reputations, even though, contractually, they were not required to do so.

REPUTATIONAL RISK AND MARKET RISK

Market risk is the risk to a financial institution's condition resulting from adverse movements in market rates or prices, such as interest rates, foreign-exchange rates and equity prices (Federal Reserve 2006). Similar to the situation with credit risk, reliable operational processes are essential for successful market and liquidity risk management. This is highlighted by a bank's use of models to evaluate and conduct banking operations. The increasing sophistication of technology used in modern banking, combined with increased regulatory scrutiny such as macroprudential supervision, has resulted in the growing use of models by banks. Successful management of the market and liquidity risks requires the operation of various models.

Any discussion regarding reputational risk and market risk will not be complete without looking at the "London Whale" event at JPMorgan Chase. Prior to this event JPMorgan Chase had consistently portrayed itself as, and was considered to be, an expert in risk management. It had a "fortress balance sheet" that ensured taxpayers had nothing to fear from its banking activities, including its extensive dealing in derivatives. But all that changed in early 2012, when the bank's chief investment office, which was charged with managing US$350 billion in excess deposits, took a huge position in a complex set of synthetic credit derivatives that, in 2012, lost at least US$6.2 billion. This was a result of a strategy to hedge credit risk, which was not well managed and controlled, and resulted in not only huge losses from changes in the value of derivatives positions it owned but also significant fines from the regulators. However, the most damaging aspect was the damage to JPMC's reputation.

REPUTATIONAL RISK AND LEGAL/COMPLIANCE RISK

The Basel Committee on Bank Supervision defines compliance risk as, "the risk of legal or regulatory sanctions, material financial loss, or loss to reputation a bank may suffer as a result of its failure to comply with laws, regulations, rules, related self-regulatory organisation standards, and codes of conduct applicable to its banking activities". Basel II defines legal/compliance risk as a subset of operational risk. Since one of the primary foci of Basel II framework was on risk measurement, reputational risk was left out of the definition of legal/compliance risk due to challenges to measure reputational risk. However, it is important to look at the boundary between this subset of operational risk and reputational risk.

Compliance failures are a primary source of reputational risk. The biggest threat to reputation is seen to be a failure to comply with regulatory or legal obligations. Failure to deliver minimum standards of service and product quality to customers is a close second. The risk that unethical practices in the bank will be exposed follows closely behind. For most risk managers, it is the failure to comply with regulatory or legal obligations that represents the biggest threat to reputation.

Since the crisis of 2008, compliance risk management has become extremely important for banks. Regulatory expectations have increased significantly. There have been long lists of new regulations banks have to comply with in a relatively short time frame. We saw unprecedented levels of fines and penalty for non-compliance with the laws such as anti-money-laundering (AML) laws. Regulators assessed a total of US$4.3 billion in penalties on BNP Paribas, HSBC,

Standard Charter and ING for non-compliance with AML. These banks have been in the headlines in a negative way with significant impact on their reputations with customers and regulators alike.

Banks have seen that compliance issues related to debt-collection practices, trading operations, Bank Secrecy Act compliance and mortgage servicing, among others, have been at the source of litigation and significant losses. Each of these issues has absorbed management time and resources that could be better spent on other matters, and they have resulted in enforcement actions and damage to banks' reputations.

Banks understand the importance of ethical behaviour and a culture of compliance. To ensure that employees adhere to ethical practices, banks have policies on codes of conduct and regular training for their employees. However, expectations concerning ethical behaviour are not a constant. Rather, they are on an ever shifting scale. In the US this was seen with the late trading and timing events in early 2000 and new regulations imposing restrictions on fees banks could charge to their customers after the financial crisis which started in 2008. Online tools make it easy for the customers to communicate their dislike towards banks' products, services and fees and it is difficult for banks to always stay one step ahead of the shifting ethical landscape. However, it is imperative for a bank to integrate ethical considerations into products, services and pricing decisions as a failure to do so has a high probability of damage to its reputation.

Community investment and philanthropic efforts, similar to ethical behaviour, are important for a bank in enhancing and managing its reputation, but, if this is not well managed, the same could become a source of reputational risk. These efforts are managed by a completely different group within a bank and risk management is generally not involved in these efforts. However, inadequacy and failure in managing the social programmes could be very damaging to a bank's reputation. There is a close linkage between the strategy behind philanthropic activities, its execution and reputational risk.

IMPACT OF REPUTATIONAL RISK ON OTHER RISKS

It is clear from the examples outlined above, and there are plenty of other examples, that different risk types are closely interconnected and, if not understood and managed well, could cause reputational risk. However, it is also possible that reputational risk could cause other risks, such as business risk and liquidity risk. If one or more stakeholders described above (Figure 4.3) perceive a bank's reputation to be of concern, then that could lead to a reduction in business, a run on deposits, lack of credit, customers choosing not to do business, etc. This could result in significant strategic, business and liquidity risk for the bank. You could say that this was one of the reasons behind failure of Lehman Brothers. Once the counterparties believed that Lehman was not strong enough to meet its short-term obligations, its reputation was damaged and that led to a liquidity crunch for the company, eventually leading to its failure.

This goes to show that, whether you believe that failure to manage other risks results in reputational risk or you believe that failure to manage reputational risk manifests in other risks such as credit and liquidity, it is imperative that understanding and managing reputational risk in a proactive manner is extremely important for all banks.

CONCLUSION

Reputation is a dynamic asset. It changes as the banks present new services and products in new markets and are held to changing ethical criteria. Reputation is as vulnerable to perceptions of failure as to failure itself. Historically, we have focused on risk areas with mutually exclusive and artificial boundaries. A more appropriate approach would be to focus each risk area with an eye towards risk factors underlying all business activities and processes. In this way, bank management would have a more accurate picture of the root cause and true level of risk within the various businesses and activities. Regardless of how a bank categorises its risks, the risk governance framework must appropriately cover risks to the bank's earnings, capital, liquidity and reputation that arise from all of its activities, including risks associated with third-party relationships. Understanding how different aspects of a bank's activities could impact on its reputation is therefore a key first step. Factors such as the development of global media/communication channels as a disseminator of reputationally sensitive information; the imposition of higher regulatory standards of governance in the wake of the high-profile market failures of the past decade; customer power, seen in their readiness to switch supplier with great ease; and governments' greater propensity to intervene in defence of public interest make understanding the boundary between reputational risk and other risk types one of the most important risk-management imperatives.

Bank management has often believed that banks succeed or fail based primarily on how well they manage credit risk. Although credit risk remains vitally important, events outlined above have shown that banks of all sizes struggle with risks that arise from failure to manage multiple risk dimensions, including reputational risk. And a failure to manage these risks, including reputational risk, could have a dramatic impact on a bank. More fundamentally, it is the evolution of information technology and the nature of financial services – what those services are, how they're managed, how they're delivered – that have really shifted the nature and sources of reputational risk.

Banks have to manage relationships with stakeholders, as outlined above, and managing reputational risk is an extremely important element in sustaining and enhancing these relationships. Reputational risk not well managed could lead to credit, liquidity or other risks. Therefore, it is extremely important for banks to understand and actively manage reputational risk in the same way they manage all other risks.

1 See http://www.bis.org/publ/bcbs107b.pdf.
2 See http://www.bis.org/publ/bcbs54.htm.

REFERENCES

Federal Reserve, 2006, *Commercial Bank Examination Manual*, November, Section 1000.1.

5

Corporate Governance Changes Following Reputational Damage in the Financial Industry

Ahmed Barakat

Nottingham University Business School, UK

This chapter presents a theoretical discussion and empirical investigation of how financial firms respond to bad-news announcements that constitute possible causes of market-based reputational damage (namely, severe operational risk events and income-decreasing financial statement restatements). This topic is examined in terms of such firms making informed changes to their corporate governance structures and practices as a result of reputational damage. The chapter begins with a discussion of why it could (and should) be crucial for financial firms to apply substantial enhancements to their "tone-at-the-top" corporate governance mechanisms[1] following material bad-news announcements. Subsequently we examine and explain the data sources of bad-news announcements, tested variables, and the selection procedure of the sample comprising bad-news announcements in 75 US financial firms during the period 1995–2009. Next we analyse the market-based reputational damage caused by income-decreasing financial statement restatements and operational risk event announcements. We also take on board the results of corporate governance changes following market-based reputational damage in US financial firms, discussing to what extent the capital markets react to such changes. The chapter concludes with relevant recommendations.[2]

BAD-NEWS ANNOUNCEMENTS, REPUTATIONAL DAMAGE AND CORPORATE GOVERNANCE CHANGES IN THE FINANCIAL INDUSTRY

The financial crisis brought to the foreground the important role the financial industry plays in the global economy. Maintaining a healthy financial sector is necessary for keeping the stability of the whole economy. Corporate governance is vital for the financial success of all public firms, including those working in the financial industry. More effective corporate governance mechanisms lead to better performance and higher market valuation (de Andres and Vallelado 2008; Adams and Mehran 2005; Caprio *et al* 2007), stronger internal controls (BCBS 2006a) and less incidence of fraud and lower operational risk exposure (Chernobai *et al*, 2011) in financial firms. Best-practice guidance from international organisations such as the Basel Committee on Banking Supervision (BCBS 2006a) emphasises that the shareholders and boards of financial firms should devote substantial effort to developing and maintaining effective corporate governance mechanisms. However, financial firms are unavoidably subject to operational risk. The Basel Committee on Banking Supervision (BCBS) defines operational risk as "the risk of loss resulting from inadequate or failed internal processes, people and systems or from external events. This definition includes legal risk, but excludes strategic and reputational risk" (BCBS 2006b, p.144). There are seven main types of operational risk events: internal fraud; external fraud; employment practices and workplace safety; clients, products and business practices; damage to physical assets; business disruption and system failures; and execution, delivery and process management (for more details, see BCBS 2006b, pp. 305–7).

The BCBS definition of operational risk and the literature-based evidence (eg, Cummins *et al* 2006; Chernobai *et al* 2011) both emphasise that operational risk event announcements have revealed serious problems in the internal control systems, fraudulent or opportunistic behaviour on the part of management and employees and ultimately weak "tone-at-the-top" corporate governance mechanisms in financial firms. Additionally, previous research found consistent evidence of the market-based reputational damage (hereafter referred to as reputational damage) caused by large operational risk event announcements (ie, losses of at least US$10 million) in the financial industry, as reflected by a drop in the market values of loss firms by more than one-to-one for internal fraud and non-fraud internally caused operational losses (Perry and de Fontnouvelle 2005; Cummins *et al* 2006; Gillet *et al* 2010).

The literature has also provided evidence showing that financial statement restatements,[3] and financial reporting fraud allegations due to violation of the Generally Accepted Accounting Principles (GAAP), could be another possible cause of big drops in the market values of public firms, and of severe damage to the reputations of their top managers and other directors and officers (eg, Srinivasan 2005; Desai *et al* 2006; Hennes *et al* 2008). Shareholders and boards of restating firms could choose to replace top executives and improve corporate governance mechanisms in order to remedy the flaws in their internal control systems, improve operating and market performance, hire fresh reputational and human capital, reduce the probability of litigation and ultimately restore the trust of potential investors and other stakeholders in the firm (eg, Farber 2005; Arthaud-Day *et al* 2006).

More specifically, previous research has found that financial statement restatements and financial reporting fraud allegations have led to increased turnover in the top management positions, ie, the CEO, chairman, president (eg, Arthaud-Day *et al* 2006, Hennes *et al* 2008). This is also true of changes in the board composition, either through the addition of more independent directors (such as audit committee members exiting their board positions (eg, Arthaud-Day *et al* 2006; Srinivasan 2005)), or through independent directors replacing executive directors in order to enhance the independent monitoring of the fraudulent or opportunistic behaviour of management (Farber 2005).

The real-world cases of reputational damage in the financial industry vividly demonstrate that many financial statement restatements are a consequence of previously incurred operational risk events. Hence, following an announcement of an operational risk event, the adverse effects of the financial statement restatement announcements on the market values of the loss firms and reputations of their top managers and other directors and officers may be dampened because such restatements become *ex ante* expected. Moreover, changes in top management positions have been known to occur immediately after the operational risk event is announced, and even before the first press cutting on the related financial statement restatement is released.

An example from the real business world is the case of William McGuire, the CEO of UnitedHealth, whose stock option of over US$1.5 billion was announced in March 2006. This was followed by an income-decreasing financial statement restatement announcement in November 2006. However, McGuire's resignation from the CEO position was announced in October 2006, before the restatement was publicly announced. The reputational damage caused by this internally caused operational risk event extended not only to the CEO but also to six other directors of the board who had been members of the compensation committee since the time of pricing the fiasco stock option grants. In an attempt to restore the trust of investors and shareholders, the board announced in October 2006 that five new independent directors would be elected during the next three years, an announcement that was again made before the date of the restatement announcement. In his comments on this operational risk event, Rajesh Aggarwal, an associate professor of finance at the University of Minnesota's Carlson School of Management, said, "The bigger issue is what does this say about the company and the management team ... Do you have an unethical or bad management team? Was the board not paying attention to accounting rules and questions of propriety?"[4] This case highlights how damaging internally caused operational risk events announced in the financial industry could be to the reputations of not only the CEO but also other directors of the board. Thus, it could be the case that the internally caused operational risk event announcement itself, not the resulting financial statement restatement, was the genuine cause of resignation. This case implies that ignoring the direct effects of large operational risk event announcements on changes in top management positions (and other tone-at-the-top corporate governance mechanisms) could lead to incorrect conclusions being drawn regarding the causes and consequences of exposure to reputational damage in the financial industry.

Some changes in top management positions result from operational risk event announcements that have not led to any financial statement restatements. A clear example of an internally caused operational risk event causing the immediate resignation of the CEO is the bid-rigging scheme involving Jeff Greenberg, the CEO of Marsh & McLennan, which was announced in October 2004 and led to his resignation in the same month. This internal fraud event was neither related to nor led to any financial statement restatement.

Back in the academic field, no previous research has distinguished between the corporate governance changes following the reputational damage caused by financial statement restatements, and by large operational risk event announcements, these being the two main types of bad-news announcements in the financial industry. Previous research has also been silent on how such corporate governance changes (ie, CEO turnover, turnovers of non-CEO executive directors and independent directors, changes in board size and meeting frequency) could help restore the trust of capital markets, which would be reflected in the stronger *ex post* stock performance of loss firms (ie, firms having bad-news announcements). Hence, using US data extracted from public sources and proprietary databases during the period 1995–2009, the following empirical study aims at filling this academic research gap and informing practitioners and stakeholders about the causes and consequences of corporate governance changes following bad-news announcements in the financial industry.

LEVELLING THE EMPIRICAL FIELD

The source of the data on operational risk event announcements is the IBM Algo FIRST database (hereafter, Algo FIRST), provided by IBM. The sample used consists of 294 large operational risk events (ie, losses of at least US$10 million) that were announced for 75 US financial firms in 198 fiscal years starting no earlier than July 1, 1995, and ending no later than June 30, 2009. The 294 large operational risk event announcements are divided into three groups:

1. internal fraud events whose announcements are expected to cause the most severe reputational damage to the loss firms;
2. non-fraud internally caused operational risk events (hereafter, other OpRisk events) whose announcements are expected to cause reputational damage to the loss firms that is less severe than that caused by internal fraud announcements; and
3. external fraud events that are externally caused operational risk events and therefore their announcements are expected to cause no reputational damage to the loss firms.[5]

Additionally, for the same 1995–2009 period in the 75 US financial firms, data on income-decreasing financial statement restatements are collected from two main sources: the US General Accounting Office's (GAO's) financial statement restatement databases of 2003 and 2006 and a manual search of the LexisNexis news database for the income-decreasing financial statement restatement announcements in the periods before January 1, 1997, and after June 30, 2006 (ie, the periods not covered by the GAO's databases). Income-decreasing financial statement restatements are used because previous research found them to cause greater decline in the market values (eg, Palmrose and Scholz 2004) and more severe damage to the reputation of directors (eg, Srinivasan 2005) than do income-increasing restatements or restatements having no effects on the previously reported net income. As a result, the final sample includes 26 income-decreasing financial statement restatements announced over 15 fiscal years, of which 17 announcements were collected from the GAO's databases and 9 from the LexisNexis news database. The distribution of the 75 sample firms by industry is as follows: SIC_60 (32), SIC_61 (3), SIC_62 (15), SIC_63 (23), SIC_64 (2). SIC_60 refers to depository institutions; SIC_61 refers to non-depository credit institutions; SIC_62 refers to security and commodity brokers, dealers, exchanges and services; SIC_63 refers to insurance carriers; and SIC_64 refers to insurance agents, brokers and service.

Table 5.1 presents descriptive statistics about the final sample of 294 operational risk announcements and 26 income-decreasing financial statement restatements in 75 US financial firms during the period 1995–2009.

The table describes characteristics of the income-decreasing financial statement restatement announcements and large operational risk event announcements (ie, of at least US$10 million in loss amount) for 75 US financial firms from July 1, 1995, to June 30, 2009. "Other OpRisk events" refers to large operational risk event announcements under the following types: employment practices and workplace safety; clients, products and business practices; business disruption and system failures; and execution, delivery and process management.

The frequency of other OpRisk event announcements (explained in endnote 5) is the highest, since the statistics encompass four operational risk event types that tend to be internally caused in nature but

Table 5.1 Bad-news announcements in the US financial industry

Type of announcement	Income-decreasing restatements	Internal fraud events	Other OpRisk events	External fraud events
Num. announcements	26	39	228	27
Descriptive statistics (in US$ million):				
Minimum loss	4.63	11.27	10.00	10.30
Median loss	41.20	29.60	48.32	24.60
Mean loss	123.95	50.73	120.91	35.84
Maximum loss	2482.61	965.36	9594.30	349.80
Distribution by industry:				
SIC_60	13	14	72	18
SIC_61	0	3	30	3
SIC_62	1	17	74	4
SIC_63	12	4	51	1
SIC_64	0	1	1	1

do not reflect any fraudulent behaviour on the part of firm insiders or outsiders. Following the sampling criteria, the minimum loss amount (US$4.63 million) comes in the restatement category, which also contains the highest mean (US$123.95 million), while the maximum loss amount comes in the other OpRisk event category (US$9,594.30 million). Considering only the operational risk event categories, it is interesting to note that other OpRisk event announcements have the minimum (US$10 million), the highest mean (US$120.91 million), the highest median (US$48.32 million) and the maximum (ie, US$9,594.30 million) loss amounts. It is also noteworthy that the minimum, maximum, mean and median loss amounts for internal fraud events are higher than those for external fraud events. Moreover, most of the operational risk event and restatement announcements are incurred by depository institutions (117), followed by security and commodity brokers and dealers (96), then by insurance companies (71), with the minimum number of announcements incurred by non-depository credit institutions (36).

Table 5.2 details the definitions and data sources of the variables measuring reputational damage following bad-news announcements (Panel A); variables measuring corporate governance changes (Panel B); and variable measuring stock performance in the US financial industry. All dollar-denominated variables are measured in 2009 US dollars. All ratios are measured in decimals.

For the contemporaneous (one year ahead) and lagged (two years ahead) corporate governance changes, the variables are measuring the CEO turnover, turnovers of non-CEO executive board directors (outgoing, incoming, sitting), turnovers of independent board directors (outgoing, incoming, sitting), change in board size, and change in board meeting frequency. Corporate governance data is collected from the RiskMetrics database and proxy statements are available from the US Securities and Exchange Commission's (SEC's) database, known as EDGAR. Additional data on the CEO turnover is collected from the LexisNexis news database. Data on stock returns is collected from the CRSP (Center for Research in Security Prices) database.

Table 5.2 Bad-news announcements, reputational damage, and corporate governance changes in the US financial industry: tested variables

Variable	Definition	Data source(s)
Panel A: Variables measuring reputational damage following bad-news announcements (Table 5.3)		
1. *Loss in market value*	The change in the market value of the loss firm during a relevant event window (ie, cumulative abnormal return in the relevant event window multiplied by the market value of the loss firm on the last trading day before the relevant event window). Cumulative abnormal return is computed according to the standard/single index market model (Benchmark is the CRSP value-weighted index).	CRSP
2. *Loss amount*	The deflated gross loss amount of the large operational risk event according to the final settlement announced or the total decrease in previously reported net income resulting from the financial statement restatement announced.	GAO databases, Algo FIRST, LexisNexis
3. *Restatement*	1 if the announcement is related to a restatement of previous financial statements that has a negative effect on the previously reported net income (ie, income-decreasing restatement); 0 otherwise.	GAO Databases, LexisNexis
4. *Internal fraud*	1 if the announcement is related to a large internal fraud event; 0 otherwise.	Algo FIRST, LexisNexis
5. *Other OpRisk events*	1 if the announcement is related to a large operational risk event in one of the following types (the "other OpRisk events" category): employment practices and workplace safety; clients, products and business practices; Business disruption and system failures; and execution, delivery and process management; 0 otherwise.	Algo FIRST, LexisNexis

Variable	Definition	Data source(s)
Panel B: Variables measuring corporate governance changes (Figures 5.1–5.5)		
1. CEO turnover	1 if the CEO has resigned, retired or been fired (except for death, promotion to a higher official rank or obligatory retirement according to an explicitly stated firm policy) in the current (or next) fiscal year; 0 otherwise.	RiskMetrics, Proxy Statements, LexisNexis
2. Turnover ratio of outgoing non-CEO executive directors	Number of outgoing non-CEO executive directors during the current (or next) fiscal year/number of non-CEO executive directors in the end of the previous fiscal year.	RiskMetrics, Proxy Statements
3. Turnover ratio of incoming non-CEO executive directors	Number of incoming non-CEO executive directors during the current (or next) fiscal year/number of non-CEO executive directors in the end of the previous fiscal year.	RiskMetrics, Proxy Statements
4. Turnover ratio of outgoing independent directors	Number of outgoing independent directors during the current (or next) fiscal year/number of independent directors in the end of the previous fiscal year.	RiskMetrics, Proxy Statements
5. Turnover ratio of incoming independent directors	Number of incoming independent directors during the current (or next) fiscal year/number of independent directors in the end of the previous fiscal year.	RiskMetrics, Proxy Statements
6. Change in board size	Total number of board directors in the end of the current (or next) fiscal year – Total number of board directors in the end of the previous fiscal year.	RiskMetrics, Proxy Statements
7. Change in board meeting frequency	Number of board meetings during the current (or next) fiscal year – Number of board meetings during the previous fiscal year.	Proxy statements
Panel C: Variable measuring stock performance (Table 5.4)		
Stock performance	Cumulative market-adjusted stock return during the fiscal year (Benchmark is the CRSP value-weighted index).	CRSP

WHAT DOES DATA TELL US?
Reputational damage caused by bad-news announcements in the US financial industry

Table 5.3 presents the results of a cross-sectional analysis of the market-based reputational damage caused by bad-news announcements in the US financial industry.[6]

It presents the results of an ordinary least squares (OLS) cross-sectional analysis of the determinants of the change in the market value of the loss firm (*loss in market value*) in different event windows around the first press-cutting date of large operational risk event announcements (ie, of at least US$10 million in loss amount) and income-decreasing financial statement restatement announcements for 75 US financial firms from July 1, 1995, to June 30, 2009. T-statistics (in parentheses) are based on heteroskedasticity-robust standard errors clustered by firm. ***, **, and * denote significance of the regression coefficients at the 1%, 5% and 10% levels, respectively. For the sake of brevity, control variables are excluded. Variable definitions are presented in Table 5.2.

In terms of proportional loss in market value, internal fraud announcements cause the greatest drop in all event windows

Table 5.3 Reputational damage caused by bad-news announcements in the US financial industry

Variable	Exp.sign	[0,0]	[-1,+1]	[-2,+2]	[-3,+3]	[-5,+5]
Loss amount	?	7.66	18.90	19.44	15.95	7.42
		(1.48)	(1.16)	(1.11)	(0.82)	(0.31)
Restatement	-	-11.65	-254.44	-1169.30	-1560.04	-2486.38
		(-0.03)	(-0.36)	(-1.71)**	(-1.70)**	(-2.14)**
Internal fraud	-	-274.18	-826.49	-535.24	-337.04	-1481.25
		(-0.41)	(-0.74)	(-0.50)	(-0.35)	(-1.23)
Other OpRisk events	-	234.13	171.68	-233.92	-244.01	-1160.92
		(0.69)	(0.26)	(-0.33)	(-0.27)	(-0.90)
Loss amount x restatement	-	-7.94	-17.98	-18.49	-13.72	-4.41
		(-1.51)*	(-1.09)	(-1.05)	(-0.70)	(-0.18)
Loss amount x internal fraud	-	-12.58	-23.06	-26.54	-24.97	-11.64
		(-2.24)**	(-1.36)*	(-1.45)*	(-1.21)	(-0.48)
Loss amount x other OpRisk events	-	-7.37	-18.47	-19.50	-15.85	-6.68
		(-1.42)*	(-1.13)	(-1.12)	(-0.81)	(-0.28)
Constant		153.75	962.08	420.88	3010.49	4083.59
		(0.12)	(0.49)	(0.21)	(1.12)	(1.15)
Num. Obs.		320	320	320	320	320
F statistic		235.37	36.63	8.25	6.95	13.89
(Prob > F)		(0.000)***	(0.000)***	(0.000)***	(0.000)***	(0.000)***
R^2		0.1750	0.1507	0.1160	0.1085	0.0905

(ranging from a drop of 11.64-to-1 in the [-5,+5] window to a drop of 26.54-to-1 in the [-2,+2] event window). Moreover, in the [0,0] event window, a one-dollar increase in the internal fraud loss amount announced causes a significant drop in the market value of the loss firm by more than 12 dollars while the same dollar increase in the restatement or other OpRisk event loss amount causes a drop of approximately 7 to 8 dollars. Similar results hold for all event windows. Collectively, these results confirm that bad-news announcements, with the exception of external fraud events, cause a severe market-based reputational damage in the US financial industry.

Corporate governance changes following reputational damage in the US financial industry

Figures 5.1–5.5 illustrate mean corporate governance changes following no-announcement and bad-news announcement years (ie, income-decreasing restatements and operational risk events).[7] First of all, Figure 5.1 shows that the CEO is immediately punished for income-decreasing restatements while there are no material effects of operational risk announcements on the CEO turnover. The contrary seems to hold for non-CEO executive directors who turn out not to be held directly responsible for income-decreasing restatements while they are immediately punished for internal fraud events (Figure 5.2, Panels A and B). The insignificance of the turnover ratio of outgoing non-CEO executive directors around restatement announcements seems rather unexpected (Figure 5.2, Panels A and B), yet there could be two possible explanations. First, the non-CEO executive officer responsible for the restatement (eg, the chief financial officer) was not a member of the board at the time of the announcement. Second, shareholders and boards consider it sufficient to punish the head of the executive team (ie, the CEO) by firing him without punishing non-CEO executive directors, especially if they are not directly involved in the fraudulent behaviour or technical errors that caused the restatement.

Furthermore, Figure 5.2 (Panels C and D) shows that shareholders and boards react to restatement announcements by restricting the entrance of new non-CEO executive directors to the board rather than firing the incumbent non-CEO executive directors. Thus, restatement announcements are associated with fewer incoming

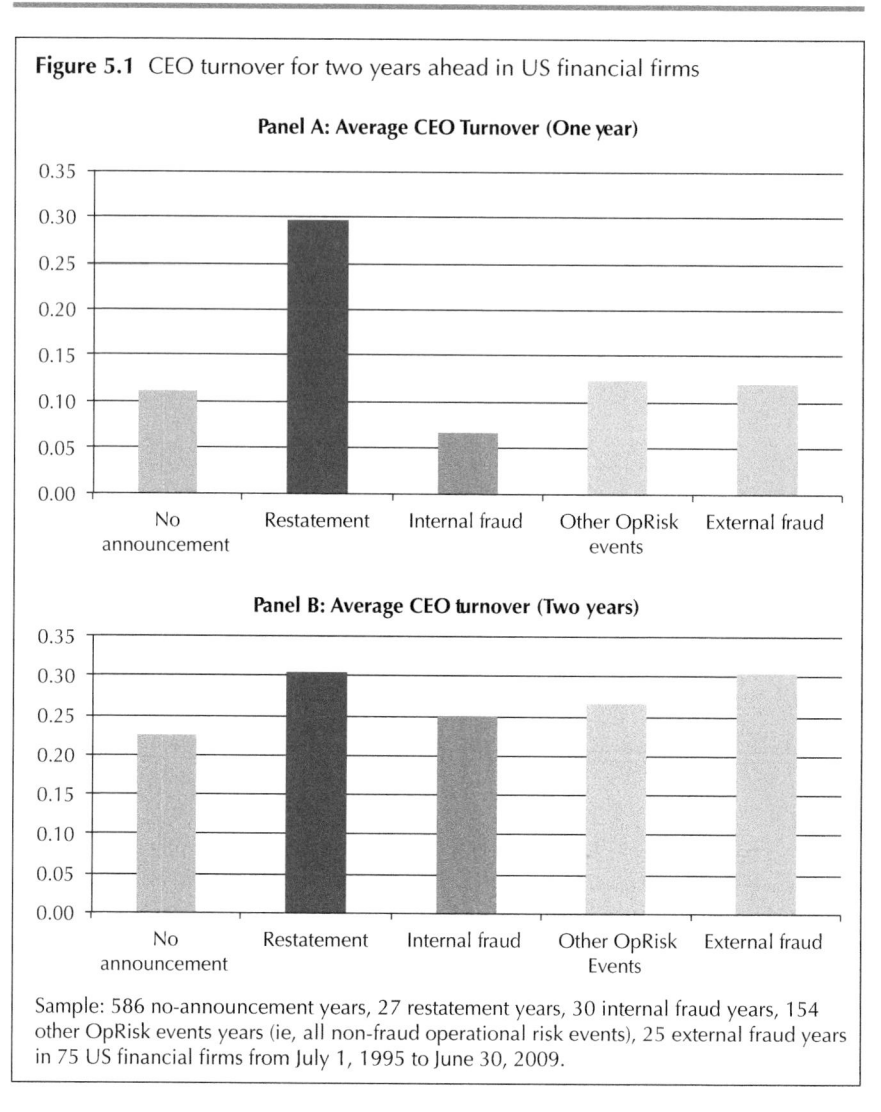

Figure 5.1 CEO turnover for two years ahead in US financial firms

Panel A: Average CEO Turnover (One year)

Panel B: Average CEO turnover (Two years)

Sample: 586 no-announcement years, 27 restatement years, 30 internal fraud years, 154 other OpRisk events years (ie, all non-fraud operational risk events), 25 external fraud years in 75 US financial firms from July 1, 1995 to June 30, 2009.

non-CEO executive directors while internal fraud announcements are associated with more outgoing non-CEO executive directors. Although they cause no reputational damage to the loss firms, external fraud announcements still motivate shareholders and boards to exclude non-CEO executive directors from the board (Figure 5.2, Panel B) and restrict the entrance of new non-CEO executive officers to the board (Figure 5.2, Panel D).

Figure 5.3 (Panels A and B) suggests that, compared with income-decreasing restatements, operational risk events are interpreted by

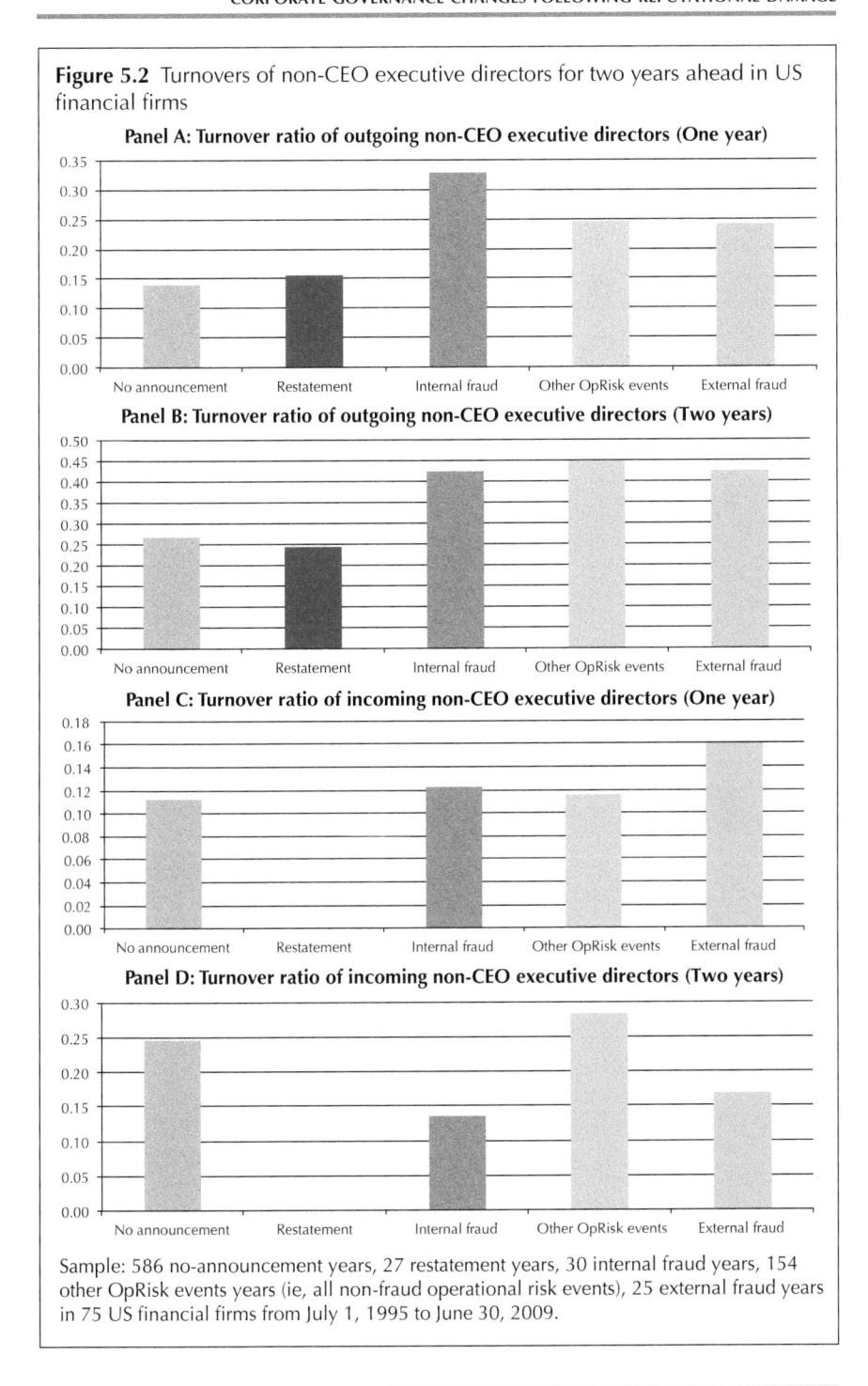

Figure 5.2 Turnovers of non-CEO executive directors for two years ahead in US financial firms

Panel A: Turnover ratio of outgoing non-CEO executive directors (One year)

Panel B: Turnover ratio of outgoing non-CEO executive directors (Two years)

Panel C: Turnover ratio of incoming non-CEO executive directors (One year)

Panel D: Turnover ratio of incoming non-CEO executive directors (Two years)

Sample: 586 no-announcement years, 27 restatement years, 30 internal fraud years, 154 other OpRisk events years (ie, all non-fraud operational risk events), 25 external fraud years in 75 US financial firms from July 1, 1995 to June 30, 2009.

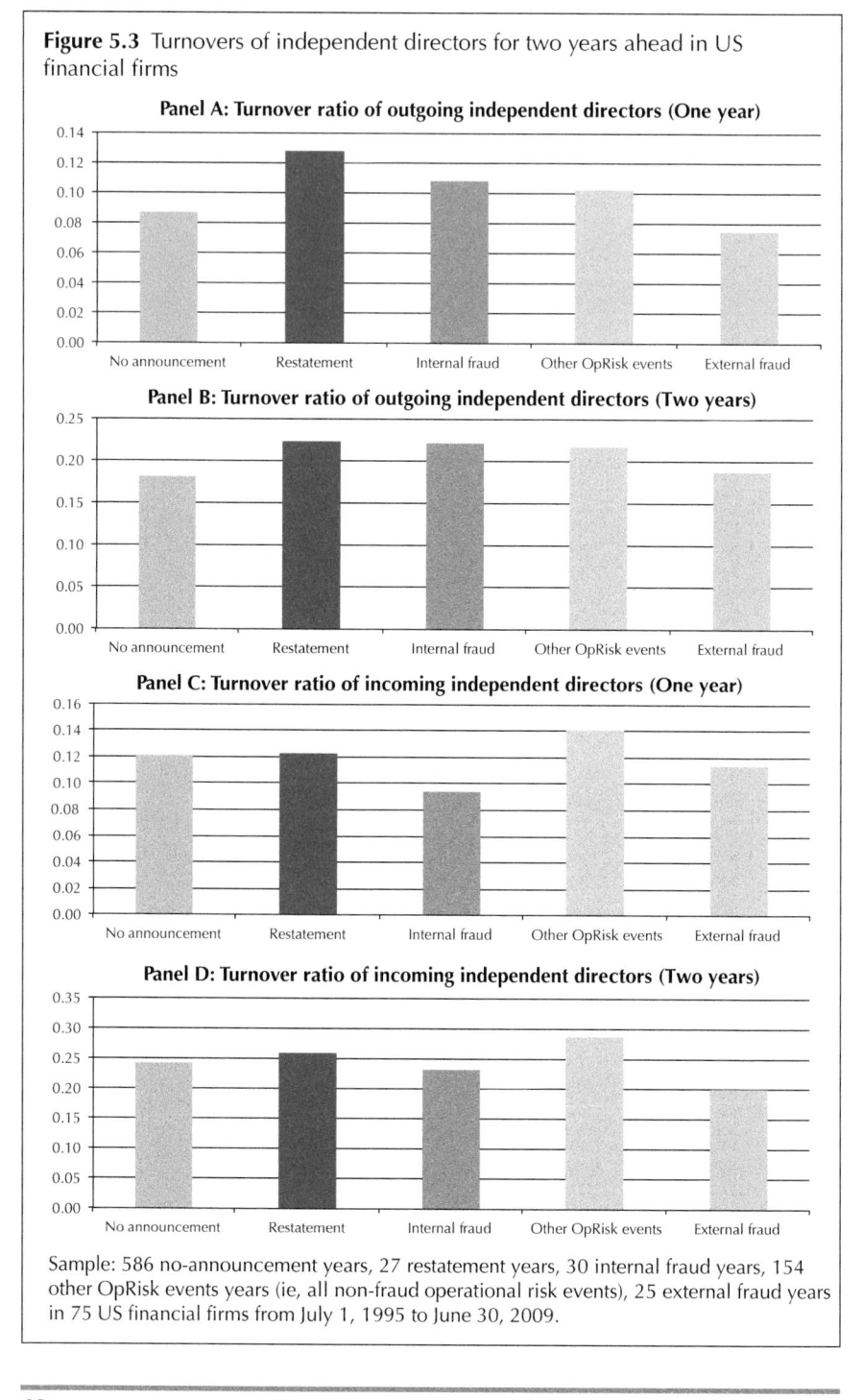

Figure 5.3 Turnovers of independent directors for two years ahead in US financial firms

Panel A: Turnover ratio of outgoing independent directors (One year)

Category	Ratio
No announcement	~0.085
Restatement	~0.125
Internal fraud	~0.105
Other OpRisk events	~0.100
External fraud	~0.075

Panel B: Turnover ratio of outgoing independent directors (Two years)

Category	Ratio
No announcement	~0.18
Restatement	~0.22
Internal fraud	~0.22
Other OpRisk events	~0.21
External fraud	~0.185

Panel C: Turnover ratio of incoming independent directors (One year)

Category	Ratio
No announcement	~0.12
Restatement	~0.12
Internal fraud	~0.095
Other OpRisk events	~0.14
External fraud	~0.115

Panel D: Turnover ratio of incoming independent directors (Two years)

Category	Ratio
No announcement	~0.24
Restatement	~0.255
Internal fraud	~0.23
Other OpRisk events	~0.285
External fraud	~0.20

Sample: 586 no-announcement years, 27 restatement years, 30 internal fraud years, 154 other OpRisk events years (ie, all non-fraud operational risk events), 25 external fraud years in 75 US financial firms from July 1, 1995 to June 30, 2009.

the shareholders and boards of financial firms as less serious indicators of the failure of incumbent independent directors in monitoring the integrity or efficiency of management. Even more, following external fraud announcements, shareholders and boards tend to support the presence of incumbent independent directors by limiting their exclusion from the board (Figure 5.3, Panel A).

Surprisingly, there is a negative association between internal fraud announcements and the presence of independent directors on board. This is an unexpected result since shareholders and boards are expected to increase the ratio of newly hired independent directors for the purpose of enhancing the board's monitoring of the integrity of management and lower-ranked employees. A possible explanation could be that, in the case of internal fraud, shareholders

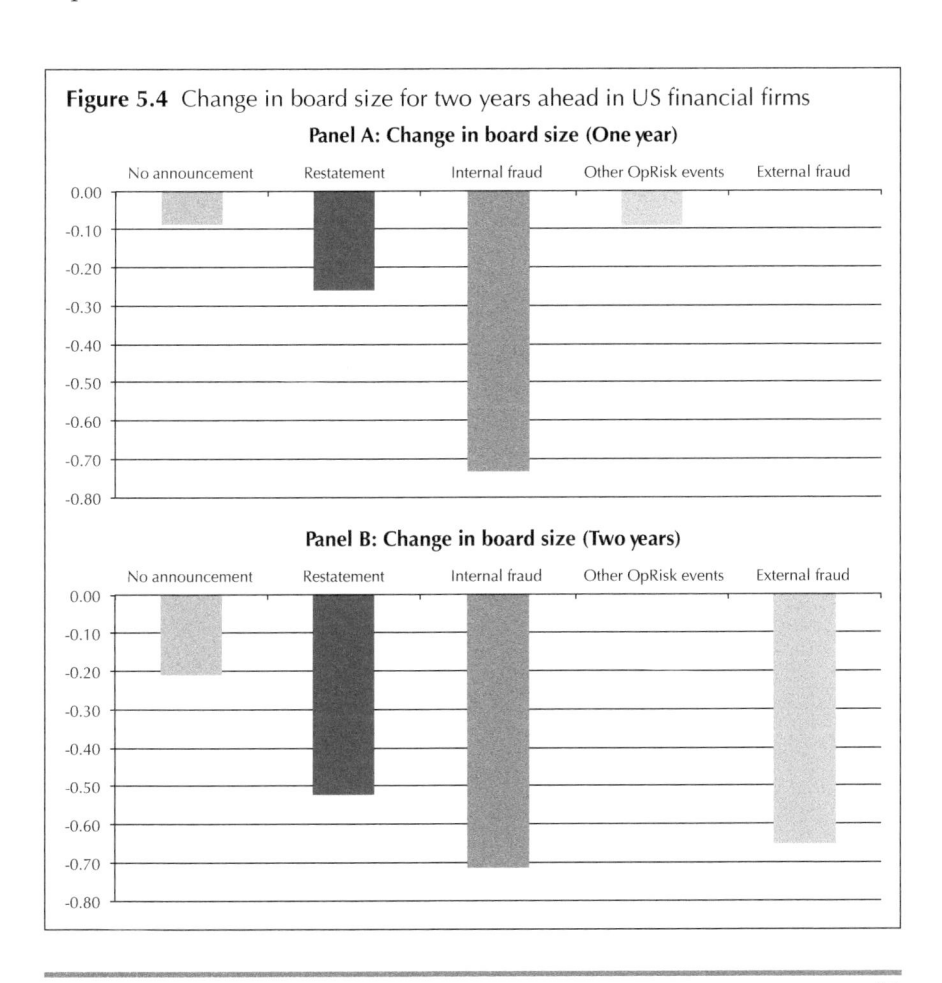

Figure 5.4 Change in board size for two years ahead in US financial firms

Panel A: Change in board size (One year)

Panel B: Change in board size (Two years)

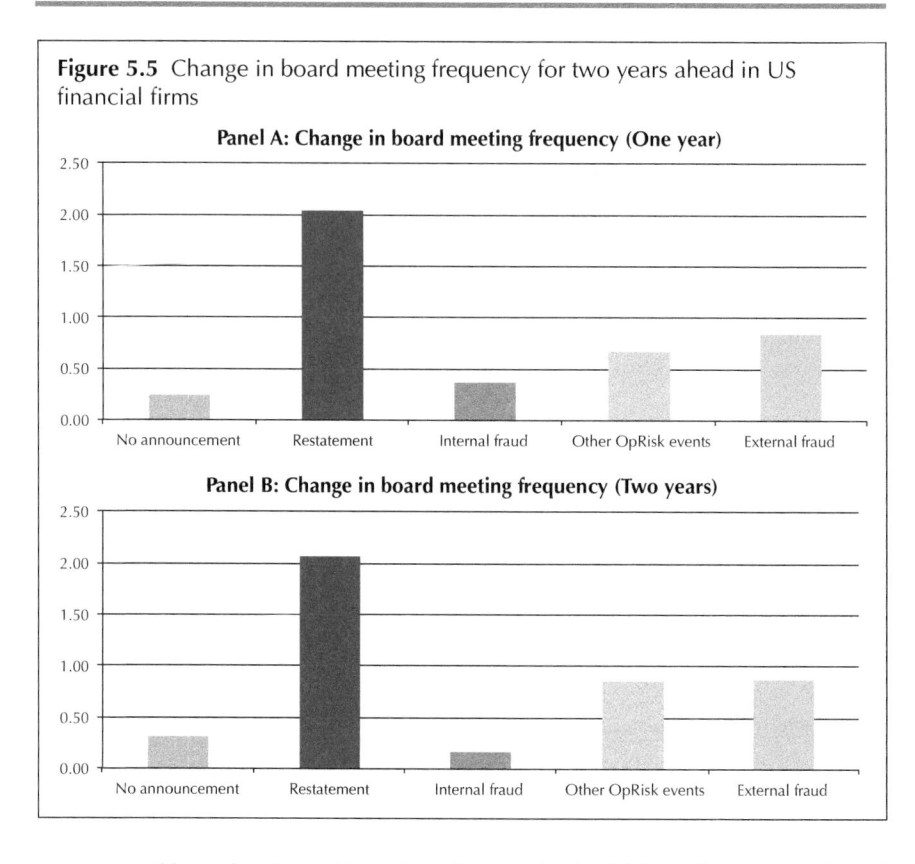

Figure 5.5 Change in board meeting frequency for two years ahead in US financial firms

Panel A: Change in board meeting frequency (One year)

Category	Value
No announcement	~0.25
Restatement	~2.00
Internal fraud	~0.35
Other OpRisk events	~0.65
External fraud	~0.85

Panel B: Change in board meeting frequency (Two years)

Category	Value
No announcement	~0.30
Restatement	~2.05
Internal fraud	~0.15
Other OpRisk events	~0.85
External fraud	~0.85

and boards attempt to reduce board size by hiring a lower number of new independent directors. This could reflect the belief of shareholders and boards that one major reason for the failure of the board to overview the installation of internal controls that are adequately efficient to prevent or detect early the fraudulent behaviour of executive officers or lower-ranked employees is inherent in the inefficient communication channels of oversized boards (Yermack 1996; Eisenberg *et al* 1998; Fernández *et al* 1998). As empirical evidence supporting this explanation, there is a strong negative association between internal fraud announcements and change in board size (Figure 5.4, Panels A and B).

Expectedly, there is consistent evidence that restatement and other OpRisk event announcements motivate the board to enhance its activity (Figure 5.5).

Moreover, it is interesting to note that boards become more active following restatement announcements than following other OpRisk event announcements. This finding suggests that the board anticipates that shareholders and capital markets view restatement announcements as more damaging to the reputation of the firm than other OpRisk event announcements. Therefore, the board might try to restore the trust of various stakeholders by more diligently enhancing its activity in the case of restatement announcements than it does in the case of other OpRisk event announcements.

How stock performance reacts to corporate governance changes following reputational damage in the US financial industry

Table 5.4 summarises the response of stock performance to various corporate governance changes following fiscal years seeing or free of bad-news announcements in the US financial industry.[8] The *ex post* stock performance (hereafter, stock performance) is measured by cumulative market-adjusted stock return (Benchmark is the CRSP value-weighted index) for one year ahead.

First of all, there is strong evidence that the CEO turnover, following other OpRisk event and external fraud announcements, has a negative impact on stock performance. One possible explanation is that capital markets interpret the immediate exclusion of the incumbent CEO in financial firms incurring other OpRisk event and external fraud announcements as a signal of an undisclosed serious flaw in the organisational structure and functioning of senior management. It is also noteworthy that the CEO turnover following restatement and internal fraud announcements does not have any significant impact on stock performance.

Table 5.4 Stock performance following corporate governance changes in the US financial industry

Announcement \ Corporate governance changes	Stock performance following:			
	CEO turnover executive directors	Increased presence of non-CEO directors	Increased presence of independent frequency	Increased board meeting
No bad news	None	None	None	None
Restatement	None	Negative	None	Positive
Internal fraud	None	Negative	Positive	None
Other OpRisk events	Negative	None	None	Positive
External fraud	Negative	None	None	None

Expectedly, enhancing board activity boosts stock performance for financial firms incurring restatement and other OpRisk event announcements. This finding implies that, for financial firms incurring restatement and other OpRisk event announcements, capital markets view the immediate enhancement in board activity during the announcement year as a positive signal that the board is dedicating more diligence to improving the efficiency of incompetent internal controls and other internal problems that might have caused these restatements or other OpRisk event losses. It seems that the same logic governs the decisions of boards and subsequent interpretations of capital markets regarding board activity in the case of restatement and other OpRisk event announcements. To put it another way, boards of financial firms incurring restatement and other OpRisk event announcements seem to enhance their activities (Figure 5.5) and capital markets seem to react positively to such enhancements (Table 5.4).

This table presents the response matrix of stock performance (ie, cumulative market-adjusted stock return during the fiscal year (Benchmark is the CRSP value-weighted index) to various corporate governance changes in 75 US financial firms from July 1, 1995, to June 30, 2009. Variable definitions are presented in Table 5.2.

Additionally, there is direct evidence that reducing the presence of non-CEO executive directors following restatement and internal fraud announcements strengthens stock performance. Therefore, capital markets seem to place more trust in financial firms that reduce the presence of non-CEO executive directors following restatement and internal fraud announcements.

Finally, capital markets react positively to an increase in the presence of independent directors on the board only following internal fraud announcements. This finding might indicate that, for financial firms incurring internal fraud announcements, capital markets view the immediate increase in the presence of independent directors on the board as a positive signal of enhancing the monitoring role of independent directors regarding the fraudulent behaviour of employees in different organisational ranks. This result also coincides with the findings of Farber (2005), who documented a positive association between long-run buy-and-hold abnormal stock returns and lagged change in the percentage of outside board directors following the announcement of fraudulent financial reporting cases detected by the SEC. Interestingly, following internal fraud announcements, the view of capital markets seems to be in opposition to the action of shareholders and boards since the latter attempt to reduce the board size by limiting the number of newly hired independent directors (Figures 5.3 and 5.4). This obvious opposition suggests that it is recommendable for shareholders and boards of financial firms incurring internal fraud announcements and opting to reduce their board sizes to first exclude the non-CEO executive directors, then limit the presence of independent directors on their boards. Hopefully, applying such a board restructuring policy, they might be able to optimise their firms' board sizes without further losing the trust of capital markets.

CONCLUSION

The findings of this chapter invite shareholders and boards of financial firms to understand the nature and extent of the market-based reputational damage, if any, that has been caused by bad-news announcements such as income-decreasing financial statement restatements or severe operational risk events. Consequently, they should properly decide on the change in the top management position, restructuring of the board composition and enhancement of the board activity that is most appropriate to alleviate any adverse reputational effects and restore the trust of their firms' stakeholders. Using US data from public sources and proprietary databases, we present a comprehensive analysis that should be beneficial to the shareholders and boards of financial firms and other practitioners in the financial industry in order to achieve a quantitative and accurate understanding and make decisions accordingly.

In this regard, this chapter presents numerous original findings. First, bad-news announcements (ie, operational risk event announcements and income-decreasing financial restatement announcements), with the exception of external fraud events, cause a severe market-based reputational damage in the financial industry. Second, financial firms respond to these bad-news announcements by implementing numerous corporate governance reforms such as replacing their CEOs (especially following restatement announcements), increasing the presence of independent directors and reducing the presence of non-CEO executive directors on the board, reducing board size (especially following internal fraud announcements) and enhancing board meeting frequency (especially following restatement announcements). Finally, capital markets seem to react positively to some of these corporate governance reforms, especially when financial firms reduce the presence of non-CEO executive board directors following restatement announcements, increase the presence of independent board directors following internal fraud announcements and enhance board meeting frequency following restatement announcements and non-fraud internally caused operational risk event announcements.

1 CEO, numbers of non-CEO executive board directors and independent board directors, board size and board meeting frequency.
2 The source of the data on operational risk event announcements is the IBM Algo FIRST database, provided by IBM. Data on income-decreasing financial statement restatements is extracted from US General Accounting Office's (GAO's) financial statement restatement databases of 2003 and 2006 and the LexisNexis news database.
3 US General Accounting Office's definition: "A financial statement restatement occurs when a company, either voluntarily or prompted by auditors or regulators, revises public financial information that was previously reported. For purposes of this report, the restatement announcement is considered the market event to be measured" (US GAO 2002, p. 1).
4 *Star Tribune* (Minneapolis, MN): "McGuire leaving over stock options; UnitedHealth chairman William McGuire, caught up in the scandal over questionable stock options, is stepping down from the board. He will leave the CEO post by Dec. 1," October 16, 2006, LexisNexis News Database.
5 Non-fraud internally caused operational risk events (ie, other OpRisk events) encompass operational losses in the following event types: employment practices and workplace safety; clients, products, and business practices; business disruption and system failures; and execution, delivery and process management.
6 Complete results of the cross-sectional analysis and a relevant event study of the market-based reputational damage caused by bad-news announcements in the US financial industry are available upon request from the author.
7 Complete results of the univariate analyses and multivariate regressions of contemporaneous and lagged corporate governance changes following the market-based reputational damage in the US financial industry are available upon request from the author.
8 Complete results of the univariate analyses and multivariate regressions of stock performance following corporate governance changes in the US financial industry are available upon request from the author.

REFERENCES

Adams, R. B., and H. Mehran, 2005, "Corporate performance, board structure and its determinants in the banking industry", *Federal Reserve Bank of New York Staff Report No. 330.*

Agrawal, A., J. F. Jaffe and J. M. Karpoff, 1999, "Management turnover and corporate governance changes following the revelation of fraud" *Journal of Law and Economics* 42, pp. 309–42.

Arthaud-Day, M. L., S. T. Certo and C. M. Dalton, 2006, "A changing of the guard: executive and director turnover following corporate financial restatements", *Academy of Management Journal*, 49(6), pp. 1119–36.

Basel Committee on Banking Supervision, 2006a, "Enhancing corporate governance for banking organisations", Bank for International Settlements, Basel.

Basel Committee on Banking Supervision, 2006b, "International Convergence of Capital Measurement and Capital Standards", Bank for International Settlements, Basel.

Beneish, M. D., 1999, "Incentives and penalties related to earnings overstatements that violate GAAP", *Accounting Review* 74, pp. 425–57.

Caprio, G., L. Laeven and R. Levine, 2007, "Governance and banks valuations", *Journal of Financial Intermediation* 16, pp. 584–617.

Chernobai, A., P. Jorion and F. Yu, 2011, "The determinants of operational risk in U.S. financial firms", *Journal of Financial and Quantitative Analysis* 46(6), pp. 1683–1725.

Cummins, J. D., C. M. Lewis and R. Wei, 2006, "The market value impact of operational loss events for U.S. banks and insurers" *Journal of Banking and Finance* 30, pp. 2605–34.

de Andres, P., and E. Vallelado, 2008, "Corporate governance in banking: the role of the board of directors", *Journal of Banking and Finance* 32, pp. 2570–80.

Desai, H., C. E. Hogan and M. S. Wilkins, 2006, "The reputational penalty for aggressive accounting: earnings restatements and management turnover", *Accounting Review* 81(1), pp. 83–112.

Doyle, J., W. Ge, and S. McVay, 2007, "Determinants of weaknesses in internal control over financial reporting", *Journal of Accounting and Economics* 44, pp. 193–223.

Eisenberg, T., S. Sundgren and M. T. Wells, 1998, "Larger board size and decreasing firm value in small firms", *Journal of Financial Economics* 48, pp. 35–54.

Farber, D. B., 2005, "Restoring trust after fraud: does corporate governance matter?", *Accounting Review* 80(2), pp. 539–61.

Fernández, A. I., S. Gomez and C. Fernandez, 1998, "The effect of board size and composition on corporate performance", in Balling, M., E. Hennessy and R. O'Brien (eds), *Corporate Governance, Financial Markets and Global Convergence* (Boston: Kluwer Academic Publishers), pp. 1–16.

Gillet, R., G. Hübner and S. Plunus, 2010, "Operational risk and reputation in the financial industry", *Journal of Banking and Finance* 34, pp. 224–35.

Gilson, S. C., 1989, "Management turnover and financial distress", *Journal of Financial Economics* 25, pp. 211–62.

Hennes, K. M., A. J. Leone and B. P. Miller, 2008, "The importance of distinguishing errors from irregularities in restatement research: the case of restatements and CEO/CFO turnover", *Accounting Review* 83(6), pp. 1487–1519.

Hermalin, B. E., and M. S. Weisbach, 1988, "The determinants of board composition" *RAND Journal of Economics* 19, pp. 589–606.

Jensen, M., 1993, "The modern industrial revolution, exit, and the failure of internal control systems", *Journal of Finance* 48, pp. 831–880.

Martin, K. T., and J. J. McConnell, 1991, "Corporate performance, corporate takeovers and management turnover", *Journal of Finance* 46(2), pp. 671–87.

Palmrose, Z., V. J. Richardson and S. Scholz, 2004, "Determinants of market reactions to restatement announcements", *Journal of Accounting and Economics* 37, pp. 59–89.

Palmrose, Z., and S. Scholz, 2004, "The circumstances and legal consequences of non-GAAP reporting: evidence from restatements", *Contemporary Accounting Research* 21(1), pp. 139–80.

Perry, J. and P. de Fontnouvelle, 2005, "Measuring reputational risk: the market reaction to operational loss announcements", working paper, Federal Reserve Bank of Boston.

Srinivasan, S., 2005, "Consequences of financial reporting failure for outside directors: evidence from accounting restatements and audit committee members", *Journal of Accounting Research* 43(2), pp. 291–334.

US General Accounting Office, 2002, "Financial Statement Restatements: Trends, Market Impacts, Regulatory Responses, and Remaining Challenges", Report to the Chairman, Committee on Banking, Housing, and Urban Affairs, US Senate.

Vafeas, N., 1999, "Board meeting frequency and firm performance", *Journal of Financial Economics* 53, pp. 113–42.

Yermack, D., 1996, "Higher market valuation of companies with a small board of directors", *Journal of Financial Economics* 40, pp. 185–211.

Part 2

Methodologies and Processes for Managing Reputational Risk

6

Reputational Risk and Prudential Regulation

Mattia L. Rattaggi

UBS

INTRODUCTION

The prudential banking regulation literature issued by a primary global standard setter such as the Basel Committee on Banking Supervision (BCBS) abounds with references to reputational risk.[1] Similar references characterise the ongoing dialogue between banks and their supervisors.

This chapter focuses first on the prudential regulation of reputational risk. Reviewing the relevant publications issued by the BCBS, it emerges that the stance taken by the prudential regulators can be characterised by (i) the absence of capital charge for reputational risk, (ii) a specific definition of reputational risk and (iii) the principle of no direct regulation of reputational risk.

The subsequent section "Critical appraisal" contrasts the definition of reputational risk put forward by the prudential regulators with the definition characterising the approach taken by the business economists. The fundamental differences are that the prudential regulators neglect internal stakeholders (the employees) and do not consider – understandably – the upsides, ie, reputational gains.

Next, we make the point that the reality of banking has consistently presented us with institutions experiencing significant reputational losses but eventually embarking on a recovery process, with substantial engagement by the prudential regulators. We then note that re-establishing a good reputation among employees is the first step to recovering the external perception of the firm.

Recovering reputation is a process that occurs over a long period and requires discipline and consistency in the effort to influence perceptions based on bottom-line improvements.

Finally we highlight that, due to their significant engagement in the broad recovery process, prudential regulators play *"nolens volens"*, a non-neutral role also in connection with reputation recovery.

In the conclusion we argue that prudential regulation could better reflect the importance of reputation recovery and the role of supervision in this process, particularly in connection with areas such as (external) communication, HR/compensation approach and the overhaul of governance and control processes. A recent consultation paper issued by the European Banking Authority (2014) seems to anticipate such development and also a more structured role of supervision in reputational risk assessment and management.

THE PRUDENTIAL REGULATION OF REPUTATIONAL RISK

A browse through the relevant BCBS literature (as discussed above) reveals an important event in June 1999, when the BCBS issued its consultative paper (CP) entitled "A New Capital Adequacy Framework" (first CP on Basel II). Recognising the importance of a rigorous control environment for the management of reputational risk and risks other than credit and market risk, the BCBS stated its intention to develop a capital charge for reputational risk (Basel Committee on Banking Supervision 1999, p. 50).

By January 2001, the BCBS had abandoned its intention. The second CP on Basel II, issued in January 2001, explicitly excluded reputational risk for the purposes of a minimum (Pillar I) regulatory capital charge (Basel Committee on Banking Supervision 1001a, p.94).

The decision not to develop an explicit capital charge for reputational risk was presumably taken during the second half of the year 2000. In the months following the issuance of the first CP on Basel II, the industry, represented by bodies such as the Institute of International Finance (IIF) and the International Swaps and Derivatives Association (ISDA), discussed at length the handling of reputational risk with the Risk Management Group of the BCBS. The industry argued that reputational risk should be excluded from capital charges out of concern for double-counting. It was observed that reputational losses are consequential. They follow credit, market or operational[2] losses. The reputation of a firm declines when it becomes known that the firm has inappropriately managed these risks. Thus, attaching capital to reputational risk would either double-count the capital attracted by these risks or mean that the capital held against these risks was insufficient – thereby questioning the calibration of the risk-based capital framework. The discussion was fundamental and focused on institution-specific issues material enough to question the viability of the firm.

The next relevant prudential regulatory episode occurred in 2004, when the BCBS issued the Basel II framework (Basel Committee on Banking Supervision 2004b, 2005c, 2005d). Pillar II ("Supervisory Review Process") comments on reputational risk by formulating the expectation that the industry further develops techniques for managing all aspects of other risks such as reputational risk. Pillar II reserves the right to the supervisors to require banks to hold capital in excess of the Pillar I minimum in case the risk characteristics of a bank suggested that capital could fall below the minimum levels. This provision is, however, not tied to any particular risk, such as reputational risk, and the BCBS also explicitly refers to other remedial actions, such as strengthening risk management, applying internal limits, increasing the level of provisions and reserves, and improving internal controls.

The financial crisis of 2007–8 led the BCBS to specify its thinking around reputational risk in the context of the securitisation process and the provision of implicit support to off-balance-sheet vehicles. In its "Enhancements to the Basel II framework" (Basel Committee on Banking Supervision 2009a) the BCBS put forward the following definition of reputational risk (Basel Committee on Banking Supervision 2009a, p. 19):

> The risk arising from negative perception on the part of customers, counterparties, shareholders, investors, debt-holders, market analysts, other relevant parties or regulators that can adversely affect a bank's ability to maintain existing, or establish new, business relationships and continued access to sources of funding (eg through the interbank or securitisation markets).

The BCBS also confirmed the consequential nature of reputational risk (Basel Committee on Banking Supervision 2009a, p. 19):

> Exposure to reputational risk is essentially a function of the adequacy of the bank's internal risk management processes, as well as the

manner and efficiency with which management responds to external influences on bank-related transactions.

For the sake of completeness, we note that Basel III (Basel Committee on Banking Supervision 2010d, 2013c) mentions reputational risk only in connection with liquidity standards, in line with the argument introduced in 2009. Finally, the Financial Stability Board (FSB), which has coordinated the overall set of measures to handle the "too-big-to-fail" problem, issued important principles and guidance from 2009 to 2013 (Financial Stability Board 2009a, 2009b, 2009c, 2010, 2011, 2013), which, however, do not affect the prudential regulatory approach to reputational risk established by the BCBS in the years before.

In conclusion, the prudential regulatory handling of reputational risk can be characterised by the absence of capital charge for reputational risk, the definition of reputational risk issued in 2009 and the principle of no direct regulation of reputational risk.

Regarding the last element, let us recognise that an effective direct regulation of the reputational risk of a bank would be of an extraordinary far-reaching nature. To be direct and effective the regulation would have to be directed at the stakeholders of the bank and specifically at their perceptions of that bank. Only by directly affecting the stakeholders' perceptions could the authorities directly limit or influence the potential for these perceptions to change, which is the reputational risk faced by the bank.

Throughout the publications, regulators make reference to reputational risk only indirectly, in the context of the regulation of market, credit and operational risks, capital adequacy, liquidity management, securitisation, compliance, KYC, AML, external and internal audits, business continuity, outsourcing, corporate governance, stress testing, economic capital and remuneration. The proper handling of such risks and practices, including the proper handling of their communication, benefits reputational risk.

The section "Reputational Risk Management" of the Supervisory Policy Manual issued by the Hong Kong Monetary Authority (2008) highlights remarkably well and comprehensively the reputational risk management aspects embedded in these key governance and risk management activities.

CRITICAL APPRAISAL

Prudential regulators and business economists associate the same dynamic to reputational risk: reputation changes encourage or discourage shareholders in investing in a firm, facilitate or complicate retaining or attracting customers and employees, stimulate or dampen the selling of products and services – affecting the financial performance of a firm.[3]

The analysis of reputational risk by prudential regulators, however, tends to focus more on the firm (ie, the object of the reputation) and on the (idiosyncratic) causes of reputational losses, than on the stakeholders (the holders of the reputation) and the way the reputation about the firm is formed. That is, stakeholders are rather implicitly assumed to act or react uniformly to changes affecting the condition of the firm.

The comparative lack of focus on the way stakeholders form perceptions limits the explanatory power of the analysis of reputational risk and dims important analytical aspects. It hampers, for instance, the ability to explain why the reputation of a firm can – as it does – deteriorate or improve even in the absence of any idiosyncratic change, or why the reputation attached to a product varies across markets, regions and clusters of the society, or why, in the face of an event affecting the firm, the impact on reputation is different in different regions, markets and societal clusters.

In reality, agents distinguish themselves by specific combinations of culture, habits, education, knowledge, socialisation, values, beliefs and experiences, all of which constantly evolve. The consequence is that each individual perception of a firm, and of changes affecting it, is unique at any point in time. Thus, given an event affecting a firm, changes in perception are going to be – to some extent – mixed and variegated across the stakeholders and this fact needs to be considered when handling reputational losses.

Business economists defines corporate reputation as "the perception of a firm by external parties, such as customers, shareholders, counterparties, investors, analysts, regulators, media, and internal parties, i.e. the employees".[4] Accordingly, reputational risk is the potential for that perception to change.

Compared with the corporate definition of reputation, the definition endorsed by prudential regulators (see the previous section) is centred on the perception by parties external to the bank, such as customers, investors, analysts, regulators. Internal constituencies, namely the employees, are neglected.

Moreover, the definition put forward by prudential regulators focuses on reputational loss, or the worsening of perceptions. While the focus on the downside is understandable, neglecting the upside hides the fact that reputational gains, the improvement of perceptions, take a much longer time to achieve than reputational losses.[5]

The aspects highlighted above are important because the reality of banking has presented us with institutions experiencing severe difficulties and significant reputational losses but eventually embarking on a recovery process. The normal case is not given by reputational losses ending with the eventual default of the institution, but rather by banks that, following severe reputational damage, avoided the default and initiated the long journey to re-establish the reputation.

The re-establishment of the reputation by external stakeholders starts with the re-establishment of the credibility of the firm and its top management by the employees. A firm with a compromised corporate identity, a failed strategy, severe financial losses, a broken corporate culture and high suffered or induced attrition rates is not well positioned to generate a recovery in the perception by external stakeholders. Improvements of employees' perception begins with the development of a corporate culture providing the required internal credibility and supporting the generation of sustainable performance. This situation will feed a virtuous circle, which, eventually, will extend positively to external perception.

Reputation can be estimated and tracked over time through methods such as "perception sampling" (carried out through interviews and polls). With respect to such approaches, however, we should never lose sight of the fact that the tracked points are not comparable. Each sample is a unique, subjective and partial characterisation of the reputation, reflecting the aggregated state of mind about a firm of the individuals constituting the sample when the polling occurs.[6] Another sample, or the same sample polled at a different time, would produce a different assessment because the generative structure of such assessment – that is, the mental state of each individual sampled – would have changed.

In sum, supervisors, rightly so, attach the greatest importance and focus to the recovery process of tattered banks and engage themselves accordingly. Yet, prudential regulation remains silent on the role of supervision in this process. We have seen that the definition of reputational risk currently endorsed by prudential regulators does not help: it undeservedly overlooks aspects such as the role of firm's internal stakeholders and the length of time required by the process of re-establishment of reputation. This state of affairs also does not commend the reality of supervision and of prudential regulation, which, following the crisis of 2007–8, has been very much focused on the recovery process.

CONCLUSION

This chapter focused on the prudential regulatory treatment of reputational risk. It highlighted fundamental elements characterising this handling, such as the absence of capital charge for reputational risk, a specific definition of reputational risk and the principle of no direct regulation of reputational risk. The critical appraisal found no reasons to disagree with these elements but identified a gap between the reputation-related pronouncements made in prudential regulation and the reality of the intense work performed by prudential regulators during the reputation recovery process.

The relevant areas of influence during this relatively long and delicate period of reputation recovery are:

❏ The process of redefinition of adequate governance and controls: through their supervisory action, regulators play a non-neutral role in the effort by management to redefine governance and control processes, which will form the basis for building a culture supportive of sustainable performance. This in turn will help recovering the reputation held by employees in the first place.
❏ Employment decisions and remuneration policy: hiring and staffing of key roles and the remuneration policy more broadly are closely connected to the stability and the quality of human resources, which are important factors supporting a rapid and effective recovery. The employees also represent an important channel to influence the perception of external stakeholders.
❏ External communication: the perception of a firm in recovery mode is highly sensitive to regulatory communication and supervisory signals, which should be oriented towards predictability and consistency and should be effectively coordinated.

In the aftermath of the crisis of 2007–8, prudential regulators enhanced significantly the depth and breadth of their supervisory activity – particularly for the bigger banks. The supervisory areas of influence of reputation management mentioned above are bound to remain active post-recovery and likely to assume a permanent character. The recent consultation paper issued by the European Banking Authority (2014, pp. 85–100) supports this direction by spelling out elements of supervisory assessment and management of reputational risk.

In the aftermath of a severe crisis, management and supervisors are united in sharing and pursuing the goal of (reputational) recovery. While this also implies shared responsibilities, it is crucial that the supervisory and management actions always preserve clear and transparent complementary roles, scopes and responsibilities – including in "run-the-bank" mode.

I am grateful to a number of reviewers for their helpful comments. The views expressed in this text are uniquely my personal views in my capacity as an industry expert.

1 See, for instance, Basel Committee on Banking Supervision (2001b: pp 67, 68, 152), (2001c: pp 8, 24), (2004a: pp 4, 7, 8), (2005a, pp. 17, 20, 23, 26, 27), (2005b, pp. 7, 10, 15), (2006a, pp. 158, 222, 303), (2006b, pp. 7, 13), (2006c, pp. 23, 31, 36), (2006d, pp. 20, 21), (2008a, pp. 9, 15, 18), (2008b, pp. 7, 11, 24), (2008c, pp. 12, 17, 18, 20, 23), (2008d, pp. 14, 16, 18, 19, 23, 24, 27, 32, 34, 35), (2008e: p 12), (2009a, pp. 5, 15, 16, 19, 20, 23, 24, 25, 26, 31), (2009b, pp. 11, 12, 16, 18, 20, 24), (2010a, pp. 17, 18), (2010b: p 35), (2010c, pp. 17, 21, 28, 34, 36, 42), (2011a, pp. 27, 29, 38, 47, 57), (2011b, pp. 11, 23, 25), (2012a, pp. 7, 8, 10), (2012b, pp. 12, 42, 50, 63, 65, 71), (2012c, pp. 14, 44, 45, 47), (2013a, pp. 24, 27), (2013b, pp. 5, 28).
2 It should be noted that the discussion based on a definition of operational risk defined as "the risk of direct or indirect loss resulting from inadequate or failed internal processes, people and systems or from external events. This definition includes legal risk. However, strategic and reputational risk is not included in this definition for the purpose of a minimum regulatory operational risk capital charge" (Basel Committee on Banking Supervision 2001a, p 94).
3 For the "business economist" view see for instance Markham (1972), Rindova and Fombrun (1998), Hall (1992), Balmer (1997), Bromley (1993), Robert and Dowling (1997), Reichheld (1996).
4 Thus, for R. Chun (2005), corporate reputation is "the summary view of the perceptions held by all relevant stakeholders of an organisation, that is, what customers, employees, suppliers, managers, creditors, media and communities believe the organisation stands for, and the associations they make with it" (p. 105).
5 As Warren Buffett put it, "it takes 20 years to build a reputation and five minutes to ruin it" (Buffet 2009).
6 See also Shamma (2012, pp. 162–3).

REFERENCES

Balmer, J. M. T., 1997, "Corporate identity: what of it, why the confusion, and what's next?", *Corporate Reputation Review* 1 pp. 183–8.

Basel Committee on Banking Supervision, 1999, "A New Capital Adequacy Framework and Capital Standards, A Revised Framework", Bank for International Settlements, Basel.

Basel Committee on Banking Supervision, 2001a, "Consultative Document The New Basel Capital Accord", Bank for International Settlements, Basel.

Basel Committee on Banking Supervision, 2001b, "Compendium of documents produced by the Joint Forum", Bank for International Settlements, Basel.

Basel Committee on Banking Supervision, 2001c, "Working Paper on the Regulatory Treatment of Operational Risk", Bank for International Settlements, Basel.

Basel Committee on Banking Supervision, 2004a, "Consolidated KYC Risk Management", Bank for International Settlements, Basel.

Basel Committee on Banking Supervision, 2004b, "International Convergence of Capital Measurement and Capital Standards, A Revised Framework", Bank for International Settlements, Basel.

Basel Committee on Banking Supervision, 2005a, "Outsourcing in Financial Services", Bank for International Settlements, Basel.

Basel Committee on Banking Supervision, 2005b, "Compliance and the compliance function in banks", Bank for International Settlements, Basel.

Basel Committee on Banking Supervision, 2005c, "International Convergence of Capital Measurement", Bank for International Settlements, Basel.

Basel Committee on Banking Supervision, 2005d, "The Application of Basel II to Trading Activities and the Treatment of Double Default Effects", Bank for International Settlements, Basel.

Basel Committee on Banking Supervision, 2006a, "International Convergence of Capital Measurement and Capital Standards", Bank for International Settlements, Basel.

Basel Committee on Banking Supervision, 2006b, "High-level principles for business continuity", Bank for International Settlements, Basel.

Basel Committee on Banking Supervision, 2006c, "Core Principles Methodology", consultative paper, Bank for International Settlements, Basel.

Basel Committee on Banking Supervision, 2006d, "Observed range of practice in key elements of Advanced Measurement Approaches (AMA)", Bank for International Settlements, Basel.

Basel Committee on Banking Supervision, 2008a, "Liquidity Risk – Management and Supervisory Challenges", Bank for International Settlements, Basel.

Basel Committee on Banking Supervision, 2008b, "Implementation of the compliance principles", Bank for International Settlements, Basel.

Basel Committee on Banking Supervision, 2008c, "Range of practices and issues in economic capital modelling", Bank for International Settlements, Basel.

Basel Committee on Banking Supervision, 2008d, "Principles for Sound Liquidity Risk Management and Supervision", Bank for International Settlements, Basel.

Basel Committee on Banking Supervision, 2008e, "External audit quality and banking supervision", Bank for International Settlements, Basel.

Basel Committee on Banking Supervision, 2009a, "Enhancements to the Basel II framework", Bank for International Settlements, Basel.

Basel Committee on Banking Supervision, 2009b, "Principles for sound stress testing practices and supervision – consultative paper", Bank for International Settlements, Basel.

Basel Committee on Banking Supervision, 2010a, "Compensation Principles and Standards Assessment Methodology", Bank for International Settlements, Basel.

Basel Committee on Banking Supervision, 2010b, "Report and Recommendations of the Cross-border Bank Resolution Group", Bank for International Settlements, Basel.

Basel Committee on Banking Supervision, 2010c, "Principles for enhancing corporate governance", Bank for International Settlements, Basel.

Basel Committee on Banking Supervision, 2010d, "Basel III: A global regulatory framework for more resilient banks and banking systems", Bank for International Settlements, Basel.

Basel Committee on Banking Supervision, 2011a, "Range of Methodologies for Risk and Performance Alignment of Remuneration", Bank for International Settlements, Basel.

Basel Committee on Banking Supervision, 2011b, "Principles for the Sound Management of Operational Risk", Bank for International Settlements, Basel.

Basel Committee on Banking Supervision, 2012a, "The internal audit function in banks", Bank for International Settlements, Basel.

Basel Committee on Banking Supervision, 2012b, "Core Principles for Effective Banking Supervision", Bank for International Settlements, Basel.

Basel Committee on Banking Supervision, 2012c, "Principles for the supervision of financial conglomerates – final report", Bank for International Settlements, Basel.

Basel Committee on Banking Supervision, 2013a, "External audits of banks", Bank for International Settlements, Basel.

Basel Committee on Banking Supervision, 2013b, "Sound management of risks related to money laundering and financing of terrorism", Bank for International Settlements, Basel.

Basel Committee on Banking Supervision, 2013c, "Basel III: The Liquidity Coverage Ratio and liquidity risk monitoring tools", Bank for International Settlements, Basel.

Bromley, D. B., 1993, *Reputation, Image and Impression Management* (Chichester: John Wiley).

Buffet, W., 2009, "US Entrepreneur and Financier", *Independent*, October 28.

Chun R., 2005, "Corporate Reputation: Meaning and Measurement", *International Journal of Management Review*, 7(2), pp. 91–109.

European Banking Authority, 2014, "Draft Guidelines for common procedures and methodologies for the supervisory review and evaluation process under Article 107 (3) of Directive 2013/36/EU".

Financial Stability Board, 2009a, "Principles for Cross-border Cooperation on Crisis Management", Bank for International Settlements, Basel.

Financial Stability Board, 2009b, "Principles for Sound Compensation Practices", Bank for International Settlements, Basel.

Financial Stability Board, 2009c, "Guidance to Assess the Systemic Importance of Financial Institutions, Markets and Instruments: Initial Considerations", Bank for International Settlements, Basel.

Financial Stability Board, 2010, "Intensity and Effectiveness of SIFI Supervision – Recommendations for Enhanced Supervision", Bank for International Settlements, Basel.

Financial Stability Board, 2011, "Key Attributes of Effective Resolution Regimes for Financial Institutions", Bank for International Settlements, Basel.

Financial Stability Board, 2013a, "Guidance on Developing Effective Resolution Strategies", Bank for International Settlements, Basel.

Financial Stability Board, 2013b, "Guidance on Identification of Critical Functions and Critical Shared Services", Bank for International Settlements, Basel.

Hall, R., 1992, "The strategic analysis of intangible resources", *Strategic Management Journal* 13, pp. 135–44.

Hong Kong Monetary Authority, 2008, "Supervisory Policy Manual, RR-1 Reputation Risk Management", available at www.hkma.gov.hk/eng/key-functions/banking-stability/supervisory-policy-manual.shtml.

Markham, V., 1972, *Planning the Corporate Reputation* (London: George Allen & Unwin).

Reichheld, F. F., 1996, *The Loyalty Effect: the Hidden Force Behind Growth, Profits and Lasting Value* (Boston: Harvard Business School Press).

Rindova, V. P. and C. J. Fombrun, 1998, "The eye of the beholder: the role of corporate reputation in defining organisational identity", in D. A. Whetten and P. C. Godfrey (eds), *Identity in Organisations: Building Theory Through Conversations* (Thousand Oaks, CA: Sage), pp 62–6.

Robert, P. W. and G. R. Downling, 1997, "The value of a firm's corporate reputation: how reputation helps and sustain superior profitability", *Corporate Reputation Review* 1(1/2), pp. 72–6.

Shamma, H. M., 2012, "Towards a Comprehensive Understanding of Corporate Reputation: Concept, Measurement and Implications", *International Journal of Business and Management* 7(16), pp. 151–69.

7
Managing Stakeholder Expectations

Sandra Dow
Middlebury College

INTRODUCTION

The 2008 financial crisis shook the global financial system and arrested economic growth. At the epicenter of the financial crisis were the too-big-to-fail financial institutions (TBTFs), which included AIG, Lehman Brothers, Merrill Lynch, Bear Stearns, Countrywide Financial, JPMorgan Chase, Bank of America, Citigroup, Wells Fargo, State Street, Goldman Sachs, Bank of New York Mellon and Morgan Stanley. In this chapter we explore whether these TBTFs met stakeholder expectations in the period preceding the crisis, at the crisis and during the post-crisis fallout. We argue that the failures in corporate governance in the financial services sector that led to excessive risk taking seem to have spilled over to treatment of other stakeholders.

Banks[1] are financial intermediaries and this intermediation function exposes them to an array of significant stakeholder issues likely unparalleled in other industries. One perspective could suggest that, since they are intermediaries, the reputations of these stakeholders may be as critical to the reputation of the bank as those reputational issues that may be internally generated. In this framework, bank reputation would most likely be linked to the corporate social responsibility (CSR) profiles of a wide range of partners that encompass the usual list of customers, suppliers, employees, government, community and suppliers of financial capital. There is merit to this perspective. However, a focus on traditional stakeholder analysis that in the extreme does not prioritise various stakeholder interests or provide guidance on appropriate governance mechanisms to address them is particularly ill suited to frame and resolve the reputational issues of the financial services sector.

The financial services sector differs from the corporate sector in a number of significant ways. Mehran, Morrison and Shapiro (2011) point out that the key stakeholders of banks are depositors, creditors and the government (through deposit insurance and implicit guarantees of bailouts for systemically important financial institutions). Indeed, 90% of bank assets are financed by debt, which lies in sharp contrast to the more modest debt levels of the corporate sector, which hover around 40–50%. In effect, shareholders in the corporate sector have far more skin in the game than do shareholders in the financial sector. Mehran *et al* (2011) draw on the academic literature to make two additional observations: (1) bank governance is designed to prioritise shareholder interests and (2) bank ownership tends to be concentrated in the hands of institutional investors whose risk tolerance is far superior to those of other financial sector stakeholders. Furthermore, the pivotal role of financial institutions as a pillar of the global financial system has meant that governments implicitly and explicitly afford their creditors (debtholders and depositors) a protection that is unheard of in the corporate sector. In brief, the governance structure of financial institutions has been set up to imitate the corporate sector, despite the stark contrasts in ownership structure, owner identity and stakeholder interests. Consequently, the governance of financial institutions has evolved into a structure that facilitates operational risk and ultimately entrenches management, encouraging not only erosion of shareholder wealth but equally securing failure to meet the expectations of other stakeholders.

Trust in the integrity of the financial system is key to its development and impact on global economic growth. Trust is equally intimately tied to reputation. Like reputation, trust is the "output" of operational decisions undertaken by financial institutions. At the height of the 2008 financial crisis, mistrust among financial institutions was measurable and palpable (Cornett *et al* 2011). Trust began to unravel in the summer of 2007, when, as noted by Acharya and Schnabl (2010), the market started to question the integrity of asset-backed commercial paper that was guaranteed by mortgage securities of doubtful value and liquidity. By the height of the 2008 financial crisis, in October, the difference between the three-month Libor and the yield on three-month US treasury bills (the "Ted Spread") had burgeoned to more than 4.5%, well above the historic norm of 0.3%. As the T-bill rate proxies for the return on nominally riskless investments, increases in the Ted Spread reflected heightened counterparty risk in interbank transactions. By autumn 2008, credit markets had frozen. Cornett *et al* (2011) reveal that loans and unused loan facilities on bank balance sheets declined by US$500 billion (of a total US$14 trillion in annual balances) in the fourth quarter of 2008. The mistrust that immediately befell the financial players at the height of the crisis percolated downward to other stakeholders. Indeed, a Gallup Poll conducted between August 27 and August 30, 2010, found that only 18% of respondents trusted the US banking system. This figure was even lower than the confidence level accorded by respondents at the height of the financial crisis and reflected a downward spiral that had begun in 2006.

This chapter addresses the issues of reputational and stakeholder expectations in the financial services sector and argues that an appropriate governance structure must be devised in order to meet the expectations of key stakeholders. Management of reputational risk must proceed by rethinking both board structure and enterprise-risk-management processes. For the most part we focus on US financial institutions that form part of the too-big-to-fail segment of the financial services industry, although we also offer some anecdotal commentary regarding reputational issues of the broader international cohort of TBTFs identified by the Financial Stability Board. We organise the discussion as follows: in the next section, we focus on the performance record of financial institutions in meeting stakeholder expectations. We show that, in the years preceding the financial crisis (at the opening of the 21st century), the interests of non-financial stakeholders were largely ignored. During the crisis period there seemed to be some improvement in stakeholder engagement, but by 2011–12 this interest had once again waned. In the section that follows we provide an overview of the governance landscape of the TBTFs as they entered and exited the 2008 financial crisis. After that we discuss necessary changes to the governance regime and risk-management practices to engage and protect stakeholders and limit reputational risk. Conclusions follow.

FINANCIAL INSTITUTIONS AND STAKEHOLDER ENGAGEMENT
The corporate objective function and stakeholder expectations

The role of business is often viewed from two divergent perspectives: shareholder wealth maximisation and stakeholder engagement. For most of the 20th century the financial paradigm prevailed. Milton Friedman's 1970 editorial in the *New York Times* exemplified this paradigm: "the Social Responsibility of business is to increase its profits". Friedman's perspective naturally emphasised shareholder hegemony. Many corporate boards even questioned whether their fiduciary duty was at stake if issues other than those defined by narrow financial parameters were tabled. There is a strong logic behind the shareholder-centric perspective that is rooted in the nature of the modern corporation. Modern corporations are complex organisations where ownership and control are separate. Such separation creates agency problems where managers (the agents) are engaged by shareholders and tasked with maximising shareholder wealth. However, managers may pursue their individual agendas to the detriment of shareholder interests. The resolution of agency problems lies in finding ways to align managerial and shareholder objectives and corporate governance provides the framework within which this is accomplished.

By the 1980s, however, the shareholder-centric approach began to be questioned openly and debated in academia. In 1984, Freeman recommended a more holistic approach to business that placed the firm's many stakeholders, including financial stakeholders, on an equal footing. Following Freeman's pioneering work, the term "stakeholder" has been both widely used and fraught with ambiguity. Stakeholders, for Freeman, were any individuals or groups that could influence or were affected by the firm's operations. Such definitions are so loose, however, that virtually everyone is a stakeholder to a greater or lesser degree. Miles (2012) confirms this state of confusion and reports that, even in 1997, there were at least 38 varied definitions of stakeholders. Her own 2011 research surveyed 493 articles that offered 435 different definitions of "stakeholder", which translated to a new definition every 1.13 journal articles in her sample.

Jensen (2001) attempted to resolve the Freeman–Friedman extremes by recommending long-term shareholder wealth maximisation, where the costs of ignoring non-financial stakeholders (the community, employees and the environment for example) are internalised. In Jensen's world, long-term shareholder wealth maximisation would promote the interests of all other stakeholders in the firm's operations. Moreover, Jensen argued that allowing management to satisfy a broad range of stakeholder interests beyond those of financial stakeholders would promote managerial agency problems and misdirect corporate resources to the point that the only winners in the game are the managers themselves. In effect, Jensen argued that shareholders, and all other stakeholders, are better off when the manager is given a single unambiguous objective to maximise long-term shareholder value. The logic is highly appealing and rarely disputed by financial economists: it is mathematically impossible to maximise more than a single objective at a time and measurement of the objective (firm value) is readily available from the capital markets. Problem solved!

If we follow Jensen's prescription, long-term shareholder wealth maximisation will be consistent with meeting both financial and non-financial stakeholder expectations. Alternatively, the source of reputational issues in the financial services sector is precisely tied to failing many, if not all, the stakeholders. During the 2008 financial crisis and the Great Recession that it spawned, credit markets froze, the housing markets collapsed, unemployment spiralled upward, and the TBTFs were bailed out with taxpayer dollars. As we later show, management had cashed out billions of dollars before the onset of the financial crisis, and, within five years of the crisis, lofty executive compensation arrangements had re-established themselves. Clearly, the financial crisis, its aftermath, and continuing post-crisis scandals in the financial services sector point to failure – not success – in meeting stakeholder expectations. Was this indicative of the Jensen model, where multiple stakeholder objectives muddied waters and allowed self-dealing managers to prevail? To answer this question, however, we require a crisp definition of the stakeholders in the financial sector and then we require a means of evaluating performance on these objectives. We begin below with performance evaluation using arbitrary criteria set out by KLD, which is a RiskMetrics database that assesses firm level social performance across several dimensions.

TBTFs: stakeholder expectations and outcomes

Assessing the extent to which stakeholder expectations are met is a complex undertaking. While, for shareholders, shareholder returns provide an easily recognised and agreed-upon metric, gauging performance for broader stakeholder expectations remains a challenge. As with the multiplicity of definitions of stakeholder identity, there is no shortage of proposed metrics. Some of these metrics are reviewed by Porter and Kramer (2006), who explain, for example, that the Dow Jones Sustainability Index at their time of writing accorded almost 50% of the Corporate Social Responsibility (CSR) ranking score to customer service while also considering economic performance as part of the ranking recipe. By contrast, FTS4Good, a competitor index, included no weighting for economic performance or for customer service. Generally, in the absence of guidance emanating from agreed-upon metrics to measure stakeholder expectations, how could performance against these metrics even be assessed? Resolving this issue is beyond the scope of the present work. Rather, we decided to investigate how the TBTFs had met stakeholder expectations over time referencing a common database (KLD STATS) used by academic researchers and practitioners.

KLD identifies strengths and weaknesses of the firm along seven non-financial dimensions: environment, diversity, employee practices, product characteristics, community, human rights,[2] and corporate governance.[3] KLD scores firms by awarding one point for each strength and one for each weakness. Thus, firms may score higher than 1 for a particular category of strength if there are several positive attributes associated with the strength. For example, a score of 2 for environmental strength could reflect policies directed at pollution prevention and recycling efforts. Similarly, firms can score greater than 1 if more than a single concern is recorded in the above-named categories. Results for the set of TBTFs are displayed in Figures 7.1–7.5 with the governance exhibit and discussion following a little later.[4] Total strengths and concerns in each recorded period (2001–2, 2007–8, 2011–12) represent the sum of strengths and concerns for all TBTFs. Note that the sample shrank through time with the disappearance of Bear Stearns, Lehman Brothers, Merrill Lynch, Countrywide and the pre-crisis merger of Mellon Financial and the Bank of New York.[5]

Figure 7.1 displays the environmental strengths and weaknesses assessed for the sample of financial institutions deemed TBTF. Seven environmental strength and concern categories are delineated. Strength points are awarded for manufacture of environmentally beneficial products and services, pollution prevention, use of renewable energy, recycling, environmentally friendly maintenance of property, plant and equipment, disclosure of environmental practices and a final catch-all category to fold in other environmental initiatives such as proactive programmes and volunteer activities. Environmental weaknesses represent various categories of fines and penalties including hazardous waste and regulatory violations. In addition to these two concern categories, environmental concerns designate manufacturers of ozone-depleting substances, substantial emissions placing the firm at the top end of the KLD sample of firms, manufacture of pesticides and chemical fertilisers, sale of products or derivatives of coal and oil, and a final miscellaneous category to capture controversies otherwise unspecified.

Attention to environmental issues in the financial services sector began to appear around the time of the financial crisis. Notably, a spike in interest was recorded in 2011 with the industry collectively reporting 29 environmental strengths. This dropped off to a collective score of 11 strengths in 2012. Not surprisingly, given the nature

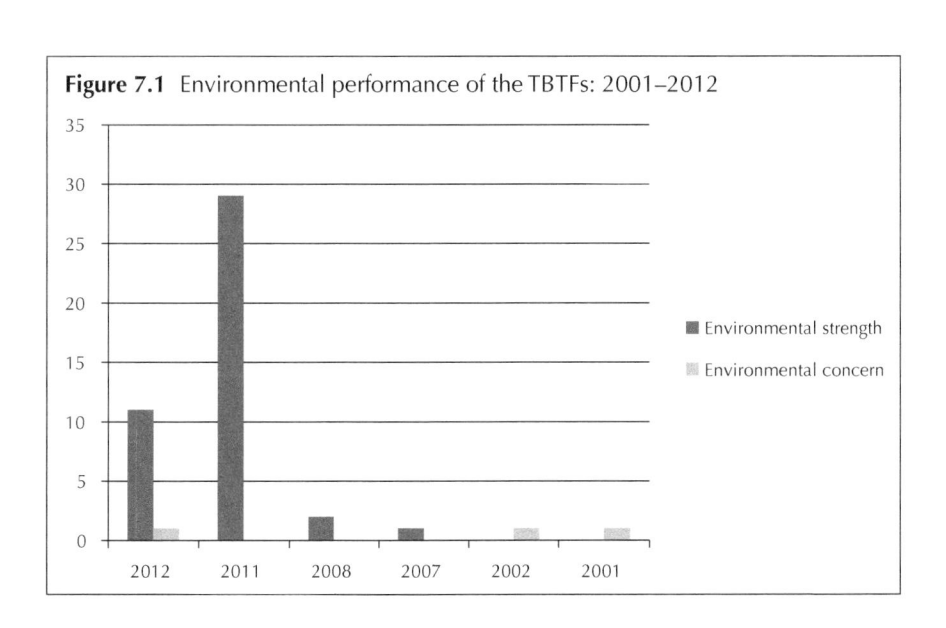

Figure 7.1 Environmental performance of the TBTFs: 2001–2012

of the financial services industry, direct environmental concerns were nearly absent throughout the period.

Community strengths and concerns for the TBTF sample are charted in Figure 7.2. KLD identifies eight strength categories, three of which refer to the level and method of charitable giving, two targeting housing and education initiatives, one aimed at policies targeting or affecting indigenous people, volunteer activities, and, lastly, an "other" category. Community weaknesses include actions causing negative economic impacts on the community (such as layoffs); policies or actions adversely affecting indigenous people; investment controversies, especially those related to the Community Reinvestment Act, which mandates availability of financial services to economically disadvantaged groups in the community; and a final miscellaneous category.

Community concerns for the TBTF segment overall rose through the first part of the 21st century peaking in 2008 at 10 total concerns for the sample. Coincident with the rise in concerns leading up to the financial crisis was the rise in strengths to 21 in 2007, falling off to 17 a year later when some of the TBTFs disappeared from the sample. In 2011 and 2012, community strengths remained stable at 10, while weaknesses had fallen to 2 in total in 2011 and disappeared completely in 2012.

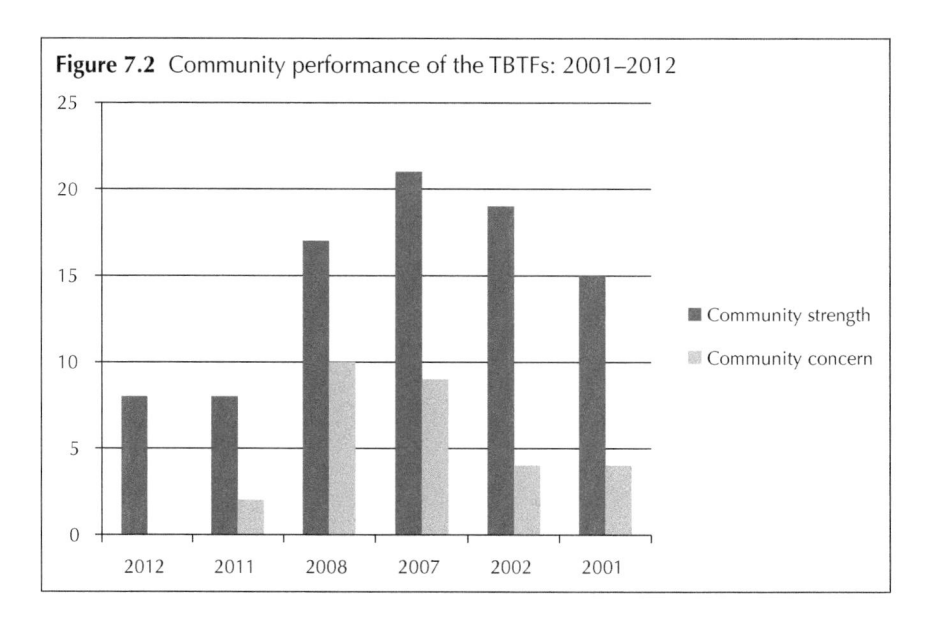

Figure 7.2 Community performance of the TBTFs: 2001–2012

Examination of KLD data reveals solid improvement in favourably addressing employee issues in 2012 compared with performance in prior years. Figure 7.3 highlights scores for the TBTF sample. By 2012, the total number of employee strengths recorded by the TBTFs stood at 39, a jump from 4 in 2011. Throughout the coverage period, the employee concern score hovered around 3. KLD awards strength points for quality union relations; cash and stock profit-sharing programmes, strong retirement benefits, quality health-and-safety programmes and other favourable employee policies not captured by the aforementioned categories. Employee concerns were recorded if there were shortfalls in any of the aforementioned categories and a final "other" that specified concerns not otherwise recorded. The turnaround in employee relations recorded in 2012 for the TBTF sample reflected an across-the-board improvement for all the financial services firms.

KLD provides an assessment of diversity strengths and weaknesses. Figure 7.4 illustrates the totals for the TBTF sample. For KLD, diversity strengths capture corporate actions that promote gender and minority representation at the CEO and board level; promotion; family benefits; employment of disabled, gay and lesbian policies;

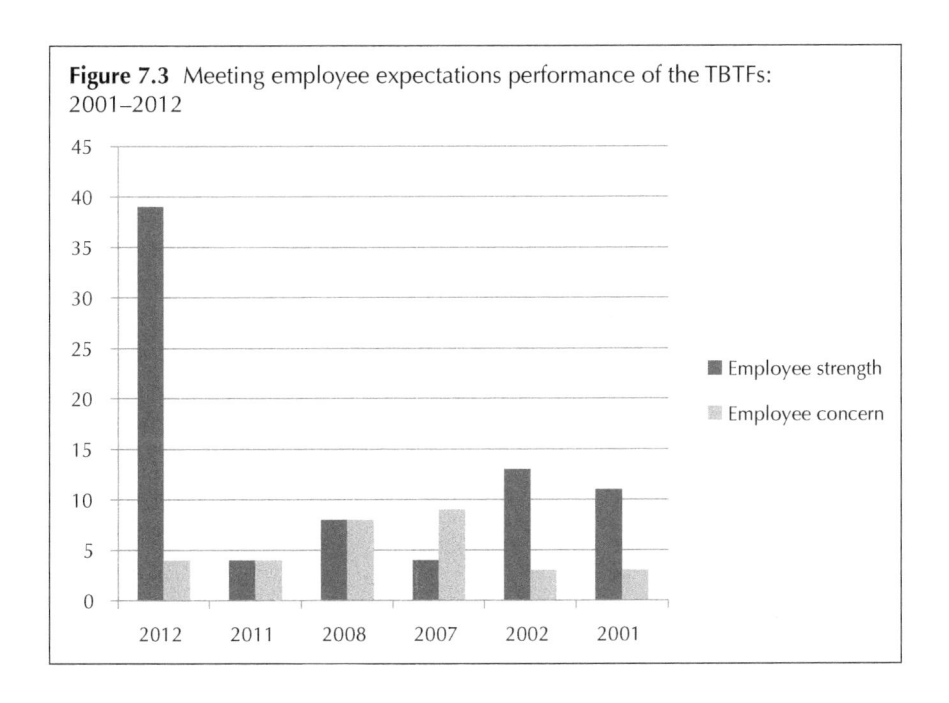

Figure 7.3 Meeting employee expectations performance of the TBTFs: 2001–2012

and a miscellaneous category. Diversity concerns are registered if fines or penalties have been levied for anti-diversity outcomes or other affirmative action controversies. Further, firms are awarded a diversity concern if women are neither on the board nor in senior line management. As usual, an "other" category rounds out diversity concerns. Diversity strengths rose steadily from 2001 through 2007, dropping off in 2008 and strengthening substantially in 2011 to a record 41 total strengths. By 2012, diversity strengths measured only 17, the lowest level of total strength for the period considered. However, over the entire period, diversity weaknesses shrank.

Product strengths are defined by KLD to include the following product characteristics: quality, an R&D/innovation component, provision for economically disadvantaged, and other. Product safety concerns, marketing concerns and other concerns round out scoring for weak product performance. Figure 7.5 summarises the total performance of the TBTF sample. The TBTFs performed dismally in total product strengths. Moreover, product concerns remained persistently elevated, reaching a peak of 27 in 2007. Although the KLD data are not sufficiently disaggregated to identify whether these concerns had to do with the toxic mortgage products, it is undoubtedly the case. What is worrisome is the spike in product

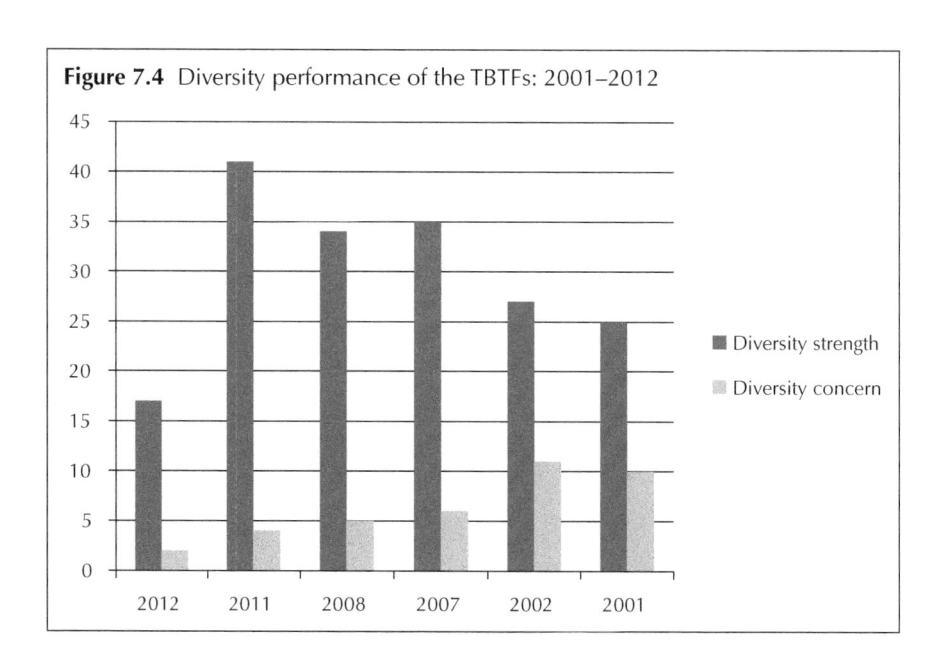

Figure 7.4 Diversity performance of the TBTFs: 2001–2012

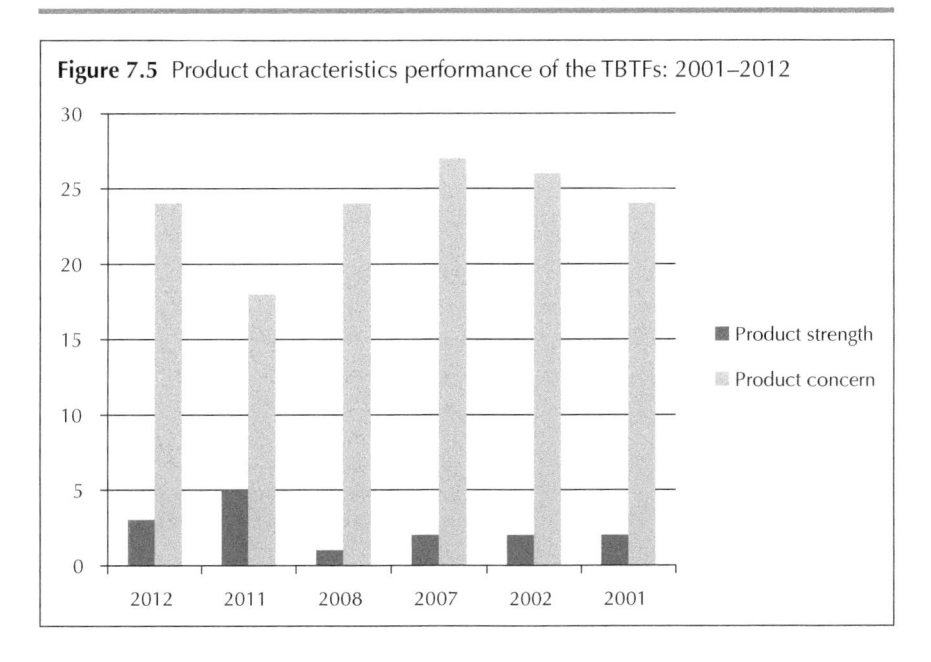

Figure 7.5 Product characteristics performance of the TBTFs: 2001–2012

- Product strength
- Product concern

concerns in 2012 to almost immediate pre-crisis levels (2007) following declines in 2008 and 2011.

TBTFs: governance and oversight of stakeholder issues

Although the analysis of stakeholder engagement among the TBTFs indicates an overall improvement in addressing employee expectations in the aftermath of the financial crisis, there is an unsettling trend indicative of poor social performance on most other dimensions. Strength in community engagement, strength in addressing environmental issues and performance strength on diversity issues all trended downwards for the TBTFs since the crisis through to 2012. At the same time, product concerns were on the rise in the aftermath of the financial crisis. On balance, it would seem that managing stakeholder interests was not prioritised as the banks emerged from the Great Recession. It is little wonder that trust in the financial system had correspondingly drifted downwards. Rather alarmingly, the poor "social" performance of TBTFs may indeed foreshadow inadequate enterprise risk management throughout the firm.

KLD provides an assessment of the quality of oversight of stakeholder issues in the governance scorecard segment of their database.

Figure 7.6 summarises this analysis. KLD classifies governance strengths as follows: limited compensation, non-majority ownership of a socially strong firm, disclosure/transparencies strengths and responsible leadership in shaping public policy. Further, there is the usual "other" strength category. Governance concerns identify issues of high compensation in excess of US$10 million for CEOs and greater than US$100,000 for independent board members; non-majority ownership in a socially weak firm; accounting concerns (added in 2006); transparency concerns in reporting social and environmental issues and public policy concerns. The "other" category rounds out the list of governance concerns.

Notably, the governance strengths and concerns surveyed by KLD are not usually the ones identified in governance literature, with the exception of compensation concerns.[6] Most corporate governance researchers tend to focus on more shareholder-centric elements of governance[7] that include board-of-directors characteristics encompassing separation of CEO and board chair, board size, director independence, multiple board appointments, tenure on the board and related party transactions. Increasingly, diversity of the board is also thrown into the mix. As for executive compensation, the main issue in traditional corporate governance literature considers alignment of shareholder and managerial interests. Thus emphasis is placed on long-term incentive compensation and limits on golden handshakes that are the antithesis of a pay-for-performance philosophy. Evaluation of shareholder-centric governance also typically includes a review of shareholder rights. Is there majority voting? Is the board staggered? Is cumulative voting permitted? Are poison-pill provisions in place? Can the market for corporate control operate without impediment? Thus, the survey of governance offered within the KLD framework departs substantively from what is usually considered by governance scholars. Nonetheless, the KLD governance metrics can serve a useful purpose when considered with these more traditional metrics, by providing a more focused view of the quality of oversight in addressing non-financial stakeholder issues.

Figure 7.6 depicts the KLD assessment of governance at TBTF financial institutions. As noted, the emphasis by KLD is on governance measures thought to influence the social and environmental outcomes of the firm. Yet, the relatively weak non-financial perfor-

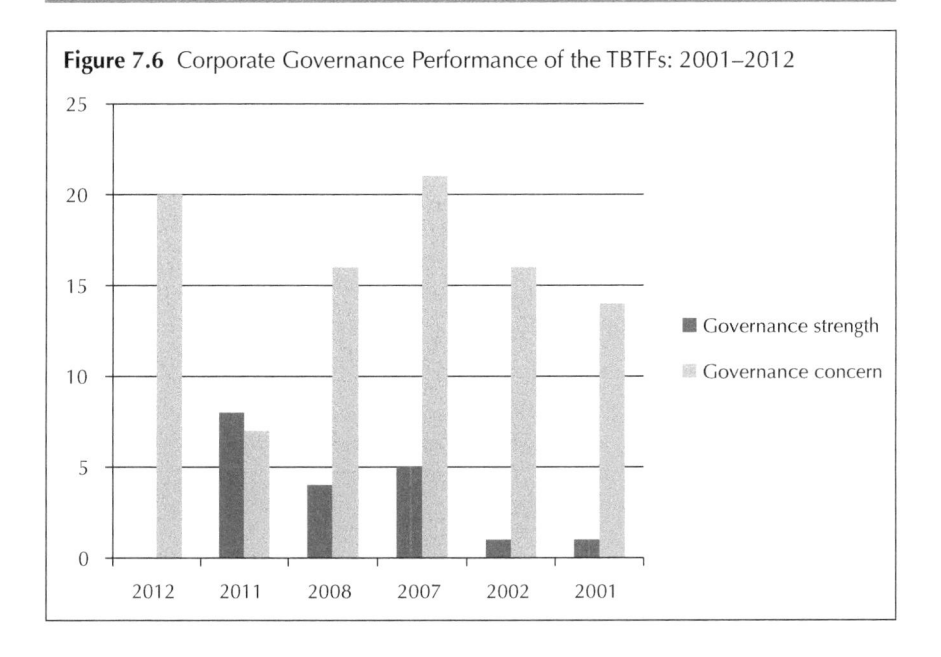

Figure 7.6 Corporate Governance Performance of the TBTFs: 2001–2012

mance of the TBTFs over the 2001–12 period seems to disabuse us of the notion that these institutions might have tried to draw attention away from economic issues to softer social issues. KLD governance concerns by 2012 were almost as high as in 2007 at 20 versus 21. Even the build-up towards greater strength in "extra-financial" governance in 2008 had completely disappeared by 2012. This situation is particularly worrisome, since the number of financial institutions counted as TBTFs in our sample shrank over the period due to mergers and bankruptcy. Might inattention to all stakeholders have foreshadowed the financial crisis of 2008 and is it repeating itself in 2012? At the very least, it would seem that there is no systematic effort to address stakeholder concerns as an integral component of overall firm governance. The performance of the TBTFs in meeting stakeholder expectations as summarised in Figures 7.1–7.5 might be interpreted as almost incidental outcomes of organisations that are not only too big to fail but probably too big to manage. There is ample anecdotal evidence to support the proposition that operational and reputational risks that compromise the interests of both financial and non-financial stakeholders had intensified in the post-crisis period and even accelerated over the 2012–14 period.

Stakeholder "disengagement" in the post-crisis period

According to the Reputation Institute (2014), the reputation of the financial services sector was for many on par with that of tobacco firms. A spate of reputational events that came to light in 2012 and 2013 added to the reputational woes of a financial services industry that was still stinging from the debacles of the financial crisis. Record fines were paid by firms for their involvement in the subprime-mortgage scandal. As the 2008 financial crisis continued to reverberate through 2014, the banking sector set aside unprecedented amounts for litigation expenses. In January 2014 *Forbes* reported that following JPMorgan Chase's US$13 billion settlement with the US government over behaviour leading up to the crisis, other major banks (Bank of America, Citigroup, Goldman Sachs and Morgan Stanley) augmented their reserves for possible litigation/fines (Flitter 2014). Moreover, new scandals began to emerge that were systemic throughout the industry, which included Libor fixing and FX manipulation.[8] Alongside these mega-reputational events was the unfortunately habitual spate of bank-specific scandals. The London Whale trader at JPMorgan's UK office placed risky bets that resulted in losses for JPMorgan of US$6.2 billion in 2012.[9] Some argued, however, that the trader was at least partially motivated by the high-risk appetite of the bank. Somewhere along the way, Deutsche Bank stopped conforming to its slogan "Everything starts with Trust". In December 2012 the bank was investigated for tax evasion and money laundering in addition to Libor fixing.[10] Deutsche's involvement in the Libor scandal produced a fine from the EU Commission of €725 million. The spotted reputational record of Deutsche Bank included allegations in 2009 that the bank spied on board members and a troublesome shareholder.[11] In other words, while some activities had consequences for the global financial system, others were aimed at a more traditional stakeholder focus and were somewhat idiosyncratic. For example, In 2012, UBS, a partner in the Libor scandal, also received a record fine (at the time) from the British Financial Services Authority over a loss of US$2.3 billion carried out by a rogue trader.[12] It was determined that UBS lacked appropriate internal controls that would have prevented the loss. While Barclays enjoyed the questionable distinction of being the first bank fined in the Libor scandal, early in 2014 a scandal of new dimensions was emerging. The personal data of 27,000 customers had been compromised. As data security breaches became more and more common in 2012 and 2013, a new kind of reputational risk emerged: how safe is the customer's data? What seemed more egregious, however, was the suspicion that Barclays attempted to cover up the data breach as the story was broken not by the bank itself but by a whistleblower within the bank.[13]

The accounts of reputational follies seem endless. *Investopedia* created a list of the "10 Most Shameful Bank Scandals of 2013".[14] The Investopedia list ranged from ethical breaches to systemic failures, but, individually and in total, the scandals damaged the reputation of the financial services sector. Included in the list were the Libor/FX manipulation and collusion by major players in international finance; and mishandling of foreclosures in the US, where indirect employees of banks entered homes not in foreclosure, changed locks and stole valuables. Enquiring whether Bank of America is the most corrupt bank, *Investopedia* noted that the bank led the list in consumer complaints in 2013 for refusing mortgage loan modification. Further, Bank of America settled a US$39 million lawsuit for gender bias at its Merrill Lynch subsidiary. Ponzi schemes (Wells Fargo) and transgressions of the Fair Housing Act (Wells Fargo) rounded out what is clearly a non-exhaustive list of social, ethical and ultimately economic breaches.

CORPORATE GOVERNANCE AND SHAREHOLDER WEALTH

With a worsening reputation from the pre-financial-crisis period onward, financial institutions seemed powerless (brought on by the sheer size of the organisations) to change their direction. Policymakers were equally frustrated as they looked for ways to curb bank excesses and, most importantly, to mitigate the threat of another systemic banking crisis. Was the disorganisation apparent in meeting non-financial stakeholders' expectations carried over to financial stakeholders? While not without detractors, many governance scholars have concluded that failures in corporate governance were the ultimate cause of the financial crisis. Less clearly understood, however, are the antecedents of failure.

The OECD (2009), in reviewing lapses in governance leading up to the financial crisis, concluded that managerial compensation arrangements at financial institutions fostered excessive risk taking that was further amplified by the lack of centralised enterprise risk management. Since compensation policy and risk management are the purview of the board, then surely there must have been significant breaches in oversight to have fostered a climate of excessive risk taking. We briefly explain below governance failures at the TBTFs using accepted shareholder-centric metrics.

Executive compensation at the TBTFs

Bhagat and Bolton (2012) are among scholars who argue that failures in corporate governance were responsible for the near unravelling of the global financial system in 2007–8. There is much speculation that executives of TBTFs were incentivised to adopt risky strategies, although empirical evidence on this topic is mixed. For example, while Suntheim (2010) and Balachandran, Kogut and Harnal (2010) find that executive compensation may have promoted excessive risk taking, Fahlenbrach and Stulz (2011) could find no support for the hypothesis that bank CEO incentives contributed to the credit crisis or depressed the performance of banks. Indeed, Beltratti and Stulz (2012) contend that "better-governed" firms, those more open to shareholder pressures, performed worse during the financial crisis. One of the puzzling aspects of the compensation–risk relationship surrounds the question of why CEOs of financial institutions who held equity in their firms would choose to lose money right along with other shareholders. The simple and unfortunate answer as illustrated by Bhagat and Bolton (2012) is that they did not lose. The Bhagat and Bolton study revealed that, in the run-up to the financial crisis, CEOs at the TBTFs had systematically liquidated their holdings. Table 7.1 (adapted from Bhagat and Bolton 2012) shows the value of net equity trades of CEOs at the TBTF institutions prior to the 2008 meltdown. CEO losses when the crisis hit represented paper losses, while their gains in the 8 years previous were "real". As Bhagat and Bolton (2012) illustrate, these CEOs took their money off the table!

Risk management: governance and appetite

Why were executives encouraged to make such risky bets? One view is consistent with managerial entrenchment where passive boards were derelict in monitoring the alignment of shareholder and managerial objectives and either failed to identify the risk appetite of the bank or neglected to design and implement policies consistent with a defined risk appetite. There is some truth to this interpretation. While an in-depth discussion of board characteristics of the TBTFs is beyond the scope of this chapter, several stylised facts are worth noting: bank board members require financial acumen, board independence is a desirable characteristic but legal independence may eclipse true independence if board members have served lengthy terms, CEO/Chair duality should be discouraged but improvement in oversight may still be impeded if the Chair is not truly independent. However, if we examine the scorecards of the TBTFs in the post-crisis period, it would seem that many banks carried over their Board members from the pre-crisis period. Data from SEC filings in 2014 reveal that six of eight TBTFs have CEOs who also chair their boards (the exceptions are Bank of America and Citigroup). We calculated the percentage of independent directors to total independent directors who were on the Boards in the pre-crisis period and found that on average 50% of board members in the TBTF group were "advising and monitoring" in the run-up to the financial crisis. It is little wonder that we observed stakeholder performance returning to pre-crisis levels. Table 7.2 summarises these general board characteristics.

The OECD (2009), in its post-crisis analysis, targeted inadequacies of the risk-management systems in financial institutions, noting an

Table 7.1 Cashout by CEO 2000–8

Name	Value of net equity trades (USD)
American International Group	$27,662,737,668
Bank of America	$1,485,014,269
Bank of New York	$5,250,286,975
Bear Stearns	$11,477,613,715
Citigroup	$18,962,730,241
Countrywide	$6,947,555,591
Goldman Sachs	$32,167,493,818
JPMorgan Chase	$4,047,358,641
Lehman Brothers	$2,839,629,839
Mellon	$1,476,234,775
Merrill Lynch	$2,213,635,723
Morgan Stanley	$8,848,339,556
State Street	$329,212,051
Wells Fargo	$3,273,128,325
Total	$126,980,971,187

Adapted from Bhagat and Bolton (2012)

Table 7.2 Board characteristics of the TBTF (2014)

	JPMorgan Chase	Bank of America	Wells Fargo	Citigroup
Board size	11	19	14	14
% directors deemed independent	90.91%	78.95%	92.86%	92.86%
Number pre-crisis directors	6	4	8	2
% pre-crisis directors	54.55%	21.05%	57.14%	14.29%
Pre-crisis directors as % indpendent board members	60.00%	26.67%	61.54%	15.38%
CEO/chair duality	Yes	No	Yes	No

	State Street	Goldman Sachs	Morgan Stanley	BNY Mellon
% directors deemed independent	12	13	15	13
Number pre-crisis directors	91.67%	76.92%	80.00%	92.31%
% pre-crisis directors	7	3	6	13
Pre-crisis directors as % indpendent board members	58.33%	23.08%	40.00%	100.00%
CEO–chair duality	63.64%	30.00%	50.00%	100.00%
CEO–chair duality	Yes	Yes	Yes	Yes

Source: SEC Filings 2014
Note: "Pre-crisis" refers to directors who were on the board as of 2007 or earlier.

absence of centralised risk management. Lehuede, Kirkpatrick and Teichmann (2012) found that boards were often ill informed regarding the level of risk their institutions were incurring. Lack of centralised risk management even led to risk-management units being viewed as an encumbrance. In fact, Lehuede *et al* suggest that many boards were overly focused on ensuring that capital-adequacy requirements were being met and devoted relatively little attention to other board responsibilities. Since the crisis Ernst Young (2013) has been conducting an annual review of risk-management practices across financial institutions. Findings published in 2013 indicate that the culture of risk at financial institutions had shifted to a culture of greater conservatism, at least according to Ernst Young's survey evidence. Nevertheless, while replete with opinion, the five-year review offered little in terms of concrete policy implementation and well-designed metrics against which risk-management success or failure could be measured. It quotes one bank executive surveyed by Ernst Young: "There is going to be a lot of attention to further detailing and operationalising the risk appetite ... Most banks have high-level statements, but I think this needs to be refined in practical limits at the business unit and country level."

The Ernst Young report did emphasise, however, that a majority of interviewees regarded reputational risk as an integral component of the overall risk-management strategy.

STAKEHOLDERS AND REPUTATION GOING FORWARD
The post-crisis governance landscape of banks seems virtually indistinguishable from its pre-crisis origins. The review of non-financial stakeholder engagement revealed a reversal to pre-crisis levels, while reputational issues both industry-wide and firm-specific featured prominently in the news in the years following the financial crisis. At the same time, policy regulators worried about the enormity of the problems created by a banking sector populated by TBTFs.

Resolution
Managing reputational risk, the risk of risks, cannot simply be an exercise in explaining why things went wrong. Managing yesterday cannot successfully create value for tomorrow. Reputational risk management must above all be proactive. For example, in 2014,

General Motors was plagued by a series of defects in its vehicles that mandated recall upon recall. The first set of recalls was prompted by allegations that faulty ignition switches had caused multiple deaths.[15] GM, however, set upon examining safety issues throughout its fleet and, as it continued to detect and recall ever greater numbers of vehicles, the stock price of GM began to react positively. Consumer confidence was restored as mistakes of the past were corrected.

Management of reputational risk in the financial services sector will, in our view, occur at two interdependent levels. First, if banks cannot find ways to better manage reputational risk, external pressure from national and supranational regulatory bodies could lead to a morass of regulations governing issues relevant to non-financial stakeholders. While critics of the financial services sector might champion such initiatives, the unintended consequence could well be overemphasis on compliance rather than proactive forward-looking measures that banks could adopt that would result in concrete improvements to the management of stakeholder concerns.

Second, banks must weigh in on qualitative risk assessment and management as well as focusing on the development of new tools to manage reputational risks associated with stakeholder issues. We think that both changes in bank governance and a significant overhaul of enterprise risk management within the bank need to occur in order to resolve reputational risk issues. Changes in governance can occur internally through bank initiatives as well as in response to national and supranational policy shifts. Concurrently, changes in risk-management practices at the bank level can produce enhanced reputational risk management at the enterprise and industry level. Thus, we recommend proactive changes in both the governance and risk-management practices within the bank.

Governance remedies

The first order of business in remedying negative reputational events must occur at the board level. Boards must renew their mandates of monitoring and advice so that enterprise risk management is understood to be one of the main functions of the board on a par with compliance and traditional management of liquidity risk and credit risk. A number of countries are enacting or studying legislative remedies for the board that include term limits for directors. While experienced directors are important, we found that roughly half of the TBTF boards consist of directors who predate the financial crisis. How can we expect a different result if the main actors remain in place? In tandem with term limits on directors, the pool of qualified directors must be expanded. There is no shortage of individuals with high levels financial and other industry expertise, and tapping such an enlarged pool can further reduce the potential for board entrenchment while providing valuable advice to management. New boards must not only focus on traditional risk management of credit and liquidity with a focus on compliance, but also expand their sphere of influence to encompass non-financial stakeholders.

The incentive structure of employee compensation requires re-examination. Many governance scholars place blame on perverse incentives that encouraged excessive risk taking as a root cause of the 2008 financial crisis. Boards must be willing to both reward and discipline managers and to carry this policy throughout various business units. There is a vast body of academic literature that discusses appropriate incentive alignment strategies focusing on C-suite executives not only receiving upside rewards from their actions but also requiring that downside risk be borne. Hence, current thinking suggests replacing stock options with phantom stock or deferred stock units. Moreover, requiring longer holding periods for securities – five to seven years – would further capture the long-term nature of extra financial risk and result in greater emphasis on attenuating reputational risk.

Compensation strategies at the business-unit level have mostly been ignored in the governance literature. Yet many reputational issues arise at the business-unit level but, due to the large size of banks, they tick away without notice until it is too late. To prevent such excess and change the culture within business units, a policy of incentive compensation linked to hours worked could be devised where incentives begin to diminish and even turn negative as hours worked increase. Although not a perfect solution, these kinds of policies within business units could ensure that throughout the bank the work–leisure tradeoff is acknowledged. These practices are present in other industries. A large private Canadian electronic parts distributor began to require all employees take their holidays following the fatal car accident of an employee who was exhausted from overwork. News media from time to time highlight the plight of medical workers required to work punishing shifts that have ended in illness or accident. Something as simple as incentivising time off as well as profit could serve as a preventive measure to avoid reputational events associated with employee relations.

In brief, the banking sector needs to rethink its governance structure at the board level and implement compensation arrangements both for C-suite and non-C-suite personnel that will incentivise attention to both financial and non-financial stakeholders. Such processes will be a key element in implementing a meaningful ERM strategy throughout the firm.

Enterprise risk management

Banks that became too big to fail arrived at a point where they also became, if not too big to manage, at least very large, unwieldy institutions. Bank size has mushroomed. Barth, Prabha and Swagel (2012) report that, in the fourth quarter of 2011, the five largest bank holding companies in the US had assets equivalent to 60% of GDP. In 1970 the assets of the five largest bank holding companies counted for only 10% of GDP.[16] We think a large part of reputational risk is an outgrowth of the size of banks. Thus, reputational risk management within the bank must acknowledge the problems inherent in their large size and adopt appropriate enterprise-risk-management processes that take a holistic view of risk management in general, with reputational risk figuring prominently in risk assessment at the business-unit and enterprise level.

Enterprise risk management (ERM) presents a relatively new focus area for both the financial and non-financial sectors. ERM is still an emerging field that offers great opportunity for the financial services sector to attenuate risk while creating value for all stakeholders. The reputational events described earlier highlight the urgency of the task. Management of stakeholder concerns that could create reputational risk must be integrated with traditional risk-management techniques to provide a holistic view of risk in the banking sector. That said, what measures concretely should the financial services firm adopt? In keeping with the theme of this chapter, we focus exclusively on stakeholder issues but caution the reader that interactions with other risk measures must be evaluated. For example, in the mortgage crisis that led up to the financial crisis, reputational risk was not considered. Had this been the case, the expected value of these mortgage portfolios would have been significantly decreased. Part of the problem, aside from inappropriate incentives, was the lack of depth in human resources that left small groups of financial engineers disseminating risk models throughout the firm. Did boards even understand or question the moves into this sector?

We encourage banks to review risk management at both business-unit and enterprise levels. The ERM function needs to be housed as a high-level business unit charged with integrating risk assessments from divisional units and also with conducting enterprise risk assessments of their own. Specifically, umbrella ERM requires that banks obtain information not only internally (from their business units) but also from important external sources such as consultants, but, more importantly, from monitoring of social media (defined broadly to include websites in general pertinent to the bank) that relate specifically to the bank, then to the industry, and events of a more general global nature. Banks should look at reputational risk management in other sectors susceptible to reputation-damaging incidents. Two candidate sectors are pharmaceuticals and oil and gas. How is risk management proceeding in these industries? How is reputation handled? In effect, one of the main ingredients of reputational risk management is information that will create forward-looking risk assessments. The kinds of tools required for ERM as they relate to addressing stakeholder concerns will take traditional risk managers out of their comfort zone of quantitative techniques to focus on information. The acquisition and integration of non-financial information obtained from non-traditional sources should greatly reduce the frequency of reputational events. However, significant financial resources must be allocated to this task. A coherent plan for ERM must be devised that recognises the threats from tail events not only in liquidity, credit and narrowly defined operational risks, but also in how these may synergistically create reputation damaging events that will ultimately devalue the bank and impose more onerous regulations than would otherwise be necessary.

CONCLUSION

Despite heightened regulation of bank capitalisation, regulatory oversight of the corporate governance fabric of financial institutions remained relatively untouched – financial institutions continued to at least nominally be guided by the financial objective of maximising shareholder wealth. As noted, many of the corporate boards at the TBTFs did not undergo a substantive overhaul in the post-crisis period. The prevailing governance regime in the financial services sector has undermined trust, which underpins not only reputation but is critical to a functioning financial system. In the years following the financial crisis non-financial stakeholders seem to be as ignored as in the run-up to the crisis.

In this chapter we have offered an analysis of the antecedents of reputational-damaging events in the financial services sector. We proposed a two-pronged solution that begins with an overhaul of bank governance and then proposes an ERM strategy that not only looks to the past but, more importantly, is forward-looking. Banks that succeed in addressing stakeholder concerns and reducing reputational risk will enjoy a competitive advantage and create value-enhancing propositions for both financial and non-financial stakeholders.

1 We use "banks" and "financial services" interchangeably.
2 Human rights performance is omitted from discussion. As evaluated by KLD, human rights strengths and concerns are highly issue-specific and for the purposes of this chapter are not relevant.
3 Governance quality, as assessed by KLD, focuses for the most part on governance quality as it relates to oversight of stakeholder issues, rather than shareholder-centric governance attributes typically considered in the finance literature.
4 The number of firms in the TBTF sample varies through time. The earliest period considered includes AIG, Bank of America, Citigroup, Goldman Sachs, JPMorgan Chase, State Street Financial, Wells Fargo, Mellon Financial, Bank of New York, Merrill Lynch, Bear Stearns, Countrywide and Lehman Brothers. The shake-out of the financial crisis and mergers eliminated Merrill Lynch, Bear Stearns, Countrywide and Lehman Brothers, and saw the merger of Mellon Financial and Bank of New York. Thus the earliest period included a greater number of TBTFs than the later period.
5 Since we wanted to illustrate how as a group the TBTFs replied to stakeholder expectations we felt that controlling for the number of firms as the TBTF cohort moved through time would distort their overall impact.
6 KLD considers only the magnitude of compensation and ignores the more relevant issue of linking pay with performance.
7 Discussions include Adams, Hermalin and Weisbach (2010); Bebchuk (2005); Bebchuk, Cohen and Farrell (2009); Gompers, Ishii and Metrick (2003).
8 See http://money.cnn.com/2013/11/20/investing/forex-probe-lawyers/.
9 See www.bloomberg.com/quicktake/the-london-whale.
10 See www.antimoneylaunderinglaw.com/2012/12/deutsche-bank-offices-raided-over-money-laundering-tax-evasion-and-carbon-trading-investigation.html.
11 See http://online.wsj.com/news/articles/SB125356686762028947.

12 See www.ft.com/intl/cms/s/0/d58c9816-37a1-11e2-a97e-00144feabdc0.html#axzz30l YILI7V.
13 See http://www.bloomberg.com/news/2014-02-09/barclays-probes-possible-theft-of-data-from-27-000-customers.html
14 See http://www.punchng.com/business/am-business/10-most-shameful-bank-scandals-of-2013/.
15 See www.reuters.com/article/2014/06/30/us-gm-recall-idUSKBN0F52MS20140630.
16 Size alone, however, does not qualify or disqualify membership in the Financial Stability Board's club of systemically important financial institutions (SIFIs). The Bank of New York Mellon and State Street do not make the list of the world's 50 largest banks, but, due to their importance in clearing and custodianship of assets, they are designated as SIFIs. For more discussion of bank size and SIFI see Barth, Prabha and Swagel (2012).

REFERENCES

V. V. Acharya and P. Schnabl, 2010, "Do Global Banks Spread Global Imbalances? The Case of Asset-Backed Commercial Paper During the Financial Crisis of 2007–09", NBER Working Paper No. 16079, June, published in *IMF Economic Review* 58, pp. 37–73.

Adams, Renee B., Benjamin E. Hermalin and Michael S. Weisbach, 2010, "The Role of Boards of Directors in Corporate Governance: A Conceptual Framework and Survey", *Journal of Economic Literature* 48, pp. 58–107.

Balachandran, S., B. Kogut and H. Harnal, 2010, "The probability of default, excessive risk, and executive compensation: A study of financial services firms from 1995 to 2008", working paper, Columbia Business School.

Barth, James R., Apanard Prabha and Phillip Swagel, 2012, "Just How Big is the Too Big to Fail Problem?", Milken Institute.

Bebchuk, Lucian, Alma Cohen and Allen Farrell, 2009, "What Matters in Corporate Governance?", *Review of Financial Studies* 22, pp. 783–827.

Bebchuk, Lucian and Jessee Fried, 2005, "Pay Without Performance: Overview of the Issues", *Journal of Applied Corporate Finance* 17, pp. 8–23.

Beltratti, A. and R. Stulz, 2012, "The credit crisis around the globe: Why did some banks perform better?", *Journal of Financial Economics* 105, pp. 1–17.

Bhagat, Sanjai and Brian J. Bolton, 2013, "Bank Executive Compensation and Capital Requirements Reform, May, available at SSRN: http://ssrn.com/abstract=1781318 or http://dx.doi.org/10.2139/ssrn.1781318.

Cornett, Marcia Millon, et al, 2011, "Liquidity Risk Management and Credit Supply in the Financial Crisis", *Journal of Financial Economics* 101, pp. 297–312.

Ernst Young, 2013, "Remaking financial services: risk management five years after the crisis", available at www.ey.com/Publication/vwLUAssets/Remaking_financial_services_-_risk_management_five_years_after_the_crisis_-_Complete/$FILE/EY-Remaking_financial_services_risk_management_five_years_after_the_crisis.pdf.

Fahlenbrach, Rudiger, and Rene M. Stulz, 2011, "Bank CEO Incentives and the Credit Crisis", *Journal of Financial Economics* 99, pp. 11–26.

Flitter, Emily, 2014, "In wake of JPMorgan settlement, big banks add to defense funds", *Forbes*, January 17, accessed February 19, 2014, at www.reuters.com/article/2014/01/17/usa-banks-reserves-idUSL2N0KR1K020140117.

Freeman, R. Edward, 1984, *Strategic Management: A stakeholder approach* (Boston, MA: Pitman).

Friedman, Milton, 1970, "The Social Responsibility of Business is to Increase its Profits", *New York Times Magazine*, September 13.

Gompers, Paul, Joy Ishii and Andrew Metrick, 2003, "Corporate Governance and Equity Prices", *Quarterly Journal of Economics* 118, pp. 107–55.

Jensen, Michael C., 2001, "Value Maximization, Stakeholder theory, and the Corporate Objective Function", *Journal of Applied Corporate Finance* 14(3), pp. 8–21.

Lehuede, Hector J., Grant Kirkpatrick and Dorothee Teichmann, 2012, "Corporate Governance Lessons from the Financial Crisis", May 1, available at SSRN: http://ssrn.com/abstract=2393978 or http://dx.doi.org/10.2139/ssrn.2393978.

Mehran, Hamid, Alan D. Morrison and Joel D. Shapiro, 2011, "Corporate Governance and Banks: What Have We Learned from the Financial Crisis?", FRB of New York Staff Report No. 502, June, available at SSRN: http://ssrn.com/abstract=1880009 or http://dx.doi.org/10.2139/ssrn.1880009.

Miles, Samantha, 2012, "Stakeholder: Essentially contested or just confused?", *Journal of Business Ethics* 108, pp. 285–98.

OECD, 2009, "Corporate Governance and the Financial Crisis: Key Findings and Main Messages", June, available at www.oecd.org/daf/ca/corporategovernanceprinciples/43056196.pdf.

Porter, Michael E. and Mark R. Kramer, 2006, "Strategy and Society: The Link Between Competitive Advantage and Corporate Social Responsibility", *Harvard Business Review*, Fall, pp 78–93.

Roe, Mark J., 2014, "Structural Corporate Degradation Due to Too-Big-To-Fail Finance", *University of Pennsylvania Law Review*, forthcoming; European Corporate Governance Institute, Law Working Paper No. 253/2014, available at SSRN: http://ssrn.com/abstract=2262901 or http://dx.doi.org/10.2139/ssrn.2262901.

Reputation Institute, 2014, "Can Banks Recover Their Reputations?", accessed February 20 at www.reputationinstitute.com/thought-leadership/white-papers.

Suntheim, F., 2010, "Managerial compensation in the financial service industry", available at SSRN: http://ssrn.com/abstract=1592163.

Wood, J., and P. Berg, 2011, "Trust in banks", Gallup.

8

Environmental and Social Risks from the Perspective of Reputational Risk

Nina Roth and Olivier Jaeggi

UBS and ECOFACT

INTRODUCTION

There are at least three reasons to have a chapter on environmental and social (E&S) risks in this book. First, such a chapter can contribute to a better understanding of E&S risks. Second – and this rationale likely resonates more with the readers of this book – E&S risks offer interesting insights into reputational risk. This is because, in the arena of E&S risks, reputational risk can occur independently of other risk types. Therefore, discussing E&S risks also contributes to the discussion about whether or not reputational risk events occur only as a consequence of other risk types (for example, credit risk, market risk, and operational risk). Third, in most banks E&S risks are still a neglected source of reputational risk, despite their importance. This is why the main purpose of this chapter is to make the case that E&S issues harbour considerable potential for damage in the here and now, and that banks take a significant risk if they underestimate them.

The chapter is organised into five sections: the first section contains a framework that describes E&S risks, particularly those that present reputational risks for banks. Here, we discuss the fact that E&S risks also occur in other financial risk types. The section is especially helpful for those readers who have not yet been exposed to E&S risks.

The second section summarises the key issues of corporate reputation and reputational risk. This section provides the greatest value for E&S risk experts who have not yet dived into the literature in this area. More details on reputational risk are available throughout this book, of course, but the aim of this section is to summarise the concepts that are relevant in the context of E&S risk management.

The third section illustrates how banks manage E&S risks, primarily from a reputational risk perspective. Interestingly, E&S risks are evolving into material compliance risks and legal risks at the time of writing. This, in turn, will likely also increase reputational risk.

Then we summarise the key statements of this chapter. We also add an outlook on how E&S risks might further develop in the future.

A BRIEF INTRODUCTION TO E&S RISK

This chapter focuses on the direct relationship between a bank and its corporate clients: a bank supports a company in its efforts to raise capital, either through loans or advisory services such as capital market transactions and private placements. In most cases the capital is used to fund the company's ongoing business operations. In some cases capital is needed to finance growth, the expansion of existing projects, or the construction of greenfield projects. While there are exceptions, such as loans to leverage a firm's financial investments, in most cases there will be a link between the provision of capital and its use to finance the operations of the client.

This is why controversies related to companies can also affect the banks that engage in business relationships with them. Controversies result from questionable business practices (eg, illegal logging), sectors (eg, the mining industry), projects (eg, large dams), and/or countries (eg, autocratic regimes). In this chapter the adjective "controversial" is used as a general term to describe business practices, sectors, projects, and/or countries that are associated with detrimental E&S impacts.[1] These impacts may be direct or indirect (eg, through the company's supply chain), and in some cases controversies are based on mere allegations and conjecture and there is little tangible information or evidence about the actual situation. Such E&S scenarios primarily occur in emerging markets and developing countries, as these countries tend to have less-developed and less-reliable sociolegal processes.

However, in the day-to-day reality of business, such E&S situations can occur in any country. New mining projects, for example, often cause controversies – regardless of the country in which they are located. In fact, some of the most controversial mining projects are found in the United States. And almost any project can lead to controversy if it has the potential to impact on a sensitive location, such as residential or high-conservation-value areas. In the words of Michael J. Kowalski, Chairman of the Board and CEO of Tiffany & Co.,[2] who is at the forefront of opposition to the development of the Pebble Mine in Alaska's Bristol Bay region, "The mine poses a dire threat to the region's pristine, highly productive ecosystem that supports the world's most important salmon fishery ... We have long believed that there are certain special places where mining simply should never take place, and we are working to make the retail jewelry industry and jewelry consumers aware that Bristol Bay is one such place. We are also urging the U.S. Environmental Protection Agency to use its authority under the Clean Water Act to prohibit mine development there."

In banking, controversial issues are often defined as environmental or social. Environmental issues include, for example, pollution of air and water, as well as impacts on biodiversity or on landscapes. Social issues include, for example, impacts on the health or the livelihood of communities, as well as poor labour standards or the infringement of human rights. In the discussion on sustainable finance, which focuses primarily on investments in equity and debt, E&S issues are usually combined with additional non-traditional issues under the umbrella term "ESG issues": environmental, social, and governance issues. The "G" component normally covers issues related to companies (eg, poor corporate governance), but can also address issues related to countries (eg, sociopolitical instability). In banking, governance issues are often dealt with in compliance (eg, money laundering), in credit risk management (eg, corporate governance) or in political risk management (eg, crisis potential). As the "G" component is often already covered in banking, the term E&S remains more common to describe this discipline in risk management.

In summary, E&S risks are those risks that occur when banks enter direct client relationships with companies that are associated with controversial issues.

There is one more important point regarding the scope of this chapter that should be discussed here. The business case for

PANEL 8.1: REPUTATIONAL RISK FOR BANKS: SOFT COMMODITY TRADING

Reputational risk can also be related to the products and services offered by banks. This is reflected in the discussion surrounding soft commodities trading and food speculation. Some civil society groups and other organisations such as the UN Food and Agricultural Organization (FAO) are concerned that trading by investors in agricultural commodities might increase food prices for consumers. Interest in commodity products has increased in recent years as a means of hedging portfolios. According to the critics, the growth in the agricultural commodities market has altered food prices. They claim that prices are being driven not only by supply and demand, but also the activities of banks.

There is no consistent academic position on the negative impacts on food prices of speculation in agricultural commodities. Most non-governmental organisations (NGOs) do not dispute that research has not led to a clear understanding of these mechanisms, but argue the "precautionary principle": if an activity is suspected of causing harm, in the absence of scientific consensus on the issue the proof that it is not harmful should be supplied by those who are involved in this activity (in this case, the banks).

NGOs' pressure on banks, particularly in Europe, has been heavy. This protest unified a diverse set of opponents, from classic anti-bank campaigners to church associations, activist shareholders and consumer protection agencies.[3] Positions taken by banks in reaction to this external pressure and public debate vary widely. Some banks have:

- exited all food commodity businesses;
- shut down agricultural trading via hedge funds;
- closed agricultural commodity funds; or
- highlighted the positive effects of banks in commodity markets by increasing transparency and liquidity, while blaming the fundamentals – such as policy changes in producing countries or poor weather conditions – as the main reason for rising food prices. These banks thus remain in the pressure groups' firing line.

After several years focusing their efforts mainly on banks, some NGOs have turned their attention to regulators. In January 2014, the EU voted in new rules in the form of an updated version of the Markets in Financial Instruments Directive (MiFID), "to address excessive [agricultural] commodity price volatility" in food markets. The World Development Movement, an NGO, praised the move, but singled out the UK government for opposing strict controls and insisting on national – rather than EU – standards, as this might result in a "regulatory race to the bottom". Still to be ratified by nation states, "the rules will limit the size of positions that traders can hold in a broad range of commodities, including food staples".[4]

managing E&S risks builds on two cornerstones. First, the risks a client is exposed to can translate into risks for the bank, such as credit risk.[5] Second, banks expose themselves to risk – at the time of writing, primarily reputational risk – if they engage in client relationships with entities that disregard minimum E&S requirements. Such requirements have been defined by international and multilateral institutions such as the World Bank Group (eg, the IFC Sustainability Framework[6]), the UN (eg, the 10 principles of the UN Global Compact[7]), and the OECD (eg, the OECD Guidelines for Multinational Enterprises[8]). Other minimum requirements are defined by voluntary initiatives, often driven by non-profit organisations or by sector associations, such as the Roundtable on Sustainable Palm Oil[9] or the Equator Principles,[10] which both mention financial sector responsibility.

The remainder of this chapter focuses on the second cornerstone of the business case – the risks that the associations with controversial business practices, sectors, projects, and/or countries present to banks – as it is here that the materiality of these E&S risks is less obvious. As mentioned above, this chapter makes the case that E&S issues harbour considerable potential for damage in the here and now, and that investment banks take a risk if they underestimate them. Several factors are changing the risk landscape of banks and, as a consequence, E&S risks will quickly become material.[11]

REPUTATIONAL RISK FROM AN E&S RISK PERSPECTIVE
This section contains a brief introduction to key concepts of corporate reputation and reputational risk, particularly from the perspective of E&S risk management. It explains why reputational risk management matters, and why E&S risk management should be part of a comprehensive reputational risk management system.

Corporate reputation
Corporate reputation is a concept that has attracted considerable interest in academic literature, business publications and other media. One of the challenges is that nowadays many different definitions of corporate reputation can be found. Barnett and Pollock (2012), for example, criticise that "distinct theoretical constructs such as image, identity, brand, status, and legitimacy have been either conflated with reputation or treated synonymously".

For the purpose of this chapter we use a definition proposed by Fombrun (2012), who advocates defining corporate reputations as "attractiveness", while emphasising that "corporate reputation should always be defined in terms of a specific stakeholder group", such as investors, customers or advocacy groups, "and a specific reference group", such as private-sector banks.

The fact that the characteristics of the stakeholder matter, comes as no surprise. We can easily imagine how a stakeholder group's perception of a firm is influenced by its specific beliefs and interests, and also by the specific type of interaction it has with the company, for example.

Just as important is the second point: the reference group. The industry sector – or subsector – in which a company is active affects its reputation. Yue and Ingram (2012) observe that "reputation seldom develops in isolation" and that therefore "reputations of organisations are interdependent". Yue and Ingram use the example of corporate social responsibility to illustrate how the corporate reputations of companies in a specific industry are interrelated when they write that "the public has become increasingly concerned about the role of corporations as responsible citizens in society. Besides pursuing profits, corporations are expected to comply with labor, environmental, human rights, or other standards of accountability." They also observe that "[r]esearchers have documented numerous cases in which an entire industry is sanctioned when one or a small group of organizations violate the expectations of social responsibility."

Among this research is that of Barnett, Jermier and Lafferty (2006), who emphasise the importance of looking at a wider range of a company's performance indicators. They believe that judgement "made by observers about a firm ... often occurs as a consequence of a triggering event" that "may arise from a firm's more visible actions and mistakes (eg, environmental damage or human rights violations) or various external events".

The brief discussion of selected views on corporate reputation led to three conclusions, which are relevant in the discussion of reputational risks related to E&S issues.

The first of these conclusions is that stakeholder expectations matter, as they influence their assessment of a company's "attractiveness". Different stakeholders have different expectations – and some will not be aligned with the company's strategies.

The second is that a bank's business practices, including those in the field of E&S risk management, will be compared to the practices of peers. It matters what peers do. Ignoring their practices is risky.

Before we move to a brief discussion of the definition of reputational risk, there is one more important point raised by Fombrun (2012) that is relevant in this context. In the chapter cited above he also raises the question of where corporate reputations come from. He believes that, in addition to stakeholders and the companies themselves, "influential intermediaries such as analysts, journalists, and other central gatekeepers linked through social networks" play an important role in developing corporate reputations. Fombrun particularly emphasises the role of the media.

This leads us to a third conclusion, which will be relevant in the discussion of reputational risks related to E&S issues, and it is that media, in the broad sense used above, play a crucial role as influential intermediaries. Interestingly, some definitions of reputational risk do not explicitly refer to these actors, and focus on stakeholders that have a transactional relationship with a bank (see below).

Reputational risk

After discussing corporate reputation, the subsequent question is: what is reputational risk? The simple answer is: the risk to which a firm's corporate reputation is exposed.

In the financial sector, several organisations have made an effort to come up with a definition of reputational risk. One of them is the Basel Committee on Banking Supervision (Basel Committee). The Basel Committee is the most important global standard-setter for risk management regulation in banking. Its mandate is to strengthen the practices of banks, as well as their regulation and supervision worldwide, with the purpose of enhancing financial stability.[12] The committee's secretariat is located at the Bank for International Settlements (BIS) in Basel, and is staffed mainly by professional supervisors on temporary secondment from member institutions. The BIS primarily acts as a bank for central banks, and is the world's oldest international financial organisation.

In the 2006 Basel II framework, the Basel Committee wrote that it expects the banking industry to develop standards for reputational risk management, but did not provide further guidance. In 2009, after an initial brief definition in 2001,[13] the Basel Committee provided a more detailed definition of reputational risk in a document entitled "Enhancements to the Basel II Framework" (BCBS 2009). It formed part of a package of guidance that addressed risk-management issues that became apparent during the global financial crisis. For the first time, detailed requirements for reputational risk management were given. However, most guidance was generic: banks are required to "have appropriate policies in place to identify sources of reputational risk when entering new markets, products, or lines of activities". When it comes to concrete measures, the same document narrows down the scope of reputational risk management to a concept termed "implicit support". Implicit support is provided when a bank decides to voluntarily cover the losses of clients to protect their client relationships and corporate reputation. The risks of the clients are now on the books of the bank.

In October 2010, the Basel Committee released "Principles for Enhancing Corporate Governance"[14] to address deficiencies in bank corporate governance that became apparent during the financial crisis. This document provides additional generic guidance relevant to reputational risk management.

The need for more concrete guidance was the primary reason behind the launch of the Forum on Reputational Risk Management in Banking in 2008.[15] Its objective is to provide a platform for dialogue and knowledge sharing on common and best practices in reputational risk management. As one of the inputs for the past forum, a set of views about reputational risk management were developed. The topic at hand, controversial client and business relationships, is seen as one of five primary potential issues that might lead to reputational risk. In short, reputational risk is seen as the "risk to earnings and capital arising from adverse perceptions on the part of existing and potential transactional stakeholders". The bank's transactional stakeholders are those parties that have a direct influence on the bank's business performance, such as clients, employees, supervisors and investors.

To address shortcomings of earlier definitions of reputational risk, these views also emphasise the role of tangential stakeholders such as NGOs, the media and the public. This reflects the view that they have an important influence on how transactional stakeholders perceive a bank's activities and business decisions.

Reputational risk is also seen as an independent risk category and not as a consequential risk only. This is because reputational risk can occur independently of other risk types, at least in certain circumstances. Take the example of a campaign organised by an advocacy group that targets a bank's business relationships with companies that produce controversial weapons or operate coal-fired power plants. The bank faces a reputational risk without having done anything related to other financial risk types. There is no credit risk, no market or liquidity risk, neither has an operational risk event taken place if the bank complied with its own policies. The Basel Committee defined operational risk as the risk of loss resulting from inadequate or failed internal processes, people and systems or from external events (BCBS 2011). You could argue that the bank's internal processes were inadequate, as they failed to address material risks. However, to address each and every issue that might become material, the bank would have to meet all expectations with its risk-management system. This makes little sense. You could also argue that it is an operational risk event, as it is an external event. However, it is unlikely that this is the kind of event the Basel Committee had in mind when defining operational risk. In the example briefly mentioned above, an advocacy group publicly targets a bank with the objective of leveraging the bank's corporate reputation ultimately to alter the business practices of a specific company or an entire industry sector. It is difficult to see this as an operational risk.

The discussion of reputational risk above leads to the following key takeaways regarding E&S issues:

❏ relationships with controversial clients – controversial owing to their business practices or their involvement in controversial sectors – can lead to reputational risk;
❏ the importance of tangential stakeholders should not be underestimated; and
❏ E&S risks present reputational risks, and, in some cases, such reputational risk can be seen as a standalone risk category.

HOW BANKS MANAGE E&S RISK

After a brief introduction to E&S risks, particularly from the perspective of reputational risks, this section illustrates how banks manage E&S risks. It provides an understanding of the topic's relevance, as well as the potential organisational set-up to control, mitigate and manage the risks involved.

Despite (a) recurring public controversies, (b) the existing business relationships between banks and controversial clients and (c) the significant E&S risks of many financed projects, the level of awareness and the depth of the corresponding risk-management systems are limited at many banks.

Banks often do not assess E&S risks as a part of their conventional risk analysis. Separate assessment tools are developed along with separate policies, procedures and subject-matter teams to perform E&S risk due diligence to identify reputational risk. Nowadays, most major global banks have E&S risk teams that are integrated in group-wide, cross-divisional-transaction due diligence processes to identify and manage E&S risks.

Banks such as JPMorgan, Standard Chartered and UBS – all with differing business models and sector and regional business focuses – have such specialised E&S risk (control and management) teams. The reporting lines vary. Many teams are part of the bank's risk management unit, others are also embedded in compliance, investor relations, corporate responsibility, communications, corporate social responsibility, sustainability or environmental management, and public affairs, as well as (to a lesser extent) directly in project finance or investment bank teams.

While this is true mainly at global universal banks, such E&S risk units are rare in second and third-tier banks. With little public pressure from NGOs, they often do not see the need to establish E&S risk units. This may be a mistake. The processes and teams established within major global banks are justified by concerns related to financial and reputational risk. The materiality of E&S risks is also confirmed by other parties: various stakeholders, including sustainability rating agencies, NGOs, activist shareholders and stock exchanges expect banks to address and manage E&S risks appropriately.

With regulatory requirements in the E&S risk arena still being the exception, the set of voluntary standards for banks in the management of such risks is expanding rapidly.

The International Finance Corporation (IFC), the private-sector arm of the World Bank Group, developed the "IFC Environmental and Social Performance Standards"[16] (the PS) in 2006.[17] The PS were originally developed to provide World Bank/IFC clients with "guidance on how to identify risks and impacts, and are designed to help avoid, mitigate, and manage risks and impacts as a way of doing business in a sustainable way, including stakeholder engagement and disclosure obligations of the client in relation to project-level activities". As the first such document and guideline, the PS were quickly adapted by private-sector financial institutions. The PS outline standards surrounding: (1) the assessment and management of E&S risks and impacts, (2) labour and working conditions, (3) resource efficiency and pollution prevention, (4) community health, safety, and security, (5) land acquisition and involuntary resettlement, (6) biodiversity conservation and the sustainable management of living natural resources, (7) indigenous peoples, and (8) cultural heritage.

The IFC asks its clients to meet these standards throughout the lifetime of the investment and establishes a control-and-monitoring process to manage E&S risks. A standard procedure for any IFC-related investment is an evaluation of the project's compliance with the E&S requirements during its lifetime by reviewing the annual monitoring reports. The report must cover the ongoing performance of project-specific environmental, health-and-safety and social activities. Deadlines for submission are outlined in the investment agreements. Depending on the project, periodic site supervisions might be conducted. The relevant documentation will be made available to the public online.

In 2003, recognising the impact and importance of the Safeguard Policies (a set of standards developed before the PS), a small group of banks agreed on a set of tenets named the Equator Principles (EP). Ten banks[18] established a risk framework to better assess and manage E&S risks for project finance-related transactions, mainly in emerging markets.

In early 2014, 79 banks worldwide were signatories to the EP. It is believed that approximately 70% of project finance transactions are managed by EP signatories. They commit to finance only projects in which compliance with minimum standards related to stakeholder consultation, indigenous peoples' rights, labour rights and the availability of environmental and social risk assessments issued by independent third parties are guaranteed.

Commitment to the EP also requires banks to disclose the number of project finance transactions assessed in their E&S risk-management units. However, NGOs often criticise the EP banks. Repeatedly EP banks have been accused of failing to comply with their own standards.

The EP have been reviewed twice (in 2006–7 and 2012–13), and now cover four transaction and product types: project finance, project finance advisory services, project-related corporate loans and bridge loans.

Recent examples of voluntary standards established by banks, partly developed together with NGOs or academia include the following.

❏ The discussion paper published by the Thun Group of Banks interprets the UN Guiding Principles on Business and Human Rights developed by UN Special Representative John Ruggie from the perspective of the banking industry. The paper "suggests an approach to risk assessment through a tailored due diligence, which may be undertaken in the core business activities of universal banks; retail and private banking, corporate and investment banking, and asset management".[19]
❏ The Banking and Environment Initiative (BEI) brings together banks and the Consumer Goods Forum (CGF) companies with the aim of eliminating deforestation in their supply chains by 2020. One compact targets the "alignment of banking standards to the CGF sustainable procurement standards for priority soft commodities (palm oil, timber, pulp and paper, soya and beef)".[20]

These voluntary standards, subscribed to by important global banks, increase the pressure on other banks to follow their path. Not complying with best practices, and in the case of the EP with common practices, presents reputational risk to other banks. In the medium term, banks might even face legal risks if they are seen as deliberately neglecting such standards.

Implementing an E&S risk-management framework
Banks need an E&S risk framework to identify and manage reputational risk and financial risks. The steps needed to implement an E&S risk framework within banks are:

1. acknowledgement of the importance of the topic at senior management level; develop a strategy for how to address these risks;
2. develop policies and procedures that reflect and enact the strategy;
3. set up an E&S risks team of subject-matter experts and programme managers to implement these policies and procedures; they should have a direct reporting line into the chief risk officer function;
4. continuously raise awareness of E&S risks in general as well as specific E&S risk procedures across the organisation;
5. report internally as well as externally about the implementation of the framework and the corresponding challenges and achievements;
6. review the implementation of the framework, based on internal and external reviews or audits; and
7. have the implementation of the framework independently audited, by internal as well as external audit functions.

As with all other risk types, "the tone from the top" is crucial (ie, Step 1 above). A bank's executive board and its board of directors need to acknowledge the importance of E&S risk. A strategy needs to be carved out based on this acknowledgement.

The strategy needs to frame the risk appetite of the bank with regard to sectors and industries, business practices, companies and even countries. Once the strategy is defined, policies and procedures need to be developed (Step 2) or adapted to enable the organisation's staff to implement it. International standards and voluntary frameworks need to be taken into account. The policies describe scope with regard to products, services, business units or transaction types. The roles and responsibilities of affected employees need to be outlined. To enhance the effectiveness of E&S risk policy implementation and to increase the internal control and awareness levels of senior management, a direct reporting line to a member of the bank's executive board or a top management committee is needed. The E&S risk team ideally includes (a) sector and industry experts who combine an advanced understanding of E&S risks with a banking background and (b) programme managers who support the implementation of the strategy and further refine policies and procedures

(Step 3). It is important to raise awareness about the relevant policies and procedures of the organisation. Owing to the complexity of E&S risks, training programmes (Step 4) for all employees are needed.

To track the challenges and achievements of the system and to build trust in the market, banks should regularly report on the level of implementation of their E&S risk-management system (Step 5). Internal reporting is best reflected by inclusion in quarterly risk reports that are submitted to senior management/the board/regulators. Internal reporting should reflect the level of policy implementation with KPIs such as: transactions screened per business unit, sector, country; changes in policies and procedures; and upcoming E&S risks (eg, Arctic drilling in Greenland, rare-earth mining in China) and how these could be tackled.

External reporting should cover E&S risks in annual reports, as well as in investor roadshows. Today, the most common place for reporting on E&S risks is the annual sustainability or corporate (social) responsibility report. External reporting is an essential part of public acceptance and enhances the credibility of an organisation's strategy. It also provides an opportunity to compare an organisation's own system with that of its peers. In the sphere of E&S risk management, open and transparent communication can substantially minimise and/or mitigate reputational risk, especially in connection with NGOs and rating agencies.

A successful management system additionally requires periodic review (Step 6) to determine flaws, challenges, and areas of improvement. To keep the system continuously improving, the development of international or voluntary industry standards needs to be tracked, as well as NGO activities and evolving issues monitored. The regulatory environment needs to be followed. Reviews of relevant E&S risk policies and their appropriateness with regard to the bank's E&S risk profile as well as the level and depth of adherence to the relevant E&S risk policies need to be performed by independent internal control groups such as internal audit (Step 7). Additional assurance and credibility can be obtained with independent third-party audit companies periodically reviewing an organisation's E&S risk management system.

OUTLOOK

This chapter has tried to shed some light on the relevance of E&S risk management. Several case studies have illustrated how E&S risks at the client level impact on the financial performance of the company in question, and thus influence (a) the relationship with the company's banks and (b) the bank's own risk exposure.

Looking ahead, successfully implemented E&S risk-management systems will not simply make E&S issues related to banks' reputational risk go away. NGOs will continue to campaign against the "financial support" or bare "involvement" of a bank with a certain controversial company, project or sector. The inclusion of controversial companies in third-party funds that are distributed by the bank will continue to present reputational risks. Also, participation in bond issues where the use of proceeds is deemed to be "general corporate purposes" remains challenging. Financial and reputational risks related to E&S issues can be addressed with initiatives at three levels: internal, peer and external. We will look at each of these in turn.

Internal initiatives
- Train relationship managers and analysts about E&S risk issues and how to address these at client level. This is to avoid surprising the client with the bank's E&S risk standards.
- Ask clients to answer non-transaction-related questions about their E&S risk issues for monitoring purposes, eg, on a quarterly basis.
- Make the inclusion of E&S risk teams in due-diligence processes for capital markets transactions in high-risk industries mandatory. Participating in all due-diligence processes for predefined high-risk sectors could make sure that E&S risks are appropriately addressed.
- Brief senior management and sector heads regularly about current and emerging E&S risks for specific industries. When considering expanding specific sector teams, E&S risk teams should be included early on to avoid frustration later. Monitor the development of international standards, voluntary initiatives and regulatory developments.

Peer initiatives
- Join peer initiatives related to E&S issues. To allow an exchange on best-practice policies, and the development of new standards

(for example, in the field of controversial weapons, human rights or soft commodities), banks should organise forums themselves in which an exchange on pressing topics or approaches to specific transactions is possible employing the Chatham House Rules. Such events, meetings or calls can also be facilitated by trustworthy external partners or be ancillary events to meetings of, for example, the EP banks, United Nations Environment Programme Financial Initiative, or the Roundtable on Sustainable Palm Oil.
- ❏ Coordinate efforts during E&S risk due diligence in transactions with peers.
- ❏ Engage in meetings with controversial clients to jointly address E&S risks.
- ❏ Engage with peers – as in the Thun Group or the BEI process (see above) – to develop topic-specific or overarching disclosure guidelines to better address E&S risks.

External initiatives
- ❏ Support financial-sector associations in further developing standards to include E&S risks in capital market disclosures and public transaction documentation. Some stock exchanges already have such requirements. The Hong Kong Stock Exchange can be considered a frontrunner in this field.
- ❏ In early 2014, the US Sustainability Accounting Standards Board (SASB)[21] published voluntary standards to be integrated into the Form 10-k, which must be filed by publicly listed companies with the Securities and Exchange Commission in the US.

CONCLUSION

This chapter has aimed to establish the importance of identifying, controlling and managing E&S risks for banks. International mandatory and voluntary standards and initiatives that apply to the financial industry have been introduced. The chapter also gave insights into ongoing recent discussions on E&S risk management for banks. Being a comparatively new risk type, it was also showcased that there is a potential for further initiatives, also from the regulator's side, and that, as in most cases, a proactive approach is best.

1. The concepts and definitions used in this section were first introduced in Jaeggi, Kruschwitz and Manjarin (forthcoming).
2. Interviewed by Rahim Kanani for Forbes.com (January 19, 2014); see www.forbes.com/sites/rahimkanani/2014/01/19/ceo-of-tiffany-co-on-ethical-sourcing-responsible-mining-and-leadership.
3. See www.wdm.org.uk/stop-bankers-betting-food/what-problem, www.foeeurope.org/farming-money-Jan2012 or www.foodwatch.org/en/what-we-do/topics/speculation-with-foodstuffs/more-information/report-the-hunger-makers/ (all sourced February 2014).
4. See www.theguardian.com/business/2014/jan/15/eu-curb-food-price-bets-traders-rules.
5. E&S risks occur in multiple financial risk types, such as credit risk, operational risk (including legal risk) and reputational risk. This chapter focuses on the last of these.
6. See www.ifc.org/sustainabilityframework.
7. See www.unglobalcompact.org/abouttheGc/TheTenprinciples/index.html.
8. See www.oecd.org/corporate/mne.
9. See www.rspo.org.
10. See www.equator-principles.com.
11. For more information on the drivers that increase the need for banks to address E&S risks systematically, see Jaeggi, Kruschwitz and Manjarin (forthcoming).
12. See www.bis.org/bcbs.
13. "Reputational risk is defined as the potential that adverse publicity regarding a bank's business practices and associations, whether accurate or not, will cause a loss of confidence in the integrity of the institution" (BCBS 2001).
14. See www.bis.org/publ/bcbs176.htm.
15. The first Forum took place in Berlin in February 2008, hosted by Dresdner Bank, the second in London in October 2008 (HSBC), the third in London in October 2010 (Deutsche Bank), and the fourth in October 2013 (RBS). For more information, see www.ecofact.com/Forum.
16. Today they are called "IFC Performance Standards on Environmental and Social Sustainability"; see www.ifc.org/wps/wcm/connect/topics_ext_content/ifc_external_corporate_site/ifc+sustainability/publications/publications_handbook_pps.
17. Based on pre-2006 Safeguard Policies.
18. ABN Amro, Barclays, Citigroup, Credit Lyonnais, Credit Suisse, HypoVereinsbank, Rabobank, RBS, WestLB, Westpac.
19. See www.skmr.ch/cms/upload/pdf/131002_Thun_Group_Statement_Final.pdf.
20. At the time of writing, the BEI "Compact" had not yet been published. Further information and updates on the Compact can be found at www.cpsl.cam.ac.uk/Business-Platforms/Banking-Environment-Initiative.aspx.
21. See www.sasb.org/sectors/financials.

REFERENCES

Barnett, M., J. Jermier and B. Lafferty, 2006, "Corporate Reputation: The Definitional Landscape", *Corporate Reputation Review* 9(1), pp. 26–38.

Barnett, Michael L. and Timothy G. Pollock, 2012, "Charting the Landscape of Corporate Reputation", in M. L. Barnett and T. G. Pollock (eds), *The Oxford Handbook of Corporate Reputation* (Oxford University Press), pp. 1–15.

BCBS, 2001, "Customer due diligence for banks", Bank for International Settlements, October 2001.

BCBS, 2009, "Enhancements to the Basel II framework", Bank for International Settlements, July 2009.

BCBS, 2011, "Principles for the Sound Management of Operational Risk", Bank for International Settlements, June 2011.

Fombrun, Charles J., 2012, "The Building Blocks of Corporate Reputation", in M. L. Barnett and T. G. Pollock (eds), *The Oxford Handbook of Corporate Reputation* (Oxford University Press), pp. 94–113.

Jaeggi, Olivier, Kruschwitz, Nina and Manjarin, Raul, forthcoming, "The Case for Environmental and Social Risk Management in Investment Banking", in K. Wendt (ed), *Responsible Investment Banking* (Springer).

Yue, Lori Qingyuan and Paul Ingram, 2012, "Industry Self-Regulation to Solve Reputation Commons", in *The Oxford Handbook of Corporate Reputation* (Oxford University Press), pp. 278–296.

9

The Relationship between Reputational Risk Management and Business Continuity

Alexander Klotz, Tibor Konya; Abtin Maghrour

UniCredit Bank AG; Transfer of Innovative and Integrative Management Solutions (tiim)

INTRODUCTION

The Center for Strategic and International Studies has provided an outlook on the most important trends that will shape our world through to the year 2035. Seven areas of change have been identified: population; resource management; technology; information and knowledge; economics; security; and governance.[1] With these trends and in particular their interconnections as outlined in the research, businesses will face a higher number of potential threats and disruptions. Together with the growing complexity of business itself, each and every disruption may cause higher and more sustainable impact.

Within this fast-paced environment in particular, banks and financial institutions are more and more exposed to the failure of business processes and outages of IT or other crucial resources. The "outage" of IT refers to a period during which IT systems are not available. The reason for an IT outage can be technical failure, human error (caused, for example, by IT administrators) or power failure.

Additionally, increasing regulatory requirements call for stronger control, monitoring and management regarding the operational stability of institutions. Anticipating risks, identifying potential disruptions and managing these scenarios are paramount for financial institutions. The reputational impact of disruptive events must also be managed in a proper way.

The importance of business continuity management (BCM) and crisis management in order to be prepared for the worst has been validated by historical catastrophes such as the events of September 11 2001.

This chapter describes the discipline of BCM, including its reputational aspects, and subsequently discusses and illustrates the link between business continuity and reputational risk management by outlining their commonalities, differences and interdependencies. The terminology "business continuity management" will be explained and illustrated throughout this chapter, with the help of some examples. The importance of a stakeholder-oriented approach within crisis management is also emphasised.

KEY DRIVERS AND TRENDS OF BCM WITHIN THE FINANCIAL INDUSTRY

Due to the financial crisis and a number of diverse and disastrous events within the financial industry, the public are more disillusioned with this sector than ever. Customers, public and politicians have little trust and confidence in the financial industry, which is certainly its biggest challenge.

Furthermore, supported by the latest technology, financial institutions work to develop customised services, implement innovative strategies and capture new market opportunities. With further globalisation, the financial sector is becoming more and more complex and financial institutions progressively face the growing importance of their IT systems. This is due to the fact that a large number of business processes are managed by IT systems. Therefore, an outage of the IT systems would cause an outage of business processes, which partially cannot be handled by manual workarounds due to the high volume of data exchange and processing.

Additionally, the financial sector is, in most industrial countries, the lifeblood of the respective economies. The growing regulatory requirements put in place will form further challenges for BCM.

In a nutshell, given the scope and speed of the last financial crisis and the growing complexity of business within this sector, BCM is increasingly important.

BUSINESS CONTINUITY MANAGEMENT

BCM concerns the identification of critical activities and processes within an organisation and ensures that they continue at predefined levels in the case of disruptive events.

A simple example of the core idea of BCM can be found in the aviation industry. In most aeroplanes you will find two pilots: the captain, who is probably the most critical resource, and his backup, the flight officer. Whatever happens to one of the pilots, the other one is able to take over in order to ensure the operations proceed as normal and if necessary save the lives of passengers and the aircraft.

A more complex example can be found in the financial industry. The outage of investment banking or trading processes can result in enormous financial damage. Therefore, the UniCredit Bank AG, for example, has prepared comprehensive backup solutions for its IT infrastructure (including IT systems and applications) as well as for its operations (eg, workplaces and business processes). In the case of an outage of IT systems or buildings these so-called backup solutions will be activated. Hence, the staff will be able to continue working with access to all required IT systems. If required, the staff will be moved to emergency workplaces and the IT systems will be switched to backup solutions. In this way the bank ensures the contingency of its processes and activities in most cases.

BCM is about developing and implementing contingency plans in order to make sure that the necessary critical processes and resources continue regardless of circumstances. It means taking responsibility for your business and staying the course, whatever happens.

It can also be described as building and improving resilience in your business through the identification of key services and products, as well as in the most urgent activities which underpin them. Once the Business Impact Analysis is comprehensively processed, it is about creating strategies and plans which will enable you to continue your business processes and recover quickly and effectively from any kind of disruption regardless of its size or cause.[2]

Above all, BCM is mandatory by law for enterprises in many countries. Just to provide a few examples, while in the healthcare industry, BCM is regulated in the US by the Food and Drug Administration and HIPAA, in the financial industry it is regulated by Basel II, the Expedited Funds Availability (EFA) act and the

Federal Financial Institutions Examination Council (FFIEC) (Noakes-Fry, Baum and Runyon 2005).

BUSINESS CONTINUITY MANAGEMENT SYSTEM IN UNICREDIT BANK AG

At the heart of every good business continuity practice sits the BCM system. BCM in the UniCredit Bank AG as well as on Group level (UniCredit Group) is based on ISO 22301.

On May 14, 2012, the International Organisation for Standardisation (ISO) published the new ISO 22301 for BCM, which was the first worldwide valid and certifiable norm for the practice. This ISO norm also replaced the only certifiable standard for UK BS 25999–2 and is applicable for all organisations[3] regardless of their size.[4]

According to ISO 22301, business continuity is defined as the capability of the organisation to continue delivery of products and services at acceptable predefined levels following a disruptive incident.[5] A disruptive incident is an event that could lead to loss of, or disruption to, an organisation's operations, services or functions.

The BCM system in UniCredit Bank AG as part of the overall management system establishes, implements, operates, monitors, reviews, maintains and improves business continuity.

From an organisational perspective, the BCM responsibility in UniCredit Bank AG is allocated to a central role (central BCM) and a number of de-central roles (de-central BCM) in order to incorporate both an overall governance function with central BCM, and the use of relevant technical expertise of de-central BCM for the business divisions, such as investment banking or commercial banking. A defined organisational structure is required in order to enable the company to understand the organisation comprehensively and manage business continuity properly in terms of countering disruptions directly where they occur.

The BCM system emphasises the importance of the following key aspects.

Programme management

Programme management is an ongoing management and governance process supported by top management and appropriately resourced to implement and maintain BCM, which is led by central

BCM in UniCredit Bank AG. This includes policy level, within the organisational structure, and in the methodologies used to manage risk.

Understanding the organisation

UniCredit Bank AG has established, implemented, and maintains a formal and documented evaluation process to identify critical processes, determining continuity and recovery priorities and objectives for them. This process is called business impact analysis. Along with the financial and regulatory impacts, the reputational impact is a key factor needed for a business process to be classified as critical.

The criticality of a process varies from organisation to organisation depending on their structure, culture, governance and other factors. A critical process in the UniCredit Bank AG is, for example, "Payments". The disruption or outage of this process can lead to significant reputational and economical damage not just for the UniCredit Bank AG but also for its clients. Therefore, it is considered as critical.

Conducting the business impact analysis can be seen as the most important step within the whole BCM system as the result provides the basis for all following activities within the system. Therefore, it is conducted at least annually to make sure that changes in terms of regulatory requirements and business processes are up to date.

Additionally, only the end-to-end analysis of critical processes enables a comprehensive understanding of the process criticality for the bank. This analysis also includes external providers, as an outage or disruption of their services can cause the same reputational damage as an internal one.

BCM strategy

Subsequent to the analysis of the organisation's critical activities, business continuity strategies will be established, which consider costs and risks of BCM strategy implementation.

Business continuity planning

The information extracted or gained from the business impact analysis is used to implement emergency plans (or business continuity plans) to take care of critical business processes. This reduces the impact of incidents and guarantees that the organisation in question is capable of restarting these critical business processes within predefined recovery times.

Test maintenance and monitoring
A test and exercise programme is an essential part of the BCM system as this ensures that the business continuity plans are fit for purpose and up to date. This step also provides quality assurance and the opportunity for continuous improvement. In the UniCredit Bank AG test and exercise programme, responses for all possible outage scenarios considering the following resources: employees; buildings; information and communication technology; services delivered by providers; infrastructure; and documents

An outage scenario describes possible events that could lead to an outage of a process or IT system. It also includes its possible impacts on critical resources as defined in ISO 22301, such as employees, buildings and others (as listed above).

BCM awareness
This step includes measures to increase BCM awareness in order to enhance the collaboration with relevant business units.

Figures 9.1 and 9.2 provide an overview of the BCM system in general and within the UniCredit Bank AG (the steps illustrated in the graph have been explained earlier in the chapter).

BCM EXAMPLE OF UNICREDIT BANK AG
A practical example for BCM in UniCredit Bank AG is the outage of one of the premises in Munich in 2013 due to a major incident.[6] The business continuity plans (which in this case would come under the heading of "loss of workplace" for critical processes) were immediately activated in order to avoid any disruption of critical activities.

In addition, the Crisis Committee was activated in order to manage the complex situation. Emergency workplaces for all employees, including for those not supporting critical processes, were subsequently organised. Furthermore, regular meetings were set up to inform all interested parties. The initial assessment of the situation made clear that the "outage" of the building would last for a few months. This meant that a long-term solution was required to ensure the recovery and stability of particular functions of the bank. In this way, the complete IT and technical set-up for all employees and workplaces was put in place.

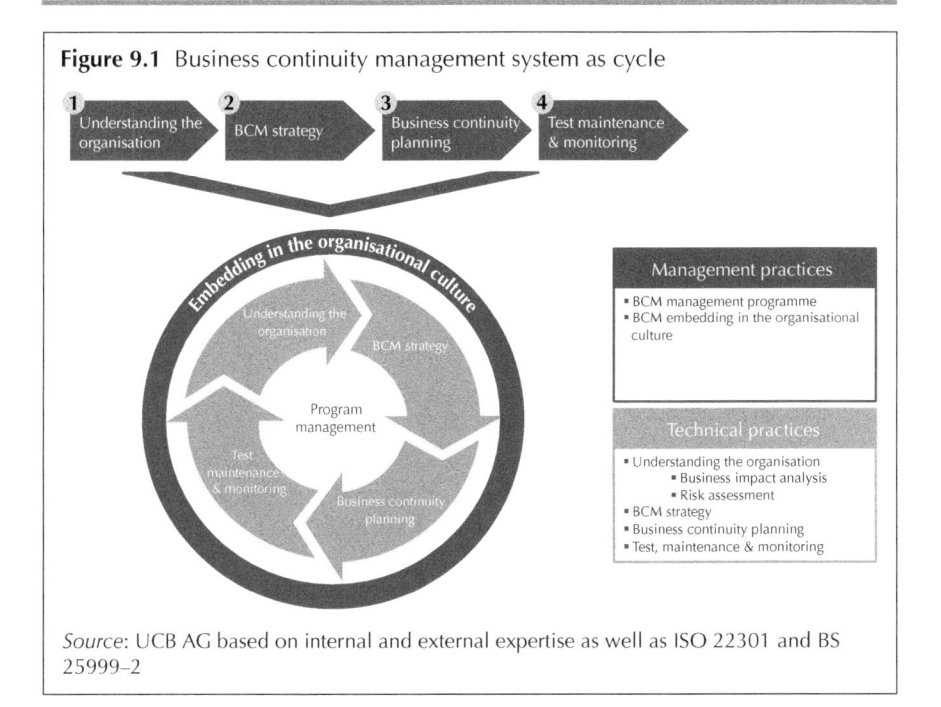

Figure 9.1 Business continuity management system as cycle

1. Understanding the organisation
2. BCM strategy
3. Business continuity planning
4. Test maintenance & monitoring

Embedding in the organisational culture
- Understanding the organisation
- BCM strategy
- Business continuity planning
- Test maintenance & monitoring
- Program management

Management practices
- BCM management programme
- BCM embedding in the organisational culture

Technical practices
- Understanding the organisation
  - Business impact analysis
  - Risk assessment
- BCM strategy
- Business continuity planning
- Test, maintenance & monitoring

Source: UCB AG based on internal and external expertise as well as ISO 22301 and BS 25999-2

Without a professional BCM set-up, and the proper crisis communication, the event might have resulted in severe damage with long-term outage of critical business processes. This would have had significant consequences for reputational risk.

REPUTATION: A MAJOR FACTOR IN BCM

The organisation's reputation within the financial industry is a driving force for success, which is complex and difficult to define. Without a positive reputation, potential and existing clients will be sceptical about doing business with an organisation, as they will be uncertain about the quality of services and products. Therefore, a financial institution facing reputational issues could lose all of its business to its competitors.

Ensuring business continuity for online banking, trading and payments is essential for every bank. Any disruption of these services would not just mean financial damage to the bank but also reputational damage realised by clients, regulators and other stakeholders. So, ultimately, reliable processes and the ability to cope with critical events is also a matter of creating or destroying trust. Hence,

REPUTATIONAL RISK MANAGEMENT IN FINANCIAL INSTITUTIONS

Figure 9.2 BCM system as workflow

Program management (1) Understanding the organisation	(2) BCM strategy	(3) Business continuity planning	(4) Test maintenance & monitoring	BCM awareness
Management professional practice				**Management professional practice**
■ BCM guidelines ■ Organisation of BCM (roles and responsibilities) ■ Determination of methodologies and procedures (business impact analysis, risk analysis, BC-planning, testing) ■ Definitions: incident, problem, emergency, crisis, catastrophe				■ Measures to increase BCM awareness (eg, intranet, events, reporting, exercises)
	Technical Professional Practice			
■ Business impact analysis ■ Identification of critical processes and their resources ■ Risk assessment for critical processes ■ Relevant risk scenarios ■ Risk mitigation measures	■ Options for continuity scenarios ■ BCM Strategy for: – People/employees/workers – Building and infrastructure – Information and communication technology – Data: electronic and paper documents – Suppliers and provided services	■ Business continuity plans for critical and systemic processes ■ Crisis management plan	■ Test and exercise concepts for critical and systemic processes ■ Procedures and templates for tests and exercises ■ Exercise plans ■ BCM reporting	

Source: UCB AG based on internal and external expertise as well as ISO 22301 and BS 25999–2

BCM is a key discipline for the operational stability and coherent reputational aspects of running a bank.

BCM adds value to reputational risk, as reputational issues are always part of the analysis and mitigating measures that are designed and developed within BCM.

Beginning with the business impact analysis, the consideration of reputational risks is a key factor in categorising activities and processes as critical in UniCredit Bank AG. Based on the results of the analysis, the potential risk of disruptions and outages of critical processes and activities is identified and can be mitigated.

Furthermore, critical activities and processes are covered by contingency plans. Therefore, in the case of a disruption or outage the recovery process is well regulated, which limits the potential reputational impact.

In addition, when a disruptive incident becomes too complex to be managed by BCM, crisis management will take control of the incident. Once that happens, communication becomes one of the most important disciplines, since it is paramount in any crisis to mitigate the reputational impact. It is important to choose a stakeholder-oriented approach and communication in order to reduce or prevent reputational risk impacts. The decision-making process of the stakeholder-oriented approach is part of crisis management planning and business continuity planning. Within this process, it is also important to identify individuals within the organisation, who will/should take care of the communication with each stakeholder in the event of a crisis event. Furthermore, it has also to be considered that different communication approaches are needed depending on the stakeholders involved. For example, the communication approach of an organisation's internal stakeholders will be different from the communication approach of external stakeholders such as regulators and customers. In a nutshell, there is a need for comprehensive planning for crisis communication.

Finally, with the help of exercises and tests the organisation can verify and ensure that its BCM plans are effective and up to date, taking into consideration all known and relevant reputational risks.

At the heart of comprehensive risk management lies the increasingly important art and science of managing reputation (Woodcock 2006). While it is commonly acknowledged that reputational risk is difficult to manage, there is mutual consent on the key elements of managing it (Alijoyo):

- understanding of stakeholders' expectations, information requirements and perceptions of the organisation;
- effective management of all categories of stakeholders, such as clients, staff, regulators, shareholders and the press;
- strong and consistent enforcement of controls on governance, business and legal compliance;
- ensuring ethical practice throughout the supply chain; establishment and continual updating of a business continuity and crisis management plan and the team required to support them;
- continuous monitoring of threats to reputation;
- a clear vision: "what we stand for and are prepared to be held responsible for";
- clear values, supported by a code of conduct, setting out expected standards of behaviour;
- an open, trusting, supportive culture;
- organisational learning leading to corrective action where necessary; and
- reward and recognition systems that support organisational goals and values.

When taking a closer look at the key elements and the methodology behind how business continuity and reputational risk are managed, it becomes clear that there are differences, commonalities and consequently interdependencies – as shown in Table 9.1.

UNDERSTANDING THE DIFFERENCE

Arguably the most obvious difference between the two disciplines is their perspective on business. While reputational risk primarily focuses on the potential reputational effects caused by different business activities or other issues, BCM looks at disruptive events and their relation to business processes themselves.

Moreover, while the focus of reputational risk is primarily on the perception of stakeholders and the public, business continuity puts its emphasis on the critical activities and relevant resources required to deliver.

A proper BCM plan is expected to deliver both preventive and reactive measures and plans to maintain or restart business processes within an acceptable timeframe. BCM and in particular crisis management activities are active and operative risk-mitigation

Table 9.1 BCM versus reputational risk

Category Type	Reputational risk	Business continuity management
Objective	Protecting brand reputation and value	Staying on course whatever happens
Scope	Managing of reputational risk	Business continuity for critical processes and activities
Stakeholder	Understanding needs and requirements of stakeholders	Stakeholder as part of the overall analysis
Trigger	Risk of loss from damages to organisation's reputation	Disruption or outage of a process, activity or resource
Process	Implementing risk assessment, determining whether the risk is acceptable	Business impact analysis/risk assessment/business continuity strategy – determine dependencies and resources including recovery objective
Solution	Providing risk-improvement activities to convert unacceptable risks into acceptable ones	Develop effective/efficient response plan
Methodology	Holistic approach	Holistic approach
Competence/people	High soft skills as well as business understanding	High soft skills as well as business understanding
Benefits	Protecting and enhancing corporate reputation for the greater benefit of all stakeholders	Maintaining continuity of the operational core competence of the organisation with less impact in terms of financial, operational and reputational risk
Internal perception	Becoming more and more important; nevertheless, it is taken for granted	Becoming more and more important; nevertheless, it is taken for granted
Quantification of added value to the organisation	Very difficult	Very difficult
Subject matter	Reputational risk	Critical processes and activities
Ability to learn	Essential	Essential
Open culture	Required	Required
Strategic level versus tactical level	Strategic level	Operational, tactical and strategic level
Response time	Step by step, adopting due process to respond and mitigate the incident	Immediately

measures. It can be said that only in the case of an incident can BCM fully prove the quality and effectiveness of its system, while, for the performance of reputational risk, the evaluation is not of major relevance.

A further difference is the response time. While BCM immediately activates existing continuity plans in order to respond to upcoming or present events, which generate significant uncertainty, reputational risk is not designed to immediately respond on an operational level.

Additionally, the obvious benefits of the two disciplines differ. Reputational risk is focused on the reputations of corporates. BCM benefits include maintaining the continuity of an organisation's competitive core competence. In other words, BCM enhances the business operations resilience while reputational risk mitigates and manages their reputational risks.

In addition the idea of reputational risk management is strongly aimed at compiling financial performance indicators, which are used to measure identified risks. This approach is a favoured methodology in order to weigh risks and translate them into financial figures. Based on the compiled figures the organisation can prepare for both known and potential (unknown) risks.

Where BCM supports the operations and business, (reputational) risk management provides figures (which give information about estimated financial impact) regarding existing and potential risks.

COMMONALITIES

Both disciplines are applicable across functional, divisional and (in a corporate group) even legal departments. BCM and reputational risk do not focus on just one specific process or business of an organisation but more on the complete value chain, taking into consideration each and every internal and external factor that could somehow have an impact on the business or reputation of the organisation.

Both business continuity and reputational risk emphasise the identification and understanding of relevant parties (ie, stakeholders) in order to assess their needs and requirements in the overall analysis.

There are activities, such as risk assessment, for which both disciplines need people with similar skills. The required "soft skills" needed to manage the stakeholders and business, and the technical knowledge needed to conduct a risk assessment, are similar for both business continuity and reputational risk. "Soft skills" refer to a person's emotional intelligence quotient – the cluster of personality traits, social graces, communication, language, personal habits and friendliness that characterise relationships with other people.

For a long time BCM and reputational risk were taken for granted and viewed more in the context of using common sense. Today, as a consequence of the above-mentioned conditions in addition to regulatory requirements, this is changing. Nevertheless, BCM and reputational risk both still need to put effort into working on awareness within an organisation. One of the reasons may be that they are neither a profit-generating unit, such as investment banking, nor one of the classic supporting departments, such as Finance and Controlling. This makes creating awareness even more important in order to promote these disciplines throughout an organisation.

Furthermore, the quantification of the added value given to the company by reputational risk and BCM is very difficult if not impossible to calculate. While reputational risk is a consequential risk having its root in other risks, business continuity deals with the continuation of diverse critical processes within an organisation. Although both support the resilience of an organisation, their work cannot be directly quantified. This is an additional factor that may explain the underestimation of reputational risk and BCM.

Another common aspect is that both disciplines need an open, trustworthy and supportive culture in order to thrive. Both depend on continuous learning and development, including corrective measures. Such culture is the breeding ground for a continuously improving discipline that relies on past experiences and the new measures that result.

Finally, both business continuity and reputational risk have a holistic approach and view. Like the BCM strategy, a risk strategy is usually also developed within an organisation.

INTERDEPENDENCIES

While reputational risk is part of the assessment conducted as part of the business impact analysis, the failure of the BCM process could end up as a reputational risk and probably a crisis for an entire organisation.

Furthermore, business processes are sometimes determined as

critical within the business impact analysis because of their reputational impact. The cash supply and the IT for ATMs are examples. If ATMs are not operating due to lack of cash or an IT outage, usually there would not be significant monetary damage for the bank. Nevertheless, a certain number of events like these, accompanied by relevant media attention, can cause a chain reaction that could end up as reputational damage. The clients might even switch loyalties and end up with a competitor.

Such connections do demonstrate that the limitations or weak points of the one discipline serve as entry points for the other.

The competencies and behaviour of those involved in these processes are additional and essential areas of interdependency, which should be mentioned. Managing reputation requires "soft skills" such as prudence, anticipating future needs and trends, understanding stakeholders' requirements and planning and taking action in a positive way (Rayner 2004). This skill set is also part of the required skills for business continuity, although, for the business impact analysis, there are more business-related and technical skills required to analyse the relevant activities and processes, as the analysis is not limited to stakeholders and associated risks. With close cooperation between the two disciplines a number of goals can be reached:

❏ use of synergy effects based on information sharing – synergy effects arise between two or more processes, units or parties that produce an effect greater than the sum of their individual effects;
❏ increase of acceptance of information and measures of both disciplines due to reduction of redundancies and duplication of work;[7]
❏ leveraging knowledge in terms of one discipline using the generated knowledge and collected experience of the other one and vice versa;
❏ increase of validity of information and avoidance of inconsistencies; and
❏ increase of innovation and creativity of both disciplines.

All these things help an organisation to build its capability to respond quickly to unforeseen changes and chaotic disruptions. They help an organisation to enhance its ability to bounce back and also to make progress with regard to speed, precision and determination (Bell 2002) and build its organisational resilience. But in particular, for the two areas in the scope of this chapter, trustworthy interaction and a culture of "sharing and gaining" are crucial in order for them to be both efficient and effective. This means a culture providing ideal conditions for open communication, transparency and trust in order to share and generate existing and new knowledge.

CONCLUSION

The quality of resilience can be found in many disciplines and sciences, eg, psychology, education, technology and even within ecological systems. Basically, resilience is the characteristic needed to enable any system to cope with changes and become stronger through the experiences and lessons learned during these changes. In trying to clarify and explain the link between reputational risk and BCM the resilience aspect is the most relevant and connecting element. Both reputational risk and BCM significantly contribute to the reinforcement of business, although in different ways and with different perspectives. In this sense they deliver results that should be considered complementary.

It is also true that BCM is an essential contributor to a modern reputational risk approach and vice versa. The interaction between the two disciplines helps practitioners to have a better understanding of potential risks, and to be able to conduct a more comprehensive analysis of all risks.

Coming back to the trends within the financial industry mentioned at the beginning of this chapter, we end with the following remarks.

- ❏ Both disciplines, which have been underestimated in the past, seem to have gained greater visibility and exposure, in particular within the banking and financial industries, due to stricter regulatory requirements (among other reasons).
- ❏ In order to regain the trust of stakeholders, and especially business partners and clients, financial institutions need to possess stable operational and IT systems and the capability to manage disruptive events. All these efforts are required for a financial institution to maintain its good reputation, which is its most valuable attribute.

❏ Therefore, it has become obvious that BCM and reputational risk management are the key disciplines within financial institutions for creating and maintaining stable and resilient systems that support the good reputation of the organisation.

As there seem to be many common elements and potential overlaps, it is decisive that the actors on both sides, in addition to professional skills, develop the ability to share and communicate properly.

1 Source: Seven Revolutions, http://csis.org/program/seven-revolutions
2 See "What is BC?" at www.thebci.org/index.php/resources/what-is-business-continuity.
3 Throughout the chapter we alternate between the words "bank" and "organisation". An organisation can be a bank, but whenever we are referring to bank-specific topics the terminology "bank" is used, to clarify exactly what we are discussing.
4 News: 12.07.2012: ISO 22301 – ein neuer Internationaler Standard für das Business Continuity Management, http://www.hisolutions.com/DE/News/Aktuell/ISO22301.php.
5 ISO 22301:2012.
6 Due to internal regulations we are not allowed to be more specific about the details of this incident.
7 To clarify this point, the assumption here is that both disciplines – reputational risk and business continuity management – involve similar activities. When people work closely together the duplication of work must be avoided in order to ensure that practitioners will not be asked the same questions by two sources, and/or will not be given the same information more than once.

REFERENCES

Alijoyo, Antonius, "Reputation Risk Series: Part 3: Reputation Risk Management", available at https://erm-academy.org/publication/risk-management-article/reputation-risk-series-part-3-reputation-risk-management.

Bell, Michael, 2002, "The Five Principles of Organisational Resilience", available at www.gartner.com/doc/351410/principles-organisational-resilience, January

Noakes-Fry, Kristen, Christopher H. Baum and Barry Runyon, 2005, "Laws Influence Business Continuity and Disaster Recovery Planning Among Industries", available at www.gartner.com/doc/483265/laws-influence-business-continuity-disaster.

Rayner, Jenny, 2004, *Managing Reputational Risk: Curbing Threats, Leveraging Opportunities,* Vol. 6 (New Jersey, Wiley).

Woodcock, Chris, 2006, "Why Reputation is a Major Factor in Business Continuity Management", April, available at www.continuitycentral.com/feature0335.htm.

10

Tracking Reputation and the Management of Perception at UniCredit

Armin Herla
UniCredit

REPUTATION IN THE BANKING SYSTEM

The end of the 2000's was marked by the subprime mortgage crisis and the insolvency of many banks, events that kicked off an unprecedented global recession. The subsequent crisis of the European sovereign debt, together with the erosion of the reputation of the financial sector, has undermined public confidence in the ability of banks to support the real economy. The 2008 financial crisis turned the spotlight on the issue of trust and has shown how essential it is for a bank to operate in a sustainable manner. This has led to an increasing focus on the long-term stability of the financial sector, as well as on the professional conduct of banks and their ability to be responsible "corporate citizens".

While reputational risks concern precise actions, events or situations, reputation itself is a more general and long-term concept. It can be seen as a result of several actions, events and situations over time, all of which build an overall perception of how a company behaves. Or, in short, reputational risk control is one of the means to achieve a good reputation as the end result. Therefore, not only is the regular monitoring of reputation necessary in order to evaluate and align measures, but so is the continuous discourse of responsibility for risk control and reputation measurement.

In this context, the established reputation of banks, namely the way in which banks are perceived by stakeholders, has a crucial role.

As a result of the major events that have put a strain on the global economy, banks have been asked to respond by adopting a strategy (risk management being one part of a larger reputation strategy, but not its only component) to satisfy all stakeholders and to define goals consistent both in the medium and long term (as detailed below). In the short term, one of the strategy options is to operate with the goal of increasing profits while disregarding their sustainability. Undoubtedly, attaining profit in the short term is a fundamental aim for a company, since shareholder satisfaction ensures the company's financial independence. However, a strategy that focuses only on profit maximisation in the short term puts at risk the sustainability of results in the medium and long terms. The adoption of sustainable practices is therefore a key factor for the smooth running of a business in the long run.

The only way a company can transform its profit into long-term value for stakeholders is to consider their interests in its decision making. The practices, the products and the processes need to meet, or indeed to exceed, the expectations of the stakeholders, and to achieve sustainability and social legitimacy (ie, an ethical consensus of sorts within society that engenders goodwill towards the company in question and in theory extends its lifetime). Social legitimacy is confirmed and strengthened by a solid reputation. Today more than ever, for a bank it is essential to act to create a solid reputation.

A structured approach to reputation management ensures that the bank in question is able to anticipate the warning signs, needs and expectations of the stakeholders.

This chapter begins by describing the ways in which reputation is analysed in UniCredit, detailing the changes that occurred after 2011. We then move on to the methodology established by the Reputation Institute, followed by a discussion of the annual UniCredit reputation survey, before concluding with an overview of the results of this survey and the impact this information has on the day-to-day running of operations within UniCredit.

THE ASSESSMENT OF THE REPUTATION IN UNICREDIT

The interest of UniCredit in reputation has its origins in 2008. The former group CEO, Alessandro Profumo, in the 2008 Sustainability Report stated (UniCredit 2008),

The creation of value means generating sustainable profits over the long run, which in turn means social legitimisation with respect to customers, colleagues, investors and local communities. Creating value means responding, as best possible, to the needs of these four stakeholders. That hardly seems like an outmoded concept to me. In fact, it seems more needed than ever.

This underlying belief has been the starting point around which the group has started to build a new connection with its main stakeholders. This approach, defined as stakeholder engagement by UniCredit, increases the main stakeholders' knowledge in order to improve the bank's ability to manage risk and resolve conflicts. Only by focusing on stakeholders' interests when making decisions and

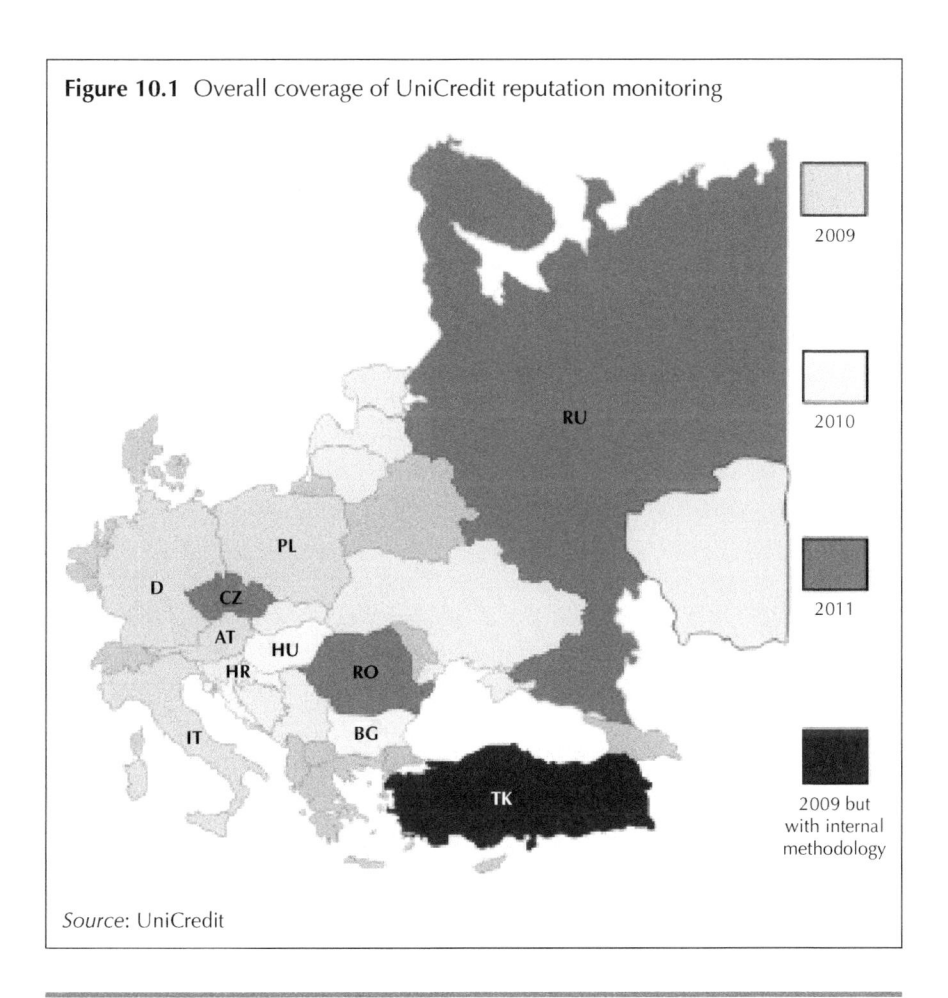

Figure 10.1 Overall coverage of UniCredit reputation monitoring

Legend: 2009; 2010; 2011; 2009 but with internal methodology

Source: UniCredit

implementing practices and products that meet or exceed expectations with the bank can the bank strengthen its reputation.

Reputation is thus of crucial importance, becoming one of the key pillars of the sustainability model alongside profitability and legitimacy. A strong reputation is based on financial performance, management skills, commitment to the community and fully realising what was originally promised.

To analyse and evaluate the perceptions of stakeholders, UniCredit implemented reputation monitoring in 2009 with the following objectives:

❑ to identify and continuously monitor key aspects of stakeholder groups in countries in which UniCredit operates; and
❑ to assess the bank's activities and its ability to meet the needs and expectations of stakeholders.

Reputation monitoring, achieved through a series of interviews, helps to identify the factors that most affect reputation.

The reputation assessment first focused on four countries, Italy, Germany, Austria and Poland, which account for approximately 80% of the bank's revenue. The process was then extended a year later to three other CEE countries: Bulgaria, Croatia and Hungary. Starting from 2011 the survey added the Czech Republic, Russia, Romania and Turkey – having already been implemented in 2009 for a total of eleven countries.

THE ORGANISATIONAL RESPONSE

Up until 2011, reputation assessment within UniCredit had been managed by the Management Identity and Communications Department. That year was a real turning point: reputation began to play a major role, not only at a strategic level but also at a commercial level. Simply put, a bank's reputation became one of the key factors that influence a customer's decision to choose between particular companies. This assumption, along with the need for customer acquisition, moved UniCredit towards a more consistent approach in monitoring and evaluating reputation.

UniCredit subsequently decided to focus on the analysis of stakeholder perception, establishing in 2011 the Group Stakeholder and Service Intelligence Department. Together with local teams, its task is to coordinate the surveys completed by customers, stakeholders, communities, employees and internal customers, as well as to analyse the business context. The department uses survey results to support the development of action plans in single countries and promote initiatives aimed at effective stakeholder engagement.

Group Stakeholder and Service Intelligence coordinated the following surveys:

- CUSTOMER SATISFACTION: this evaluates and monitors the perceptions and the expectations of customers regarding products and services;
- BRAND IDENTITY: this evaluates the level of knowledge of the UniCredit brand and its position among main competitors;
- PEOPLE SURVEY: this evaluates the involvement of the employees in their workplace and their feelings; and
- INTERNAL CUSTOMER SATISFACTION: this evaluates colleagues' satisfaction of services received by internal offices/divisions/departments.

The outcome of each survey is communicated to the relevant departments in order to improve service quality.

REPUTATION ASSESSMENT
The methodology of the Reputation Institute

To evaluate its reputation, UniCredit chose to work with the Reputation Institute, which uses an independent methodology.

The philosophy of the Reputation Institute focuses on the thought of its founder, Charles Fombrun, that "a corporate reputation is a perceptual representation of a company's past actions and future prospects that describe the firm's overall appeal to all of its key constituents when compared with other leading rivals" (Fombrun 1995).

According to this approach corporate reputation is the result of a mixture of three components: the direct experience of the brand (ie, purchase of products, services, experience in points of sale, financial investments and/or jobs offered by the company); what the brand says about itself by marketing, communication and advertising; and

Figure 10.2 The reputation model

Direct experiences
- Products
- Customer service
- Investments
- Employment

What company says/does
- Branding
- Public relations
- Marketing
- Social responsibility

What others say
- Media (traditional, social)
- Topic experts, leaders, friends/family

Perceptions
- Trust
- Respect
- Admiration
- Good feeling

Corporate reputation

Source: The Reputation Institute

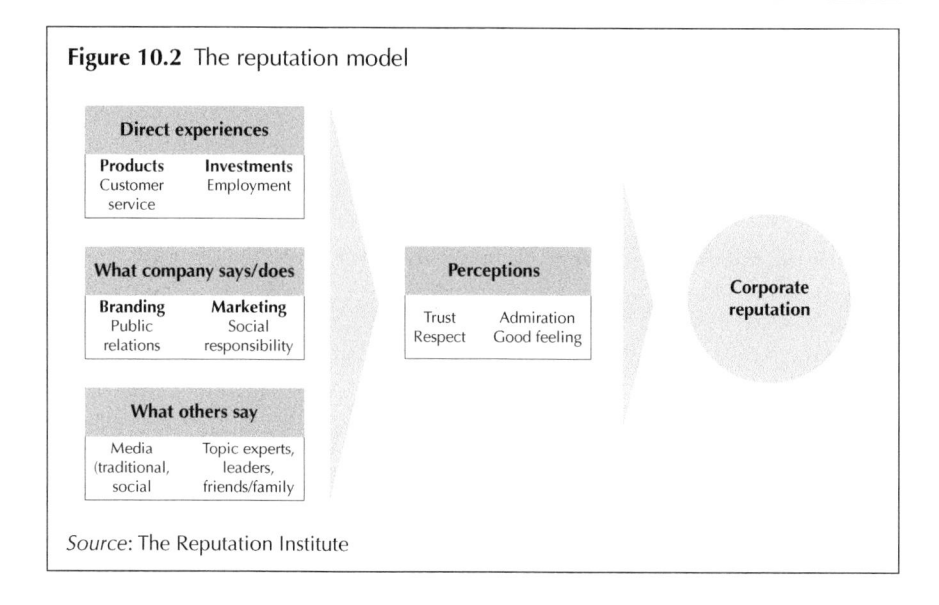

what is said about the brand (for example, by the media, opinion leaders and experts, friends and families).

Corporate reputation has its origin in the emotional bonds of key stakeholders, which has a profound effect on company business, and ensures their support and trust.

The RepTrak model developed by the Reputation Institute is based on this concept. RepTrak Pulse measures the degree of admiration and trust that stakeholders express towards the company and assess the strength of their emotional bond. This index is measured on a scale of 0 to 100 and gives the opportunity to benchmark with the results obtained by major competitors.

The seven key dimensions of reputation as defined by the Reputation Institute are: performance, products and services, innovation, citizenship, leadership, work environment and governance. Each of these dimensions provides the stakeholder with their perception of the company.

RepTrak evaluates the degree of the emotional bond between company and public and determines which dimensions have a greater impact on the recommendations expressed by the stakeholders.

The intent of RepTrak is to identify the strengths and weaknesses of the company and all the areas on which to make concrete actions to improve the overall reputation. UniCredit also uses this model to evaluate the relationship between bank and stakeholder.

The questionnaire administration

At UniCredit the definition of reputation is based on an annual survey conducted in the main countries of the group for all categories of stakeholders. The interviews are based on the methodology of the Reputation Institute.

Method of administration

The UniCredit survey (which is customised but draws inspiration from the Reputation Institute questionnaire) is based on the CATI system (Computer-Assisted Telephone Interviewing), telephone interviews lasting about 25 minutes. In 2012 in Italy and in the Czech Republic, the CATI system had been joined by the CAWI system (Computer-Assisted Web Interviewing), which is an online questionnaire. The use of the two systems together has reduced errors in the measurement of reputation, and has increased the response rate for both surveys among the young and professional. The survey is carried out annually (except in Turkey, where it is carried out every two years) over a period of four to six weeks (in September and October).

Target

The target of the questionnaire includes many different types of stakeholders. Respondents are divided into three major groups: customers, non-customers and opinion makers. Customers are categorised according to their respective income threshold and are commonly classified as one of the following:

- mass market;
- affluent;
- private banking customers;
- companies segmented on the basis of total revenue; and
- opinion makers, which includes NGOs, consumer associations, trade associations, local governments, public institutions and opinion leaders, religious movements, cultural associations, media, trade unions and professional associations.

Questionnaire

The reputation questionnaire is based on 40 items and lasts about 25 minutes. The answers are provided according to a Likert scale – from 1 to 7 – and respondents are asked to express their degree of agreement/disagreement about certain assumptions.

The questionnaire is divided into five main parts.

1. RepTrak Pulse: This part measures the emotional value that respondents have towards UniCredit, from overall reputation, to trust, to admiration and esteem.
2. rational items: This part assesses reputation, utilising the seven dimensions defined by the Reputation Institute, as detailed above. The questions vary depending on the country and the target segment.
3. supportive behaviours: This part measures the respondents' propensity to purchase, recommend and invest in UniCredit.
4. sources: This part includes questions related to exposure to media.
5. others: The final part contains general demographic questions.

Overall results

When analysing UniCredit reputation these are the key factors common to all countries:

❏ for individuals and business customers, the key element is governance (ie, the proper and ethical behaviour of the professional relationship, the transparency and openness to dialogue and confrontation) as well as the offer of products/services tailored to meet the specific needs of the customers; and
❏ for stakeholders the key factor that improves reputation is the bank's ability to provide support to families and its capacity to contribute to the economic growth of the area.

MANAGING OF RESULTS AND ACTION PLANNING

The next phase is the analysis of the survey and the communication of the results to the key stakeholders. The goal is to share with the stakeholders the reputational degree of UniCredit and to compare it with that of one of its main competitors. The survey results are the starting point for an analysis of the current situation and to develop action plans for the future.

Externally to UniCredit, the survey results are explained in several ways.

- ❏ The Sustainability Report is published on an annual basis, and describes the link between business strategies and the main activities of the group. The Sustainability Report explains the company's approach to business in general and its main priorities. The report also explains how the group develops its business with a customer-centric commitment in mind, paying attention to its environment in an ethically minded capacity. Part of the report is dedicated to reputation management and contains information about reputational risk-management systems and monitoring and risk prevention.
- ❏ A press conference is held by the CEO of each country branch. During the presentation of the annual financial results, the CEO also presents the results of the investigations into reputational issues, highlighting the drivers of both customer satisfaction and the reputation of the branch, with both contributing to the ultimate financial results.
- ❏ Within UniCredit the results of good reputation management practices are communicated to the employees in each business area: (1) the Group Stakeholder and Intelligence Service team, after analysing the data contained in the Reputation Survey (which details, for example, trends, stakeholder groupings, and strengths and weaknesses in particular areas), illustrates the results of the survey to the board or to the CEO of each country branch; (2) yearly sessions with the manager of each department are organised to analyse the data in depth, during which the results of reputation management practices are correlated with customer satisfaction and brand identity; and (3) in each country branch the results are discussed with the operational risk managers

The results of the various investigations into reputational issues are a starting point for examining areas that need to be improved, helping to implement an action plan at UniCredit. Each function, after analysing the data, formulates an action plan with the main activities for the following year.

Each action plan is divided into four parts:

- ❑ the key areas for improvement, which became clear from the results of the survey;
- ❑ the key actions, activities and initiatives planned for each improvement area;
- ❑ key performance indicators that measure the degree of realisation of a particular action; and
- ❑ the period of time within which the decided action will be implemented.

The group's Stakeholder Group and Intelligence Service, along with the local service and stakeholder intelligence team of each country, are responsible for collecting the action plans of the different functions and for monitoring the results. Through each of these action plans, the priorities of the group begin to take shape, with decisions about how to implement good practice to meet customer needs and improve their perception made for the subsequent year.

CONCLUSIONS

The reputation management practices that are implemented annually by UniCredit are undoubtedly a great investment in terms of time and resources. The UniCredit view on reputation is that a good reputation ensures sustainability in the long term and reinforces customer satisfaction.

REFERENCES

Fombrun, Charles J., 1995, *Reputation: Realizing Value from the Corporate Image* (Boston, MA: Harvard Business School Press).

UniCredit, 2008, "Sustainability Report", available at www.unicreditgroup.eu/content/dam/unicreditgroup/documents/en/sustainability/reporting-and-metrics/sustainability_report_2008.pdf.

Part 3

Best-Practice Examples

11

Successful Recovery from Reputational Crises: Legitimate versus Illegitimate Risk Case Studies

Steffen Bunnenberg
Bunnenberg Bertram Rechtsanwaelte

INTRODUCTION

This chapter will give you the tools necessary to recognise and handle crises of reputation correctly. In this matter it is of the utmost importance to understand how such crises work and what their origins and sources are. We are going to take a look not only at the reputational crises concerning banks specifically, but also at those affecting other industries that are in that way assignable to the banking industry. That is the only way to learn the right response for future reputational crises.

After a private testing institute rates a financial service provider's performance as inadequate, although it does not even offer the services in question, the sales plummet. Discontented customers, laid-off staff and disguised competitors converge on evaluation websites and blogs. And, in the spirit of the financial crisis, the established press gladly investigates banks, their providers and the wealthy as soft targets in any envy-fuelled debate, or lets itself be exploited by a competitor, selling commissioned studies under the guise of freedom of speech that praise the sponsor and denigrate the rival.

Banks, their associates and the wealthy fear for their reputation, and rightly so. They are caught in a quagmire of justification if they do not react properly. In the worst case, potential clients and associates will not even consider the companies in question any more. They have fallen off the grid. After all, the interested party can hardly contact everyone personally, only the top five. How would you, for instance, search for a good hotel? Would you call up hotels with poor reviews and ask if it is true what you read and see in the pictures? No potential customer or business partner would go to such lengths. The consequences of a crisis of reputation are almost incalculable. Disastrously, a crisis of reputation can remain completely unnoticed.

In the first section of this chapter we are going to take a look at reputational crises from a legal point of view. We are going to distinguish between the three different types of reputational crises to understand the proper response to the particular kind. In the next section we will deal with how to react to the first kind of reputational crisis: a crisis based on legitimate claims. In the section following, we will take a closer look at the adequate response to the second kind of reputational crisis: one that is provoked by the use of illegitimate claims. The most difficult cases, the ones that you cannot clearly assign to a legitimate or illegitimate claim, are going to be presented in the most relevant fourth section. The relevance of this section derives from the circumstance that in real life the claims in a reputational crisis are mostly of a hybrid nature and not at all "black or white". The contents in this section are forums, search engines, the press, tests, blogs, review platforms (in general), employer assessment websites and future kinds of reputational crises. Thereafter, in the fifth section, we are going to take a look at the hidden advantages of a trial. Last but not least, the chapter will wind up with the conclusion and a summary of all the dos and don'ts we have found so far in the case studies.

For legal reasons, please notice that, since all the provided examples are real-life-examples, we were not able to go into every detail and have had to change some facts to anonymise the companies or the crisis in that the reputational crisis has not been discussed in public or the client has not discussed their reputational issues in public; the latter is usually the normal case.

FORMS OF CRISES OF REPUTATION FROM A LEGAL PERSPECTIVE

For identifying the crisis and the correct responses, we must differentiate between two groups: the legitimate and the illegitimate claim.

Legitimate claims are those claims that are in accordance with the truth. They do not create a false impression and do not leave out necessary information. Illegitimate claims are false claims or claims creating a false impression, also incomplete claims, meaning they leave out essential information.

This distinction is important, since different claims warrant different reactions for averting a crisis of reputation. In short, if the claim is legitimate, no legal steps are necessary. These would probably prove unsuccessful or even detrimental, since every legal action includes an escalation. What is of importance is a direct communication with the claimant. This communication should not go through third parties, but be established by the company itself.

If it is an illegitimate claim, legal actions are possible and in general necessary. Not acting will often be construed as a sign of weakness, inviting further attacks. Just as it is in sports: if you neither defend nor attack, you lose.

Mixed cases are much harder to validate. They incorporate both legitimate and illegitimate claims. Here we have to meticulously and precisely analyse the situation and develop solutions accordingly. The right mixture of direct communication and legal actions is the adequate answer.

The following are examples depicting possible situations and solutions concerning different kinds of crises of reputation.

LEGITIMATE CLAIMS

Handling legitimate claims and legitimate criticism is simple. Here it is important to listen and communicate directly. Ignorance will not help. Three examples will highlight that.

One partly bizarre example that rose to fame in Germany is the wave of indignation that broke out of the blue on the Facebook page of Ing-Diba Bank in 2012. In December of 2011 the bank had commissioned an ad in which basketball player Dirk Nowitzki eats a slice of pork sausage in a butcher's shop. This enraged vegetarians and vegans. Angry posts appeared on the company's Facebook page: the commercial supposedly implied that only by eating enough meat could you grow as big and strong as the professional sports star. Yet the bank also had customers who objected to eating meat and fought against industrial livestock farming. A heated discussion broke out on the Facebook page between vegetarians and meat eaters that quickly moved away from its origin, until it had nothing to do with the commercial in question any more – let alone the services of the bank – growing into a fierce dispute between vegetarians and vegans. In accordance with their "principles of openness and transparency" ("*Leitbild von Offenheit und Transparenz*") the institute opted for de-escalation, calling for mutual respect in a few posts and devising house rules for the discussion. Then they let the dispute run its course for two weeks. On January 17, 2012, Ing-Diba terminated the discussion, explaining that the Facebook page was to be used for the core business of the bank, since customers wanted to be informed about the services and products they provided. New comments would therefore be deleted.

By and large, the bank's reaction was received well. No reputational damage remained. The reasons for this: the wave of indignation did not concern the bank's core business. During the dispute, many customers defended the bank. So the bank's job was simply to provide a framework for the discussion and end it at the opportune time. It was not necessary to take a stance regarding the content. Momentarily, the institute generated intensive media interest. Afterwards the press validated this as a positive example of how to deal with such waves of indignation.

If a company's services are at the core of the discussion, eg, the duty to inform customers about product specifications, as, for instance, mentioned in the Markets in Financial Instruments Directive from the European Union (MiFID), handling the crisis becomes more difficult. This can be illustrated by a similar case concerning a different industry, the telecommunication sector. When a customer complaining about poor network quality was put off by the company claiming he was "a singular incident", he built the website "We Are Singular Incidents" ("*Wir sind Einzelfall*"), where all dissatisfied customers converged and shared their experiences with the company's bad network coverage.

Since these posts were publicly accessible, soon other readers learned of the website when they were researching the company's services. Shortly after that, the press picked up on the website. The company reacted with openness, transparency and direct communication. Subject matter was mainly about legitimate shortcomings. Therefore, the company felt obligated to explain the shortcomings and technical problems. The company could even reach an agreement with the administrator of "We Are Singular Incidents" and publish responses on the website. The only reason this incident didn't result in a damaged reputation was the company's quick and rational reaction. It directly contacted the website's operator and took the problems seriously. It presented itself as open, transparent and ready to communicate. Thus, it was rewarded.

The complexity of a product generally minimises the risk of a reputational risk. The reason for that is simple: in order to kick off a public discussion about misbehaviour according to duty of information, you have to have the ability to explain a complex product with plain words. That's not a capability of every human being. But within the era of the Internet and the acceleration of information, it needs only one capable human being to kick off a public discussion. An example of that theory and the importance of the right timing can be seen in another – slightly older – case from a different industry: the computer sector. The global computer manufacturer Dell learned the lesson years ago. Jeff Jarvis, a well-known US journalist versed in the world of media, ordered a computer from Dell and experienced problems when he switched it on for the first time. He spent endless hours on hold to finally receive advice from people in countries far away. Even repairs did not help. If one problem was solved, another reared its head. This went on for months.

In July of 2005 – utterly frustrated – he published an article on his blog titled "Dell sucks". As mentioned above, it needs only one human being to start a crisis. Thanks to Google, the article spread enormously fast. It was available worldwide and many potential customers were interested in his experiences. In the course of just a few days, more and more people visited the website. Many of them commented on the article, firing up its importance. The article moved up and up on Google. It was linked more and more. When finally the press took notice, Dell was stupefied. "Just watch, don't touch" was its official answer concerning the Internet articles.

This attitude finally led to massive problems. Sales plummeted while the number of dissatisfied customers rose. The company's share value was cut in half. In the end, the head of marketing offered to replace the computer. But, in the meantime, Jarvis had decided on a competitor's device and only wanted his money back. The company complied and reimbursed him.

Eight months later, in April 2006, Dell started to rethink its attitude. Dell employees began to talk to the customers. They reacted to legitimate claims in form and content. Something had happened that the company had probably not foreseen. After the employees solved their customers' computer problems, the company was rewarded with positive comments in their blogs. Bad PR changed into good PR.

Yet the initial damage to their reputation was enormous and almost caused the ruin of a renowned global computer manufacturer. Only direct communication had prevented the worst.

Rethinking had proved beneficial, a fact that became apparent when a few years later Dell was confronted with the fact that one of its notebooks was highly flammable. This case led to a worldwide recall of the notebooks and could have resulted in major reputational damage. But Dell reacted very well: the company assigned several important employees to read blogs and respond to criticism.

These three examples – no matter what kind of industry they have emerged from – clarify the new form of communication necessary when dealing with legitimate claims. Let us summarise.

Don't ...
- just watch and ignore the issues. The public will discuss them with or without the person or company concerned.

Do ...
- assign (important) employees (not those from the outsourced call centre) to read blogs and respond to criticism;
- install compliance rules such as "principles of openness and transparency" and devise house rules for your social media channels;
- provide a framework for the public discussion and determine it at the opportune time; and
- react to legitimate claims in form and content, explaining the shortcomings and problems.

Yet, unfortunately, there is not only the case of legitimate criticism, but also of illegitimate claims. We will now focus on those.

ILLEGITIMATE CLAIMS

Illegitimate claims are untruthful claims, the creation of false but plausible impressions, insults or statements omitting essential information.

Handling such claims is more complicated. That is the nature of the matter. We are not confronted with illegitimate claims on a daily basis. If someone is presented – face to face – with a falsehood, that person can clarify or refute the issue right away. Doing so when defamation or libel is involved proves more difficult. Here illegitimate claims are presented to third parties. The person concerned might only later or in the worst case never get news of those untrue, harmful statements being spread.

The Internet caused a true boom in this kind of infringement. Every single person becomes the publisher of their own claims. On assessment websites and product pages, third-party claims are channelled and highlighted.

When you type a company or product name into your search engine combined with a swearword, you quickly find unlawful claims regarding product or company. Thus even seemingly unimportant opinions can reach a dramatic relevance.

Unfortunately, it is still common not to react to illegitimate claims, to ignore or downplay them. This is wrong and dangerous, as the following examples will show.

Imagine you are planning a big M&A transaction, but there is a hedge fund manager who is specialised in short selling. Needless to say, a falling stock price would be helpful. The hedge fund manager therefore spreads rumours about the poor financial situation of the company, unsold products and the expiration of an important patent. Of course, in reality, the financial situation is in best order, there are no unsold products and the patent will be extended. Nevertheless, the company neglects to respond publicly to the claims due to the fear of causing even more problems with a public statement. Meanwhile the stock price has been cut in half.

Here is another example. A couple of years ago, a financial company contacted our law firm. In a test, the company had been compared with other competitors and received a comparatively bad grade. Yet so much time had passed between the publication, notification and mandating of our firm that the client's entitlement could not be secured with a provisional court order any more. The final verdict, in favour of our client, was announced 15 months later. During that entire period of time the test was circulated in the media and has also been used by our client's competitors as USP. But since the test was carried out erroneously, thus producing illegitimate claims, the client's entitlements could finally be secured in court and the test was not permitted to be published anymore. With a faster reaction, our client's damage could have been contained.

The above examples demonstrate that the main challenge when handling illegitimate claims is a quick reaction. As the short-selling case showed, you have to act as soon as possible or the public opinion will be defined in the false way. In the worst case, the M&A transaction will not be finished, because of a rising lack of interest of your business partner.

In many cases the affected party is entitled to certain claims that warrant an accelerated process to preliminarily protect them. Germany – and, similarly, other countries – grants aggrieved parties entitlements to injunctive relief, counterstatement, repeal, compensation and reparation.

As mentioned repeatedly, time is of the essence here, since such a process presupposes urgency. Every court evaluates the term "urgency" in a different way. A general guideline for the time span is one month after the matter was discovered (according to German measurements). So, if no steps are taken within the first few days or a week after gaining knowledge of the illegitimate claim, it risks being unable to preliminarily protect the entitlement. The only road left then is to go through the principal proceedings, meaning a regular lawsuit must be filed. Yet this can take quite a long time. Many months may pass until a first ruling. Half a year may pass until the court's decision is legally binding. If the opposing party appeals to the court, a final decision may take years. And, during this time, the illegitimate claim can be distributed even further. The company will have a reputational damage that – as time goes by – becomes even harder to reverse.

Therefore, when dealing with illegitimate claims, it is important to act fast. When nothing is done, the aggrieved party may well find itself in a crisis of justification. In the worst case, it will never take notice of the potential customers turned away from it beforehand. Even associates and important potential clients use the Internet to get information on the potential new partner. The public, globally accessible image is crucial for future business relations.

If the interested party can choose among more than three companies as potential associates, those companies whose reputation on the Internet is not positive are not considered. Interested parties will not question the published articles and illegitimate claims. They will not call upon the aggrieved party and ask for clarification. They will simply choose another company.

There are few ways other than to negotiate, with the help of a lawyer, and take legal action when handling illegitimate claims. To uninvolved third parties it is always difficult to determine who is in the right. Generally speaking, uninvolved third parties will not want to be roped into a "struggle for the truth". Only when a court has determined the claims to be illegitimate will trust be restored.

Don't ...
❏ just watch and ignore illegitimate claims or play them down; wait too long or you will lose the possibility to protect your rights with an interim order.

Do ...
❏ analyse the issue and check your legal options (you might be entitled to injunctive relief, counterstatement, repeal, compensation and reparation); and
❏ act fast: you might have the right to stop the illegitimate claims immediately and thus avoid reputational damage.

INDIVIDUAL CASES

Often we cannot distinguish between a legitimate and an illegitimate claim. There is no unit control, no one miracle tool for all possibilities. The individual case is authoritative. This applies especially to legal practice. Every case must be judged individually and every court has to strive anew to reconcile the conflicting interests.

Testimonies do not stand for themselves. In general, they are embedded in the context of news coverage. There are, for example, several articles about a company depicting it critically. They include truths, falsehoods, appropriate and inappropriate impressions and probably lack some essential information that would nevertheless paint a very different picture for the reader.

Consider the following example: "25,000 customers cheated out of 400 million euros? State Police and Federal Financial Supervisory

Authority cracked down on Dresden's financial giant Infinus AG". Thus read the headlines of several national newspapers at the end of 2013.[1] An investigation into possible fraud and damage to investors was initiated across the country and 30 properties belonging to the financial group were searched.

The above-mentioned news caused many investors to panic and try to retrieve their money. They liquidated their assets, although Infinus did not have any financial difficulties up to that point. Press releases and legal means such as counterstatements and revocations might have averted the investor's overreactions. Although the everyday press is bound by due diligence and its own codes, this circumstance may also pose a threat to a company's reputation especially when negative newscasts continue over a long period of time.

Deutsche Bank, for example, has been battling negative headlines for a long time. Nowadays you can even find summaries of the shattering reports: "Unlawful interest deals, possible price-rigging with the gold price and exchange rates – there's hardly an international financial scandal where Deutsche Bank is not a suspect."[2]

And, when information like that is published in a renowned newspaper, public suspicion will be aroused, no matter what, and cause harm to the reputation of those concerned, even more so when such stories appear for months or even years. "Something must be true about this," the reader begins to assume.

Through the power of search engines, those articles and judgement calls remain retrievable, placed well in the Top 30, for all eternity. Even "youthful follies" thus become researchable today, and generate a source for future news coverage.

Striking the right note in such cases depends highly on the channel of communication. You can't decree that legal actions must be implemented *per se* when an article contains an illegitimate claim. The evolution of communication culture, the Internet and direct communication warrants a differentiated analysis. The following examples will look at successful and unsuccessful strategies in regard to crises of reputation, according to different communication channels such as forums, search indexes, the press, tests, websites, blogs, reviews and employer assessment sites and standards of corporate social responsibility (CSR).

Forums

The following case is a very special one. Although it does not concern the banking industry, it is of great importance, because it shows that you have to check your legal options very carefully.

In 2011 an Internet user put up an anonymous forum. In it, he published completely invalid claims and insults concerning a company and its directorate. Because of the many technical possibilities the Internet offered, his identity has never been discovered. All deposited data was anonymised. The forum itself was set up in a way that new links leading to the same article were created automatically every time an article was clicked or a comment was left. This led to a pretty good search engine optimisation with the search engine providers. If you typed the name of the company or its directorate into one of the big search engines, 90 of the first 100 hits led to this forum.

The reputational damage was enormous. Henceforth the CEO had to explain himself to employees, customers and associates repeatedly. Sales plummeted. The company could barely acquire new business.

At first, the company tried search engine optimisation. But this helped only marginally, because, among the top 100 hits, only a few more appeared leading to sites controlled by the company. The attacks from the anonymous forum were still retrievable and included in the search index.

The only possibility left was taking legal action, since the claims were almost exclusively illegitimate and unjustified comments. But against whom? The identity was hidden.

The company decided against attacking the forum directly – not only for legal and factual reasons, but also strategic ones. It did not wish to heat up the conflict even more. Instead, it contacted the search engine operators, making them aware of the infringement and initialising the links to be blocked from the search index.

But in 2011 the search engine operators were not prepared to handle cases that had spread so widely – neither factually nor legally. Furthermore, there was still no confirmed High Court decision. Nevertheless, the company succeeded in having 99% of the almost 3,000 links blocked.

It took over half a year. The awareness for the forum that had been fired up mainly by the search engine operators died down. The energy of the forum's proprietor let up. After nine months the forum could no longer be found on the search index. The crisis of reputation had been successfully averted.

This case shows that there are instances where it will not pay to contact the operator or attacker directly. Sometimes a direct communication by the attacked is an incentive for the attacker to publish more libel. Key to the success here was rendering the articles invisible on the search engines.

Press

The next example will show the fatal role the press can play in damaging a reputation. In a large bank, a vacancy on the board of directors had to be filled. There were several applicants. Just before the end of the application period, right before the weekend, an anonymous person pressed criminal charges against one of the applicants, citing suspected granting and accepting of unlawful advantages. The anonymous complaint was drafted so expertly that the prosecutor had to order an investigation. At the same time, the complaint was leaked to the press, still right before the weekend, which instantly led to news coverage of the investigation against the applicant. The timing was perfect. Countermeasures were impossible due to the weekend. His reputation was ruined, even though there was not a grain of truth in the accusations.

The candidate did not get the position and in applications to other firms had to defend himself on a regular basis. This would have stayed this way, had he not taken legal actions. Working with a highly specialised defence attorney, he succeeded in shutting down the investigation by the start of the following week.

Within days the candidate enforced his right to publish a counter-statement, and his entitlement to an injunction regarding the press. Because of these victories it became easier for him to clarify the incident in all interviews.

Yet the news of the investigation was not only published by the regular press, but was also disseminated as a press release through the many free press portals on the Internet. More than 100 blogs were connected to those portals, spreading the news of the investigation even further.

Roughly 500 websites reported on the candidate and the lawsuit. Working through and deleting the reports took about half a year.

Many blogs deleted the press release right away. With others, their search index results had to be blocked. Only then was the reputation mostly restored.

Search engines – index and auto-suggest
Another threat to a company's reputation (besides the search suggestion) is the search index itself: even if a forum or blog is only a singular, small website, it can quickly become the centre of attention. The examples of Dell and the forum highlight this.

Through search engines, negative publicity can easily move into the top 50 search engine hits. When an Internet user enters the name of a bank or a financial service provider into the search engine, they might find on the first page of the search results (apart from the company's homepage) several links leading to forums on shoddy business practices, dishonest counselling or derelict real estate. In these cases it is also possible and advisable to have the entries in the search engine's index blocked.

The next example attempts to demonstrate what a drama a simple search index hit is able to cause. In 2013 a company comes to know that one of the employees is supposedly a "Nazi". A clarifying meeting within the company is set up and company and employee mutually agree to part.

Yet both business partners and employees continue to inquire about the company's alleged ties to the political right. At first, the management is surprised since the whole case seemed at an end. Thereafter they find out the reason for the agitation: a Google search of the company reveals several hits in the top 10 leading to articles "exposing" the former employee as a "Nazi" and referring to his work for the company.

The company is thus erroneously presented to the reader as belonging to the extreme right. Yet the company is – as any other corporation – politically neutral and not allowed to ask employees what their political affiliation or religion is. Nevertheless, the readers associate the company with the extreme right scene. Taking actions against those unwarranted articles and blogs, especially those identifying the company by name, was not possible. The person(s) responsible hid behind their veil of anonymity.

The only course left for the company was once more to ask the search engine operator to block the links. The company checked its legal options and achieved an injunction against the search engine. The search engine was now compelled to block all index entries.

So we can see that there is an easy answer regarding how to handle unlawful entries in a search engine's index: taking legal action to have the links in question blocked is the only reasonable path.

Another threat to a company's reputation is the autosuggest function of search engines. In 2010, two words appeared automatically in the Google search window when the name of a company dealing in the financial sector was typed in: "Scientology" and "fraud". These are the so-called search suggestions Google offers users as they enter their search words. The user can thus choose from word combinations that supposedly occur often. Yet these search suggestions can also create an unwarranted impression: that the company in question is in cahoots with a religious sect, for example, or that it is being investigated for fraud. The reputation is at risk, because an impression is forced on the user of the search engine, even though they have nothing to do with the actual image of the company.

In 2013 the Bundesgerichtshof (Federal High Court of Germany) ruled correctly that Google's suggestions in the search window are not "purely technical, automated and passive", but that Google itself "processed the user queries with a special program creating the word combinations" and therefore is responsible for the suggestions. "If an affected party brings an infringement of his personal rights to the search engine's operator's notice, the operator is held accountable for prohibiting such infringements in the future." The company concerned won the lawsuit and other organisations can now rely on this ruling.

On May 13, 2014, the European Court of Justice (ECJ) ruled in a pioneering judgment (case C-131/12) that the operator of an Internet search engine may be responsible for personal data in the index. The ECJ obliged Google to delete sensitive data from the index and thus established a right to be forgotten. The judgment was based on the European Data Protection Directive (95/46 EC) and strengthens the protection of personal data and the right to privacy on the Internet.

In the initial case, a Spanish citizen had complained to the Spanish Data Protection Agency (AEPD, or Agencia Española de Protección de Datos). When he typed his name into Google, a text from the online archive of the Spanish newspaper *La Vanguardia* appeared in the index. The text was more than 10 years old and reported on his social debts and the seizure of his property. His complaint against the newspaper itself had no success, because the reporting was factual and thus lawful.

However, the AEPD assessed the complaints of the man against Google Spain and Google Inc. differently, requesting that the search engine operator delete sensitive data from its index and also to prevent access to such information in the future. Google took legal action against the decision of the Spanish court and the court submitted the question to the ECJ for a preliminary ruling.

Now the ECJ's decision is as surprising as it is radical: there is no avoiding the Data Protection Directive. Even automatically operating search engines have a responsibility. In particular, search results are able to considerably affect fundamental rights such as the respect for a private life and the protection of personal rights. Although a search engine automatically and continuously "detects published information on the Internet", according to the ECJ, this procedure constitutes a "collection of data" within the meaning of the Directive. Furthermore, Google will hereinafter retrieve, record, organise, store, disclose and make available the data in question. In the opinion of the ECJ, there is no doubt that these actions embodied a "processing" within the meaning of the Directive. This is, according to the ECJ, the case even if this information and personal data were already published unaltered in other media. Google is the "responsible party", in particular because the data processing happens in addition to the activities of the site operators. Therefore, the search engines have to ensure the protection of these rights within their means.

The ECJ took a completely new direction in obligating Google to delete search results from the index even if the reporting is itself lawful. This means that there is a right to have material deleted not only on evidence of defamatory content (libel, false statements), but also if the original site keeps the report in its archives, as in the case of the Spaniard. The reason: the search engines allow any Internet user entering a name to obtain a structured overview of a person. The effect of this intervention into the private lives is massive, because, according to the ECJ, without the search engine it is difficult to link together certain aspects of the private life of a person published on the Internet. It could also happen that originally materially correct data from legitimate reporting over time does not match the provisions of the Directive any more. According to the ECJ, the economic interests of the search engine company cannot justify such a serious interference. There would rather have to be a legitimate interest of the Internet user concerning this information. An example for a legitimate interest could be, for instance, if the case concerns someone who plays a role in public life.

But there is one problem: the decision is not directly applicable for companies. The European Data Protection Directive grants rights only to individuals. Whether in the future a company will have a right to be forgotten remains to be seen. There are very good arguments and it does seem possible. But the ECJ has to enhance the law.

Tests and (private) institutes

A reputational crisis that normally can only be fought by legal means is one set off by bad reviews from a testing institute. Institutions such as the German Stiftung Warentest are bound by certain quality standards, by their government mandate and through being partially financed by taxes. Being free of advertisements means such institutes are independent from manufacturers, and also the tests warrant a high degree of transparency.

But nowadays there are also many private testing institutes whose independence is not as thoroughly ensured. They try to circumvent the requirements of customer tests, ie, by switching to soft criteria while marketing the test as a performance trial. The customer cannot distinguish between such subtle differences and often reads the test only fleetingly. This leads to a discrepancy between the test's presentation and its actual criteria.

Mistakes in the methodology, lack of objectivity, questionable "facts", erroneously formed control groups and so forth can render the tests invalid.

In 2010 a private testing institute compared financial service providers who only worked for a fee with providers working without a fee (but on commission). Interestingly, although the private testing institute had been unwilling to pay the fee for the consultation, it still reviewed and compared the consultation. In the ensuing trial, the testing institute could not prevail. The victorious financial service provider was taken off the whole test.

In a case shortly after, a private institute tested several "asset administrators" based on the quality of their "investment consultation". One of the biggest European financial service providers was tested as well and deemed inadequate, a verdict that was published on the institute's website, for the whole world to see.

The private testing institute had failed to consider that the products tested as "asset advice/investment consultation" were not offered by the provider. The company had previously committed to the legal supervisory authority to neither offer nor carry out investment consultations for private customers. Here, as well, legal action was the solution. After a provisional court order the private testing institute agreed to no longer name the bank in relation to the test. The bank was removed from the ranking.

In cases like this the affected companies should fight their rating both inside and outside the court. Economic interests in those tests and their ramifications are extremely high. A negative rating by a "respectable institute" can lead to severe customer loss and major profit setbacks.

Blogs

Nowadays, any Internet user can create a blog with nothing more than a few clicks. Thoughts can be digitised and eternalised. Any customer, any employee, any competitor becomes their own opinion's publisher.

Between 2002 and 2013, the financial service provider AWD slipped into a crisis of reputation that lasted 11 years. The company did not survive it. And that is why this case is so informative. It was not only an insulated wave of indignation. For years blogs and discussion forums and even whole websites targeted AWD. Sources of the criticism were both employees and customers.

In the summer of 2002 an exchange forum for former AWD employees was put up under the domain www.awd-aussteiger.de ("awd-ex-employees"). Within a few months, several thousand articles were posted by former AWD personnel, telling of their financial, social and interpersonal problems due to their work for AWD. Among other things, the company was held responsible for their spiralling into debt.[3]

A formerly high-ranking manager of AWD spilled his inside knowledge through his blog.[4] Customers also attacked the financial adviser, accusing him of systematic misguidance. Lawsuits followed.

For many years AWD fought off the accusations. Many sites linked to the blogs and forums are not retrievable any more. Comments were deleted, websites shut down. But AWD also suffered setbacks, trying to ban domains like www.awd-unzufriedene.de ("awd-displeased") and lost in court. It was like fighting the Hydra. Whenever one head was cut off, two grew in its place. And the middle head was immortal.

The damage AWD suffered was beyond repair. Its decisive mistake: AWD treated every claim across the board as illegitimate. That did not work. The company had not listened and had not differentiated between the claims. It either ignored the complaints nor fought them too vigorously. Yet over the years too much criticism had piled up. Too much of it was discussed in the press. The AWD victims felt violated.

In 2013 there were still many websites detailing the shortcomings of AWD. Those will still exist in the future. Not so AWD. After more than 10 years of negative news stories the trademark was dissolved in 2013.

What could AWD have done better? The company should have differentiated between legitimate and illegitimate claims and combined the correct reactions to both types in the right manner. Naturally, AWD would have had to counter unjustified criticism. But maybe the idea would have emerged to set up a fund for the "AWD victims", as is often done in the US when a company is faced with class action lawsuits.

It is important for the company to both communicate and respect freedom of speech. At the same time it must point to certain constraints, thus securing and consolidating the company's values, because, if mistakes are admitted, company policies changed or willingness to listen demonstrated, critics generally open up to the company in question – and are themselves ready to listen. When the critic sees that their actions have consequences, that a company tries to improve, and actually respects the critic for pointing out its shortcomings – the "enemy" becomes a friend. The critic might even accept the company's values and distinguish between legitimate and illegitimate claims. Their formerly negative reviews turn into positive statements, as happened with Dell. Illegitimate criticism or illegitimate claims become isolated, while the company's new friends support and understand that it is fighting such untruthful declarations. Thus, critics can become comrades-in-arms and supporters of the company. Where they used to threaten the company's reputation, they are now active in building it up.

Review platforms (in general)

In the banking industry, as in most others, the meaningfulness of review platforms is rapidly growing. Publishing a review (of a product or a service) can be done by pretty much everyone and is a matter of only a couple of seconds. And whether it turns out good or bad is both subjective and prone to have consequences. Let us examine some.

- "We have terminated our account for the third time and every time we get the answer, the signature is wrong. This bank seems to have trouble giving back the deposited money" – Review of the Bank of Scotland.[5]
- "Zero Stars! Absolutely unrecommendable. Not one promise regarding our business funding was kept and the whole process took 4 months instead of 6 weeks!" – Review of the Sparkasse Berlin.[6]
- "… yet when it's about construction financing they put up obstacles, don't call back and make everything more complicated than it needs to be. You have to strip down for them and have everything questioned, so much time passes until the financing, if it ever gets to that" – Review of Deutsche Bank Berlin.[7]

Reviews like these scare off new clients. Customers looking for baseless "revenge" out of spite find a perfect playground in anonymous review platforms.

How to handle such reviews? At first, the afflicted company is at a disadvantage. It does not know who published the review. Neither does it recognise the specific case in question. Therefore it is necessary to get the facts straight as quickly as possible. Sometimes it turns out that the review is not even based on a case the company has actually handled, for it is not unusual for competitors to post such a destructive review themselves.

Luckily, in legal terms it is not up to the company to prove that it was not a customer but a competitor who posted the review. In Germany (unfortunately, not in all of Europe or the rest of the world) the company in question (regardless of its location) is in general not burdened with proving the falsehood of the claims. Instead, the publisher must prove their claims' veracity. The review portal itself has to decide whether it reveals the user's name or not. If it does not, it must accept fighting for the user's opinion as if it were its own, or delete it.

If it transpires that the incident actually happened and therefore the claim is clearly legitimate, legal steps would be inappropriate. With regard to this case, listening and communicating is the proper procedure. If necessary, a company must admit mistakes and clarify the facts. Many review platforms offer companies the chance to reply directly to negative reviews.

If the (negative) incident in question is made up, legal steps are the accurate way to go. Time limits force action, lest a company risk failing to combat illegitimate claims effectively (proof of urgency). In the worst case, a company can secure the deletion of a review (ie, enforcing its entitlement to an injunction) within a few days through a provisional court order.

Yet, even if a company initiates legal action, this is no final decision for litigation, because, at the moment the portal provider is notified, the aim still is to illuminate the facts of the case. Following the notification, the provider will forward the statements to the reviewer and ask them to respond. Now the critic or portal user has a chance to state their case and verify their claims. If they do not respond or do so in an inadequate manner, the portal must delete the review. If the provider judges the response to be adequate, it has to pass on the reviewer's statement to the company and offer a chance to reply. After this, the portal provider must decide: does it want to fight for the review or not? Experience tells us that, in 99% of all our cases, the reviews were deleted.

Employer assessment websites
Another new phenomenon is employer assessment websites. Already there are a large number of successful websites asking employees for their opinion on their employer. Depending on the number of evaluations posted, a public image emerges. This image must not necessarily correspond to the actual image of the company.

The consequences of this often prove dramatic. Since nowadays applications are most of the time initiated online, a look at an employer assessment website is only "one click" away. Most often, the company will not even notice.

Even very big companies with more than 10,000 employees frequently have reviews only in the double-digit area, with half of them being very negative. This is often due to a few former employees who in the heat of the moment post 10 or 20 bad reviews, carefully distributed over the course of several months. Also, competitors are known more and more to put up fictitious accounts of their rivals' services. Such actions are of course illegal. But, if the competitor makes full use of the technical possibilities the Internet provides, it can hardly be traced back to it. The only thing helping then is to have these reviews blocked. Content-wise, all illegitimate reviews can be challenged, since most of them entail untruthful claims or have not even come from a former employee.

Even when the company concerned takes the criticism to heart and initiates structural changes, the review will stay on the Internet. Years later, a promising candidate might rather apply somewhere else.

The human resources manager and directors of a big financial service company were wondering after a while why they no longer received the best applicants. One look at the employer assessment website brought the answer. Despite the fact that the company had about 2,000 employees, there were only about 100 reviews and among those 50 negative ones. The company did not know who published the negative reviews, nor did it know the cases in question. We had to assume that some of the negative reviews originated from competitors and/or former employees. In addition to that, many of the claims were untrue.

The company thereafter got the facts straight and checked the legal options. After it took legal action, all negative reviews could be extinguished. To prevent negative reviews, the company furthermore started an internal guide for conflicts in order to show the employees how to file their claims.

The growing importance of these kinds of reviews can be shown by the following survey. According to Bitkom (one of the largest German associations for IT, telecommunications and new media), every third Internet user between the age of 30 and 49 has visited an employer assessment website at least once. Yet one's own employer is seldom reviewed. Only every fifth person in that age range graded current or former employers.[8] And naturally the weight of one individual review is even heavier when there are only a few for a particular employer.

Therefore, companies should take criticism seriously, but at the same time be ready to fight unsubstantiated criticism as they would fight illegitimate claims.

CSR standards – the future cases of reputational crises

Not observing guidelines on corporate social responsibility (CSR) can lead to a reputational crisis. Around the key word "compliance", several scandals have emerged already: journeys on the company's aircraft and high-class prostitutes at Volkswagen in 2005; spying on employees at Deutsche Telekom in 2008; rampant bribery at Daimler in 2010. However the "Soft Law" (ie, declaration of intent) is not yet justiciable, that is to say subject to action in a court of law. Often the abdication of a high-ranking representative will suffice (Volkswagen); in isolated cases heads of department go to prison (Telekom); or fines are paid (Daimler).

These kinds of conflicts will be harder to fight in the future, because currently the EU, several courts in Germany and other parties are working on making the adherence to CSR standards justiciable. There are good reasons for this: voluntary commitments used by the company to advertise itself become more and more relevant to the customer. Such claims can influence a decision to buy the company's product(s) or a willingness to work with or for the company.

A corporation's ethical commitment increasingly becomes the centre of attention for its customers. It is not simply about the product any more, but also about the company behind it.

If a corporation does not adhere to its own voluntary commitments, the press and blogosphere will of course have a field day. Even competitors now can act as "white knights", pointing to the shortcomings of their industry's "black sheep" and initialising legal actions. Therefore, companies should already strive to observe the business standards by way of compliance.

THE HIDDEN ADVANTAGES OF A TRIAL

Going to trial can mean more than merely seeking an injunction. A trial offers an advantage that is not apparent at the start of a reputational crisis: a promising proceeding can considerably strengthen your position in negotiations.

In 2012, a businessman fought against several illegitimate claims in an online article. The reason for this was not the publication of the article, but its continued presence on the Google search index.

If you typed the company name into Google – without any addition – the article appeared among the top 10 hits. For months it doggedly stayed there. Even search engine optimisers could not push it back. Many months passed until this company decided to take legal action. But, since so much time had passed, it could no longer secure its entitlement via a provisional court order, and had to file a regular lawsuit instead.

In the hearing the court made it absolutely clear that most of the company's claims were justified, yet left room for a settlement. Because of the prospect of success, the publisher and the businessman came to an agreement in favour of the latter. His bargaining power enabled him to force important points he actually had no legal claim to. Mostly, he was interested in soft criteria, for example the rules regarding search engine optimisation for the article, and changing the subjective (and therefore unassailable) headline. A few days after these adjustments, the article lost a significant amount of significance for the search engine providers and shortly after did not appear even in the top 100 index hits on Google. Without legal measures, this goal would have been unattainable.

CONCLUSION

All explanations and examples in this chapter have referred to developments in Germany. The main reason for this is the author's position as a specialised lawyer working in that country. Details may vary from country to country. Yet the European Court of Human Rights' jurisdiction leads to a continued harmonisation in personal rights practice in Europe, as well as those decisions from the ECJ. There are no significant differences to legal norms in Germany. In part, the European Court sides even more with the victims, offering them more protection of their rights than many national courts.

Concerning the procedures, the European Court has already

paved the way for a simplified enforcement of libel in Europe. Even though some details still have to be worked out, it is generally accepted that a company can call for a ruling on all damages caused within the realm of the European Union. Any company harmed by Internet publications may appeal to a court either in its own country or in the country where the creator of the articles is based.

The company may also call upon the courts of any member state in whose territory the published content was or is accessible. In that case the local courts are responsible only for deciding on damages that occurred in their own territory.

If a court has to rule on damages that occurred in the whole realm of the European Union, it must consider the specific national legal situation by way of expertise. If in any of these countries no law has been breached, no damages can be claimed there. Yet this does not apply if the European Court for Human Rights decides that libel did occur.

Therefore, it can be reasonable to concentrate a lawsuit on those countries with the biggest potential, choosing territories with a comprehensive jurisdiction and a victim-friendly stance. Besides Germany, this applies to Britain and perhaps Italy and France.

Also, on the national plane, the question arises which court to appeal to. Libel/press law is one of the most complicated legal areas. There are specialised courts, but their positions are known to change. A court that five years ago would have ruled benevolently towards the victim may not do so any more.

If legal actions are considered, having a specialised lawyer answer these process-related questions fast is as important as clarifying the facts of the case itself.

Distinguishing between legitimate and illegitimate claims helps handling a reputational crisis. If a claim is truthful, attempting to ban it will not help. Rather, communication and revision prove successful. If the claim is illegitimate, the company must not stand for it, but take legal action.

In the 1980s it was usual not to attack statements. After a short time they were forgotten and could be retrieved only with a lot of effort. Today, illegitimate claims persevere permanently. Once they are on the Internet, search engine providers render them continuously retrievable. No expensive research by expert personnel is necessary to find illegitimate claims. Anything is just one click away.

In cases of negative reviews, companies are instantly in a crisis of justification, often without their even knowing. Associates and customers turn away from them and take their business to competitors. Good candidates no longer apply for vacancies. Business rivals use any opportunity to create a better public image. The more services become similar and interchangeable, the bigger the risk of a reputational crisis.

Complexity surges with mixed cases, when texts contain both legitimate and illegitimate claims. There is no patent remedy. The possible reactions can be as varied as the scenarios that bring them about. Direct communication and asserting lawful claims are the essential building blocks of the right strategy.

Any response to a reputational crisis should consider the particular medium in which the libel is mainly circulated. Countermeasures to a vegetarians' wave of indignation will not follow the same principles as fighting an untruthful review by a private testing institution, an anonymous attack on a forum or utilising prosecutors and press.

To react properly to a reputational crisis, a company should become well versed in the fields of PR and marketing as well as in the legal aspects surrounding a potential incident. The right combination of PR and legal specialists is key. On the one hand, press releases promoting transparency should be publicised and a clear communication implemented. On the other hand, the company should be ready to stop the spreading of falsehoods with a cease-and-desist warning or provisional court order (within a month of first gaining knowledge).

Today, a holistic approach is necessary that cannot be limited to the consultants. It is almost grossly negligent to allege that only PR consultants or only lawyers could make a comprehensive criticism "disappear". Such behaviour is highly dubious. It shows the thinking of the 1980s. The correct reaction to criticism nowadays is imperative, showing respect for freedom of speech and direct communication, but also consequential proceedings against illegitimate claims. Effective security means forming a specialised team that goes beyond the mere business consultant's field of expertise, for successfully repelling the potentially far-reaching consequences of a reputational crisis.

Final checklist

Don't ...

- ❏ just watch or ignore the issues or play them down;
- ❏ wait too long or you will lose the possibility of protecting your rights with an interim order;
- ❏ ignore those websites that are currently not in the top 10 of Google and other search engines – they might come up more quickly than you expect;
- ❏ put too much effort into legal actions to solve the problem if legitimate claims are the matter of discussion; and
- ❏ put too much effort in communication to solve the problem if illegitimate claims are the matter of discussion.

Do ...

- ❏ use search engines to monitor the public reputation of the company and the directorate;
- ❏ monitor regularly all important review platforms and especially employer assessment websites;
- ❏ analyse the issues and check your legal options as fast as you can; and
- ❏ immediately distinguish between legitimate or illegitimate claims.

If legitimate claims are the matter of discussion ...

- ❏ assign (important) employees (not those from the outsourced call center) to read blogs and respond to criticism;
- ❏ install compliance rules such as "principles of openness and transparency" and devise house rules for your social-media channels;
- ❏ provide a framework for public discussion and conclude it at the opportune time; and
- ❏ react to legitimate claims in form and content; explain the shortcomings and problems.

If illegitimate claims are the matter of discussion ...

- ❏ know your rights: you might be entitled to an injunction, counterstatement, repeal, compensation and reparation;

- ❏ act fast: you might have the right to stop the illegitimate claims immediately;
- ❏ render the article invisible on search engines by deleting the article itself or rendering the article invisible on search engines; use the help of your specialised lawyers;
- ❏ check your legal options if there are (partly) illegitimate claims and combine legitimate and illegitimate dos and don'ts and clearly draw the border between those kinds of claims, with the intention of being hard and fair; communicate directly and enforce your rights at the same time;
- ❏ point out certain constraints, thus securing and consolidating the company's values;
- ❏ be truthful to yourself; and
- ❏ communicate and respect the freedom of speech.

Keep in mind ...
- ❏ you cannot fight claims you simply do not approve of – the technical advantages of the Internet will help the freedom of speech;
- ❏ in extremely time-sensitive cases it takes only hours to get an injunction, depending on the court that grants it;
- ❏ even if the person or persons responsible is/are hidden behind a veil of anonymity, you can block the search results; and
- ❏ the importance of review platforms grows: every third Internet user between 30 and 49 visited an employer assessment website at least once.

---

1 For examples, see the follow articles: www.bild.de/regional/dresden/razzia/infinus-insider-packt-aus-33357458.bild.html; www.focus.de/finanzen/banken/razzia-bei-finanz dienstleister-400-millionen-euro-infinus-soll-25–000-anleger-geprellt-haben_aid_1152192. html; www.handelsblatt.com/finanzen/recht-steuern/anleger-und-verbraucherrecht/ finanzdienstleister-infinus-soll-25–000-anleger-betrogen-haben/9036296.html.
2 See http://www.zeit.de/2013/51/banken-finanzskandale.
3 See http://verein-der-ehemaligen-awd-mitarbeiter-ev.de.
4 See http://vonahmaximilian.wordpress.com.
5 See http://www.yelp.com/bis/bank-of-scotland-berlin.
6 See http://www.yelp.de/bis/berliner-sparkasse-landesbank-berlin-berlin.
7 See http://www.yelp.com/bis/deutsche-bank-berlin-8.
8 See http://www.bitkom.org/de/presse/8477_76188.aspx.

12

Reputational Risk Management Across the World: A Survey of Current Practices

Thomas Kaiser

KPMG in Germany and Goethe University, Frankfurt

INTRODUCTION

Reputational risk (RepRisk) can be defined as a risk of unexpected losses due to the reaction of stakeholders (eg, shareholders, customers, and employees) to an altered perception of an institution.

The activities of reputation management serve the purpose of affecting the public perception of the bank, as experienced by the stakeholders. In contrast, reputational risk management is concerned with the systematic identification and assessment of incidents that could jeopardise the goal of reaching or keeping up with this perception, as well as the deduction of risk-management measures. Reputational risk can arise in every business area of a financial institution. Therefore, appropriate management processes should cover the organisation as a whole.

At the time of writing, there are neither specific regulatory requirements nor other market standards for reputational risk management beyond the general requirements of Pillar II risks as defined by Basel regulation and the respective local implementation thereof.

In the absence of specific regulatory requirements, several leading banks began to implement their own reputational risk-management process around the turn of the century. This was put in place mainly due to the focus of senior management on that type of risk, rather than any sense of regulatory urgency.

Since that time, regulators in various countries have put different degrees of focus on reputational risk. Together with cultural and strategic differences between banks, this focus has led to a heterogeneous development of the discipline of RepRisk management in banks in different countries.

Although regulators have stated publicly since the financial crisis that reputational risk should be a concern for the banks, they too (at the time of writing) have limited insight into the topic. The demands of regulators towards reputational risk management depend on which authority is governing the bank. Some regulators have asked banks to come up with a qualitative reputational risk-management framework because they want them to have a process in place to deal with that risk type, while others have remarked that firms should instead have a buffer in their economical capital to deal with RepRisk events. In the end regulators will probably insist on a buffer – it can be argued or at least acknowledged that reputational risks are already included in economic capital, as they are built into other risks. But, although firms therefore already measure the impact of reputational risk, the question is whether they measure the potential impact or just a small portion of it.

KPMG conducted a survey among the global systemically important banks (G-SIBs) in late 2013 and early 2014. Risk-management professionals in KPMG in those countries where the G-SIBs are headquartered have been asked to answer a brief set of questions for the G-SIBs they are working with. Some KPMG professionals also discussed these questions with their respective clients. As of March 2014, out of the 28 G-SIBs, responses for 10 had been collected. They cover all relevant geographical areas (Europe, North America and Asia) to a similar degree. Due to the relatively small number of responses, the survey should not be seen as fully representative. Also a differentiation of the results by region was not feasible.

The results of this global survey have been compared with those of a broader, but geographically more focused KPMG reputational risk study that was conducted and published in 2012. This latter survey also aimed to illustrate the current state and planned activities of reputational risk management, but with only leading German financial institutions as its foundation. The questionnaire has been completed by 18 institutions out of the 23 firms that were asked to participate. Thirteen participants belong to the 20 biggest banks in Germany, while the remaining five were made up of medium-sized banks and building societies.

This chapter presents the results of both surveys side by side, outlining for the reader what can be learned from these responses and how these lessons might be applicable to their own working practices. As the number of questions of the German survey was larger than that of the global one, a comparison of results was not possible in all cases.

SURVEY RESULTS
Fundamentals
1. How do you define RepRisk? (Global and German study)
The starting point of the treatment of reputational risks is a clear definition of this risk, and its differentiation from other related types of risk. In several regulatory papers reputational risk is sometimes defined as a consequential risk, as a trigger to other risks, but rarely as a risk type in its own right. These points of view do not negate each other, though, because for each of these alternatives, supporting examples exist that prove their value.

For instance, an inappropriate statement from the board of directors should not be seen as a consequential risk to a primary risk type but it should rather be treated as a reputational risk in its own right. The negative public perception of a certain statement can result in a decrease in sales, thus reputational risk can be seen as a trigger for other risks (in this instance, this would be business risk). Reputational risk has to be defined as a consequential risk in case there is an underlying loss of another risk type preceding the reputational loss. These reputational risks should primarily be mitigated by the management of other risk types (for example, avoidance of flawed advice through sales trainings). The most frequently occurring category of consequential risks is that of losses arising from operational risks such as fraud, legal actions due to flawed advice, and IT breakdowns. Even so, other types of risk, such as credit risk, market risk, liquidity risk, strategic risk and business risk, can be a trigger for reputational losses.

At the time of writing there is no market standard for this. Two-thirds of the surveyed institutions define reputational risk as an independent risk category for both the G-SIBs and the German study

187

Figure 12.1 How do you define RepRisk?

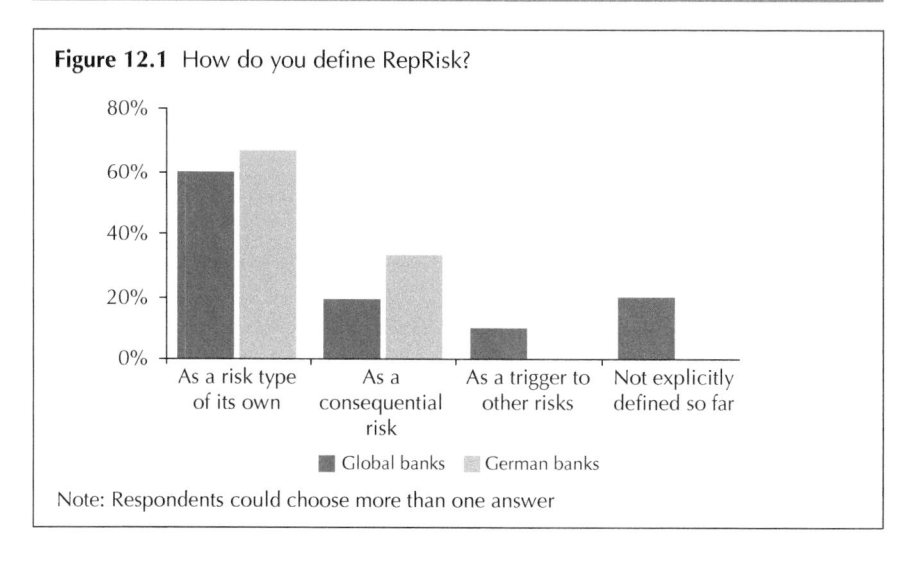

Categories: As a risk type of its own; As a consequential risk; As a trigger to other risks; Not explicitly defined so far. Series: Global banks, German banks.

Note: Respondents could choose more than one answer

(see Figure 12.1). The majority of the remaining third define reputational risk as consequential risk. It is recommended, therefore, that attention be paid to reputational risk as a trigger of other risks.

A comprehensive analysis of relations between reputational risks and other risks should help to identify and manage reputational risks separately.

2. Have you categorised RepRisk as material in the context of your risk inventory? (German study)

A central point concerning the treatment of reputational risks is materiality. According to the revision of the German minimum requirements for risk management of December 15, 2010, financial institutions have to complete a risk inventory in which the materiality of all risks that the institution is facing has to be defined. This decision has a significant impact on the further implementation of risk-management processes as well as on the expectations of regulators and auditors. The negative consequences of RepRisk events are difficult to quantify, but there are striking arguments for categorising reputational risks as material, especially with a view to the discussed interdependencies with other types of risk. The financial crises of 2007–8 showed that reputational damages can have consequences in terms of liquidity shortage or decreasing business volumes.

Therefore, it is not surprising that the majority of German banks categorise reputational risk as material (see Figure 12.2).

Figure 12.2 Have you categorised RepRisk as material in the context of your risk inventory?

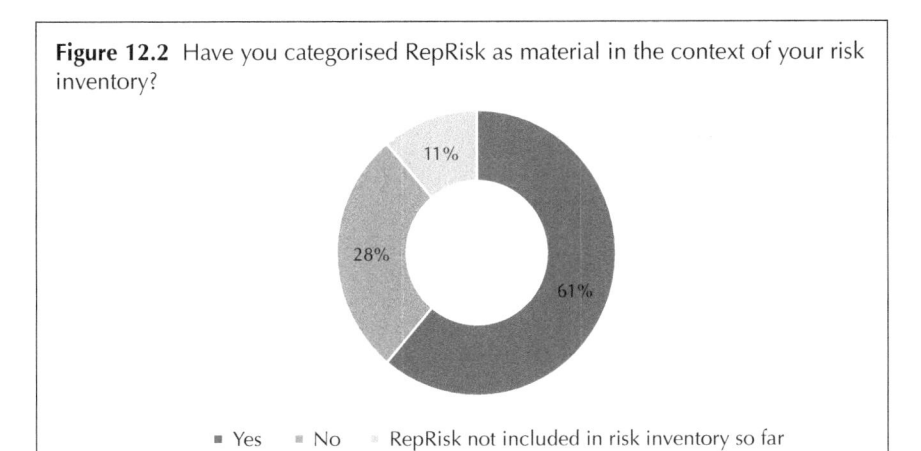

- Yes — 61%
- No — 28%
- RepRisk not included in risk inventory so far — 11%

It can be assumed that, in light of developments as of the time of writing, an evaluation of reputational risk as not material will be difficult to prove to regulators in the medium term – especially for large international institutions with a focus on capital markets.

Governance

3. How did you implement reputational risk in your risk strategy? (German study)

Possible components of an appropriate risk-management process for reputational risks will be discussed in what follows. At the time of writing there are no concrete regulatory requirements concerning reputational risks. Therefore, financial institutions have the freedom to set up their own specific governance framework. This includes the implementation of a risk strategy, the introduction of awareness-building with employees and the prioritising of stakeholders.

The relationship between taking reputational risks and the realisation of potential returns is mostly indirect. Obviously, some business decisions can result in higher returns on the one hand and an increased reputational risk on the other. The risk strategy for reputational risk should consider this relationship as well as resulting qualitative and eventually quantitative limits.

The results of the German survey show that there is still potential for the development of risk strategies. The majority of banks consider reputational risks within an overarching risk strategy. Only one-fifth of the participants have a separate strategy for reputational risk (see Figure 12.3).

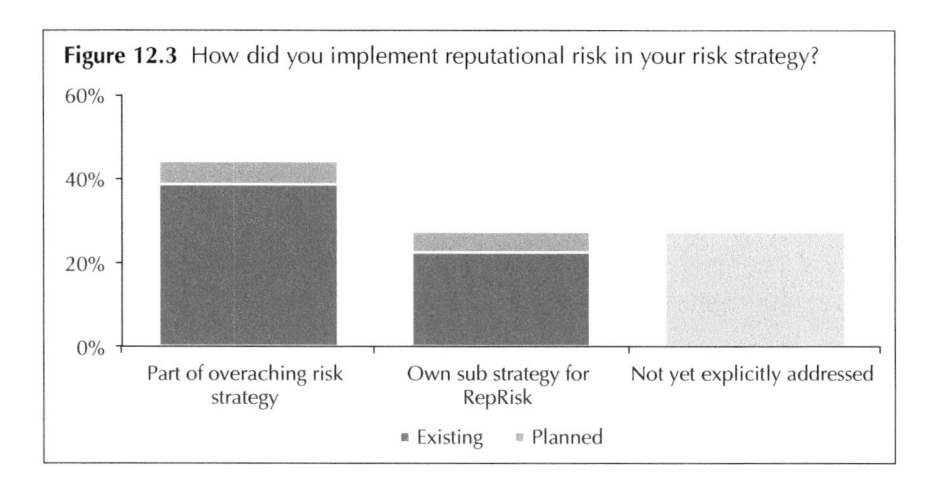

Figure 12.3 How did you implement reputational risk in your risk strategy?

- Part of overaching risk strategy
- Own sub strategy for RepRisk
- Not yet explicitly addressed

■ Existing ■ Planned

The effective management of risks requires a clear definition of the risk strategy, which should be closely aligned with the business strategy.

4. How did you build awareness with your employees for reputational risk? How did you establish a risk culture? (German study)

Employees at all levels of the hierarchy should contribute to the management of reputational risk. An appropriate risk culture should be established and the employees should be made aware of the topic. The challenge is to establish an understanding for the topic as a whole, as this is the basis for an efficient management of reputational risk. Every employee should be capable of understanding the causal chain between the primary risk – as a trigger for the consequences of other risks – and reputational risk. Reputational risk management requires experience-based judgement in many cases.

The interviewed institutions in Germany have obviously recognised the necessity of establishing a risk culture. They use different tools such as newsletters, workshops and a variety of other methods detailed in Figure 12.4 to create sensitivity to this risk in their employees.

Figure 12.4 How did you build awareness with your employees for RepRisk? How did you establish a risk culture?

■ Existing ■ Planned

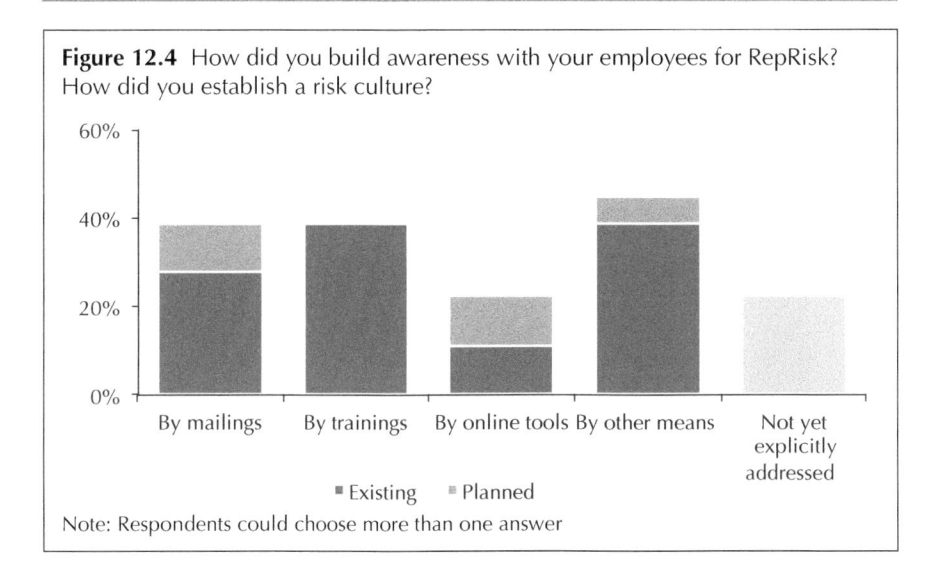

Note: Respondents could choose more than one answer

5. Which stakeholders did you prioritise within your RepRisk-management framework? (Global and German study)

Reputational risk arises when the expectations of individual stakeholders have not been fulfilled. It is important to identify relevant stakeholder groups and to judge their impact on the business of the institution. Certain transactions are perceived differently by different stakeholders. For instance, the profitable financing deal of a power plant can result, from a business point of view, in a positive response on the one hand, but on the other hand lead to a strong negative reaction by the public. As there is usually only a limited budget available for preventative and reactive measures, a system of the prioritisation of stakeholders is highly recommended for efficient management.

The study found that only 55% of the G-SIBs and 60% of the German banks had already prioritised their stakeholders. German banks gave the highest priority to customers, whereas employees had only a low priority. The survey shows that the G-SIBs have a different point of view, as they categorised not only customers but also employees and regulators with a high priority (see Figure 12.5).

Figure 12.5 Which stakeholders did you prioritise within your RepRisk-management framework?

[Bar chart showing percentages (0% to 80%) for German and Global responses across categories: Customers, Employees, Business partners, Shareholders, Creditors, Regulators, Rating agencies, NGOs, Others, Not yet explicitly addressed. Legend: German ■High ■Medium ■Low; Global □High ■Medium ■Low]

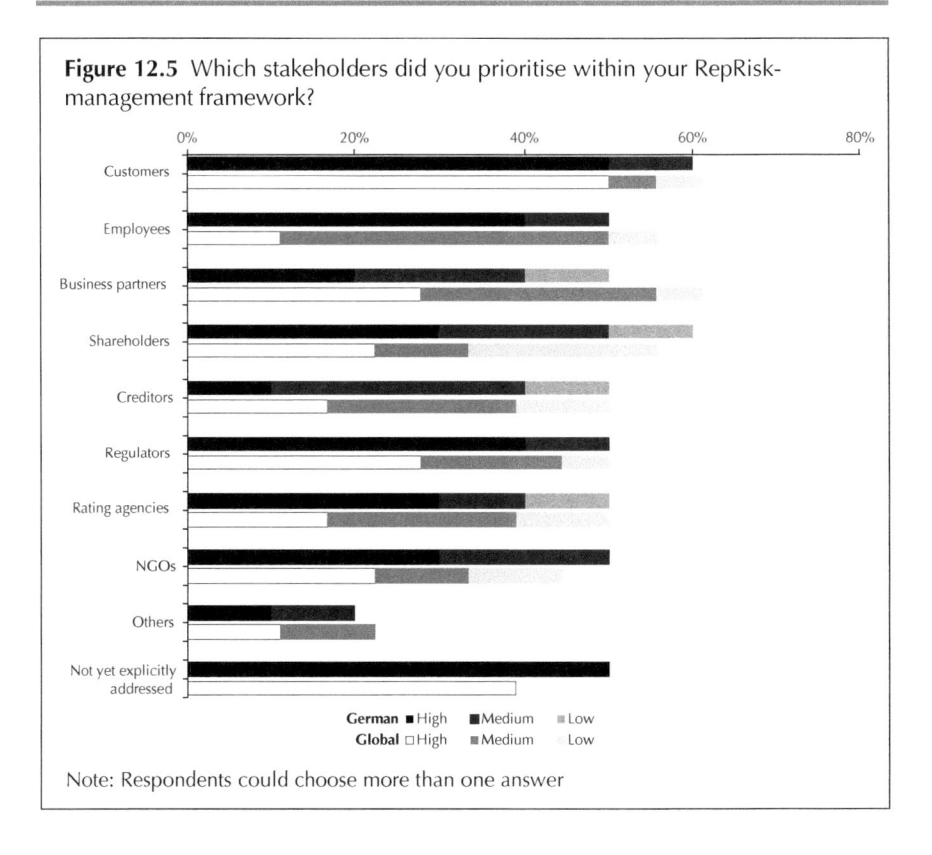

Note: Respondents could choose more than one answer

6. How did you embed RepRisk into your risk committee? (German study)

Operational risk (OpRisk) as well as reputational risk is of concern for the whole institution. A regular exchange of the individual business areas concerned with actual and potential reputational risk can be very beneficial. Therefore it makes sense to consider reputational risks within the existing decision-making committees.

As of March 2014 there was no common opinion whether reputational risk necessitates standalone risk committees or can be embedded in existing committees, or whether a committee is necessary at all (see Figure 12.6).

Especially with a view to the increasing importance of risk concentrations and dependency structures in economic capital models, there should be a stronger integration into the corresponding decision committees.

Figure 12.6 How did you embed RepRisk into your risk committee?

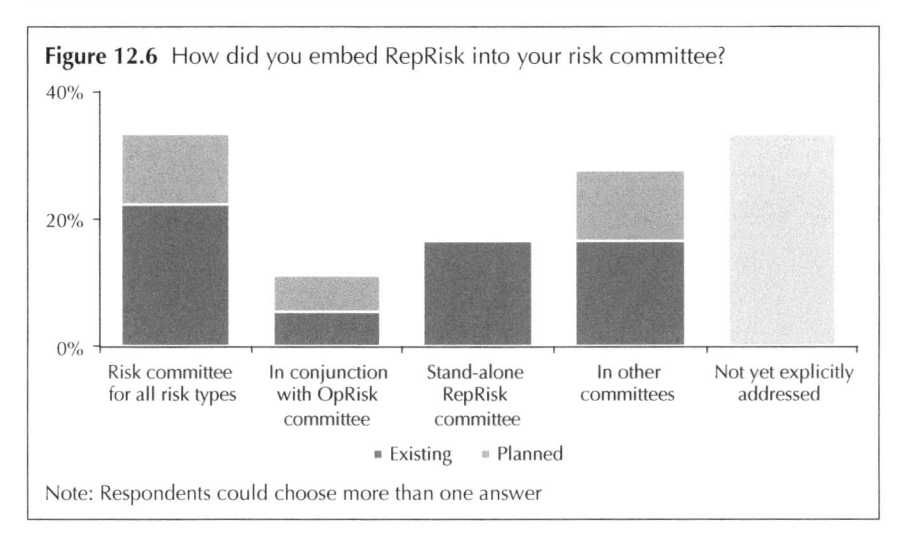

- Existing
- Planned

Note: Respondents could choose more than one answer

7. How did you embed RepRisk into the organisation? (Global and German study)

There is no standardised treatment from the risk-management point of view for reputational risks. The same problem persisted during

Figure 12.7 How did you embed RepRisk into the organisation?

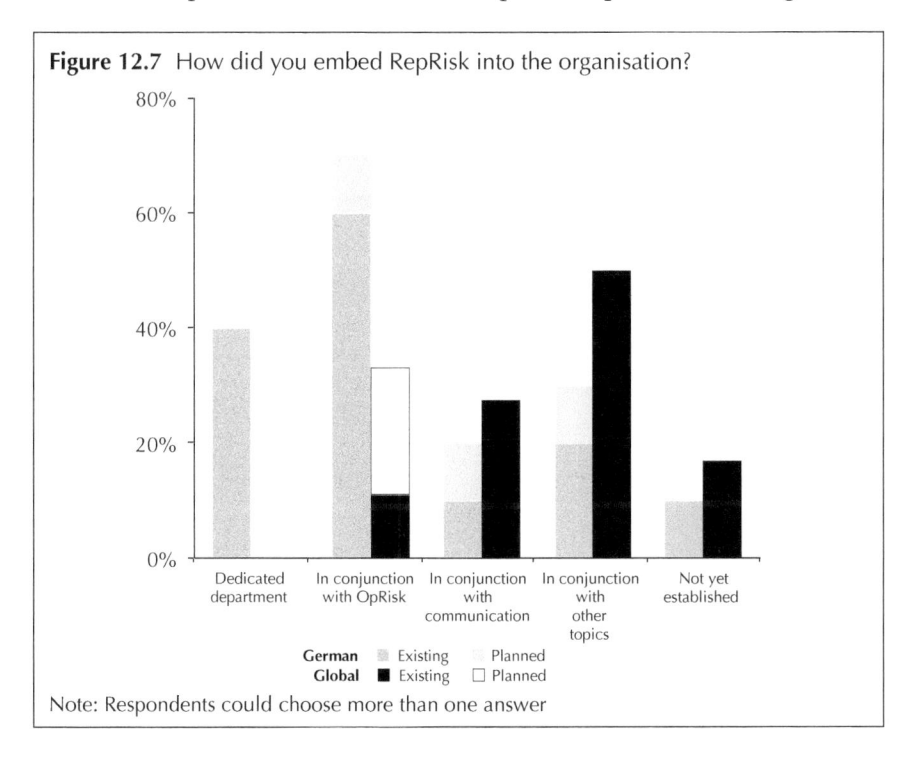

German: Existing, Planned
Global: Existing, Planned

Note: Respondents could choose more than one answer

the establishment of the management of operational risks in the past. The global survey found out that 40% of the G-SIBs already had a dedicated department and 60% embedded reputational risk in conjunction with operational risk, while 50% of the German banks embedded reputational risk in conjunction with other risk types and one-third in the communication department (see Figure 12.7). As reputational risks arise often as a consequence of operational risks, it is not surprising that the institutions try to benefit from the effects of the synergy that would occur when embedding reputational risk within the control and management of operational risk.

Identification and assessment
8. How do you conduct risk identification and qualitative risk assessment? (Global and German study)

The systematic identification and assessment of material reputational risk is the basis for the effective management of those risks. There are no standardised methods for conducting the necessary processes. It is especially unclear whether reputational risk can be quantified, or whether it is merely subject to a qualitative assessment.

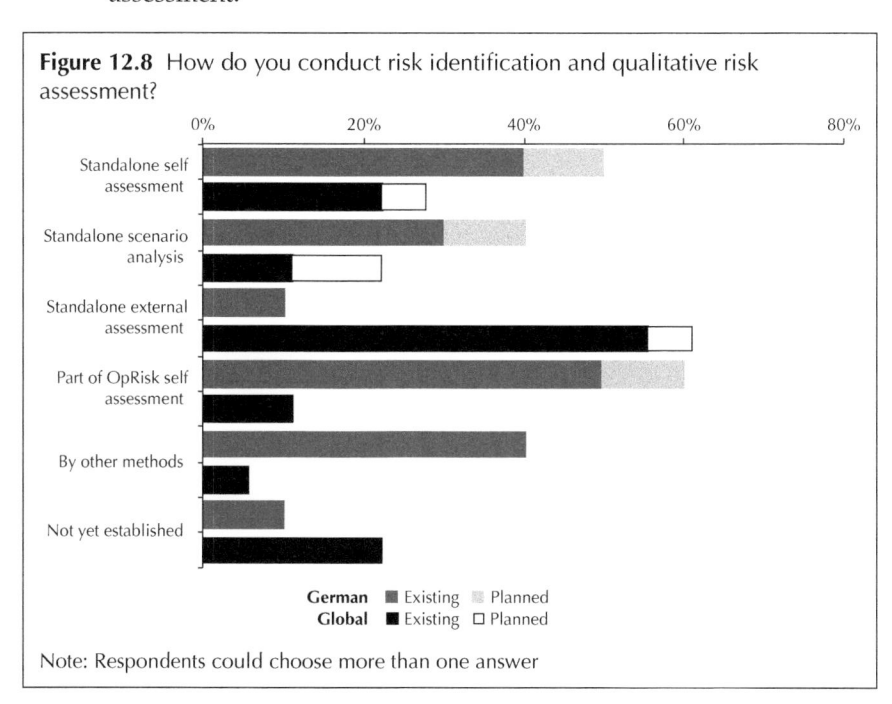

Figure 12.8 How do you conduct risk identification and qualitative risk assessment?

Note: Respondents could choose more than one answer

The survey responses demonstrate that the banks put their main emphasis on the self-assessments (see Figure 12.8). Other methods that are mentioned in the survey as indicators of reputational risk issues are expert opinions, interviews with senior management, risk inventory and analysis of press and social media.

9. How do you register losses due to RepRisk? (German study)
Knowledge of a reputational event after it has occurred is equally important for management. *Post hoc* reputational risk occurrences are subject to various interactions with other types of risk. Sometimes they are a consequential risk triggered by operational and strategic risks and sometimes they are a trigger to other risks, such as business and liquidity risk. Therefore, a systematic collection and categorisation of individual, self-contained risks is difficult. Nevertheless it seems reasonable to create a database as well as to draw conclusions from the experiences of others.

The study shows that German banks have started to create a system for the collection of different events related to reputational risk. The collection of press reports and the monitoring of social media were mentioned as examples of such other methods. Some institutions have already recognised the benefits of external information by using externally collected losses (see Figure 12.9).

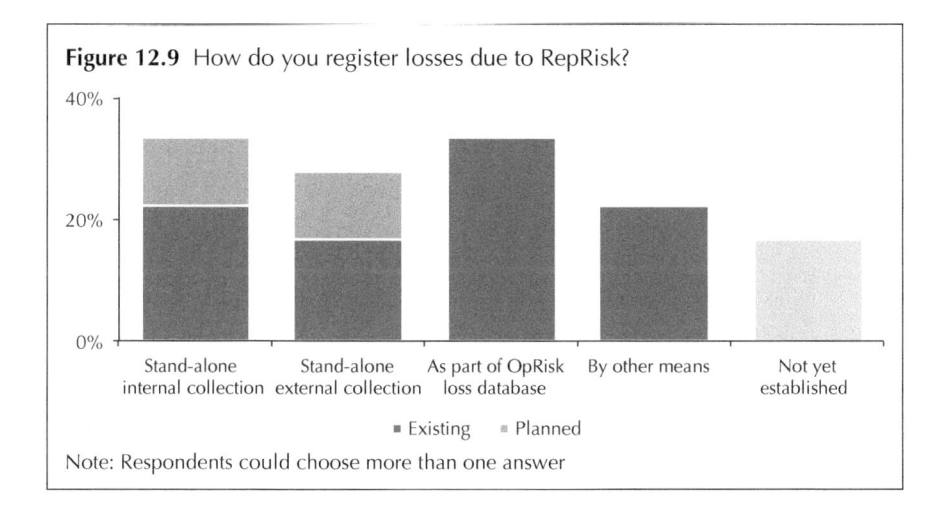

Figure 12.9 How do you register losses due to RepRisk?

Note: Respondents could choose more than one answer

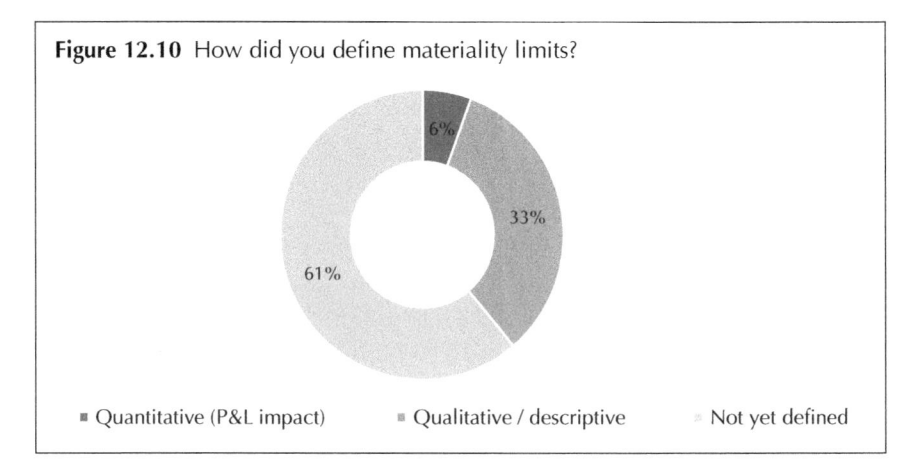

Figure 12.10 How did you define materiality limits?

- Quantitative (P&L impact): 61%
- Qualitative / descriptive: 33%
- Not yet defined: 6%

10. How did you define materiality limits? (German study)
A complete identification and assessment of all reputational risks is neither possible nor expedient. Therefore, the use of materiality limits is a possibility for clearly differentiating between similar risks. The quantification of profit and loss would be reasonable and desirable, but is currently very difficult to realise. Alternatively, there is the possibility of making use of qualitative scales (eg, low, medium, high) to approximate the monetary impact or to use qualitative/descriptive methods to define the materiality of a reputational risk. The survey found that very few institutions had defined materiality limits so far and those were in most cases of qualitative nature, building upon expert opinion rather than hard facts (see Figure 12.10).

11. How did you implement an early-warning system for RepRisk? (German study)
Usually, qualitative and quantitative assessments are performed only on an annual basis. Therefore, additional information that can possibly provide an early-warning signal at a higher frequency is necessary.

Most of the surveyed institutions had not implemented an early-warning system at the time the survey was conducted (see Figure 12.11). Another method that has been explicitly mentioned is press monitoring. A small degree of implementation of early-warning systems is probably the result of the insufficient organisational implementation of reputational risk-management practices in the

Figure 12.11 How did you implement an early-warning system for RepRisk?

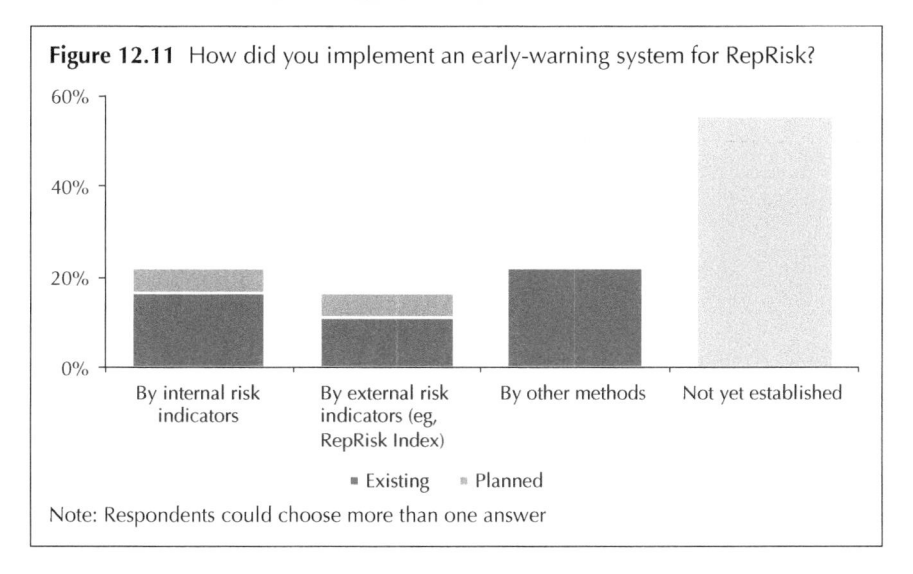

[Bar chart showing percentages for: By internal risk indicators, By external risk indicators (eg, RepRisk Index), By other methods, Not yet established. Legend: Existing, Planned]

Note: Respondents could choose more than one answer

risk-management process as a whole, or maybe this is just due to a lack in capacity.

12. How did you consider RepRisk in the risk-bearing capacity concept? (Global and German study)

Material risks should be considered within the context of the risk-bearing capacity concept, and, if they are not, there needs to be an explanation about why this is the case. Quantified and aggregated risks have to be compared with the available risk-bearing capacity in order to be able to recognise and take measures against potential shortfalls.

The lack of accepted approaches for quantifying reputational risk are a significant obstacle to including that risk type into the risk-bearing capacity concept according to these results because the presence of a buffer requires at least a certain amount of quantification in order to function. The decision to consider reputational risks as part of an overarching buffer for non-quantifiable risks requires an explicit breakdown of this buffer into its individual components according to regulatory requirements.

The global study shows that the G-SIBs consider reputational risk as an individual buffer, but most of them have no explicit model in their risk-bearing capacity. In contrast, German banks do consider reputational risks to be part of an overarching buffer (see Figure 12.12).

Figure 12.12 How did you consider RepRisk in the risk-bearing capacity concept?

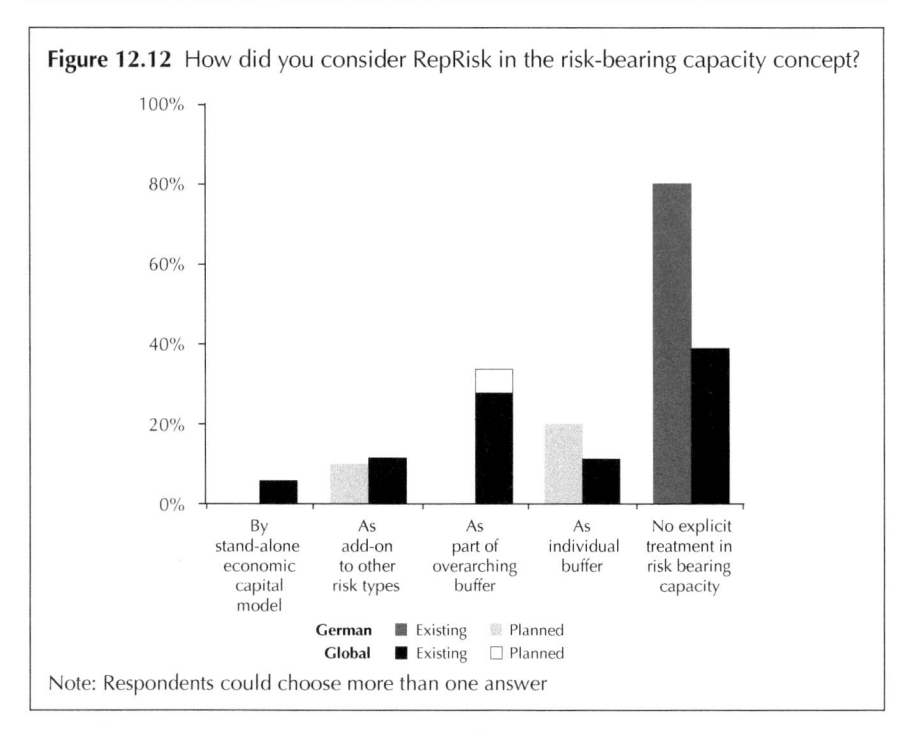

x-axis categories: By stand-alone economic capital model | As add-on to other risk types | As part of overarching buffer | As individual buffer | No explicit treatment in risk bearing capacity

Legend:
German ■ Existing ▨ Planned
Global ■ Existing □ Planned

Note: Respondents could choose more than one answer

13. How did you embed reputational risks in your stress testing? (German study)

At least since the financial crisis regulators have paid a large amount of attention to stress tests. The objective of stress tests is to examine the consequences of comprehensive macroeconomic and risk-

Figure 12.13 How did you embed reputational risks in your stress testing?

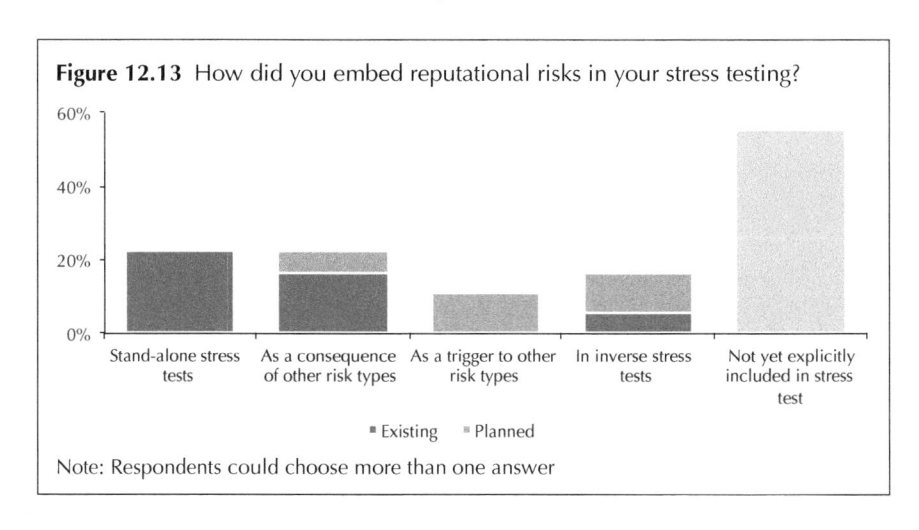

x-axis categories: Stand-alone stress tests | As a consequence of other risk types | As a trigger to other risk types | In inverse stress tests | Not yet explicitly included in stress test

Legend: ■ Existing ■ Planned

Note: Respondents could choose more than one answer

specific stress scenarios on the capital requirements, on the profit-and-loss account and on the liquidity of an institution. Stress testing should embed reputational risk into consequential risks or as a trigger of other risks.

The survey shows that the consideration of reputational risks within stress testing is not a prioritised topic so far (see Figure 12.13).

14. How did you include RepRisk in risk management/mitigation? (Global and German study)

Particular attention while managing reputational risks should be paid to risk mitigation, as the main objective of risk management is to prevent or minimise the consequences of reputational losses by reactive measures. In general these consequences can be distinguished between external consequences (ie, decreasing customer loyalty and satisfaction, decreasing turnover) and internal consequences (ie, the decrease of employee satisfaction or an increase of fluctuation). Therefore the sound organisational implementation of a reputational risk-management framework is necessary for effective management as a whole.

The majority of the German banks declared that they had defined the roles of dedicated organisational units, whereas only 10% of the

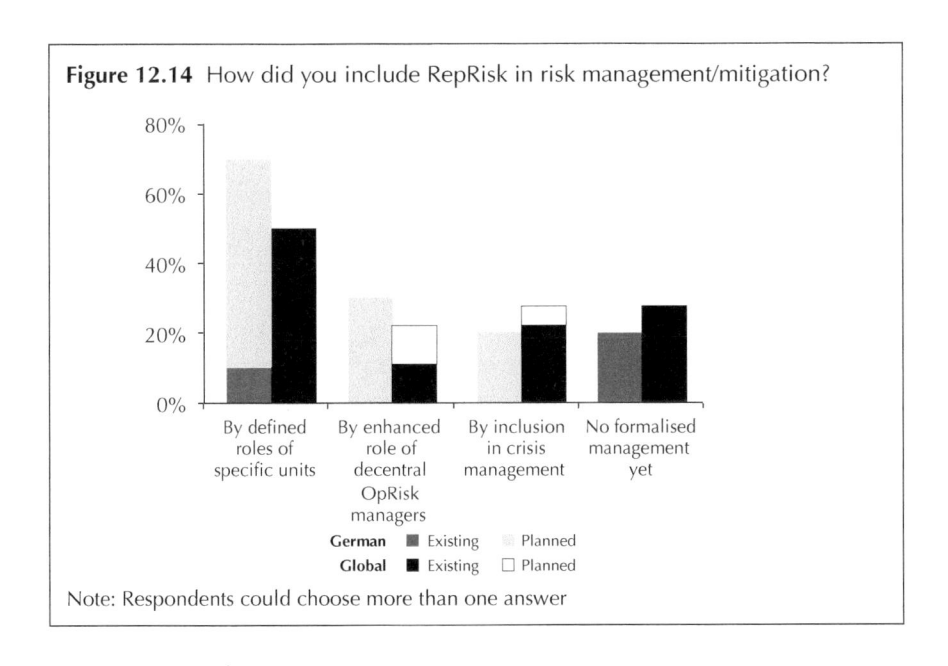

Figure 12.14 How did you include RepRisk in risk management/mitigation?

Note: Respondents could choose more than one answer

G-SIBs had any such defined roles (see Figure 12.14). However, the inclusion of reputational risk within risk management is explicitly planned in particular. Those institutions that are planning to extend their reputational risk framework intend to enhance the role of the decentralised operational risk manager, or to include reputational risk management within crisis management.

The organisation of the way in which reputational risk management is implemented should consider the day-to-day operation of the business in question, as well as internal processes during a reputational risk crisis. Existing structures such as crisis management and corporate communication can be used for that purpose.

15. In which transaction/change processes did you explicitly include RepRisk? (Global and German study)

The management of reputational risk can take place on the portfolio level. Alternatively, it can be implemented in the set-up of individual processes in order to achieve risk mitigation. Due to limited capacities both within the central risk-management function and on a divisional level, a step-by-step introduction of reputational risk-management thinking into individual transactions and change processes is reasonable.

The survey revealed that the focus at the time it was conducted was on new product processes, credit business and outsourcing which was mainly due to concrete regulatory requirements. Furthermore, the G-SIBs pay high attention to trading businesses, service providers and projects (see Figure 12.15).

Reporting and monitoring

16. How do you report about reputational risks to your senior management? (German study)

The results of the identification and the assessment of reputational risks, and especially the measures for their active management, should be reported to the management board. Regulators will be interested in those reports due to the importance of reputation for the business development and the public perception of the institution.

The result of the survey shows that very few institutions have a standalone reporting system for reputational risks.

Reputational risk reporting as part of general risk reporting seems to be reasonable, but the institution should pay sufficient attention to

Figure 12.15 In which transaction/change processes did you explicitly include RepRisk?

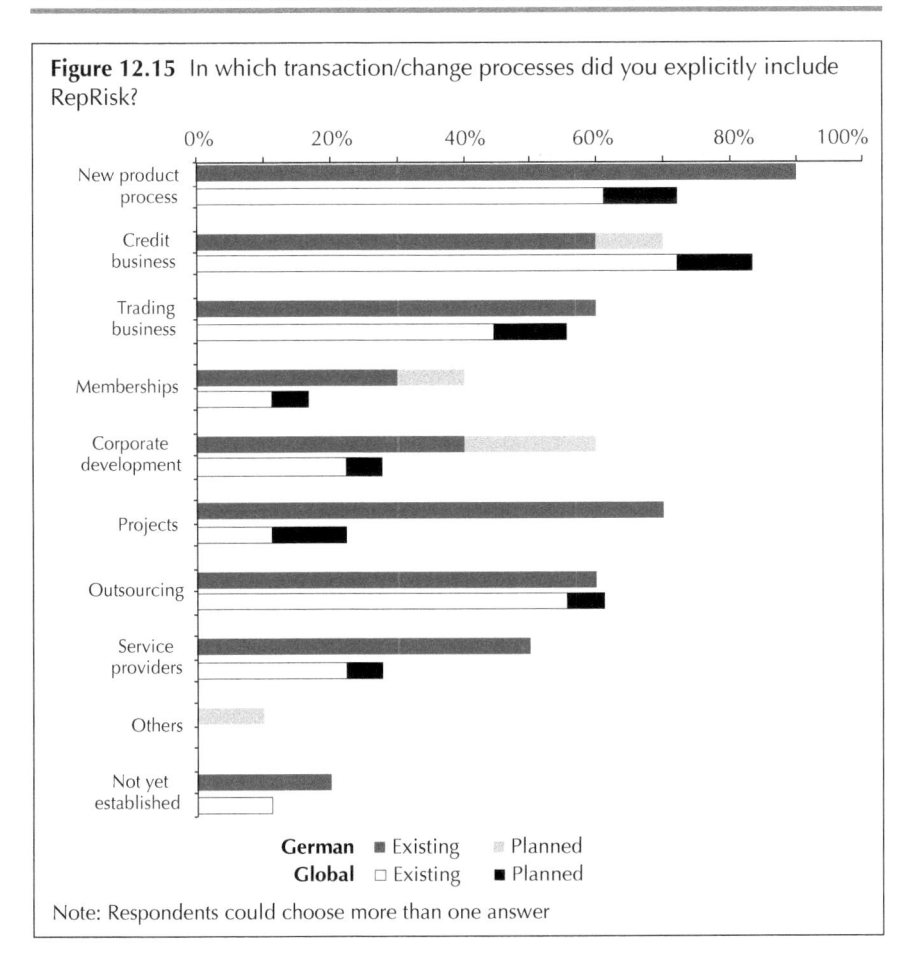

Categories (top to bottom): New product process, Credit business, Trading business, Memberships, Corporate development, Projects, Outsourcing, Service providers, Others, Not yet established

Legend: **German** ■ Existing ▨ Planned
Global □ Existing ■ Planned

Note: Respondents could choose more than one answer

Figure 12.16 How do you report about RepRisk to your senior management?

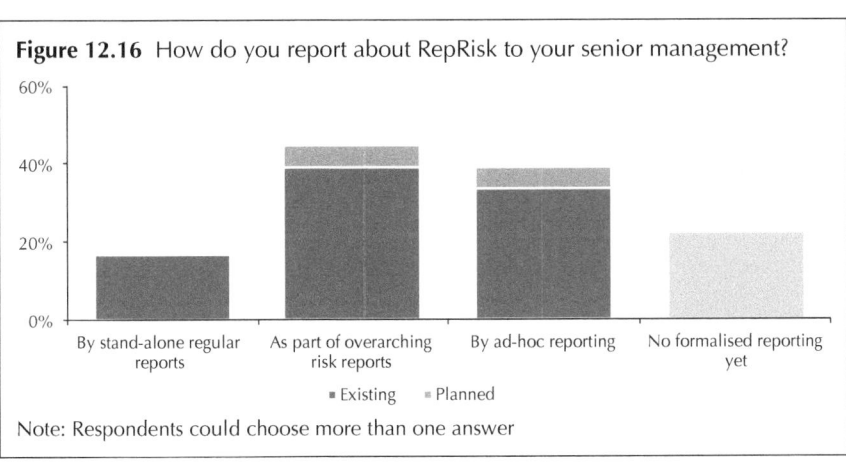

Categories: By stand-alone regular reports; As part of overarching risk reports; By ad-hoc reporting; No formalised reporting yet

Legend: ■ Existing   ▨ Planned

Note: Respondents could choose more than one answer

this topic separately as well as in unison with general risk. Ad hoc reporting should complement rather than replace regular reporting (see Figure 12.16).

17. Is there a monitoring process for RepRisk measures? (German study)
Reputational risk measures should be documented and monitored in a database to have an overview of their effectiveness. The whole life cycle of the measure and its realisation, including initiation, implementation, changes of scope and budget execution of the control of effectiveness, should be monitored.

One-third of the institutions involved in the survey have already instituted a monitoring system for reputational risk measures (see Figure 12.17).

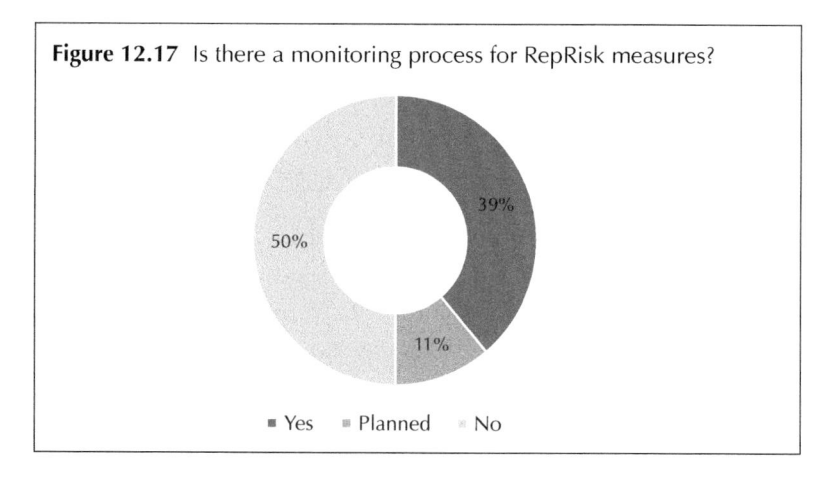

Figure 12.17 Is there a monitoring process for RepRisk measures?

- Yes: 39%
- Planned: 11%
- No: 50%

CONCLUSION

The management and controlling of reputational risks at the time of writing is in an early phase of development and there are different points of view concerning governance, methods and processes. Setting up a reputational risk-management framework is difficult when questions remain over its definition and which department should be responsible. The results of the survey show that a significant number of institutions either already systematically integrate reputational risk into their overall risk management, or have started to develop a risk-management framework.

In terms of establishing a methodology for reputational risk management, the obvious approach is for banks to utilise the tools and instruments created for operational risk management and to modify them accordingly, as demonstrated in several other chapters of this book.

Firms should take advantage of the learning curve from operational risk – it took operational risk 8–10 years to become a relatively mature discipline, but by using existing toolsets it should probably take reputational risk less time to mature.

REFERENCES

Kaiser, Thomas (ed), 2007, *Wettbewerbsvorteil Risikomanagement. Erfolgreiche Steuerung der Strategie-, Reputations- und operationellen Risiken*, Erich Schmidt Verlag (Berlin).

Kaiser, Thomas, 2008, "The rules of honour", *OpRisk & Compliance*, June.

Kaiser, Thomas, 2010, "Reputationsrisikomanagement in Banken", *Zeitschrift für das gesamte Kreditwesen* 1, February.

KPMG, 2012, *Reputationsrisiken – Management und Controlling. Status quo und Perspektiven der Weiterentwicklung im Finanzsektor* (Frankfurt).

RISKUniverse, 2012,"Managing your reputation", *Risk Universe*, October.

13

Governance as the Starting Point for a Reputational Risk-Management Process

Carsten Steinhoff and Rainer Sprengel

Norddeutsche Landesbank and Portigon Financial Services

WHY REPUTATIONAL RISK NEEDS GOVERNANCE

The reputation of a company is clearly one of the main factors for its success. It needs hard work and a long time to build up a sound reputation in the market. Unfortunately, it can be destroyed immediately by one single event. Examples of tragedy and misfortune can be found in the press on nearly every business and every day. With the increase in new communication technologies such as Twitter, Facebook and mobile computing, the environment has become more dynamic and dramas evolve much faster than ever before. To limit the damage, many of those cases need a highly flexible crisis intervention in case of a critical event.

Behavioural aspects and the impact of single people's actions have continuously increased. An example of how unexpected a reputational effect can be is Josef Ackermann, the former CEO of Deutsche Bank, who made a two-fingered V-for-victory gesture on his first court appearance for the Mannesmann trial. That truly was a disaster for Deutsche Bank's market perception. This example shows how different the causes of reputational damage can be and that, in future, risk awareness will probably be the most important factor for risk reduction. As a consequence, these "soft" insights have to play a role in a reputational risk programme and in building up a governance framework. Governance here means more than a "who is responsible for what?" question. We choose a broader definition that considers actors and responsibilities as well as tools and processes that are useful for a reputational risk-management framework.

Even if reputational risk is not new and, as with operational risk, should be part of any managerial decision, many financial institutions have only now begun to address reputational factors systematically and to build up a reputational risk framework. It is more than useful to review the companies' activities and managerial decisions as early as possible for reputational damage and be prepared.

In this chapter, we will first examine some factors that from our point of view are necessary to support this preparation and to set up a reputational risk framework. While neglecting crisis intervention, which is more a communication than a risk-management task, we will rather focus on structures, tools and processes that are necessary for a preventive strategy.

After that, we assess the current state of reputational risk management by reflecting requirements and expectations, showing different stages of maturity and focusing on strategy aspects. The next section looks at actors and responsibilities and gives practical advice about how to start building a framework and who should be part of it. Following that section, we take a closer look at instruments and processes that are necessary to support the whole framework, whereas a common taxonomy will be set as a starting point. The last section concludes.

ASSESSING THE STATUS QUO
Regulatory requirements versus stakeholders' expectations
In contrast to many other fields risk management currently has to deal with, reputational risk is not mainly driven by regulation. The efforts to build up, maintain and protect the corporate reputation frameworks represent financial institutions' self-interest and in most cases reflect common sense. On the other hand, there are many rules and restrictions that define the basis for reputational risk management and limit the spectrum of the finance business, especially of possible clients. Amongst others:

❏ corporate governance standards;
❏ laws that limit the business activities of financial institutions;
❏ international agreements restricting specific areas (eg, War Weapons Control Act or the proscription of cluster munitions);

- human rights;
- environmental management and protection;
- supply-chain issues, eg, product safety, employment practices; and
- government relations, anti-corruption/anti-bribery rules, export restrictions.

Beyond these rather compliance-relevant aspects, reputation – and subsequently the risk of damaging it – is determined by stakeholders' expectations. Possible stakeholders are: customers, employees, regulators, politicians, shareholders/owners, external analysts, local communities, NGOs, investors, suppliers and the communities in which the company operates. Naturally, the demands of these stakeholder groups are different, partially opposed. The central question is what each group will require in order to maintain or extend its confidence in the company. This should be part of frequent stakeholder dialogue that should be embedded in a reputational risk framework; we will discuss this later in more detail.

Stages of managing reputational risk

A study for the German market stated that governance structures are in many cases rather rudimentary and inconsistent, and that a best-practice approach does not seem to exist (KPMG 2012, p. 5). Nevertheless, we see three different types or stages in developing a reputational risk governance. The simplest approach is a decentralised and rather implicit consideration. This setting aims to comply with all external rules by setting policies and guidelines and to act (or react) by means of communication. In rare cases, a reputational risk committee is set up. However, no coordinative function or systematic reputational risk toolkit exists. This approach can be observed in almost all smaller financial institutions and also in a number of larger ones. The main strategy is defence/avoidance.

In the second type, a responsible role for reputational risk is established to coordinate all activities within a coordinated framework. Reputational risk is part of the institution's risk strategy, stakeholders are defined and a reputational risk committee is installed.

In the third and most advanced structure, reputational risk management is embedded into the main business processes. The framework is supported by tools that allow a view on future trends and lessons learned from the industry, eg, press database, reputational risk assessment and risk indicators. This setting is aligned to manage upcoming reputational risks. The whole framework is coordinated centrally and the strategy is to foresee reputational problems and minimise them.

RepRisk strategy

Reputational risks form an inherent part of a financial institution's business. They are mostly caused by social developments in combination with own behaviour, which are either not (completely) known or cannot easily be foreseen at the time the business is completed. For example, after the incident in Japan's nuclear power station in Fukushima, non-governmental organisations focused on institutions active in the financing of Germany's nuclear industry.

The objective of the RepRisk strategy is to mitigate or avoid these or other major reputational risks as far as possible, while taking into account cost–benefit aspects. Major reputational risks can be those that result in significant and sustainable negative effects on the financial institution's business and/or its benefits. Risk and business strategy should be combined. If a financial institution carries out its regular risk inventory assessment and finds that there is a substantial reputational risk, we suggest to referring to these risks as being concrete in a subordinated risk strategy. Recommended in this case is a separate reputational risk strategy.

In addition, the RepRisk strategy should mention those committees and subcommittees that directly relate to RepRisk (eg, Reputational Risk Committee, Credit Risk Committee and New Product Approval Committee).

In the financial industry, reputational risks are analysed, assessed and "limited" on the basis of qualitative criteria due to the many subjective factors involved. "Portfolio rules and criteria for exclusion" as well as an established "Reputational Risk Process" can be mentioned as main strategy elements.

❏ institutions should define individual fields of business, in which business is generally not allowed or on a restricted basis only. Guidelines – as, for example, compliance regulations, policies for social and environmental issues/financing in the nuclear

industry/financing regarding coal-fired power generation – should be set up, reviewed on a regular basis and mentioned in the strategy.
- ❏ The RepRisk process for the assessment of reputational risks with regard to clients, new products and transactions should be described in the strategy, referring to the respective responsibilities. Within the scope of this process, the identified reputational risks are compared with the institution's risk tolerance. In this context, the risk tolerance is not a centrally defined number, but is based on the experiences of the experts involved with regard to how far individual risks can be accepted – the result is a corresponding vote (approval, approval with conditions, rejection).

The roles and responsibilities of RepRisk management will now be briefly explained.

ACTORS AND RESPONSIBILITIES
Who should be part of the reputational risk framework?
The brief answer as to who plays a role in a reputational risk framework should be: everybody in the company. Compared with other risks, reputation can be affected not only by management decisions but by any stakeholder activity. Rumours or inadequate behaviour on the parts of single persons will lead to a negative impact as well as unfavourable credit or investment decisions (eg, in "nasty" industries). Hence, the reasons for a reputational damage are so various that we think a good risk culture is fundamental to good reputational risk management.

Nevertheless, this approach to reputational risk must be managed within a framework. It must not be a standalone discipline but has to be included in the enterprise-wide (risk) management. It is not a "pure" risk topic, but should be seen as a communication and strategy challenge as well. Some main players within the governance should be:

- ❏ The board: The tone from the top is one of the main drivers for a good risk culture and the underlying company culture. Integrity, credibility and continuity are the foundation for reputation capital.

❏ Strategy Department: The company's strategy should minimise negative reputational effects of strategic positions. Having a 360-degree view of all stakeholders and possibly negative effects in mind should avoid negative impressions in the long run.
❏ Corporate communication: Good communication is necessary to build confidence, to maintain it constantly and to interact immediately in the sense of a crisis management in case any issues arrive.
❏ Compliance Department: Mostly, compliance is responsible for setting guidelines for both compliant and ethically accepted investment decisions. This includes institution-specific guidelines and policies to comply with industry standards (eg, weapons of war) or policies to fulfil the company strategy (eg, no credits for nuclear power plants).
❏ Risk Control Department: Risk Control is responsible for all stages within a risk-management cycle, namely risk strategy, questions of risk identification and quantification and a complete management reporting. We will elaborate on that later. Reputational risk is gradually growing in importance within risk offices, after not playing a large role in recent years. There can be various reasons for that. First, it is not regulated, eg, by Basel II. Second, as a "soft risk" it did not fit into rather quantitative frameworks. Third, risk management was widely spread in the departments already mentioned. To get a full picture of the risk situation, reputation must not be excluded.

The natural connection between these corporate functions is developed differently. Some of these topics are usually not part of a risk-management framework in the sense of using the same language and similar tools as, eg, sustainability or communication. Other connections are on the rise but not yet embedded in the "risk world", like compliance, for example.

Economic action always played an important role in corporate behaviour and reputation. Since the financial crisis it became obvious that only sustainable business activities can lead to continuous success in business. Moreover, the importance of ethical issues rapidly increased. The so-called ESG (environmental, social, governance) issues need to be considered in the context of sustainability, ie, that success can be achieved only if all operations are environmentally friendly and socially responsible, meaning that they comply with responsible corporate governance. Sustainability management is no longer a "freaky green" discipline but necessary for investment decisions and therefore a must-have, too. So financial institutions need a sustainability strategy that is designed in such a way that each employee represents sustainable values internally and externally, and that is incorporated into the institution's business strategy. As a part of product design and marketing – sustainable products in particular, such as the financing of renewable energies – sustainability became a key factor for all business activities. These factors become an important module on the reputational risk roadmap.

Companies are then rated by sustainability rating agencies with regard to the extent to which they act sustainably, so that, in particular, institutional investors invest more and more money in consistently highly rated financial institutions, or investment policies allow them to contract only with sustainably rated companies. In addition, sustainable initiatives such as the Global Reporting Initiative have developed quite a few criteria that examine and evaluate sustainability reports of many companies. While other industries have been working on sustainability intensively for many years, the finance sector is currently still lagging behind; however, the importance rapidly increases. Sustainability processes are often driven directly by the CEO, and sustainability units or boards are set up.

As an aspect of sustainability, the stakeholder management of a company plays an important role. In a first step, all stakeholders need to be identified. Afterwards, each of them needs to be fully analysed and subsequently they need to be set in relation to both each other and the company. A competitive stakeholder dialogue can identify not only opportunities but also risks as, *inter alia*, reputational risks can be reduced. As a result, in some cases management objectives need to be readjusted. How successfully a company works with its stakeholders is also evaluated by sustainability rating agencies and sustainable initiatives.

Sustainability instruments should be derived from a reputational risk agenda and the governance should be perfectly intertwined so that:

❏ objectives for sustainability complement and specify reputational risk strategies;

❏ sustainability issues are part of all RepRisk steering tools; and
❏ ESG stakeholders are part of an ongoing stakeholder dialogue.

Set up the framework

To set up a reputational risk framework, it should first be disclosed which processes and policies that can be relevant for the framework are already available. Plenty of what is necessary to manage reputation in most companies already exists, although it is not labelled "RepRisk". The main challenge will be to synchronise different views and definitions, working instructions, actions, policies, tools and reports. Steps of a framework initiative could be:

1. an inventory of relevant modules (eg, rules/processes for credit approval, outsourcing, new-product processes, customer complaints, stakeholder information);
2. setting of standards for the basics (eg, definitions, categories, metrics, database);
3. approval of a reputational risk strategy;
4. deriving an appropriate governance structure; and
5. enhancing the resulting framework with risk-control tools.

The last step is necessary because, in most cases, rules exist, but there is no risk-control inventory that will support the structure by forward-looking elements and common reporting. These forward-looking elements identify threats in a structured manner, eg, by press research and a self-assessment. They also help to foresee trends that could be relevant for the company's reputation.

To start with a reputational risk framework, we suggest thinking about the arrangement of the five different elements that are shown in Figure 13.1.

In the diagram, a basic framework (1) will help to avoid negative effects right from the beginning. A common definition of reputation sets the basis, and a reputational risk strategy that is consistent with the company strategy should be linked to it.

A set of instruments (2) should help to identify reputational risk issues as early as possible and to build up a "knowledge base" to know which issues are currently on the "radar screen". An expert-based RepRisk survey, as we describe later, offers a structured *ex ante* analysis of potential hotspots. A RepRisk event database as seen in

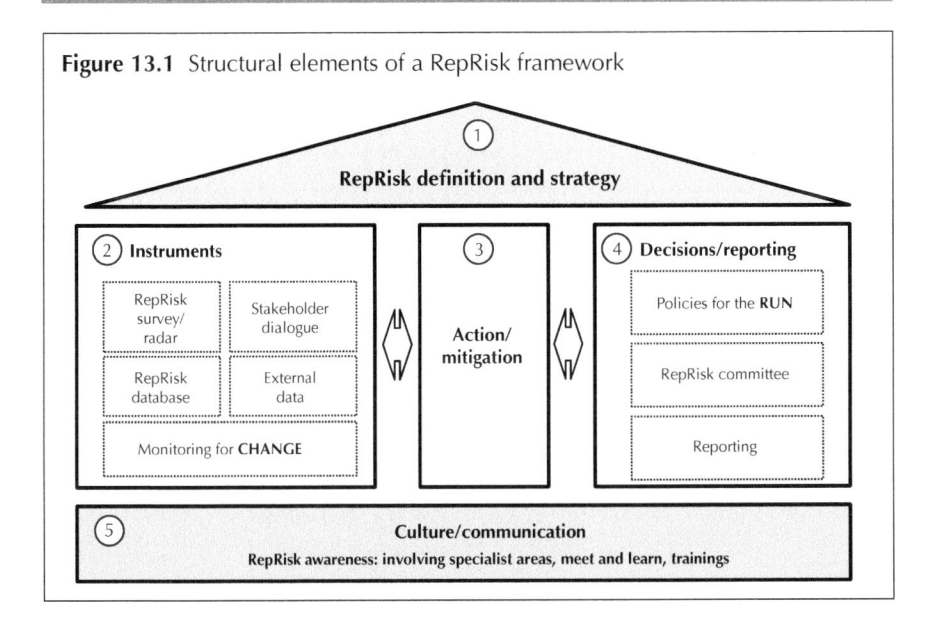

Figure 13.1 Structural elements of a RepRisk framework

```
                              ( 1 )
                    RepRisk definition and strategy

  ( 2 ) Instruments              ( 3 )          ( 4 ) Decisions/reporting

   RepRisk      Stakeholder                      Policies for the RUN
   survey/      dialogue       Action/
   radar                       mitigation
   RepRisk      External                         RepRisk committee
   database     data

   Monitoring for CHANGE                         Reporting

  ( 5 )              Culture/communication
        RepRisk awareness: involving specialist areas, meet and learn, trainings
```

operational risk management is very useful to amend the *ex post* view and to encourage lessons-learned processes; where appropriate, the existing loss databases can also be extended to reputational risk events. External databases provide examples of issues that are worth looking at. Knowing the stakeholders' needs and expectations is another factor of the "knowledge base". All processes that bring about change to the institution (eg, outsourcing, new-product approval) should be reviewed for their reputational impact, too. It is useful to set up an assessment that is comparable for all changes for these processes as well. A set of general rules for the "run" processes should support the framework that defines a set of general rules and limits for reputation-relevant actions. These instruments should be connected to each other as far as possible (eg, based on common categories or measures) in order to provide a view on the current reputational risk situation at a glance.

Moreover, decision and reporting processes (4) that supplement the instruments have to be designed. Since general rules should have priority, a set of policies ensures that fundamental reputational issues are commonly managed (eg, code of conduct, investment rules and general principles). We call these "run" processes and define them – in contrast with the change processes – as decision processes within a stable context. Furthermore, a RepRisk board should be installed that makes event-related decisions in case the policies do not fit. Tailored reporting will enable the management to have a recent and complete view on the currently highest relevant reputation issues on the issue radar. Results from the RepRisk instruments as well as from the decision processes allow reasonable actions and mitigation (3). Since communication and risk culture are at the core of good reputational risk management, we consider it here again (5).

As we think that decision processes are crucial in that framework, we will have a closer look at them now. Strategic decisions within the scope of the RepRisk strategy should be taken via a RepRisk committee with board attention or ultimately by the full board. Strategic decisions should be prepared by the respective specialist (Sustainability Unit, Communication, Compliance, Legal). In order also to meet the respective regulatory requests, we recommend the decisions be reviewed by a RepRisk Control Unit within risk controlling and be presented to the committee (Haackert *et al*, 2013, p. 7).

For event-related risk decisions (single transactions or change processes), a suitable process should be put into place with decision powers for specialists or a senior RepRisk committee. The relevant roles and responsibilities for this process should be documented in RepRisk guidelines and manuals. A possible process for event-related decisions is shown in Figure 13.2 (Sprengel 2012, p. 7).

❑ The business unit responsible for the transaction (eg, market area, project leader) should be obliged to give their first RepRisk

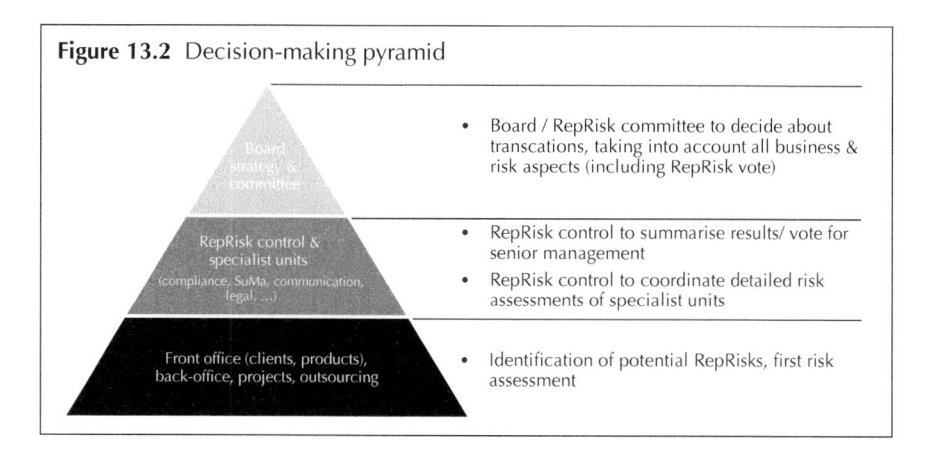

Figure 13.2 Decision-making pyramid

Pyramid level	Description
Board strategy & committee	• Board / RepRisk committee to decide about transcations, taking into account all business & risk aspects (including RepRisk vote)
RepRisk control & specialist units (compliance, SuMa, communication, legal, ...)	• RepRisk control to summarise results/ vote for senior management • RepRisk control to coordinate detailed risk assessments of specialist units
Front office (clients, products), back-office, projects, outsourcing	• Identification of potential RepRisks, first risk assessment

assessment as soon as possible. They should explain the underlying risk drivers and transfer the result to a superior RepRisk Control Unit for further analysis.
❏ Subordinated areas (eg, Credit Analysis, Market Risk Management) should – as a second line of defence – make the superior RepRisk Control Unit aware of transactions that incur RepRisk.
❏ In a next step, RepRisk Control should – in addition to its own analysis – request more detailed risk assessments of other RepRisk specialists (Compliance, Sustainability Management, Communication, Legal and so on).
❏ RepRisk Control should prepare the assessments in a management-related way and lead to a clear vote (approval, approval with conditions, rejection). The fulfilment of conditions should be tracked.

The vote should be an integral part of the company's further decision and escalation processes (eg, credit decision process, new-product approval process, outsourcing decisions).

INSTRUMENTS AND PROCESSES
In this section, we give examples of instruments, methodologies and related processes with regard to RepRisk-management that are established in practice. Currently, no standardisation could be observed in this area. The described components might also be combined.

Scaling/matrices
Many institutions initially defined reputational risk as a consequence of operational risk incidents; furthermore, holistic or integrated approaches to operational risk are on the rise. For that reason, we think that a similar toolkit and scale for operational and reputational risks is self-evident. When creating a methodology, it is fundamental to get a common understanding of what reputational risk means and to set different levels of reputational severity. To measure different levels of reputational risk, we believe it is quite useful to rely on a common tool, and propose a risk matrix or heat map that is suitable for operational and reputational risk. While the monetary impact of operational risk cannot always be estimated reliably, this is even harder for reputational risk.

We suggest a common matrix to make risk comparable as well as a "corporate language" for risk management, not only for reputational risks. That will provide recognition effects and a clear structure for risk governance, too. In Figure 13.3 you can find an example to set up that matrix: the scale of financial impact is equalised to different dimensions of reputational impacts. In this section, we show headlines for illustration only. To use the matrix, every single dimension should be defined by clear descriptions (eg, "very long-lasting negative international press"). To represent the whole variety of reputational problems to the company, we allow different scales. The maximum value defines the impact. Regarding the likelihood scale, we suggest distinguishing between an *ex post*

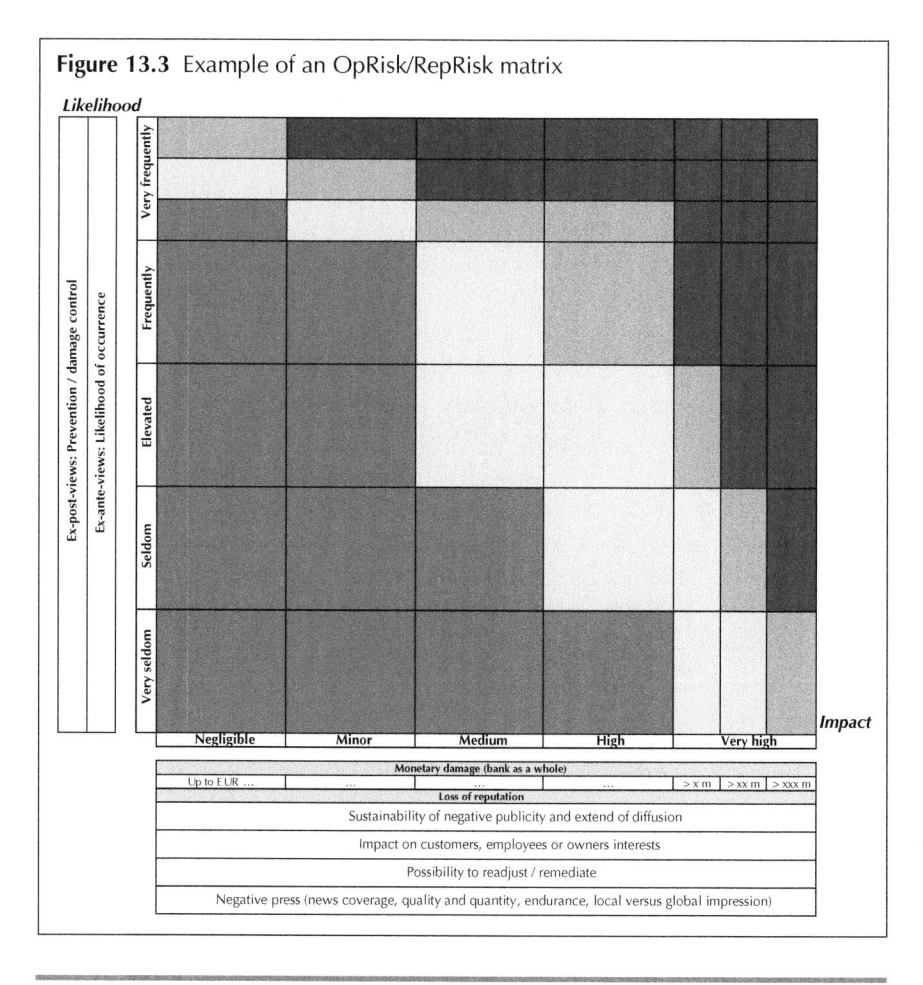

Figure 13.3 Example of an OpRisk/RepRisk matrix

Likelihood

Ex-post-views: Prevention / damage control
Ex-ante-views: Likelihood of occurrence

Rows (top to bottom): Very frequently, Frequently, Elevated, Seldom, Very seldom

Columns (left to right): Negligible, Minor, Medium, High, Very high

Impact

Monetary damage (bank as a whole)						
Up to E UR …	…	…	…	> x m	> xx m	> xxx m

Loss of reputation

Sustainability of negative publicity and extend of diffusion

Impact on customers, employees or owners interests

Possibility to readjust / remediate

Negative press (news coverage, quality and quantity, endurance, local versus global impression)

and an *ex ante* view. Thereby, incidents and hypothetical risks can also be assessed. The risk matrix can be regarded as both an assessment tool and a reporting instrument. The heatmap clearly defines information and escalation needs. For example, in the case of a "dark" flag, the risk tolerance is exceeded and immediate action is mandatory.

Since the same scales are used throughout all processes assessing reputation, all reputational information is now comparable. That creates a coherent and complete picture and enables a better management reporting.

Database, categories and risk factors

Reputational risk can roughly be categorised as internally and externally caused events. On the one hand, there are internal factors such as statements of the board and employees, the way the company does business, how processes are designed or carried out and the way the company complies with laws or deals with ethical aspects. While some of those aspects are purely risk awareness/culture topics and need good communication in case of an incident, other factors can be proactively handled very well by policies and internal controls. On the other hand, externally driven factors such as rating and market trends can be dealt with by knowing the stakeholders' needs and proactive operational actions.

During the setting-up of an efficient, institution-wide reputational risk management-strategy with the related instruments and processes, it is recommended that a suitable database structure at an early stage be considered. Thereby, a systematic recording and subsequent analysis of RepRisk-relevant information is ensured. The concept of such a database should be based on the question of which information is finally intended to be prepared, and provided in which format and to whom.

Based on the business scope and the respective exposure to RepRisk, it is useful – as a first step – to fix broad RepRisk categories such as "customer", "country", "industry/sector", "products/transactions". As a second step, risk drivers in the form of RepRisk factors – if necessary divided into first and second levels – can be mapped. As a matter of fact, the category "customer" could, via "know-your-customer" or "compliance" processes, show "reputation of customer" on the first level, while a corresponding risk factor on the second level might be "sustainably negative information shown in World Check, press, internet or other sources". In the category "industry/sector" the first level might display the risk factor "risk industry/sector", followed by the second-level risk factor, "gambling/betting". In case RepRisk-relevant information is additionally being obtained by commercial providers, categories and factors of internal and external data sources should be directly harmonised, in order to link both sources.

We recommend internal use of the information derived from the ongoing business as a kind of "checklist", providing an informative basis for potential RepRisks. These will support decentralised units when assessing RepRisk-relevant issues. At the same time, we refer to existing internal regulations for risk mitigation, as, for example, compliance regulations or policies for social and environmental issues. The risk categories and risk factors should be regularly reviewed and developed.

For standardised RepRisk processes – as for example the processing of a RepRisk process resulting in a final vote – information can be saved within the database in an audit-approved way. In case of a considerable number of RepRisk cases to be processed, workflows should be included in the database if necessary, for example between central RepRisk Control and the decentralised units or other RepRisk specialist units. A link to the measures derived from the RepRisk processes or the defined requirements can easily be provided via a database.

Identification by expert-based methods

Financial institutions should assess their major reputational risks based on a regular process. So far, no best-practice methodology exists; however, it is be useful to refer to already established OpRisk-management instruments. Expert-based methods are a good way to collect information about future risks. We will describe two possibilities for an *ex ante* assessment of reputational risk: a questionnaire-based bottom-up approach that we call a RepRisk survey; and an approach that is rather top-down and structures different sources of information by expert knowledge.

The RepRisk survey (RRS) is the regular, cause-oriented examination of both the financial institution's reputation and reputational risks by experts within a self-assessment. From these analyses, risk-reducing measures can be derived. The assessment of the reputation and reputational risks is carried out using a systematic procedure. The following RRS objectives can be identified:

- the most important drivers of the reputational risk in the relevant businesses of the financial institution;
- a general overview of all reputational risks as a decision basis to reduce the risk on the basis of cost–benefit aspects or to accept it; if applicable, further, linked risks (eg, OpRisk) are identified, which might be covered by an insurance;
- cost savings by the reduction/avoidance of potential reputational risks by a systematic risk prevention;
- recording of the institution's current reputation based on stakeholders, deriving recommendations to positively influence the reputation;
- fulfilment of regulatory requirements; and
- a positive effect on national/international regulators, owners and customers, rating agencies and advisers, which regard the systematic management of reputational risk as increasingly important.

Figure 13.4 Elements of a RepRisk survey

Overview of RepRisk survey		
Component	Definition/objectives	Enquiry procedure
1 Issue management	Identification of risk events that had or might have a materially negative influence on the institute's reputation. Early-warning function, risk prevention, realisation of opportunities.	Structured interview, including the recording of identified issues (related to component 1) and (related to component 2) assessment of risk potentials in the organisational units (basis:risk factor list, methodology OpRisk assessment).
2 RepRisk self-assessment	Identification and assessment of risk drivers in the organisational units. Preparation of risk map, derivation of preventive measures.	
3 Reputation assessment	Assessment of the institute's current reputation in addition to 1 and 2. Derivation of trends and recommendations for action per shareholder group.	Analysis of media attention and reputation analysis, interviews with stakeholders.

Figure 13.4 provides a brief overview of the three RepRisk survey components, the respective objectives and the implemented inquiry procedures.

Issue management (1) provides an early-as-possible and complete identification of events that already had or might have a negative impact on the institution's reputation and of which RepRisk Control might not yet be aware. In an interview, current events as well as – if applicable – past cases (recommendation: maximum one-year review) are recorded in a structured way and briefly analysed. "Lessons learned" resulting from past events can help to react in an appropriate way in future similar events.

Current events have an early-warning function (depending on the lifecycle phase of the issue). They offer the possibility of working against a potential reputational risk and often provide the chance of an increased reputation among stakeholders (eg, via the acknowledgement of problem prevention).

The RepRisk assessment (2) is based on established OpRisk assessment methodologies. The objective is to identify and assess the risk drivers in the respective assessed organisational unit. In addition to providing risk evidence within this organisational unit, the RepRisk assessment also aims to display and analyse the results on a cross-business-unit basis via a "RepRisk risk map". Based on a risk classification (eg, low, medium, high risk potential, if necessary backed by the probability of occurrence or statements regarding the potential media attention), action recommendations or measures are derived as a next step.

In addition to the risk-oriented components "issue management" and "RepRisk self-assessment", the component "reputation assessment" (3) addresses the assessment of the current reputation itself. The objective is to derive comments on the trend development per stakeholder group by taking into account existing analyses referring to reputation – for example, media attention – and reputation analyses or interviews with stakeholders. On the one hand, this might result in action recommendations to positively influence the institution's reputation. On the other hand, high scorings show the institution's strengths and corresponding possible chances.

The result of the RepRisk survey is more qualitative and subjective, which serves as management information as well as a steering instrument if combined with respective action recommendations or measures. Based on that, it is possible to assess consequences of reputational risks on the institution's liquidity; the inclusion of reputational risks in the risk-bearing capacity model (plausible derivation of an overall risk amount); and the inclusion and effects of reputational risk within the scope of stress tests.

To complete the picture, the RepRisk survey cannot stand alone and should be enriched by real-life-information, eg, from incidents or press data. A second approach, which we call "RepRisk radar", primarily uses objective information to assess reputational risks. To identify emerging risks, press research should be established. Most companies do media screenings to have a frequent view of their own media coverage. This kind of response analysis can help a company to react, but can be of little help in foreseeing emerging risks. There are different providers offering data that can be used for a reputational risk analysis to identify trends or lessons learned from competitors. In Germany, the database ÖffSchOR, which collects press data for operational risk, was enhanced by reputational risk information (Steinhoff and Monien 2012). All entries are rated with regard to their reputational effect. An easy scoring model helps to quantify the documented impact. Scoring factors consider which stakeholder groups are affected, the intensity of reporting and quantifiable effects on the company, eg, the stock price. Incidents that show upcoming trends or might probably affect the whole market are flagged.

This kind of data is tailored to identify trends very quickly and can be used for building up a RepRisk radar. Beyond the external data, other data sources can be considered and combined in this assessment. The RepRisk survey can be one of those. The idea is very simple and the results can be obtained by a panel of experts to:

❑ collect threats from the knowledge database (different sources, eg, press data, stakeholder analysis, incident database) that could have a serious impact on the company's reputational risk;
❑ cluster similar causes, if appropriate, to obtain a manageable size, and use the chosen categories for reputational factors (eg, external versus internal causes and subcategories); and
❑ assess the current risk for the company by setting bubbles into the radar screen: the more a risk is in the centre, the more risky it is.

Figure 13.5 Example for a simple RepRisk radar

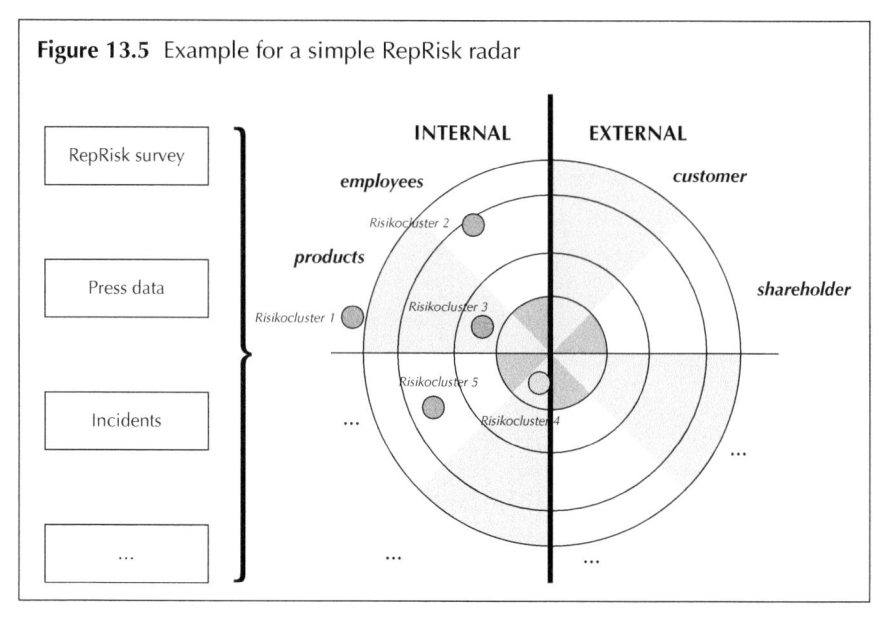

[RepRisk survey; Press data; Incidents; ...] — INTERNAL / EXTERNAL radar with quadrants: employees, products, customer, shareholder; showing Risikocluster 1–5.

The radar screen should show all important RepRisk issues and make it possible to visualise and relate the impacts to each other. As an example we look at different threats that have been assessed in the RepRisk survey. Maybe many departments complain about new requirements from various new regulation and the potential loss of reputation when implemented incorrectly. On the other hand, press data shows increasing fines on these topics. Even if the individual impact might be vague for the moment, different risks can be shown as being relevant (or not, and removed from the radar) and a relative order can be expressed very quickly and more detailed analysis started subsequently.

We suggest that, as an ongoing tool to collect key risk topics and to show them quickly without a formal assessment, a process is necessary. The RepRisk radar can be used for risk reporting as well as for challenging the completeness of the risk identification process.

Stakeholder analysis/stakeholder dialogue

Traditional approaches of a financial institution focus on the risks within the organisation. They do not, or only partially, take into account the expectations and requirements that external third parties – stakeholders – have with regard to the institution. However, as the reputation of the financial institution is closely linked to the trust of its stakeholders, both stakeholder analysis and stakeholder dialogue are important within the scope of the RepRisk management.

At first, stakeholders who mainly influence reputation and business should be defined. After that, their requirements and expectations should be considered. As a next step, those dangers and risks should be identified, which might change the stakeholders' perception. Afterwards, it must be decided which of those risks the company accepts and in which way a communication about these risks towards its stakeholders is carried out.

If, for example, a financial institution is strategically active in the project-financing segment (eg, dam construction, raw-material production), both the projects themselves and the financing institutions will probably have to take into account the risk factors "banishment of indigenous people", "breach of environmental obligations or international laws" or even "child labour". If this results in (assumed) risk concentrations in a single institution or the project consortium, the stakeholder group of non-governmental organisations will draw attention to it and might even start a special campaign – which then negatively affects the financial institution's reputation.

With regard to such a strategic positioning, it is useful to discuss potential topics with the NGOs in a regular exchange meeting that is moderated by a jointly selected, independent third person. Both sides can explain their point of view and the financial institution can, within the scope of its RepRisk – and sustainability management especially – provide information on measures and decision processes that add to a minimisation/avoidance of the above-mentioned risks. When professionally prepared and carried out, this stakeholder dialogue might result in building up reputational capital on a medium-to-long-term basis.

Reporting

Based on the results of the identification and assessment of reputational risks, action- and receiver-oriented reports should be created regularly and presented to the operating units, the board and/or the Risk Committee as well as to the supervisory body.

Dependent on materiality and criticality of the reputational risks and taking into account the implemented risk-mitigating measures, we recommend integrating these measures appropriately in the overall risk reports.

The basis can be a statistical reporting related to individual decisions and divided into decision categories (approval, approval with conditions, rejection) as well as sectors and/or locations. Over time, superior sensitive risk areas with substantial risk drivers will be derived from this. These should be reported in wider time intervals, added by the respective assessments of the RepRisk specialist units and completed by respective recommendations for action (eg, decision on new/extended portfolio guidelines). Summarising risk assessments from the RepRisk survey or risk analyses with regard to change processes should be reported additionally on an event-related basis. Especially in case of critical developments, both the implementation status of the introduced measures and the fulfilment status of relevant regulations should be additionally reported.

CONCLUSION AND OUTLOOK

In this chapter we looked at governance as a starting point for building a reputational risk-management framework. Starting with a sound strategy, a toolset should be developed that makes a current 360-degree view of reputational issues possible. We found that it is crucial to know as much information as possible about the stakeholders of the financial institution and their expectations of the company. In brief, reputational risk is about how to fulfil (or disappoint) their expectations. Furthermore we gave some ideas for tools that support that all-encompassing view. A mix of different views and data sources will suit these purposes and combine an inside and outside view.

But it should be emphasised that too much theory should be avoided and the whole framework for reputational risk management has to remain practical (ie, in the form of the use test). For that reason, we focused in this chapter on approaches that are easy to implement. From our point of view, a rather qualitative and expert-based approach fits best, since many reputational risks cannot be expressed by numbers. The gut feeling should be adhered to and indeed prioritised.

"Trust is the start of everything," Deutsche Bank claimed in an advertising campaign. The adequate management of reputational risks enables financial institutions to maintain and expand that trust by identifying or foreseeing as many threats as possible. While reputational effects have been taken into account rather implicitly in the past, a structured reputational risk management gains more and more attention. Within the scope of a complete risk governance, it is increasingly considered by the financial industry.

To manage those risks appropriately, a complete overview is vital – and a corresponding infrastructure or governance is essential to support managerial action. This chapter shows structures and components for a – from our point of view – practice-oriented RepRisk governance. The text focuses on a qualitative steering of reputational risk. An approved methodology to quantify reputational risk and provide capital underlying for these risks is (so far) not foreseeable – and also not reasonable, according to our experience.

For the future, we expect further dynamics with regard to aspects of reputational risk – even from the regulators. Bundling the different risk types that are today often managed in an isolated way and by different tools would be a step in the right direction. It could be supported, eg, by a harmonised "language" of risk categories, matrices or a joint analysis of consequences resulting from an event.

The views presented in this chapter are those of the authors and do not necessarily represent models or policies of their companies.

REFERENCES

Haackert, M., et al, 2013, "Best Practice des RepRisk-Managements", *Risikomanager* 20.

KPMG, 2012, "Reputationsrisiko – Management und Controlling. Status quo und Perspektiven der Weiterentwicklung im Finanzsektor", available at www.kpmg.com/DE/de/Documents/reputationsrisiko-management-controlling-2012-KPMG.pdf

Sprengel, R., 2012, "Einbettung des RepRisk in die Bankprozesse", *Risikomanager* 9.

Steinhoff, C., and M. Monien, 2012, "External Data: More love at Second Sight", in *Operational Risk: New Frontiers Explored* edited by Ellen Davis, pp. 211. London: Risk Books.

14

Managing Reputational Risk in a Major European Banking Group

Davide Bazzarello
UniCredit

A broad geographical presence was a major asset for UniCredit Group, as it could increase the diversification of risk and revenue. At the same time, managing reputational risk in a consistent way across the world posed many challenges and required a clear governance structure, an even stronger involvement of the senior management, clear group policies and guidelines as well as dedicated committees and defined information flows between different company functions on any type of decision taken with respect to reputational risk.

THE IMPULSE FOR REPUTATIONAL RISK MANAGEMENT
After the 2008 financial crisis, many market scandals were brought to light and tainted the reputation of all banks. The misuse and the aggressive selling of structured products, the subprime bubble in the USA, the intensive usage of derivatives, Libor-rigging investigations and top management compensation all put banks under huge pressure and scrutiny. In fact it was quite shocking for the public to realise that millionaire bonuses were paid out while the real economy was so gloomy, unemployment was surging, economic support from many banks was reduced as loan applications were rejected, and in some cases governments (ie, taxpayers) were obliged to bail out banks with public money. All these factors and many others led the overall banking industry to rethink its approach to reputation and the importance of tracking and managing it.

Big scandals aside, there were many impulses to properly tackle reputational risk. Keeping or increasing market shares, and indeed remaining in the market arena, required a sound reputational risk framework to be embedded in daily business life. Some banking actions and behaviours were detrimental to customer experience, making them feel they were not at the centre of the firm's business model. How did customers react to complex products sold as plain vanilla instruments, and what about services not in line with market practices, poor post-sale support and order execution errors? What was the reaction when banks were financing controversial industries? The result in many cases was that clients decided to leave the bank, striking a blow for both the reputation and the financial statements of the bank in question.

High-quality service for customers was then of paramount importance in every business, and banking is not an exception. The customer experience evolved with the markets and social conditions, and the relationship between clients and banking institutions tended to move towards a higher level of expectation. Equally important was to have a good reputation from an employee point of view. The commitment and engagement levels of employees were definitely linked to how a firm was perceived internally. Was there a good balance between work and private life? Was meritocracy and equality applied consistently?

In addition to customers and employees, regulators also increased their scrutiny and raised expectations on the conduct and financial stability of banks.

Last but not least, investors were asking more and more for a strategic view, for innovative thinking and for the keeping of promises as far as commitments on financial ratios were concerned. In fact, the capability of the top management to keep such promises was very positive for the reputation of their bank. Of course, this equation stood the other way round: failing to meet the results promised by top management was really detrimental for some other banks.

In a nutshell, keeping up with the expectations of different stakeholders was of paramount importance, and forms the basis of a sustainable business. Failure to keep up with those expectations could suddenly or gradually destroy the reputation of the banks in question, paving the way for business-model failure in the future.

To shed some more light on these topics, and present some solutions identified by UniCredit Group, this chapter unfolds as follows.

In the next section, "How to Manage Reputational Risk in a Group", we outline the governance guidelines that should be applied in order to ensure that a sound reputational risk framework is in place. We also introduce the "inside-out" and "outside-in" approaches. Subsequently, in "Assessment methodology", we demonstrate a more detailed version of how reputational risk assessment has been applied at UniCredit. In "Special policies for specific cases" we focus on specific business areas within credit operations that could lead to significant reputational risks and therefore require specific policies. Finally, in "The role of the holding committees", we provide some concrete ideas about how different UniCredit subsidiaries committees have interacted in the past with group committees as far as decisions on reputational risk matters were concerned.

HOW TO MANAGE REPUTATIONAL RISK IN A GROUP

In order to assure sound and consistent reputational risk management, implemented with integrity, many principles needed to be developed internationally after the crisis.

First of all a special focus was put on the governance set-up, starting from a clear definition of what reputational risk was. In our experience reputational risk is defined as the current or prospective risk to earnings and capital arising from adverse perception of the image of the financial institution on the parts of customers, counterparties, shareholders/investors, regulators or employees (stakeholders).

This definition highlighted that almost every action could adversely affect UniCredit Group's ability to maintain existing, or establish new, business relationships and continued access to sources of funding. Reputational risk was thus defined as multidimensional, and reflected the perception of other market participants. Furthermore, it existed throughout the organisation, making exposure to reputational risk essentially a function of the adequacy of the group's internal risk-management processes. This was in addition to the manner and efficiency with which UniCredit management responded to external influences on bank activities.

In this respect the involvement of corporate governing bodies (eg, Strategic Supervisory Body, Management Body[1]), each within the scope of its respective tasks and duties, was crucial. It was definitely necessary when dealing with all the relevant decisions regarding the definition of UniCredit's framework for reputational risk management and control.

The strategic supervisory board established strategic reputational risk-management guidelines and rules, periodically reviewing them on either a yearly basis or every two years, in order to ensure their ongoing effectiveness. It was also a way to inform UniCredit subsidiaries or the group in a timely fashion about the risks to which they were exposed, so that they could understand and approve the procedures for identifying and assessing risks. On top of that, the Strategic Supervisory Board ensured on a continuing basis that tasks and responsibilities were assigned in a clear and appropriate manner. This goal was achieved through the approval of the group's policies by the Strategic Supervisory Board, followed by updates, which further defined and clarified various relevant roles and responsibilities. Finally, it implemented the establishment of a system that provided accurate, complete and timely information concerning reputational risk management and control.

At the same time the Management Body was, and is, responsible for the establishment and maintenance of an effective reputational risk-management and risk-control system, implementing strategic policies. It also specified the responsibilities of the units and functions involved in a manner that clearly assigned tasks and avoided potential conflicts of interest. For example, while the first assessment of reputational risk aspects was assigned to the business functions, the definition of the methodology to be applied for such assessment was made the responsibility of the risk function. Finally, it established the necessary internal reporting flows to the corporate governing bodies and control functions so that they could have the information necessary to fully understand and govern reputational risk factors.

The corporate governing bodies (both of which are responsible for strategic supervision and management) of UniCredit Group subsidiaries were informed of the reputational risk profile and the reputational risk-management policies established by the corporate governing bodies of the UniCredit parent company.

In addition, the same corporate bodies of UniCredit subsidiaries, each within the scope of its respective duties and within the constraints set forth by applicable local laws and regulations, were (and are) responsible for implementing, consistently with the circumstances of each group member, the reputational risk-management strategies and policies established by the UniCredit parent company. To this end, the holding company involved the competent bodies of the subsidiaries in the decision-making process concerning reputational risk-management procedures and policies.

Looking at these concepts, it should be clear that, without proper strategic decisions and buy-in by the most senior managers, there have been few chances to get the framework working.

Besides the senior management support, there was another big challenge in the implementation of a sound reputational risk framework. The cascading down, from major company functions to the most junior employee, of a reputational risk culture, was not an easy task. It was even more challenging taking into account the complexity embedded in the international footprint of UniCredit Group.

Since reputational risk was considered a risk that affected the group risk profile, several holding-company and legal-entity bodies and functions played a role, with specific responsibilities in the management of reputational risk related activities.

Here we provide some examples to let this concept be better understood. Looking at the reputational risk that could be triggered by fines committed by financial authorities for bribery or for usury or money laundering or IT systems malfunctioning, what functions should be in the loop? Who should take care of the issue in its reputational implications? The compliance, risk, business or audit departments, or somebody else?

Usually, when reputational risk was concerned, the compliance function was engaged to, along with competent business functions, solve the root causes of that risk. Risk management also had a prominent role as it could be utilised to measure or assess the level of risk associated or the impact in terms of reputational risk. Media-relations functions could take care of drafting a public statement if necessary, or screen social-network reactions and relevant weblogs (or blogs).

In order to have a streamlined process for reputational risk control and management, a clear organisation of duties and responsibilities should be then defined. Of course, many options could be identified, but, irrespective of the chosen governance framework, any strategic decisions on reputational risk management at group level should fall under the responsibility of the holding company. In general, as regards internal risk measurement systems, the holding company was responsible for taking the strategic decision to adopt such systems and to establish their essential features. It was also responsible for implementing the reputational risk-measurement and risk-control processes overseeing the proper functioning and the ongoing upgrading of the methodological, organisational and procedural aspects of the systems.

In order to avoid any possible conflict of interest, the functions in charge of reputational risk management and control should rely on the greatest independence. In other words the assignment of relevant responsibility was done through a dedicated structure, independent and separated from the risk-taking functions. On one side, a corporate function could play the role of defining clear policies, guidelines and operative instructions on how to cope with reputational risk: how to identify reputational risk triggers, how to assess their potential impacts, how to monitor the risk-profile evolution and finally how to mitigate these risks. On the other side, local functions, ideally mirroring the independence and the structure of the corporate function, should also be set up in the major legal entities (eg, classified according to internal rules such as the total value of assets and the number of clients). These local functions applied the methodology developed and properly inform local senior management about the results.

One of the many options on the table, and one that, in the end, was chosen by UniCredit, was to have a two-tier approach that can be labelled the "inside-out and outside-in approach".

The basic concept behind this was quite simple. The inside-out component refers to an assessment of the key vulnerabilities of a firm, which were identified and evaluated together with the outside-in component, which entails a detailed screening of the different opinions of stakeholders. Their feedback on the subject of bank reputation was integrated into the day-to-day functioning of the bank.

In other words, the inside-out component meant that, in order to manage and to better understand potential reputational risks, it was necessary to have a clear understanding of where reputational risk lay within bank operations. This could be achieved through detailed and pervasive risk mapping or interviews with senior management, or again by looking at events that happened to a competitor. This was done by leveraging techniques very familiar to risk people (eg, scenarios analysis, risk mapping). The inside-out component was then mainly allocated to the risk function.

Another factor for assigning the inside-out activities to risk people was their experience in operational, market and credit risks. These risks could very often be at the heart of reputational risk as triggers. We realised that money laundering was actually an operational risk, as was IT malfunctioning. Equally, breaching international laws on terrorism financing or internal rules on legal but sensitive sectors were operational risks, too, respectively in the payment and credit processes. Adding reputational risk to the usual and well-rooted operational risk assessment was a relatively quick win.

Of course, due to the nature of the reputational risk triggers, the task was also supported by many other functions that were brought on board and whose contribution was necessary, such as compliance, legal, business and credit operations.

The outside-in was mainly assigned to the Corporate Sustainability and Media Relations Department, which was in a better position to understand both the mood and the "hot topics" in the agendas of the different stakeholders. Their continuous checking, performed through interviews with UniCredit customers, or by screening websites where UniCredit was quoted or, again, checking newspaper comments about UniCredit, was extremely important and provided useful insights into the risk functions that allowed the department to properly assess the firm's exposure to reputational risk. In fact, reputational risk assessment was not performed once, but regularly in response to the changing requirements of the stakeholders. Properly monitoring the attitudes of the stakeholders became vital (see Figure 14.1).

Similarly to the inside-out step, the outside-in saw a plurality of teams involved in addition to the two core leading ones. For example, Investor Relations was engaged to better understand the view of shareholders and bondholders about the reputation of UniCredit reputation, and the Human Resources Department was encouraged to have a deeper understanding of employees' thoughts about UniCredit's reputation.

Both the inside-out and the outside-in components were of paramount importance and were performed on a regular basis using

Figure 14.1 Inside-out, outside-in approach

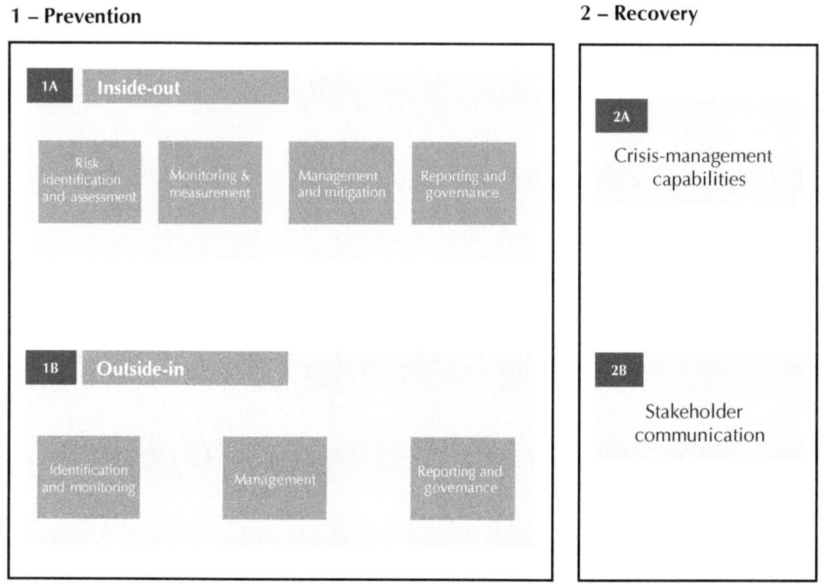

1 – Prevention

- 1A Inside-out
  - Risk identification and assessment
  - Monitoring & measurement
  - Management and mitigation
  - Reporting and governance

- 1B Outside-in
  - Identification and monitoring
  - Management
  - Reporting and governance

2 – Recovery

- 2A Crisis-management capabilities

- 2B Stakeholder communication

structured information flows between the different departments of UniCredit subsidiaries and the parent company.

ASSESSMENT METHODOLOGY

Defining a good risk-assessment methodology meant defining how the information gathered from the outside-in and inside-out approaches could be merged and interpreted. The approach that could be followed is to deconstruct the problem into smaller components, namely into the firm's exposure to specific reputational risk events and into the impact should such an event occur. Many algorithms could be applied and analysed to capture interdependencies between these two components; however, a qualitative assessment can be quite easily implemented as described below.

We decided to start from concrete experience and well-known risk such as that of fraud. For a commercial type of bank, savings security is definitely a value for customers. Although we might imagine that this is secured by all the players in the market, we noted an interesting phenomenon when fraud did occur. When fraud received newspaper attention, and when prominent people became involved, the branch that suffered an internal fraud ("internal" meaning that at least one employee was actively involved in the fraud), the weeks and months after the public disclosure of the facts of the case had a reputational risk effect. Indeed, for some weeks or months there was a higher-than-average rate of clients leaving the affected branch of the bank, compared with other bank branches. Clients abandoned completely or significantly reduced the amount of money deposited or under management or custody. At this point we posed ourselves a simple question: "How should we have assessed the reputational risk?" The drivers were all there: the significant amount of money that disappeared, the fact that the news was repeated everywhere in the media, and a more-than-reasonable expectation from clients to have their money in a safe place.

In Figure 14.2 you can see a very simplified version of UniCredit approach to the assessment of reputational risk, in relation to the aforementioned example.

Figure 14.2 highlights in the y axis the assessment of the probability of triggering a reputational risk when an internal fraud occurs. This is related to the probability of having wide media coverage of such fraud, spreading concern to many customers with regard to bank safety. In the x axis the probability of having a severe internal fraud in a branch is assessed. The combination of the two dimensions

Figure 14.2 Reputational risk analysis

Probability of trigger reputational risk if fraud occurs			
	Medium (L,H)	High (M,H)	High (H,H)
	Low (L,M)	Medium (M,M)	High (H,M)
	Low (L,L)	Low (M,L)	Medium (H,L)
Low	Low		

Degree of exposure to primary "trigger" risk

Figure 14.3 Stakeholder reaction

Intensity of potential reaction (eg, based on number of clients leaving)	Medium (L,H)	High (M,H)	High (H,H)
	Low (L,M)	Medium (M,M)	High (H,M)
Low	Low (L,L)	Low (M,L)	Medium (H,L)
	Low		

Client focus on the topic (are they sensitive?)

shows an overall assessment of the reputational risk exposure stemming from the inside-out approach.

Figure 14.3 highlights in the y axis the assessment of the potential magnitude of the reaction of the major stakeholder, who in our example would be the customers of the branches where media coverage was most significant. The x axis shows the level of client's attention to the topic: "Would the customer react to the reputational risk event?" The combination of these two dimensions shows an overall assessment of the stakeholders' reaction following an outside-in approach.

SPECIAL POLICIES FOR SPECIFIC CASES

Another important piece of a sound reputational risk framework for UniCredit Group is represented by a practical "toolbox", the contents of which would enable the user to assess and handle specific cases of potential reputational risk. Beside the shared set of policies and guidelines that illustrated the responsibilities and tasks of the different functions involved, and the information flows between such functions, some user-friendly and pragmatic guidelines had to be clearly written and properly communicated through the organisation in order to manage banking transactions. Typical transactions falling into this category refer to financing projects, individuals, corporates dealing with sensitive sectors such as weapons, nuclear production and transportation, gaming and many other sectors that could trigger severe environmental and social issues. Ideally, a complete set of topics would be prepared as reputational risks could also be found in the new-products approval process; in outsourcing initiatives; in any important decision on employee conditions; and in the substantial adherence to international and local laws, especially when dealing with countries perceived as non-cooperative jurisdictions. An example of the last of these would be cases of money laundering and terrorist financing.

For an international group such as UniCredit, one of the biggest challenges was to define guidelines that could fit different legislations and also different public-opinion stances towards the same topic. High-level principles, such as the respect and transparency towards UniCredit employees, clients and local communities, were then recommended and deep and open discussion on the business consequences of the implementation of such guidelines was encouraged. After such principles were identified and shared, clear and simple operative processes for running the business needed to be designed that could cover the overall lifecycle of a transaction. This would start with client knowledge and acquisition (ie, "know your customer"), moving through the transaction origination until the approval by the competent manager or committee is reached, according to each firm's delegation of powers. This is important, as the relationship manager could be in country A, while the client could have their headquarters in country B, while running their particular business in country C. Without a proper group-wide standard process, the possibility of having reputational risk issues could not be excluded.

However, as no single policy or process could cover the full range of possible transactions and peculiar situations, an ultimate decision body was empowered to have the last word. Likewise, the guidelines and processes of such bodies, namely the responsibility of the reputational risk committees, were implemented both at the level of UniCredit subsidiaries and at that of their parent company, with a flow of information established between them.

In Figure 14.4, an overview of how different reputational risk triggers could be handled is illustrated according to different existing banking processes.

For every topic defined as a reputational risk trigger, a special

Figure 14.4 Stakeholder reaction

	REPUTATIONAL RISK TRIGGER	DECISION TAKER	INVOLVED DEPARTMENTS
Credit process	Transactions (credit/non-credit such as payments …) on sensitive sectors (eg, weapons, nuclear, mining, water infrastructure)	Credit committee	Credit operations and risk
Hybrid*	Transactions that could lead to financial sanctions	Credit committee	Compliance (KYC, AML)
Others (non-credit processes)	Transactions involving non-cooperative jurisdictions potentially leading to taxation issues	Chief financial officer dept	Tax affairs
	All transactions triggering potential conflicts of interests (COIs)	Compliance dept	Compliance

* The risk analysis leverages on compliance processes; the recipient in case of escalation is the credit committee (compliance is a member).

policy is provided that helps UniCredit employees to properly carry out an adequate reputational risk assessment without significantly changing existing processes. If we look at the first row of Figure 14.4, we can see that every deal managed in the credit process that falls into defined "sensitive sectors", such as financing a new nuclear plant or supporting firms in the mining business, is subject to a reputational risk analysis by the Credit Operations Department as well as by specialised reputational risk functions. In the end, the Credit Committee decides whether to underwrite the risk, approving the deal or not.

THE ROLE OF THE HOLDING COMMITTEES

The Group Operational & Reputational Risks Committee (GORRIC) in UniCredit was responsible for monitoring operational and reputational risks at group level; evaluating incidents significantly affecting the overall operational and reputational risk profile; informing the Group Risk Committee of operational and reputational risk strategies, policies, guidelines, methodologies and limits; and regular reporting on operational and reputational risk portfolios.

The GORRIC was responsible for ensuring consistency in operational and reputational risk policies, methodologies and practices across business functions and legal entities. It controlled and monitored the group operational and reputational risk portfolio and risk-mitigation actions. The GORRIC met with consulting groups, discussing a number of topics to be passed on to the Group Risk

Committee. The GORRIC discussed, for example, specific reputational risk events, the crisis-management capabilities and stakeholder communication coherently with the reputational risk-management framework, and was able to provide advice on such matters as the implementation of special policies on request of any governing bodies of UniCredit's parent company or subsidiaries.

The GORRIC convened to discuss, and when necessary, to approve, such topics as special operational and reputational risk policies and the idea of a single-transaction evaluation in the case of grey areas in reputational risk policy or in case of escalation when submitted by the relevant competent committee at local level (business units or country subsidiaries). Local UniCredit subsidiaries could be asked to approve transactions beyond their delegated powers (such as transactions with a notional monetary amount that is higher than defined limits) or transactions where they did not feel comfortable taking a decision without knowing the opinion of a UniCredit parent company ahead of time.

The GORRIC was also in charge of dealing with residual areas, meaning specific business beyond the scope of existing special policies. Potential reputational risks could be spotted almost everywhere, and at that time we had some cases that were not listed in any relevant guidelines or processes. Therefore, to better serve the client and provide quick answers regarding the feasibility of specific transactions it was decided that we should assign the Group Operational and Reputational Committee, in addition to its previous powers, a non-binding-opinion (NBO) power, which would express the view of the Group on the subject of uncommon cases (see Figure 14.5). In such cases the GORRIC is usually asked, by the Group Transactional Committee (GTC) to provide its view on the matter.

The NBO relevant to the reputational risk of the holding company was a necessity for any transaction, from reputational risk special policy to a group subsidiary Reputational Risk Committee recommendation. It was also mandatory in the case of specific topics that might expose the group to a relevant reputational risk, irrespective of whether the matter was covered by the principles and rules in force according to the process as illustrated in the flowchart in Figure 14.5.

The group committee received on a regular basis, usually quarterly, an information flow for all the credit files (ie, information on

REPUTATIONAL RISK MANAGEMENT IN FINANCIAL INSTITUTIONS

Figure 14.5 The non-binding opinion process

NBO Request flow chart

[1] Proponent requests the NBO in any case of reputational risk due to:
- Transaction / Credit with amounts > or < defined holding company threshold
- documentary business

[2] Legal entity reputational risk competent body provides a first opinion to the request

◇ If the opinion is negative move to activity 3
   If the opinion is positive move to activity 4

[3] Considering the legal entity negative opinion, the NBO request is rejected

[4] Considering the legal entity positive opinion: the NBO comes in charge to the competent group transactional committee (GTC). GTC can, in any case, asks the support of other functions for NBO issuing

◇ In case the competent GTC has no doubts the NBO process moves to activity 5
   If the GTC considers to have doubts regarding reputational risk policies' grey areas or specific but not covered topics, the NBO process moves to activity 6.

[5] The NBO is released and communicated to all the involved functions. In any case the NBO shall be communicated to the group reputational risk function. The competent GTC reports on regular basis to the GORRIC about the implementation of the group reputational risk policies

[6] Further to GTC request, GORRIC provides the NBO required. In case of GORRIC negative evaluation, the proponent may escalate to the group risk committee

[7] Decision released by senior business management

Proponent: [1] NBO REQUEST

Legal entity reputational risk competent body: [2] LE REPUTATIONAL RISK OPINION → RESULT? → NEGATIVE → [3] NBO NOT SUBMITTED / POSITIVE →

Competent group committee: [4] IN CHARGE TO ISSUE NBO → DOUBTS? → NO → [5] NBO RELEASE / YES →

GORRIC: [6] NBO RELEASED → RESULT? → POSITIVE → END / NEGATIVE →

Group risk committee: [7] DECISION RELEASED

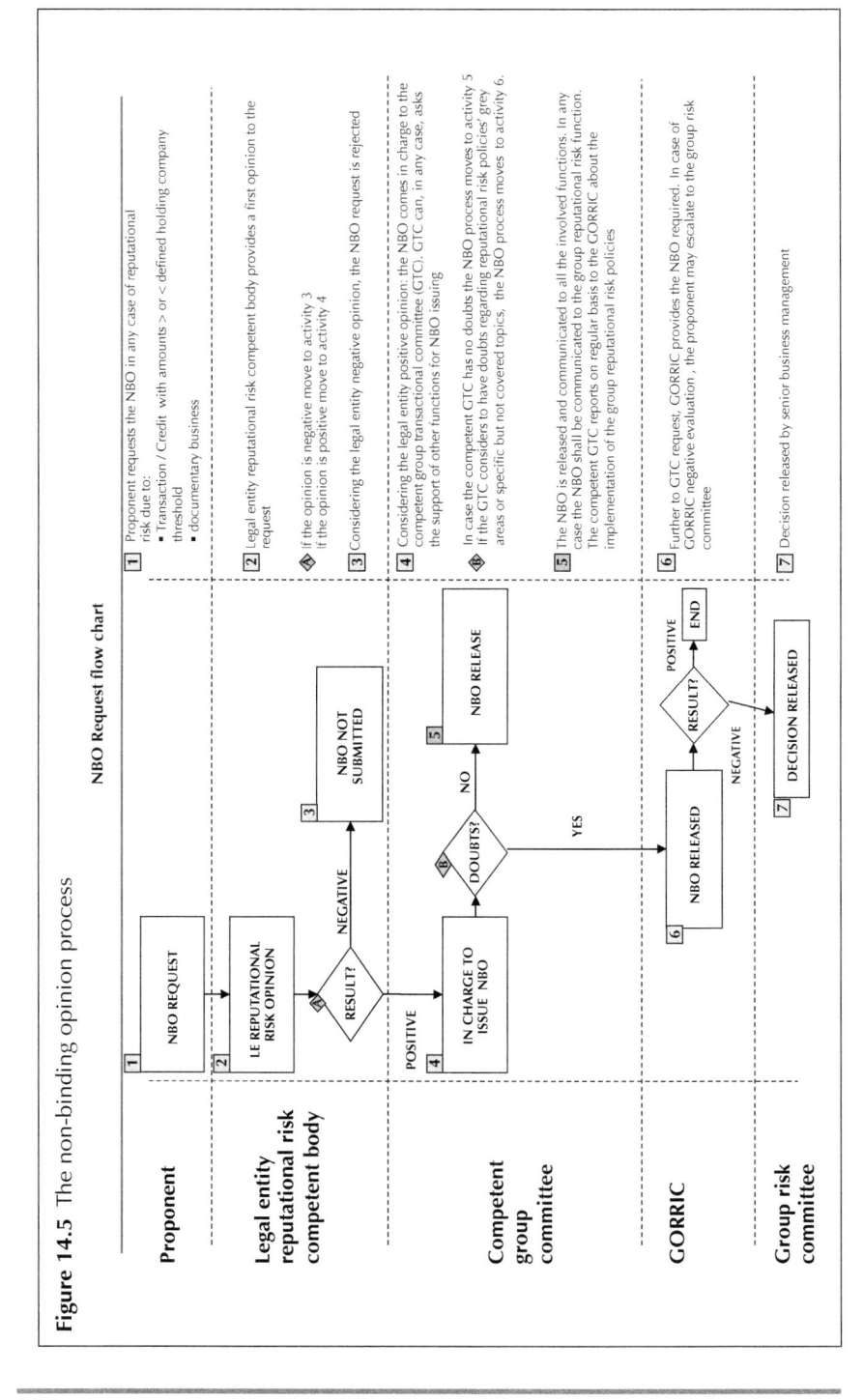

credit applications filed by customers to get credit facilities) that included reputational risk aspects, from other committees in charge of credit files approval. This was important in order to have an overall picture of how the group and each business unit or country was managing reputational risks in credit transactions. According to the information received, a reporting package for superior committees, such as the Group Risk Committee, was prepared on a regular basis to keep the top management of the group reputational risk profile informed. A positive secondary effect was to have ongoing feedback from the top regarding whether the group positioning was perceived as appropriate, and in case the business required the prompt provision of useful inputs to steer it in a particular direction.

Figure 14.6 shows a simplified version of a report that was used to monitor the credit transactions in sensitive sectors across UniCredit subsidiaries. It reported by single country the number of transactions with a breakdown by business sector (eg, nuclear, defence/weapons).

Figure 14.7 shows a simplified and illustrative report detailing credit transactions with potential reputational risk impacts. A breakdown by approval type (with or without conditions, rejected) is also provided.

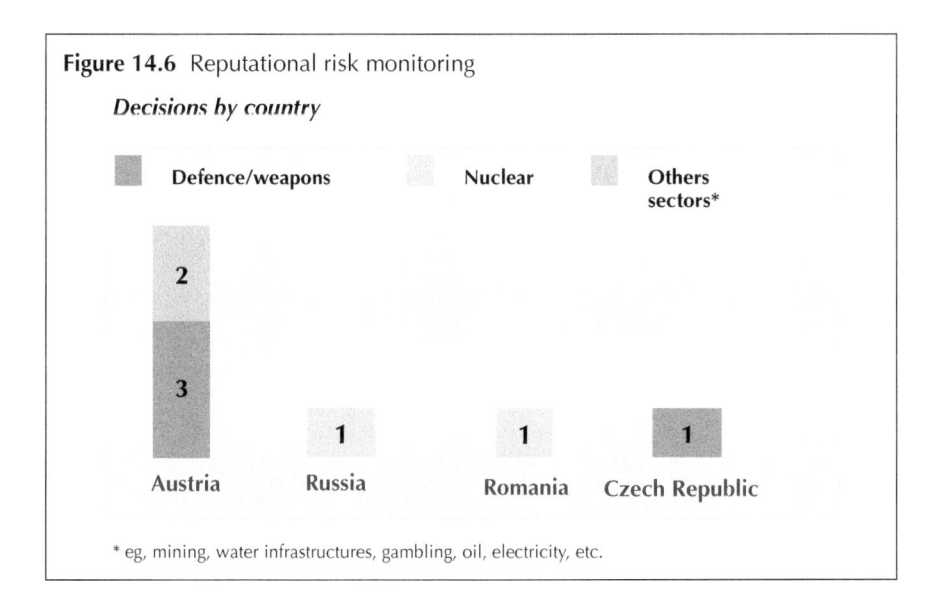

Figure 14.6 Reputational risk monitoring

Decisions by country

	Defence/weapons	Nuclear	Others sectors*

Austria	Russia	Romania	Czech Republic
2, 3	1	1	1

* eg, mining, water infrastructures, gambling, oil, electricity, etc.

Figure 14.7 Transactions reporting details

Decisions details

Decision	Defense weapons	%	Nuclear	%	Other sectors	%
Approved as submitted	3	75%	1	50%	2	100%
Approved with conditions	1	25%	1	50%	-	-
Not approved	-	-	-	-	-	-
Total	4	100%	2	100%	2	100%

Focus on Defense / Weapons

Country list	Number of positive decisions	Country importer
Low risk (A)	1	K
Medium risk (B)	1	Y
High risk (C)	2	Z
Embargoed	-	
All purpose	-	
Total	4	

CONCLUSION

Running business in different geographies did add some new challenges in terms of setting up and running a proper and sound reputational risk framework. An international presence simply reinforced the need for tackling common issues between local and global players. The need for a clear definition of reputational risk; the organisation of a clear framework for governance; the strong involvement of decision-making bodies; and a simple methodology were common challenges. The real difference could be found in the necessity, for a multinational group, to define adequate information flows and delegation powers between countries, along with robust training on the different commercial networks (ie, the branches in different countries where UniCredit operated).

Last but not least, the different perceptions of the stakeholders on an international level necessitated an intensive sharing process of methodologies for reputational risk before these could be implemented. All of this can be applied to the banking sector, too. Indeed, all businesses must come to an understanding of the potential consequences of any decisions they take within the context of reputational risk. For example, the energy industry has for a long time faced the need to become greener, as the public has become increasingly well informed on the subject of pollution and its implications. If a firm operating in this sector has factories or laboratories in different countries with potentially different attitudes towards such sensitive matters, then it must face the issues we present in our chapter. Do businesses within the energy industry have a full understanding of the most sensitive subjects for their stakeholders (ie, clients, investors, employees and local communities)? In other words, do they have an outside-in approach?

Equally, such businesses should identify their own way of assessing the financial and reputational impact if something goes wrong. For example, what happens if clients in rich areas of the world realise that a specific energy company exploits natural resources from poorer countries just to improve its profitability? Would they have an inside-out approach?

In our view a sound and well-implemented reputational risk framework, based on the inside-out and outside-in approaches, can help any company to pre-empt and mitigate reputational risks arising from day-to-day operations. But in no way can this be achieved without the involvement of the company's top management and without spreading a common risk culture across the jurisdictions where a company operates.

1 The expression "Strategic Supervisory Body" refers to the governing body that, pursuant to the provisions of the applicable corporate bylaws, is responsible for establishing management policy (for example, by way of the examination and approval of business or financial plans, or strategic corporate operations). The expression "Management Body" refers to the governing body responsible, either by legal entitlement or delegation, for the management of current operations, which involves the implementation of the policies established by the supervisory body.

15

The Implementation of the UniCredit Group Approach

Thomas Beil
UniCredit Bank AG

INTRODUCTION

In 2009, as one of the first major European financial institutions, UniCredit Bank AG, as part of UniCredit Group, began to implement risk-management processes aimed at managing reputational risk (RepRisk). Initially, the focus was on setting RepRisk special policies to cover the most important and frequent cases of reputational risk on the business side, such as cases related to weapons finance or nuclear energy. Within the organisational framework of UniCredit Group, these special policies were proposed by the UniCredit Group (Italy) head office. The local implementation at UniCredit Bank in Germany was subject to extensive debate at the management board level. Although, at the time, RepRisk management was not subject to any regulatory requirements, the top management of UniCredit Bank began to pay particular attention to RepRisk-sensitive issues.

Since those days, RepRisk has become an increasingly important topic, not only in terms of protecting the bank's reputation but also in terms of complying with regulations and requirements that have gradually come into existence and that aspire to ensure the creation and maintenance of a comprehensive system of RepRisk management. Still, currently, at least within the domestic banking industry, RepRisk-management procedures are at a relatively low-level developmental stage. This is hardly surprising, as RepRisk still is a "young" risk category, in particular in comparison with the venerable risk categories of credit and market risk. Nevertheless, increasingly, RepRisk management is becoming an integral component of the risk-management function in many financial institutions.

In order to significantly improve UniCredit's approach to RepRisk management, the bank started a particular project in 2012. The main objectives of the project were (i) to establish a comprehensive identification, evaluation and mitigation of RepRisk; (ii) to implement a consistent reporting of RepRisk; and (iii) to ensure that RepRisk is appropriately taken into account within the bank's stress-testing activities. As part of the project, a RepRisk control unit was established, organisationally located within the area of the chief risk officer and functionally integrated into the Operational Risk Control Unit.

The results of the above-mentioned project, which will be described in this chapter, are completely in line with the group-wide RepRisk framework. To some extent, however, the new methodologies and innovative solutions developed by UniCredit Bank expanded the group approach significantly.

Further contributing to the risk culture of UniCredit Group, UniCredit Bank started a broad communication offensive directed to the bank's managers as well as to all of the bank's employees. The purpose of this effort was to increase the awareness that (i) RepRisk may lurk in any banking transaction or decision; (ii) it may be hidden in various asset portfolios; and (iii) the potential negative impacts on business can be threatening to the stability of the bank's profitability. The management of UniCredit Bank put particular emphasis on this communication offensive as, in its view, at the time, RepRisk had still not been sufficiently valued in the context of the bank.

"We all are reputational risk managers" is the slogan we used at UniCredit Bank to call on and encourage every colleague to get involved into the new bank-wide RepRisk effort and to take ownership in the management of potential RepRisk.

In the following sections we will begin with the description of the specific definitions that apply to UniCredit Bank in order to understand the approach of UniCredit Bank. Subsequently, the governance system in place will be outlined in order to describe the rules and responsibilities of the bank's RepRisk management. Following on from this, the two core process tracks and valuation issues are characterised and a brief description of the reporting will be added to complete the process descriptions. Finally, the RepRisk unit's interfaces to the ICAAP[1] risk-management system will be outlined. The final section concludes and gives an overview of the bank's first experiences in this area.

REPRISK DEFINITIONS AT UNICREDIT BANK

In this section the specific definition of RepRisk as defined by UniCredit Bank AG will be outlined, with the main elements of the definition explained.

At the beginning of the RepRisk-management project referred to above, some important basic questions had to be answered. How should RepRisk be defined, given internal and external requirements? Which relationships to other risk types, such as operational risk, credit risk and liquidity risk, need to be considered? How could RepRisk management be integrated into the bank's overall risk-steering methods (ICAAP)? Who are the relevant stakeholders? What are the primary drivers for RepRisk? And what other risk categories might be triggered by RepRisk issues?

UniCredit Bank AG defines RepRisk thus:

> Reputational Risk is defined as the risk of a negative effect on the P&L caused by adverse reactions of stakeholders due to their altered perceptions which, in turn, may be triggered by the materialisation of a primary risk.

Figure 15.1 highlights important attributes of UniCredit's working definition of reputation and reputational risk. UniCredit Bank's definition of RepRisk includes a number of key elements, which are characteristic of the bank's specific view of RepRisk.

UniCredit Bank's RepRisk definitions contains some core elements which will be described as follows:

Profit-and-loss effect

Prevention of the materialisation of RepRisk in the negative sense is the primary focus of RepRisk management. Prevention not only includes possible direct effects to the profit and loss (P&L) but refers to the bank's reputation in general. For example, if the bank engages in business in a sector that is associated with RepRisk (such as mining), a negative press report may not directly result in a loss for the bank but, nevertheless, negatively affect the reputation of the bank. Thus it is important that transactions be handled via the bank's RepRisk management in an appropriate way.

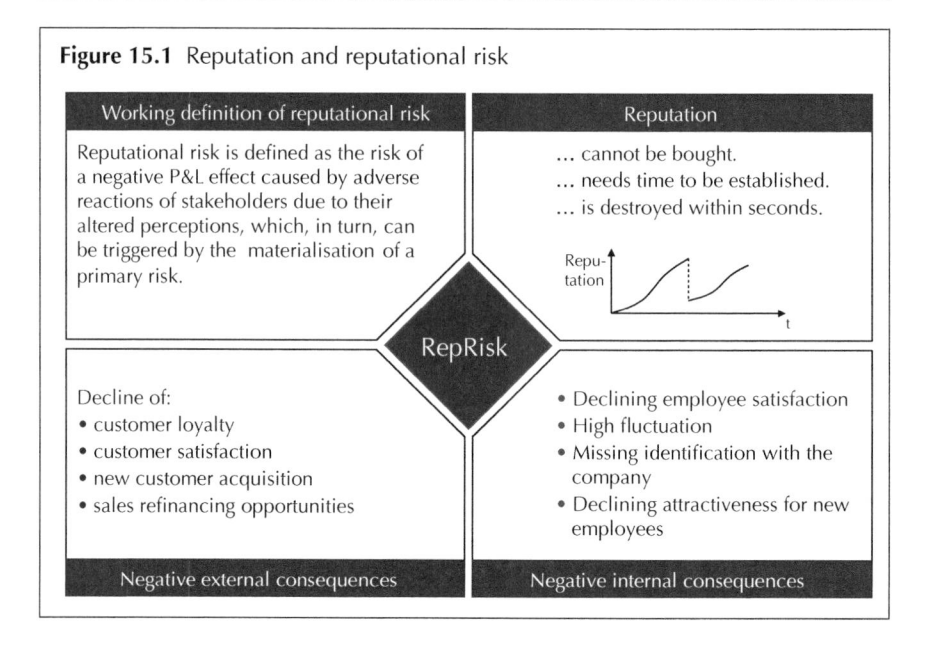

Figure 15.1 Reputation and reputational risk

Working definition of reputational risk	Reputation
Reputational risk is defined as the risk of a negative P&L effect caused by adverse reactions of stakeholders due to their altered perceptions, which, in turn, can be triggered by the materialisation of a primary risk.	... cannot be bought. ... needs time to be established. ... is destroyed within seconds.

RepRisk

Negative external consequences	Negative internal consequences
Decline of: • customer loyalty • customer satisfaction • new customer acquisition • sales refinancing opportunities	• Declining employee satisfaction • High fluctuation • Missing identification with the company • Declining attractiveness for new employees

Apart from this general approach to RepRisk management, primarily for the purpose of RepRisk control, UniCredit Bank AG's definition of RepRisk includes potential direct negative P&L effects, which might arise from negative reputational events (such as press campaigns). This is considered to be a necessary element in order to ensure a consistent evaluation of RepRisk within the RepRisk-management process.

According to the bank's RepRisk framework, these potential P&L effects are estimated; that is, although not numerically quantified, they are classified as falling into a certain range (ie, categorisation of risk into low/medium/high). Within the UniCredit RepRisk management framework, an identified RepRisk without potential direct negative P&L effect(s) is not pursued any further.

Stakeholders

Every RepRisk has to be associated with a relevant stakeholder, ie, a group of interest that, through its negative reaction, bears the potential to affect the profitability of the bank. This is important because only an estimate of a stakeholder's reaction to a RepRisk allows the bank to project an associated P&L effect. In this context, relevant stakeholders can, to some extent, have a direct influence on the bank's reputation. An example of this can be found when many customers leave the bank due to a negative press campaign or frequent/long-running IT problems that paralyse the cash dispenser.

Accordingly, UniCredit Bank has defined the set of its core stakeholders: first of all the customers, but also creditors, rating agencies, employees and regulators.[2] There are important other stakeholders (such as media, non-governmental organisations (NGOs), suppliers etc.); however, the bank views these as groups who exert their effect on the bank's reputation only indirectly via affecting the core stakeholders.

Figure 15.2 shows the relationship between the core stakeholders and the other stakeholders.

Links to other risk types

For a universal bank such as UniCredit Bank, the classic risk categories, such as credit risk, market risk, operational risk, liquidity risk and business risk, are a key focus of risk-control activities. In the context of RepRisk, UniCredit refers to these risk types as "primary risks".

RepRisk potentially arises from primary risks as an additional risk. This means that, if, for example, the bank has identified an operational risk, a reputational risk could arise as a consequence.

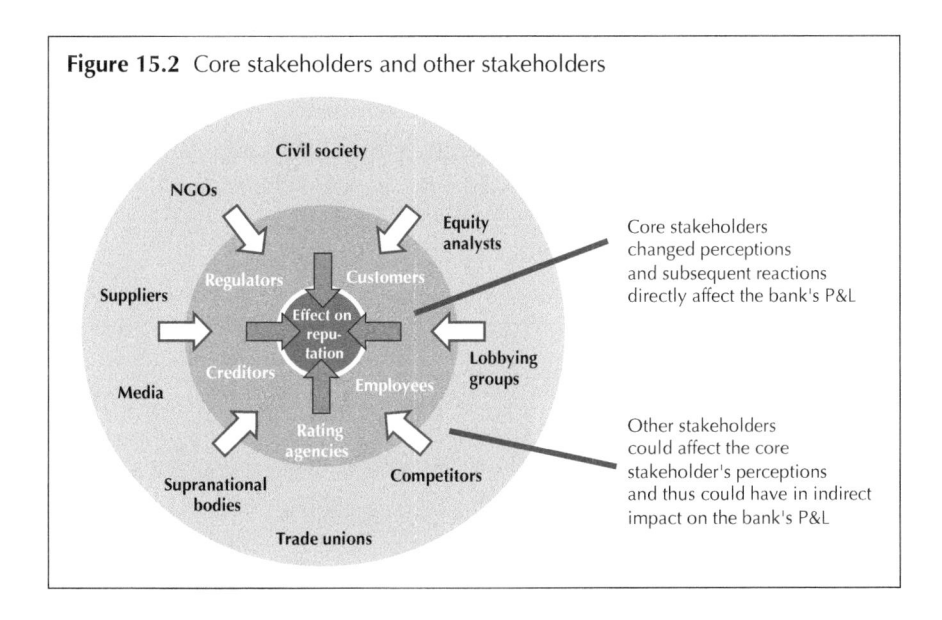

Figure 15.2 Core stakeholders and other stakeholders

However, the causality can also be directed in the opposite direction, ie, RepRisk events can also negatively affect primary risks. For example, in the case of a bank run, reflecting the limited reputation of a bank, liquidity risk will rise abruptly and significantly.

Finally, RepRisk does not have to be linked to a primary risk at all. For example, if a high-level representative of a bank makes statements that get a negative perception, the associated RepRisk is not related to any other primary risk. Thus RepRisk may occur:

❏ as knock-on effect to a different risk category (primary risk;
❏ as an independent risk (no causal relationship with any other risk type); or
❏ as a risk triggering other types of risk.

Overview of the UniCredit RepRisk-management process:
UniCredit's approach to RepRisk management is characterised by the idea that the RepRisk-management process should cover all parts of the bank, screen all portfolios and systems and trigger a decision in all cases in which RepRisk is involved. Put another way: UniCredit's RepRisk-management process is set up such that any "blank spots" (ie, departments not covered by the risk-management process) in the organisation are avoided. The key objective of RepRisk management (described in detail below) is to prevent negative reputational events, such as press campaigns or high customer "churn rates", which might provoke adverse reactions by the core stakeholders. However, UniCredit Bank does not run a zero-risk strategy. Instead, it will take RepRisk to an extent that is tolerable (eg, in the case of mining financings, the customer must comply with all relevant standards, in particular international security, social and environmental standards).

In that context, it is useful to highlight the border that, at UniCredit, separates RepRisk management and reputation management. RepRisk management attempts to avoid the materialisation of RepRisk by implementing suitable risk-management processes. Reputation-management processes, in contrast, deal with RepRisk that has already materialised. As in most financial institutions, in addition, the classic function of reputation management is the continuous and proactive development of the bank's reputation. Underlining this clear separation of duties at UniCredit, RepRisk management is part of the risk-management function whereas reputation management is located in the communications department, as is typical in the banking industry.

Thus, from the perspective of UniCredit Bank, some key characteristics of RepRisk are listed here.

❑ RepRisk is not just a result of risk, but can also be a risk *per se* (as will be shown below, this characteristic affects the structure of risk identification and assessment).
❑ Only events that are associated with expected material effects on the income statement are considered RepRisk events.
❑ RepRisk does not affect the income statement directly; that is, RepRisk exerts its effects on the income statement only indirectly, through other risk types (mainly business risk). This has ramifications for the handling of RepRisk within the ICAAP capital calculation as well as for stress testing (ICAAP interfaces are discussed later).
❑ The management of reputation is not part of RepRisk management but lies in the hands of the communication and press departments and/or the stakeholder management functions.

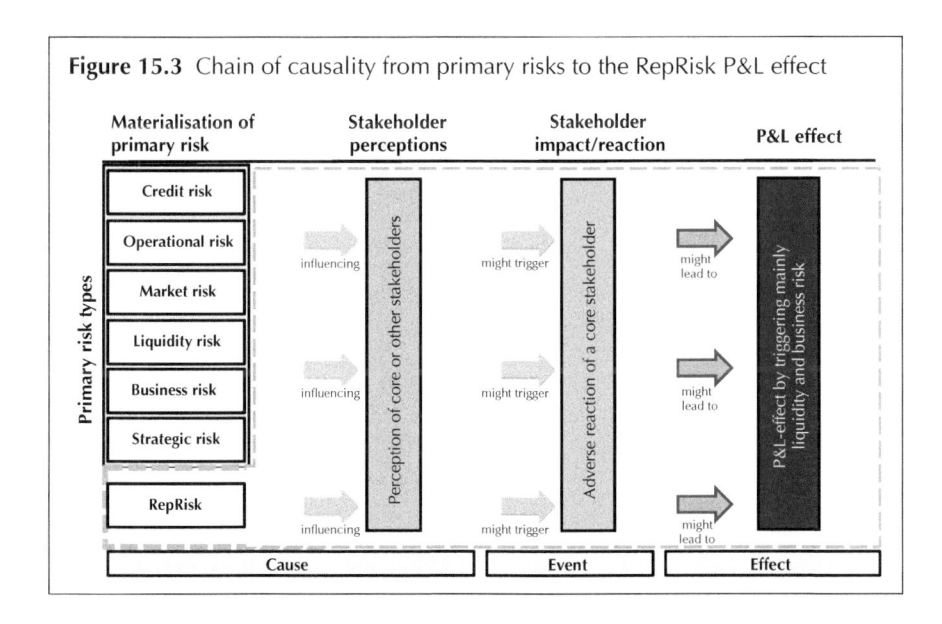

Figure 15.3 Chain of causality from primary risks to the RepRisk P&L effect

THE REPRISK GOVERNANCE SYSTEM

At UniCredit Bank AG, RepRisk Control is part of the risk-management function. Driven by the fact that the infrastructure and the systems in place for the management of operational risk could easily be adapted to the purpose of RepRisk management – and the fact that there exist essential links between both risk types – the governance system in place for RepRisk is mainly based on the previously existing structures, roles and regulations for operational risk, including the extended functions of the operational risk managers who additionally shoulder the responsibility as RepRisk manager.

"We all are reputational risk managers", as we have previously mentioned, is the slogan at UniCredit Bank to express that each employee bears responsibility for RepRisk management as an integral part of their function. Thus the distinct business divisions, business lines and competence lines (central functions) are all involved in the RepRisk-management effort and bear a correspondingly large responsibility (ie, they form the first line of defence). Within these entities, operational risk managers (ORMs), officially

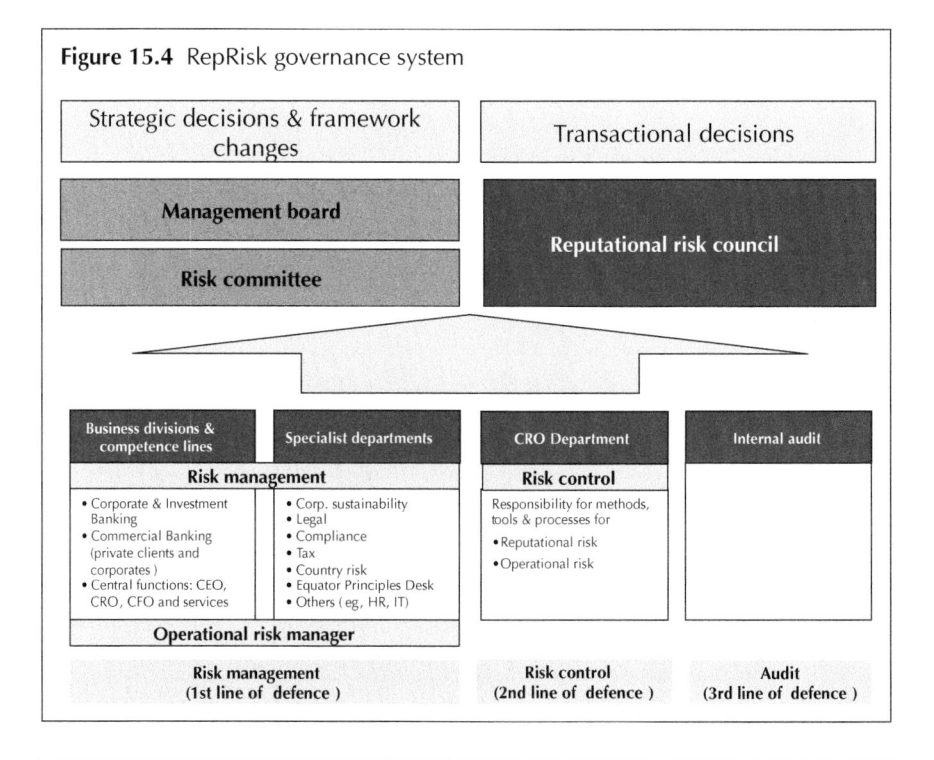

Figure 15.4 RepRisk governance system

Strategic decisions & framework changes	Transactional decisions
Management board	Reputational risk council
Risk committee	

Business divisions & competence lines	Specialist departments	CRO Department	Internal audit
Risk management		Risk control	
• Corporate & Investment Banking • Commercial Banking (private clients and corporates) • Central functions: CEO, CRO, CFO and services	• Corp. sustainability • Legal • Compliance • Tax • Country risk • Equator Principles Desk • Others (eg, HR, IT)	Responsibility for methods, tools & processes for • Reputational risk • Operational risk	
Operational risk manager			
Risk management (1st line of defence)		Risk control (2nd line of defence)	Audit (3rd line of defence)

appointed by senior management and organised along the business divisions and the competence lines of the bank, hold the key role for the coordination of the efforts with respect to identification and evaluation of RepRisks. In addition, certain advisory tasks for RepRisk management are carried out by the corresponding existing specialist functions – such as specialists for corporate sustainability management, compliance issues or taxes.

The Operational Risk Control Department acts as an independent control centre with responsibility for methods, processes, tools and reporting (second line of defence). The internal audit function, finally, represents a third line of defence for RepRisk (as for all other risk types).

Strategic decisions in the area of RepRisk (for example, with respect to risk-management concepts or risk models) are taken by the risk committee, an institutionalised body charged with making or preparing decisions in all areas risk management. Ultimately, important decisions have to be approved by the management board. Both bodies – the risk committee and the management board – are the recipients of the official RepRisk reporting.

For decisions on individual business-related RepRisk issues – eg, those concerning potential RepRisk in business transactions or new products – the bank has established the Reputational Risk Council (RRC). The RRC decides on single requests on the basis of a formalised application and approval process.

All rules and responsibilities concerning RepRisk management at UniCredit Bank are fixed in a number of distinct internal operating guidelines and general policies. Beyond that, the bank has issued a series of special policies that address RepRisk-management approaches in certain critical sectors as well as RepRisk-related tax and compliance issues. The regulations of the RepRisk framework have been implemented at UniCredit Bank AG as well as at the most important subsidiaries of HVB-Group.

Figure 15.5 illustrates the technical, managerial, structural and procedural components of the bank's RepRisk-management framework. The most important elements will be presented in the following paragraphs.

Figure 15.5 RepRisk management requirements

Description	Level
Part of firm-wide risk strategy	Strategy
Implementation of a RepRisk control and extended processes for identification, measurement and reporting New policies/RepRisk	Governance
RepRisk definition and categories, stakeholders	Definitions & structures
Top RepRisks, RepRisk council cases	Reporting
Preventive and reactive mitigation, action tracking	Mitigation
RTB:* Self-assessments, senior management interviews – CTB:** transactions and activities	Identification & measurement
Single case assessment, action tracking	IT system

* Run the bank
** Change the bank

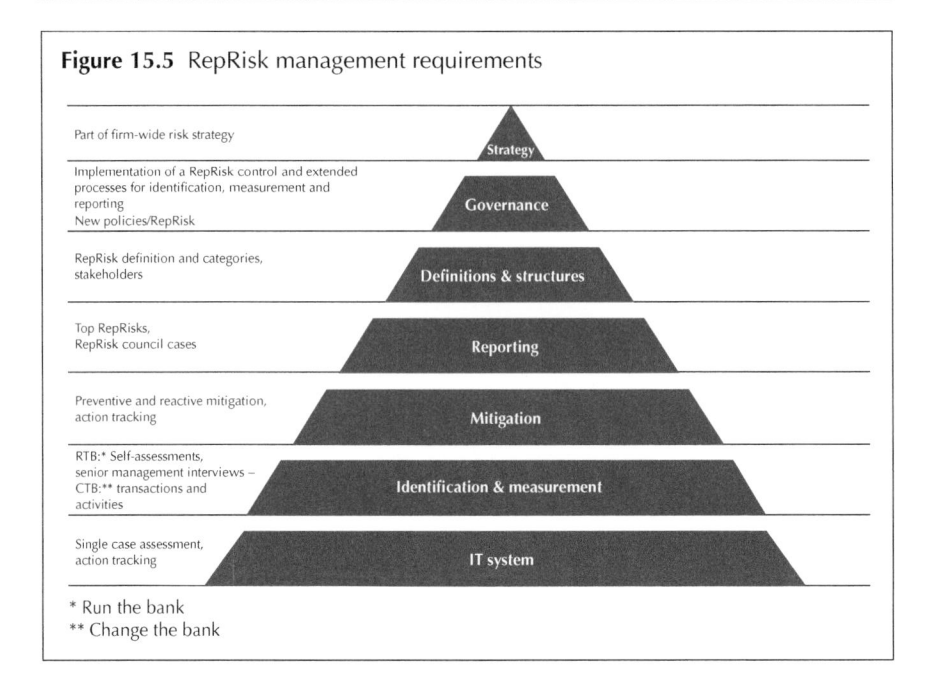

REPRISK IDENTIFICATION AND ASSESSMENT

UniCredit Bank has implemented a holistic approach towards RepRisk management. The RepRisk-management process has to cover all activities and portfolios in the bank. In principle, all new activities bearing potential RepRisk – in particular business operations and transactions – must be examined with regard to RepRisk issues. At UniCredit, the scope of these tasks is outlined under the so-called "change-the-bank" (CTB) approach. Parallel to that, all existing areas of the bank are subject to regular (minimum of once a year) checks for potential RepRisk in portfolios, systems and processes. These tasks fall under the "run-the-bank" (RTB) approach.

Change the bank

The CTB approach was developed to deal with RepRisk in all new activities, such as business transactions, products, markets, projects, outsourcings and special investments (eg, special-purpose vehicles (SPV)). In the case of business transactions, the focus is on financings and guarantees in industry sectors and on payments that are associated with RepRisk, eg, in the context of international financial

Figure 15.6 RepRisk identification

View	Identification & measurement	
	Micro-perspective	Embedded mitigation
Inside-out	**Transaction-oriented CTB**	Business transactions
		Special investments (eg, SPV)
		Outsourcing
		New-product process
		Projects
	Macro-Perspective	Ex-post mitigation
	Portfolio-orientied RTB	Self-assessment
		Senior mangement interviews
Outside-in	**Stakeholder**	Stakeholder manager
		Stakeholder survey

sanctions regulations. At times also customer-specific aspects have to be considered (know-your-customer (KYC) process[3]).

CTB policies
For issues of particular importance, generally bearing higher potential RepRisk, UniCredit has adapted a set of special group-wide policies regulating the management of RepRisk. A first group of policies relates to corporate sustainability management. These policies set a framework for business transactions with customers in "critical" industry sectors that are associated with RepRisk, such as weapons, nuclear power and mining. Another set of policies deals with compliance issues, in particular financial sanctions, anti-fraud and anti-money-laundering regulations. Tax-related reputational issues are addressed in the tax policy.

In practice, however, although of importance, there are many RepRisk issues that cannot be regulated via a policy. At UniCredit, they are managed as particular cases via the CTB process.

CTB process

All CTB activities (as described above) initially have to be examined with regard to RepRisk by the employee involved in and responsible for the activity (proponent, eg, relationship manager or product manager). In particular, this employee has to verify that the relevant policy rules have been observed by matching the new business transaction with the regulations in the respective policy.

If a potential risk or a breach of policy has been identified, the proponent has to prepare an application for decision to the RRC, the body in charge of taking decisions on CTB RepRisk issues. The RRC has two members, the chief risk officer and the head of the business division responsible in the particular situation. The process of preparing the application is always supported by a specialist from a particular field (eg, from, corporate sustainability, compliance topics, tax affairs or accounting) who, as such, possesses expert knowledge in that field and supports the process by adding their assessment, classifying the particular risk according to its threat potential and providing an opinion to the decision maker.

The CTB process is institutionalised in a formalised way, using application forms particular to the bank that have been developed specifically for RepRisk cases. Within this process, a formal risk classification by the applicant (into low/medium/high – see below) is not required since the CTB process is not exclusively focused on P&L-relevant RepRisk issues. Operational risk control is involved in the process with quality checks and the submission of the request to the RRC.

The RRC will make the final decision on whether an activity in question can be continued or is to be discontinued. If necessary, according to a particular policy or in case of a customer of group-wide interest, the relevant bodies of UniCredit SpA will get involved, in addition.

Figure 15.7 gives an overview of the process.

Run the bank

Not only new activities may bear RepRisk. Instead, RepRisk may also be hidden in the bank's existing portfolios or systems. In order to bring those hidden risks to the fore, UniCredit Bank AG has implemented the run-the-bank (RTB) process, which runs parallel to the CTB process. On an annual basis, the RTB process is executed in two

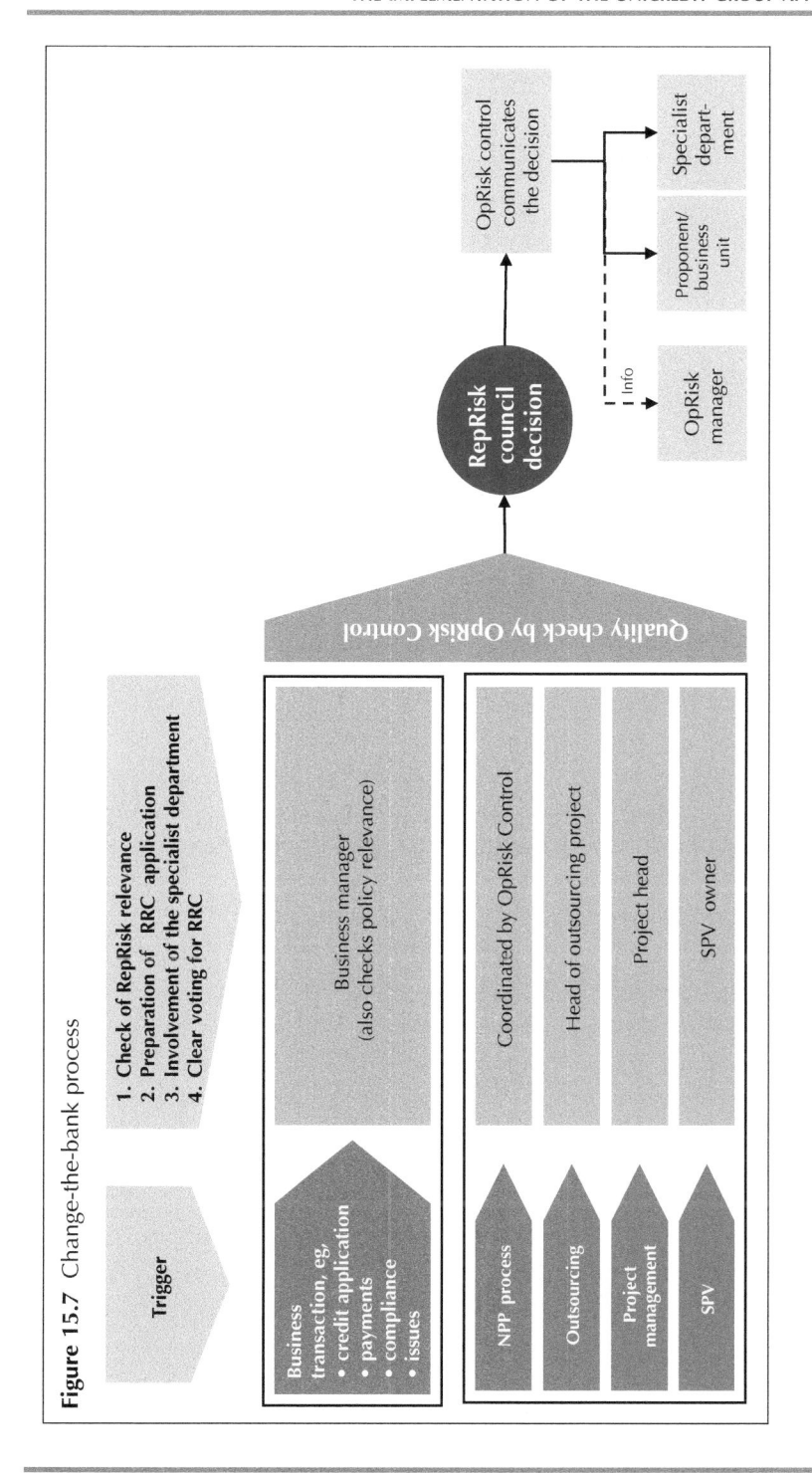

THE IMPLEMENTATION OF THE UNICREDIT GROUP APPROACH

Figure 15.7 Change-the-bank process

Figure 15.8 Run-the-bank process

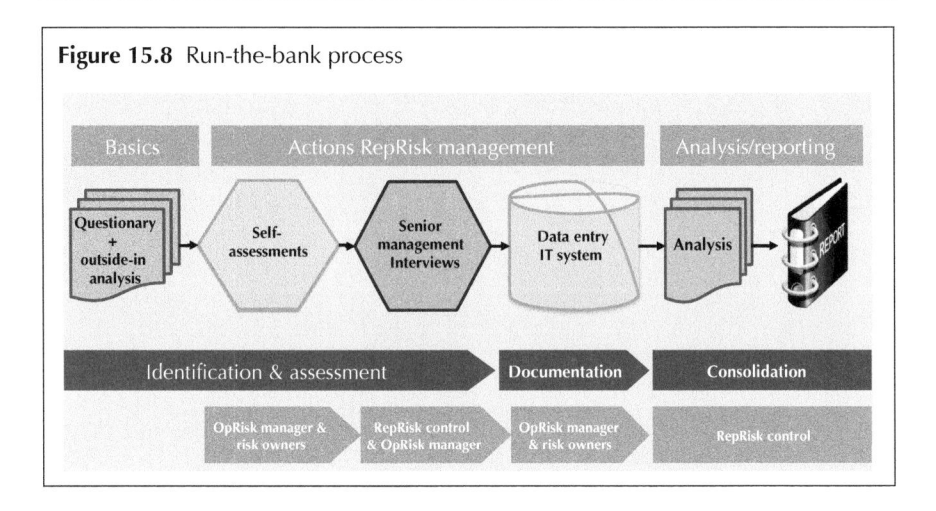

consecutive steps: risk self-assessments and senior management interviews.

Figure 15.8 shows an overview of the different RTB-process steps

Step 1: Risk self-assessments
The RTB process starts with risk self-assessments that are performed by appointed "risk owners", ie, employees holding important functions such as team heads, process managers, product managers. These risk self-assessments are supported by the operational risk managers of the corresponding business areas and carried out using a questionnaire that covers all relevant RepRisk aspects and that is used in a common format across the bank. The operational risk manager of a business area or competence line will discuss with the respective risk owners of their area each question of the questionnaire in order to identify potential material RepRisks that either are triggered by certain primary risks or represent RepRisks that arise independently.

Reprisk questionnaire and assignment of stakeholders
Starting points for the RepRisk questionnaire are the primary risk categories (including RepRisk itself). For each primary risk category, specific questions and examples are outlined. The interviewee has to check each position and tick off whether or not a particular RepRisk is recognised. In order to implement the necessary recording of the association of particular RepRisks with particular stakeholders, for each identified RepRisk, the potentially affected stakeholders are

THE IMPLEMENTATION OF THE UNICREDIT GROUP APPROACH

Figure 15.9 RTB questionnaire (structured/compact illustration)

Primary risk	Relevant question/ examples	Affected stakeholders					No stakeholder affected
		Customers	Creditors	Rating agencies	Employees	Regulators	
Credit risk							
Market risk							
OpRisk							
Liquidity risk							
Business risk							
Strategy risk							
RepRisk							

Figure 15.10 RTB classification tables

General parameter (expectations)	Customers Earnings	Creditors Refinancing rate	Rating agencies Rating	Employees Fluctuation rate or hiring costs	Regulators Measures & sanctions
Insignificant					
Low					
Medium					
High					

	Probability
Low	
Medium	
High	

assigned in the questionnaire (ie, if a potential reputational risk is identified, the type of stakeholder who would likely be affected should be indicated).

The RepRisk questionnaire forms the basis for the subsequent risk self-assessments as well as for the planning of mitigation actions at divisional and departmental levels. Moreover, the results serve as input to the senior management interviews (described below). Also, the RepRisk questionnaire is documentation for internal and external audit and proof of RepRisk assessment and management.

Once the risk owner (described at the beginning of Step 1) has identified a particular RepRisk, they also have to propose a risk evaluation and make an effort to determine appropriate countermeasures, to the extent that this is possible.

Reprisk evaluation

At UniCredit Bank, RepRisk is evaluated according to expected reactions of stakeholders (see Figure 15.3). This methodology is implemented via the use of preformatted classification matrices whose two dimensions are (i) the expected intensity of the stakeholders' reaction and (ii) the estimated probability of the event (see Figure 15.10). Given the basic difficulty in evaluating the possible consequences of stakeholders' reactions, UniCredit refrains from quantifying RepRisk numerically but rather classifies it into "low", "medium" or "high" risk.

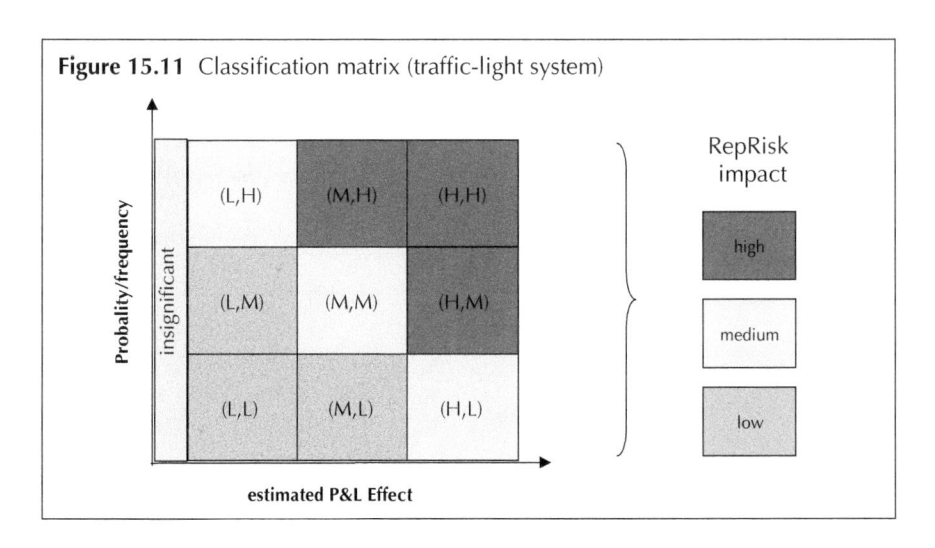

Figure 15.11 Classification matrix (traffic-light system)

In order to deduce and represent a final classification of a RepRisk, UniCredit Bank AG uses a simplified nine-field matrix (in comparison with the group solution), the axes of which correspond to the above-mentioned two dimensions.

Step 2: Senior management interviews
Based on the results of the risk self-assessments, the senior managers of each area, supported by the relevant operational risk managers, are interviewed with regard to RepRisk by Operational Risk Control. In the course of these interviews, the senior managers review the RepRisks identified in the risk self-assessments. The senior managers can modify risks, delete risks or add further risks. They have the final say, also with respect to proposed countermeasures. Beyond their assessments for their own areas, the senior managers are interviewed on RepRisks related to other departments, to UniCredit Bank AG in total and to UniCredit Group in total (referred to as "cross-divisional general RepRisks").

Results
The above-explained senior manager interviews are conducted on a yearly basis, ie, an annual screening cycle. At the end of each screening cycle, Operational Risk Control consolidates the results of the interviews, clusters identical or similar risks[4] and prepares a management report that contains the most important RepRisks of the bank. In case of "cluster risks", Operational Risk Control determines an average evaluation. Finally, similar to the procedures applied in the recording of operational risks, the (finally confirmed) RepRisks as well as the associated countermeasures are captured by the risk owners in the bank's IT system.

IT SYSTEM

In order to create an infrastructure to capture RepRisk, UniCredit Bank could build upon an existing IT system that originally had been designed for OpRisk purposes and that, just making a few modifications and supplements, easily could be cloned and adapted to deal with RepRisk.

The RepRisk IT system is used for capturing RTB risks. It contains risk descriptions, risk evaluation details, primary risk sources, affected stakeholders and determined countermeasures. With respect to countermeasures, the system enables an ongoing monitoring. Reports can be generated, customised to user needs and exported.

REPRISK MITIGATION AND REPRISK REPORTING
CTB: embedded risk mitigation
As described above, the CTB process is designed to identify RepRisks for new activities before they are executed. Thus risk mitigation is part of the regular CTB process in the sense that excessive risks won't be entered into in the first place. Still, taking into account all aspects of an activity, the RepRisk Council may approve an application despite the identification of potential risks or may set conditions to be associated with a transaction or other activity. In case of rejection, a transaction/activity must not be executed.

RTB: *ex post* risk mitigation
In contrast to the CTB process, in the context of the RTB process, risks can be mitigated only via the determination of countermeasures. These countermeasures have to be approved by senior management as, typically, costs and effort are associated with them.

In some cases, especially in cases related to strategic issues, it may be difficult to define effective countermeasures without affecting other objectives. Thus some risks will be taken without mitigation measures. On the other hand, in other cases, we may be able to draw on existing measures, eg, in cases where an operational risk is the primary risk. For example, if the bank has identified an operational risk within IT infrastructure and an associated RepRisk (as some consequences also might affect customers and regulators), countermeasures defined for the operational risk also, indirectly, treat the RepRisk. Nevertheless, further countermeasures may have to be discussed in addition.

Once countermeasures have been determined, the risk owners have to monitor the execution of these measures on a regular basis. To the extent necessary, measures will have to be adjusted or replaced.

Second-level controls
Based on UniCredit Bank's RepRisk framework, Operational Risk Control is responsible for controls to monitor the results of risk self-

assessments, the correctness of data processing and the implementation of determined countermeasures. The general parameters for these second-level controls include quality (accuracy), completeness and timeliness.

Reporting
The data and information gathered via the RepRisk processes (CTB and RTB) are analysed by Operational Risk Control on a regular basis and reported to senior management and the management board who, in turn, can make decisions with respect to further mitigation activities.

INTERFACES TO INTERNAL CAPITAL ADEQUACY ASSESSMENT PROCESS (ICAAP)
According to UniCredit's model of the chain of causality (see figure 15.3), the P&L effects of RepRisk implicitly are included in the P&L effects associated with other risk types. In that context, the question arises whether the bank has to reserve distinct economic capital for RepRisk as a separate risk category, or if RepRisk is sufficiently dealt with via the capital reserved for other risk types. This question needs to be adequately addressed as required from a regulatory perspective, ie, by the so-called Internal Capital Adequacy Assessment Process (ICAAP).

Some examples
❑ Declines in revenue due to RepRisk events will be reflected in the historical time series of revenues that, in turn, is fundamental in the determination of business risk.
❑ Effects of RepRisks on liquidity and funding costs are taken into account in liquidity risk calculations.
❑ Increasing operational risk losses due to RepRisk will be accounted for in the operational risk model.

UniCredit Bank refrains from distinct economic capital calculations for RepRisk. Depending on the outcomes of future RepRisk assessments, its management may decide to change its attitude in this regard and, possibly, decide on further measures.

More severe or extraordinary scenarios are already being considered in the context of stress-testing activities and the bank's recovery planning. With respect to stress testing, alternative chains of causality are taken into account. For example, scenarios modelling the effects of RepRisk on liquidity and turnover or costs are being considered in stress testing with regard to liquidity risk and business risk.

SUMMARY AND EXPERIENCES SINCE IMPLEMENTATION

The main objective of RepRisk management is either to avoid RepRisk entirely through prevention-oriented processes or to ensure that RepRisk is entered only to a limited extent on the basis of conscious decisions. The embedding of RepRisk management into the risk culture of UniCredit Bank promotes and already has promoted awareness of this risk category.

Risk culture, in turn, is not a target in itself but rather serves the purpose of achieving risk-management objectives. The risk processes in place are supposed to ensure the primary objectives of (i) an effective risk management and (ii) a high degree of transparency of the risks of the institution. At UniCredit Bank, these two key objectives are addressed via two approaches:

❏ change-the-bank approach, which implements RepRisk management via different sector policies (eg, weapons industry or mining financings) and various compliance policies as well as via risk limitations in the context of individual decisions; and
❏ run-the-bank approach, which provides transparency with respect to latent RepRisks in the bank's existing systems and portfolios and, to the extent possible, triggers risk-mitigation actions by determining appropriate countermeasures.

Viewed in its entirety, RepRisk management represents both a prevention strategy and a mitigation strategy, which, in a process sense, precede the business continuity management and the crisis management of the bank. UniCredit Bank AG expects that increasing risk awareness and improving communication of risk information will contribute to a gradually clearer picture of the risk situation of the institution.

From an organisational perspective, the development of new processes and functions, the organisational set-up, the IT-system and the training of operational risk managers, risk owners and specialists were finalised by the end of 2012. Given thorough preparation, including the above-mentioned communication measures, the new system and processes were started without problems at the beginning of 2013.

Following the release of the new RepRisk-management system, only a few minor modifications had to be implemented on the side of the change-the-bank processes (update of rules of procedure, especially approval regulations). Following a short adaptation period, the bank's employees accepted the new, more formalised procedures (as opposed to those of the former process mode).

On the side of the run-the-bank processes, the complete newness of these processes led to an exciting first screening cycle. Indeed, for a number of months, all involved participants (Operational Risk Control, operational risk managers, risk owners and senior managers) went through a learning process. One of the first and important recognitions was the fact that RepRisk frequently arises in either an identical or similar way. Thus, it was straightforward to summarise and cluster RepRisk. Another insight was that, for many of the important RepRisks, operational and strategic risks often appear as the main drivers (primary risks). Furthermore, it became clear that, with respect to its effects on other risk categories, RepRisk primarily affects risks in the business risk category (as opposed to risks in the categories of market risk, credit risk and so forth). In summary, we obtained a rather clear and robust picture of the bank's potential RepRisk as borne by the senior managers of the institution.

The implementation of UniCredit Bank's extended RepRisk management concept has been accepted as a considerable contribution to the bank's risk culture and as an integral part of the bank's risk-management processes. Indeed, the holistic approach with two process tracks, the release of further sector policies (eg, for mining and dam buildings), the regular reporting and the considerable number of risk self-assessments, interviews and RepRisk Council decisions have all contributed to an increased awareness for RepRisk issues. At UniCredit Bank, we have had interesting and committed discussions with senior managers who indeed support the RepRisk-management process. The above-mentioned specialists have also been well integrated in the risk-management process. In the end, the increasing number of enquiries and not-policy-driven RepRisk

Council requests prove that, today, RepRisk management is alive at UniCredit Bank AG and well integrated into the institution.

1 ICAAP – the Internal Capital Adequacy Assessment Process – is a requirement for financial institutions under Basel II to ensure that, in particular, among other requirements, material risks of the firm are understood by its board and that a sufficient and appropriate risk-management effort is in place.
2 In this enumeration, shareholders are not included since, in the case of UniCredit Bank AG, there is only one shareholder: UniCredit SpA.
3 The KYC process is based on Article 8 in the EU Anti-Money-Laundering Directive and requires a deeper eligibility check for the customers of banks and insurers.
4 A number of risks listed by the senior managers result from the same or very similar primary risk (eg, misselling items) with similar RepRisk effects and therefore get summarised in a common description and valuation (so-called cluster risks).

16

Promotional Banks: An Introduction to Reputational Risk Management

Heidi Rudolph
KfW Bankengruppe

While the reputation of a commercial bank has a big influence on its business model, as commercial banks could conduct their business and manage their business branches on their own, the mission of promotional banks is clearly defined by the fact that is a promotional bank as such. Further, the mission of such banks is in many cases influenced and regulated by their special shareholders (ie, the state) and even prescribed by law. As an example the European Investment Bank (EIB) is legitimated based on Article 308 of the treaty on the functioning of the European Union. The KfW in Germany is based on the law concerning KfW and the KfW's articles of association. The use of government guarantees[1] and the type of business of German promotional banks was further regulated within Understanding II, a common understanding between the European Commission and the German federal government, reached in 2002. The mission of and differences between common institutions are described throughout the chapter.

Some of the reputational risks arising from business transactions cannot be merely turned off by changing or stopping certain components of the business, eg, their promotion in financing environmental protection. UBS as an example of a commercial bank that gave up almost its whole investment banking in 2012 as a consequence of huge losses in the investment sector due to internal fraud cases and related court proceedings. The reputational risks of promotional banks need to be dealt with by strong reputational risk management instead.

Development banks are special financial institutions that aggregate foreign aid and offer assistance in general by issuing loans to the countries in need. One of the most important is the World Bank Group. Promotional banks might also interact in foreign aid but further promote the investment activities in defined fields, eg, environmental projects or infrastructure extension. The promotional banks are a supplement for commercial credit institutions and act in particular in the public interest, as also development banks do. The mission of a promotional or development bank is not its growth or the achievement of huge profits but the promotion of investment in needy countries, structures or social, environmental or economic projects. They call this their public mission.

Promotional banks are in the public eye, as they are involved in all types of investments in which the public are implicated directly, as private borrowers, or indirectly (for example the promotion of urban planning and infrastructure projects). Their investments are customised and set up in line with the development of political, economic or social topics. As the business of promotional banks is influenced by these external factors, their business strategy needs to be adapted to fit the external expectations of their shareholders, and consequently the risk strategy has to be adjusted to fit the special product portfolio that promotional institutions offer.

Many of the promotional banks are backed by government guarantees to fulfil their particular mission. Their most significant goal is to fund investments in important social fields by granting loans, in many cases at discounted interest rates. Activity in important social fields on the one hand while, on the other hand, the bank is working in a risk-sensitive manner represents a big challenge, as these fields are not free of risks. In many cases, these fields engender particular risks and need special investments and development programmes (which will be further discussed in the section "Reputational risks in promotional banks"). Promotional banks are asked to find a way to balance needed investments with the risks involved. Integrated sustainability measures are therefore more important to directly control the institutions' risk appetite.

Promotional institutions (which are the same as promotional banks) enjoy public confidence as they act in the public interest. They invest in fields where other institutions are not allowed to or not willing to invest. Further, promotional banks backed by government guarantees can offer attractive products to their clients or take care of investments that are requested by the government. Also, the public are more focused on these institutions as they and their products are part of public and political discussions and consciousness. The reputation of promotional banks is strongly connected to the reputation of their stakeholders. Any related risks need to be mitigated by well-defined communication processes as well as enhanced image cultivation.

As promotional banks are in general financial institutions, they are also subject to auditors and regulations. In some cases, even more comprehensive regulations need to be considered with regard to the broad activities of the promotional banks. As in the end all promotional banks are owned by public authorities (ie, particular federal governments), they have to fulfil more or less political goals. The understanding and mission of the institutions is determined either by special laws or by the institutions themselves. Nevertheless, the institutions have to focus on corporate governance and compliance as much as every other credit institution needs to do.

Europe's leading public financial institutions are the European Investment Bank (EIB, bank of European Union), Caisse des Dépôts (CDC, France), Cassa Depositi e Prestiti (CDP, Italy) and KfW Bankengruppe (KfW, Germany). In general, they follow the same mission while their organisational structures differ.

In Germany a special set of promotional banks was created, consisting of 19 institutions. Seventeen of them operate at a state level in line with the German federal state structure. Their goal is to promote investments in their state by offering loans at reduced rates of interest. The two others, KfW and Rentenbank, are active throughout the whole country. In addition, KfW also invests globally, eg, with promotional programmes in foreign aid. Essentially, the rules are not determined by each state, but the relevant missions and projects are geographically determined by the relevant state (for example, KfW can finance projects throughout Germany).

The VÖB, the Association of German Public Banks, summarised the goal of German Promotional banks (VÖB 2013) as follows:

> In carrying out their public mission, promotional banks engage in financing small and medium-sized enterprises, infrastructure and

the housing sector. They also provide special programmes for environmental protection and agriculture, for financing technology and innovation and for supporting cross-border promotional measures. In doing so, they cover a wide range of financing services. They provide loans, guarantees and equity finance, allocate and transfer public subsidies, they give advice in matters of development and finance and can also engage in agency agreements under public contract.

Because of their mission, promotional banks offer special financial investments and products by using widespread overall budgets and by covering a huge part of the included risks, especially when political or social developments ask for more investment programmes (although the programmes do not achieve the needed profits, or political and social structures seem to be insecure). As Philippe Maystadt, former president of the EIB, said at the annual meeting of the Board of Governors in 2009, a broader range of financial products is demanded than ever before. This includes the promotional banks taking increased but controlled risks with the goal of supporting change and encouraging forward-looking ideas.

REPUTATIONAL RISKS IN PROMOTIONAL BANKS

What are the basic stakeholders of promotional banks and do they differ from other institutions? In general, the stakeholders do not differ that much. Taking into account that promotional banks are all the same credit institutions and also have to consider the rules and regulations of banking authorities, the expectations of the usual stakeholder groups – such as customers, investors, shareholders, auditors, the public and employees, as well as rating agencies – influence the business of promotional banks.

The origin of reputational risks in promotional banks is not that different from what can happen in other institutions. But, as public expectation is varied, these institutions face a lot of reputational risks just by their special mission.

As the promotional institutions act in the public interest and their core business lies in the public mission itself, the focus of the domestic public is higher than for commercial institutions. The strategic decisions and plans of the government have a direct impact on the promotional programmes described earlier in the chapter. Additionally, promotional banks at the national level carry out dedicated tasks on behalf of the federal government. The government's decision in Germany to intensify the support for business start-ups or provide student loans, for example, has led to the creation of specific promotional programmes at the institutions in charge, eg, KfW. Similarly, the agreed-upon accelerated phase-out from nuclear energy and the energy turnaround in Germany influence the environmental programmes and products. Governments and shareholders provide new directions. Consequently, the financing of renewable energies has been further enhanced while the investments in coal-fired power plants or nuclear energy have been reduced. The financial products, investments and behaviour of promotional banks are continuously discussed alongside political events.

Due to their involvement in the support and financing of environmental and climate protection, promotional institutions have also caught the eye of environmental organisations. Nongovernmental organisations (NGOs) such as independent pressure groups shape and have an impact on public opinion, for example regarding governments or financial institutions. Predominantly they engage in social and eco-political topics. As the protection of the climate and the environment has become more and more important and significant to society as a whole, environmental issues are being discussed more openly by the public. Consequently, the perception of private persons is as important as the perception of environmental organisations or NGOs. As promotional banks offer special loans not only to developing and transitioning countries, municipalities or companies, but also to private persons directly, they have to focus on the different expectations of each.

The reputation of promotional banks is under permanent surveillance, and public interest – including the expectations of NGOs – is the key driver of reputational risk management and even more so for banks' sustainability management. Public perception is continuously developing and is influenced by many factors. Just consider the public opinion towards nuclear power. Even before the nuclear disaster in Fukushima, triggered by a natural catastrophe, the use of nuclear power plants has been heavily criticised. Nevertheless, with the events in Japan, the public dislike of these energy sources has increased rapidly. Just before the natural disaster the use of nuclear power plants, for example, in Germany was part of the energy portfolio and more or less accepted throughout the country. After Fukushima each new investment in nuclear energy has been criticised not only by environmental protection organisations but also by a majority of the public. Promotional institutions have to react to changing public perception. The promotional programmes for energy business need to be adapted or even stopped as the financing of nuclear power will not be further accepted by the public.

For another example, you could have a look at the financing of projects that invest and support coal-fired power plants.[2] Until 2013 financial institutions all over the globe promoted investments in the building or renewal of these plants. Since 2013 public pressure on promotional banks and country governments increased. Gradually, governments are reacting, and have influenced the increasing promotion of coal power.

The promotional banks follow not only because of the reputational risks arising but also due to issues of sustainability and their responsibility. The financing of coal power will not stop completely but the projects will be further regulated and restricted to special cases, with the following exceptions even more intensively discussed. One of the promotional banks on the state level in Germany, KfW, states in its published position paper on coal-fired power plants:

> In developing and emerging countries – particularly in countries with their own large coal reserves and in neighbouring states – coal-fired power plants are an important option in the long run to improve energy access. They offer a high level of security of supply with relatively low electricity generation costs. In this way, coal-fired power plants can serve as an important building block for economic development and thus for fighting poverty. However, the aim of the cooperation with the partner countries is to promote means of sustainable development through the gradual integration of renewable energies in the energy supply system.[3]

The perception of the public on these matters does not necessarily take all the different implications of the investments into account.

With regard to their respective public missions and widespread product portfolios, promotional banks have different objectives. In addition to the focus on environmental projects such as renewable energy and the construction of new energy-efficient homes, they support, for example, the creation of new jobs and the development of local industries. It can be recognised that promotional institutions support urban development, including noise-control measures for private households, and also finance the development of infrastructure initiatives such as road construction and the creation of new airports, as the right infrastructure is a key factor for the promotion of local industries, which in turn provide new jobs, help fight poverty and develop regions that are lagging behind.

The perception of and relationship between environmental, climate and sociopolitical concerns has always been problematic. Therefore, it is not surprising that the different promotional programmes are continuously analysed in a critical way and the promotional business constitutes a steady reputational risk for the promotional banks concerned. The promotion of renewable energy sources can be mentioned as an example. In principle, the focus on the sustainable use of energy is appreciated by the public. Nevertheless, the funding of solar-power storage units is criticised severely in some countries as the investments in this area does not necessarily strengthen sustainability as a whole. A similarly controversial subject matter, the further development of wind power, is considered by many to be a good thing. But the development of such plants is not welcome everywhere. Therefore the funding of these plants by promotional banks will also be vetoed by some of their stakeholders.

The described different objectives on renewable energy sources above do not exclude each other completely but require strong credit processes, including clearly defined rules and requirements, and strong sustainability management, as well as the implementation of sustainability principles. Furthermore, the promotional banks in question need to intensify the dialogue with their stakeholders in order to make public and explain their promotional views and positions. The different perceptions of their stakeholders need to be identified and understood.

STAKEHOLDERS' REACTION

As described above, the special nature and diversity of the portfolio of promotional banks increases their reputational risk exposure. But how do stakeholders react?

The perception of promotional banks' business differs a lot between the different stakeholders. Additionally, their reactions can be found to have a more qualitative than quantitative impact, as shown in figure 16.1.

As promotional banks are owned by public institutions and are

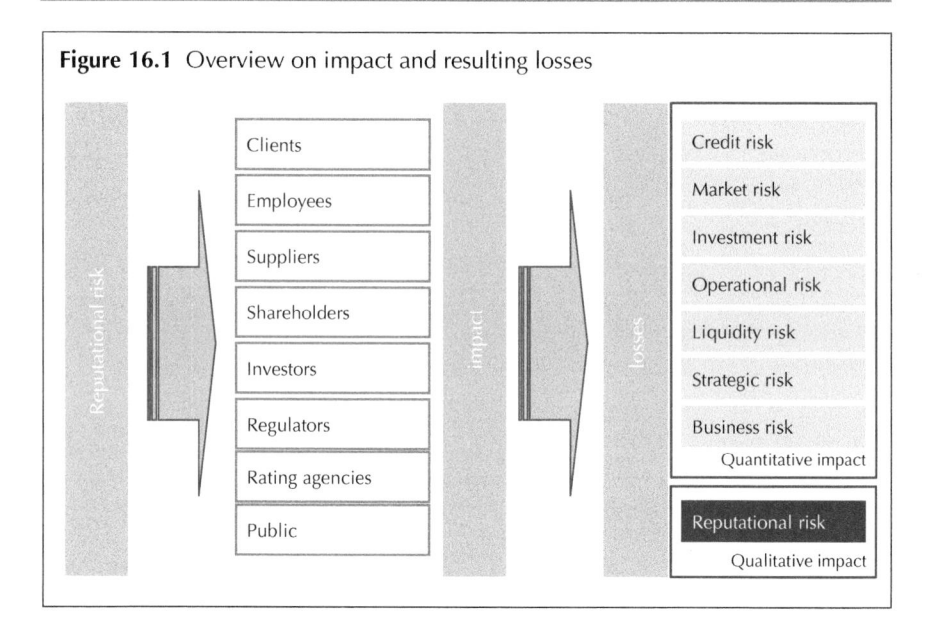

Figure 16.1 Overview on impact and resulting losses

Reputational risk		impact	losses
	Clients		Credit risk
	Employees		Market risk
	Suppliers		Investment risk
	Shareholders		Operational risk
	Investors		Liquidity risk
	Regulators		Strategic risk
	Rating agencies		Business risk
	Public		Quantitative impact
			Reputational risk
			Qualitative impact

often backed by government guarantee, the possibility of liquidity risk as a consequence of a reputational risk event is reduced. Ratings of promotional banks are often linked to the ratings of their shareholders, which are public institutions or states. Therefore, investors are interested in working together with them in the long run. But what investors demand is a professional organisation that manages and mitigates its risks, especially the ones arising from operational failures or deficient processes. Promotional banks need to implement strong operational risk management, including a working internal control system as well as reasonable compliance structures.

As the product portfolio of promotional institutions is multipurpose and versatile, they look after a wide range of different customers. Therefore, reputational risks arising in one part of the product portfolio do not necessarily affect all customers to the same degree. As the products of promotional banks are unique and individual and the customer cannot obtain them somewhere else (or only in a less desirable condition) they will not terminate contracts directly due to an occurrence of reputational risk. Furthermore, as promotional banks do not suffer the classic deposit-business-involving risks such as a bank run, neither the widespread withdrawal of assets nor the termination of customer contracts needs to be taken into account when managing the outcomes of reputational risks. The degree of interdependency of reputational risks with other risk types as business risks, credit risks or liquidity risks as a consequence is therefore lower than in commercial institutions. Do stakeholders therefore not react at all on reputational risks? Of course this is not the case. What can be observed is a lack of confidence in the products and in the work of promotional banks rather than a more measurable, quantitative consequence.

As described above, the public (including the NGOs) is highly interested in the investments that are made by promotional banks, as these should act in the public interest. The public monitors the behaviour of the banks closely. Its reactions can be recognised easily, eg, by increasing coverage in the press, letters of enquiry, or even demonstrations against the decisions or business of promotional banks. These reactions are also highly visible to customers or other stakeholders such as employees or rating agencies.

A lack of confidence as well as increased coverage influences the shareholders' view of the promotional bank in question. Shareholders might influence, for example, the precise tasks and development funds that can be spent on promotional activities. They can also demand the revision of frameworks and organisational structures, for example the reorganisation or modification of internal processes.

As for the special social mission and understanding of the social responsibility within promotional banks, this is one of the reasons why many employees decide to work in such an institution. Their reaction to reputational issues seems to be less severe than in other institutions because their business model is more or less unique in the financial sector. A fast change to another institution with the same values and understanding is not that easy. Furthermore, promotional banks offer good working conditions for their employees, including health programmes, work–life-balance strategies and internal sustainability goals, as well as adequate payment. While an increasing fluctuation in staff might not always be the consequence of reputational events, employees actively demand the implementation of corporate governance structures, the recognition of sustainability principles and effective organisational structures and processes from their management.

CONCLUSION: REPUTATIONAL RISK MANAGEMENT AND CONTROLLING PROCESSES

To manage reputational risks, promotional banks should focus on four fundamental pillars: sustainability; marketing and communication; compliance; and corporate governance.

Sustainability

Promotional banks need to define their own mission by respecting common sustainability guidelines. The sustainability goal should be described precisely and should be in line with the corporate social responsibility of the institution in question. It is necessary to define concrete sustainability principles that can be focused not only outside but also in-house. To fulfil these principles and to achieve the set goals, a sustainability management system has to be implemented. With regard to the special risk exposure of promotional banks it is necessary to identify the ecological, social and/or ethical risks of projects at an early stage and to act accordingly. Promotional banks need to prove that they have concentrated on the special risks of their business and have to explicitly explain their activities to their different stakeholders. The company's risk strategy needs to take the underlying sustainability principles into account.

Marketing and communications

Marketing and communications manage and review the reputation of the institution itself. They transport the ideas and principles to the stakeholders, internally as well as externally. Further, they periodically scan the media channels to identify possible reputational risk events by analysing stakeholders' expectations. Additionally, promotional banks analyse the view of their customers and the public in general to better align their business and products to the needs and expectations of this group of stakeholders. As described above, the perception of social, political or environmental topics can change in a very fast and not always predictable way. As a consequence, the communications departments and sustainability teams of promotional banks are closely linked to each other. The defined mission statement, the values that have been specified and the concrete realisation of both in the company need to be made public in order to offer the highest possible level of transparency to the stakeholders. A consequent dialogue with the stakeholders is essential. The more they are getting informed and involved, the better reputational risks can be mitigated or even avoided from the beginning. In case of reputational issues, communications departments need to establish close contact with those responsible for sustainability. The communications and risk control departments need to work together to connect themselves to business transactions.

Compliance

To prevent the institutions from operational as well as reputational risk, institutions need to implement a compliance framework. In this respect, promotional banks are not that different from commercial institutions, but because of their own mission statement and corporate social responsibility they galvanise themselves, and are galvanised by their stakeholders, to a higher level of compliance. Systems for data protection as well as for the prevention of conflicts of interest, money laundering, the financing of terrorism, corruption and fraud have to be in place. The related rules, processes and controls need to be continually adapted to the corresponding legal and regulatory legal framework and market requirements. The framework should be completed by regular compliance trainings for employees. With compliance the institutions commit themselves to the adherence of market standards and respect for the interests of the stakeholders.

Corporate governance

Corporate governance takes into account the principles and standards of good corporate management and supervision, which help to improve the management of the relevant enterprise and supervision by its bodies, raise awareness for good corporate governance and perform the tasks of the enterprise better and more efficiently. Similarly to the contents of compliance, stakeholders expect professional corporate governance structures, especially from promotional banks, as they expect and demand the same from their partners or clients.

These four elements build a framework, provide principles for the business operations of promotional banks and manage their adherence to these principles. Reputational risks are here considered more or less independent of the stakeholder. Nevertheless, besides the analysis of reputational risks as a consequence of other primary risk types such as operational risk, the described risk-management processes are an integral part of the risk-controlling cycle. The risk-controlling processes complete the established management system through a standardised validation of the identified risks, as well as principles for a consistent handling of the risks throughout the whole institution. As the impact of reputational risks in promotional banks is different from stakeholder to stakeholder and difficult to quantify, it is necessary to validate the risks according to the stakeholder. Additionally, it is necessary to involve the right people. Here the risk-controlling function needs to identify the contact people responsible for the single stakeholders within their organisation. The risk assessment by those in charge can comprise a qualitative risk valuation as they are able to determine the precise impacts and are able to develop suitable risk-mitigating measures.

The views expressed in this article are those of the author and they do not necessarily represent those of KfW Bankengruppe.

1 The shareholder of the promotional bank (eg, the federal or state government) takes over parts of the credit risks and guarantees for the borrowers. In case that the loan cannot be paid back, the state or the federal government takes the risk. As a consequence of the government guarantee, the creditworthiness of such promotional institutions equals the creditworthiness of the state or federal government that supports their refinancing on the capital markets.
2 Promotional banks finance industry sectors such as the energy industry, which uses the loans for building further nuclear or coal-fired power plants. These plants have been heavily criticised by NGOs due to their effect on the environment.
3 See https://www.kfw.de/nachhaltigkeit/KfW-Konzern/Nachhaltigkeit/Nachhaltigkeits management/Leitsätze-und-Richtlinien/Positionspapier-Kohlekraftwerksfinanzierung/ index.html – KfW position on financing coal-fired power plants.

REFERENCES

VÖB, 2013, "Promotional banks in Germany – Acting in the public interest", August 1, available at http://www.voeb.de/de/publikationen/fachpublikationen/publikation_ foerderbanken_englisch.pdf.

17

Reputational Risk Management in a Global Insurance Company

Claudia Meyer and Maurice LeBlanc

Allianz SE

Whereas the previous chapters of this book dealt with reputational risk management in banks, this chapter discusses how reputational risk management was successfully implemented and lived in an international insurance company.

For both banks and insurance companies the most important value is the brand or franchise value and its good reputation. Without good reputation and trust, these companies cannot sell their products to clients; nor are they able to contract intermediaries that support the purchase of insurance or asset-management products; nor are they able to refinance themselves in the market under ideal conditions. When a direct or indirect reputational incident occurs in an insurance company or bank, a lot of effort and money need to be spent to manage the stakeholders' expectations and to reduce the financial and non-financial impact of the event. As it is difficult to assess the future lost profits or influence on the share price from a reputational risk incident, the proactive management of stakeholders' expectations is a key success factor by which companies should align their reputational risk-management strategy.

When dealing with indirect reputational risks events triggered by risk events in other risk categories, such as internal fraud or corruption (ie, operational risk), both banks and insurance companies are largely impacted on and respond to these events in a similar manner. Conversely, when it comes to direct reputational risks, there are some distinctions and unique challenges differentiating the two industries. In particular, whereas a bank has the option to close client accounts and modify security portfolios relatively quickly, an insurance company may be locked up in a long-term insurance contract. This means banks are often in a better position to deal with reputational risks and reputational issues even after the underlying transaction has occurred, while insurance companies must be more focused on screening transactions prior to entering into any commitment.

For example, when agreeing to underwrite a large infrastructure project, such as a hydroelectric dam, the commitment of an insurance company can be for a period of five years, ten years or even longer. This means that a careful assessment of potential reputational risks that could arise must be conducted upfront as part of the underwriting process and consider factors related to the project, such as environmental impacts, the rights and conditions of the labour force and forced resettlement.

This chapter is a case study in the management of direct and indirect reputational risk in a globally leading insurance company that has won numerous environmental social governmental (ESG) awards. The reader should gain a feeling for how reputational risk management is embedded in the daily business of an insurance company, including the handling of issues that are specific to insurers.

DEFINITION OF REPUTATION AND REPUTATIONAL RISK

Reputation is defined as trust in value-based and stakeholder-oriented performance. That leads to a definition of reputational risk as an unexpected drop in the value of the share price, the value of in-force business or the value of future business caused by a decline in the reputation of the company or one or more of its subsidiaries from the perspective of its stakeholders.

Reputational risk can be split into direct and indirect reputational risk.

❏ Direct reputational risks are those reputational risk events caused by any company behaviour that alone might have a negative impact on important stakeholders' perception of the company.

Figure 17.1 Direct versus indirect reputational risk

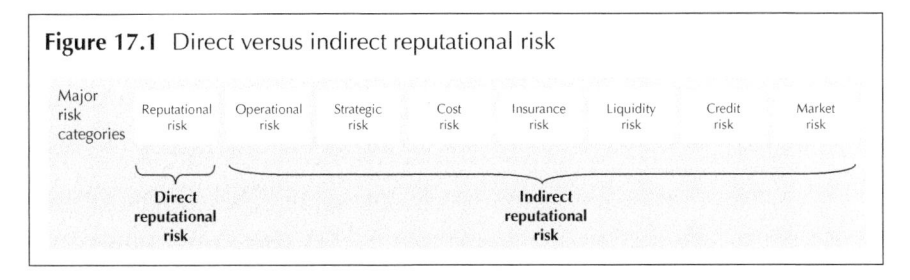

Major risk categories	Reputational risk	Operational risk	Strategic risk	Cost risk	Insurance risk	Liquidity risk	Credit risk	Market risk
	Direct reputational risk	Indirect reputational risk						

❏ Indirect reputational risks are those reputational risk events caused by a risk event in one of the other major risk categories (ie, operational, strategic, business, insurance, liquidity, credit, market risk) that triggers an additional loss in the value of the company due to reputational damage.

Reputational risk management versus reputational issues management

The term "reputational risk management" refers to proactively avoiding or mitigating the potential damage that might result from a future reputational risk event (*ex ante*). Measures to limit damage from a reputational risk event that has already occurred are referred to as "reputational issues management and crisis communication" (*ex post*), as shown in Figure 17.2.

Generally speaking, it is deemed more efficient to enact processes to avoid reputational issues in the first place than to deal with them once they have arisen. More specifically, if a simple process is in place to screen key business transactions in sensitive areas the potential reputational risk event may be avoided entirely upfront (albeit at a trade-off against profit). However, this ultimately requires less

Figure 17.2 Reputational risk management versus reputational issues management

Reputational risk → Reputational risk event → Reputational issue → Reputational crisis

Ex ante | Ex post

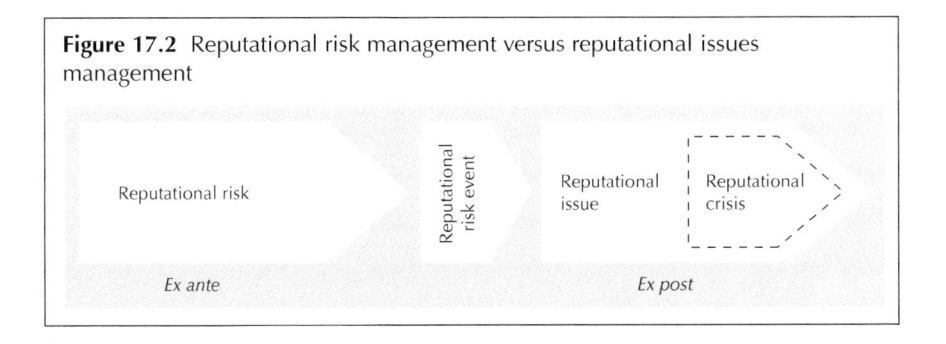

effort and management attention than continuously engaging in "crisis-management" activities.

REPUTATIONAL RISK IN THE CONTEXT OF THE BUSINESS AND RISK STRATEGY

A core corporate objective of the insurance business strategy was operational profitability accompanied by sustainable competitiveness. In order to protect the company and support its goal to be the most valuable brand in financial services, reputational risk principles were also defined in the global risk strategy as follows: indirect reputational risks, resulting from the occurrence of non-reputational risk events (especially from operational or compliance risks), were to be identified, assessed and managed through the top risk assessment process and operational risk and control self-assessment (RCSA) process.

When launching new products or services or onboarding new customers, an assessment of the potentially direct reputational risks was required. The impact of reputational risk events were mitigated using a coordinated communication and crisis-management approach. The reputational risk-management approach needed to support the fulfilment of legal and regulatory requirements, including Solvency II, as well as any applicable risk standards defined by national regulatory bodies.

To address the fact that serious reputational impacts may arise from compliance-related events, the company also focused on fostering integrity among employees by implementing a code of conduct, providing regular trainings and applying sanctions when ethical lapses occurred or corporate rules were breached.

In the context of the operational risk-management framework, which is the most relevant risk category for triggering indirect reputational risk events, reputational risk management principles were established aiming to:

❏ recognise and understand the reputational risks present in the company's operational risks;
❏ learn from past reputational risk events and events that resulted in, or could have resulted in, lost profits and a reduction in the franchise value;
❏ foster risk awareness among all employees and establish a risk

culture conducive to the open discussion of reputational risks; and
❏ reduce reputational risk impacts and other consequences.

FROM REPUTATIONAL RISK STRATEGY TO REPUTATIONAL RISK APPETITE AND LIMITS

The risk strategy to mitigate reputational risk foresaw the establishment of risk tolerances for the two areas: risk tolerance for direct reputational risk; and risk tolerance for indirect reputational risk.

Risk tolerance for direct reputational risk

The risk tolerance was defined based on a set of mandatory group guidelines for sensitive reputational areas identified by the company. In some areas, guidance was provided to allow (green signal) or prohibit (red signal) defined activities. In other areas, case-by-case decision-making based on qualitative guidance was required. If a group-sensitive area was not yet regulated via a specific group guideline, or the group guideline was not precise enough for a specific case, the local risk function was required to refer the case to the central group risk function for decision making (see below for a detailed description of the management of direct reputational risks).

Risk tolerance for indirect reputational risk

The risk strategy required an evaluation of the indirect reputational risks for all top risk scenarios and operational risks with scope of the qualitative risk management processes designed to ensure an adequate control environment is in place (ie, top risk assessment (TRA) and risk and control self-assessment (RCSA). With results of the TRA process the company's board of management (BoM) decided on an explicit risk tolerance via a target risk appetite for reputational impact and probability.

REPUTATIONAL RISK GOVERNANCE

As reputational risk was defined as a separate risk category for the company, a specific reputational risk-management guideline was implemented for the group as a supplemental document to the overarching risk policy and risk strategy. Also, at the subsidiary level, the risk functions were required to have a local risk policy in place that

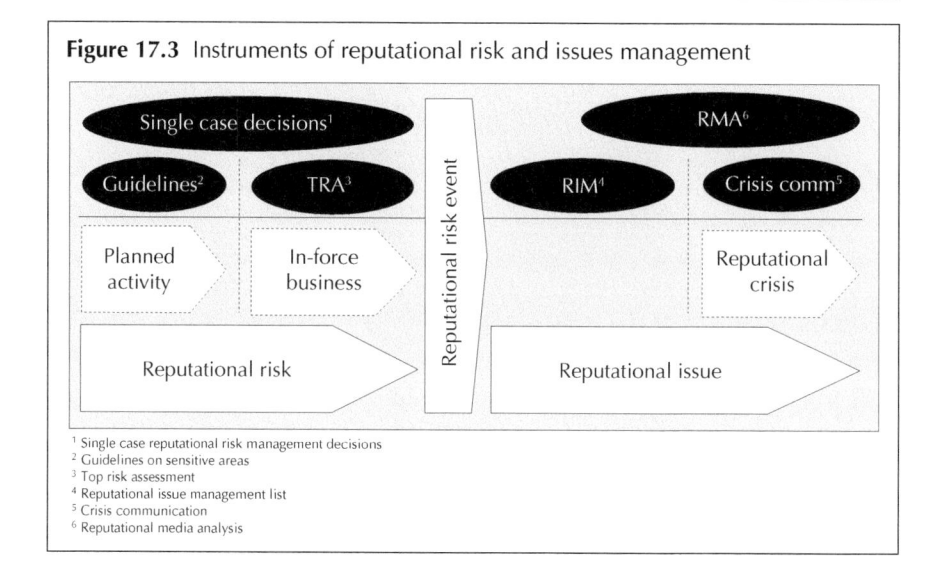

Figure 17.3 Instruments of reputational risk and issues management

[Figure 17.3: A diagram showing instruments of reputational risk and issues management. On the left side (Reputational risk), ovals labeled "Single case decisions¹", "Guidelines²", and "TRA³" are shown above boxes labeled "Planned activity" and "In-force business". A vertical axis labeled "Reputational risk event" separates the left and right sides. On the right side (Reputational issue), ovals labeled "RMA⁶", "RIM⁴", and "Crisis comm⁵" are shown above a box labeled "Reputational crisis".]

¹ Single case reputational risk management decisions
² Guidelines on sensitive areas
³ Top risk assessment
⁴ Reputational issue management list
⁵ Crisis communication
⁶ Reputational media analysis

defined the subsidiary's reputational risk and issues management activities, including:

❏ local roles and responsibilities;
❏ reputational risk strategy; and
❏ all steps in the local risk and issues management processes.

In addition, the local policy needed to describe rules for how to address reputational risks from outsourced or vendor activities in the respective service level agreements.

Roles and responsibilities in indirect RepRisk management

The following lists the roles of involved persons, functions and committees, including their key responsibilities and how the various roles interacted.

Board of Management Committee

The BoM was responsible for approving the risk tolerance for top risk scenarios from the TRA with a substantial direct or indirect reputational risk. The BoM or Risk Committee was responsible for deciding on reputational risk guidelines for sensitive areas and on indirect reputational risk appetite in the context of its decision-making on the other major risk categories.

Risk Committee
The Risk Committee (RiCo) was responsible for proposing the reputational risk appetite and respective action plans in the context of the TRA. The RiCo undertook a comprehensive discussion of reputational risks and issues at least once a year and acted as the final escalation body in case a subsidiary did not wish to accept a transactional veto issued by the chief risk officer (CRO).

Chief risk officer
The CRO was involved in direct reputational risk cases via his authority to restrict business transactions on grounds of the company's reputational risk tolerance.

Risk function
The risk function was responsible for proposing and updating a consistent governance framework for all reputational-risk-related activities in accordance with applicable regulatory requirements and the group's general risk-management strategy. For the RiCo, the risk function proposed, together with the communication function and a dedicated environment, social and governance function (ESG), new and updated guidelines for sensitive areas.

Additionally, the risk function was responsible for monitoring and challenging the reputational risk assessments and mitigation activities of the subsidiaries and reporting to the risk committee on a regular basis important matters regarding reputational risk.

Communication function
The communication function (COM) was responsible for monitoring on a regular basis how the company was perceived by the public (ie, reputational media analysis (RMA)) and thereby played a major role not only in managing reputational issues, but also identifying the sensitive reputational areas for the company.

For all case-by-case decisions on reputational risk at the group level, COM provided an initial assessment of the reputational risk impact – based on consideration of each stakeholder group – along with a corresponding recommendation to group risk function on how proceed with the case. Moreover, COM reviewed and challenged the direct and indirect reputational risk assessments for all risk scenarios in the TRA. Whenever reputational risk events would occur and trigger reputational issues, COM was also responsible for coordinating the reputational issues management process (RIM), including the development of communication strategies and management of crisis communications.

Compliance function
The Compliance Department was responsible for providing GR with *ex ante* information about potential reputational risks related to sanctions and embargoes, whereby the compliance function did not identify the need to restrict a transaction from a compliance perspective, but recognised a potential reputational risk.

Business managers and employees of the first line of defence
The first line was primarily responsible for identifying, assessing and actively managing reputational risks when, for example, new products were launched, potential mergers or acquisitions were considered, or underwriting and investment decisions were made.

MANAGEMENT OF INDIRECT REPUTATIONAL RISK
Top risk-assessment process
As reputational risk may also be a consequence from the occurrence of risk events within other risk categories, it was important not only to assess frequency and financial impact of the risk in diverse risk categories, but also to identify and assess any indirect reputational risks that could cause significant harm to the company. As part of a top-down assessment, where board members were the ultimate risk owners and second-level managers from the first line of defence were the risk experts (interview partners), material risks that could threaten the company were identified, assessed, managed and monitored. Specifically, the following risk types were considered in the top risk-assessment process, including direct reputational risk:

❏ market risk;
❏ credit risk;
❏ business risk;
❏ strategic risk;
❏ insurance risk;
❏ operational risk;
❏ liquidity risk; and
❏ reputational risk (ie, direct reputational risks).

For each risk identified under a given specific risk category the risk tolerances were required to be additionally determined, which meant that targets were set for frequency, severity and indirect reputational impact and other non-financial impacts. If the actual risk score was higher than the target, further mitigation actions needed to be implemented. This was also valid for the indirect and direct reputational risk assessment.

As the reputational impact of operational risk incidents (eg, internal fraud or unauthorised activities) could be quite significant, stringent standards were also set to additionally assess indirect reputational risk in the operational risk control self-assessment process, which is described below.

Operational risk control self-assessment process

Through the operational risk control self-assessment (RCSA) process, which was facilitated by the risk-management function on an annual basis, all major operational risks and corresponding key controls were identified, assessed, managed and monitored together with the respective business process owners. Besides assessing the frequency and severity of each operational risk in scope of the RCSA, the business was also responsible for assessing the reputational impact. As part of the RCSA process a risk response from the business was required for each risk, where a decision was made not to accept the operational risk as adequately managed. This response specified further mitigation actions to be implemented and, where appropriate, included the mitigation of risks that could lead to the indirect reputational risk event.

The nature by which reputational risk considerations were integrated into the RCSA process meant that, although the RCSA was first and foremost defined as an operational risk-management process, it was also very much a reputational risk-management process in the sense that even risks with a low potential operational risk impact would still be subject to increased oversight of mitigation and control effectiveness if the potential reputational impact were high. For example, a company may incur incremental costs due to an advertising campaign where advertisements were subsequently deemed inappropriate due to missing knowledge of regional traditions, customs or social norms. At its core the costs incurred to rectify such a situation would be considered operational losses. However, from an impact perspective the potential reputational damage associated with this scenario is much more significant.

Evaluation of reputational risk impact
The evaluation of reputational impacts was quite difficult, especially from the perspective of assessing concrete financial amounts, eg, lost profits for the next years, loss of clients or distribution partners, reduction of share price or reduction of company value. Therefore both direct and indirect reputational risk impacts were rated on a 1–5 scale using qualitative criteria contained in a reputational risk assessment matrix, whereby a 1 translated into "no reputational impact" and a 5 translated into a "very high" reputational impact. The matrix provided a set of qualitative assessment criteria for every major stakeholder group, including:

- clients;
- investors;
- regulators;
- distribution or other business partners; and
- employees.

The qualitative impacts of the direct (business activity) and indirect reputational risk were estimated under the assumption that stakeholders become aware of the underlying reputational issue. Each scale described qualitative examples for each stakeholder group for an easier and consistent assessment of the reputational risk impact.

The overall reputational risk rating for a top risk or RCSA risk was taken as the highest single score from each stakeholder group. It is important to note that not only the impact on the subsidiary itself was considered, but the possible impact on other subsidiaries or the entire group as well (the matrix was calibrated to support the identification and assessment of reputational risks for the group company). Additionally, the subsidiaries were allowed to use additional criteria when assessing the local reputational risk impact, reflecting subsidiary-specific circumstances.

Reputational risk management
Wherever the actual reputational risk score exceeded the target score, proactive reputational risk management was a key success

factor. The business, together with support of the communication and risk function, elaborated *ex ante* communication and crisis plans and exercised so-called "war games" to be better prepared and cope with media attacks whenever a risk triggered a high reputational impact and heightened media awareness.

Reporting
The risk function documented all reviews of single cases in a database and created a respective repository, which supported reporting to relevant stakeholders such as the risk committee, board of management and supervisory board.

Monitoring
Continuous monitoring of reputational risks resulting from operative business (eg, investment and underwriting transactions, new products) was primarily the responsibility of the respective managers and employees of the first line of defence. In the event that a significant increase in the reputational risk related to a specific piece of business was identified, the first line of defence was required to re-perform a reputational risk evaluation and decision process in the same manner as originally conducted.

The investor relations function tracked incidents of public interests with high media awareness, including reputational risk impacts, and monitored and reported on share price movements as a result of such incidents on a monthly basis to senior management and COM.

DIRECT REPUTATIONAL RISK-MANAGEMENT PROCESS
This part of the chapter deals with the direct management of reputational risk as part of the daily operative business.

General strategy
The general strategy of the company was to implement a process for the management of direct reputational risks that ensured all transactions from investments and insurance business with potential to generate a reputational risk impact exceeding the tolerance of the company were identified by business process owners and referred onward to appropriate experts for further consideration.

In practice, despite well-defined sensitive-area guidelines and a universal reputational risk assessment methodology, direct reputational risk management existed as a purely qualitative process highly subject to professional judgement and the particulars of each case, including consideration of broader business impacts outside the narrower lens of reputational risk.

Establishment of sensitive areas

The starting point for embedding direct reputational risk management into business processes was the establishment of a general risk strategy and tolerance for exposure to specific controversial topics, such as mining or weapons production, against which the company wished to protect itself ("sensitive areas"). These sensitive areas were in general universally applicable to all areas of the business rather than relating to a specific processes or types of transactions.

This initial step required a fairly extensive amount of brainstorming in order to conclude on a comprehensive list and consistent grouping of what these sensitive areas should be – and relied on a combination of professional experience, common NGO points of criticism, media analysis and the input of third-party providers, as well as, most importantly, the company's particular philosophy towards various environmental, social and governance issues.

After the initial list of sensitive areas was established, a further refinement was carried out that more precisely defined what types of characteristics, behaviour and so forth for each sensitive area would be a source of concern from a reputational risk perspective. This refinement ultimately helped steer both what business the company was willing to engage in as well as how the company would react in the event that a reputational issue arose.

For example, in one instance there was extensive media awareness driven by NGO criticism of food commodity investments that claimed that active trading in these investments was correlated with an increase in food prices. Depending on companies' reputational risk appetites, the reaction to these allegations differed markedly. Some financial institutions decided to abandon food commodity trades immediately and widely publish the decision in the media to bolster their image, whereas other companies initiated long-term dialogues with NGOs while continuing to trade in the criticised investments.

Embedding reputational risk assessment triggers into business processes

In the context of the entire approach towards direct reputational risk management, the establishment of sensitive areas was a rather straightforward step, with engaged experts dedicated to achieving a workable, high-quality conclusion. Truly successful direct reputational risk management, however, required processes and tools to be in place that enabled, at the transactional level, the triggering of a more thorough reputational risk assessment where appropriate. This resulted in transforming the sensitive areas into a very simple "triggering" format to be applied by individuals who were only marginally interested in reputational risk management, complicated in part by factors such as:

❑ who performs the activity and how much influence the company has over their behaviour;
❑ what the incentive structure is for these individuals to adhere to corporate reputational risk strategies and processes; and
❑ how knowledgeable the individuals are in recognising and fairly assessing or escalating reputational risks.

Underwriting

The most basic form of implementation consisted of providing underwriters with a list of key words (ie, the sensitive areas) and instructions so that any business related to these areas could first be cleared with the designated individual or function responsible for conducting a more detailed reputational risk assessment. More elaborate details regarding the company's broader reputational risk strategy and position towards the sensitive areas were normally not put forth to underwriters, since (a) the unnecessary detail would only serve to confuse or complicate and (b) it could not be assumed that the underwriters possessed the level of expertise to conduct the assessment themselves, were interested in the quality of the assessment or were objective towards the outcome. As such, the key objective was to put a process into place that would be consistently applied and present a minimal additional burden directly on the underwriters.

Roll-out of the process occurred through embedding the relevant requirements into the underwriting guidelines of the company and covering underwriter responsibilities for reputational risk management during either topic-specific or general training sessions.

Investments

In contrast with the "keep it simple" approach applied to underwriting, on the investment side it was necessary that investment managers and parties responsible for investment manager selection possess a relatively deeper understanding of the reputational risk strategy of the company and the finer points of the defined boundaries. This was in large part due to the fact that they exercised much more autonomy in conducting reputational risk assessments and mitigating reputational risks, and typically referred reputational risk issues on for further consideration only if a preliminary risk assessment breached certain potential impact thresholds.

Complicating this situation was the degree of influence the company exercised over internal versus external investment managers. To address this and ensure adequate alignment of the ESG philosophy of the company with that of external managers, specific guidelines were created that established rules for the selection of external investment managers and the minimum ESG standards they must have adopted into their investment strategies.

Conducting reputational risk assessments

Despite the above-described differences between when and how independent reputational risk assessments were triggered within underwriting and investment processes, the end result for both was performance of a more thorough reputational risk assessment by a knowledgeable, objective individual. The exact placement of this individual or function within the company was not deemed to be of critical importance, but typically was within the underwriting integrity/oversight function, the risk management function or a dedicated ESG function.

The individual conducting the assessment was expected to possess a thorough understanding of the reputational risk strategy of the company and application of the sensitive-area guidelines. Using this knowledge they would work closely together with, for instance, the underwriter or investment manager to understand the details of the case and ultimately conclude on how to proceed, including, where appropriate, further risk-mitigating actions to be implemented as a precondition to accepting the risk.

The starting point for each assessment was the application of a universal reputational risk-assessment methodology to arrive at a risk score on a scale of 1–5. This methodology considered the potential impacts of the reputational risk materialising on investors, customers, business partners, regulators and employees of the company. Results of this assessment served as the primary indicator for whether or not the reputational risks accompanying the proposed transaction were tolerable, not tolerable, or tolerable only on condition of further mitigation. However, also factored into the decision was consideration of broader business impacts such as the entire portfolio of business with the customer, whether the customer was of particular strategic importance or how much influence might be exercised over the customer (eg, whether or not the company was a passive participant in a shared contract).

Standard procedure called for all risks rated 3 or higher on the 1–5 scale of the standard reputational risk-assessment methodology to be escalated to the risk function (ie, in the event that the risk function was not already the party responsible for conducting the assessment in the first place) and, possibly, the communications function as the key perception experts. It was then the risk function's decision whether to block the transaction or escalate it to the corporate centre risk function for further consideration.

Escalation to the corporate centre

Risks escalated to the corporate centre risk function by subsidiaries were subject to further assessment that also took into account particulars of potential reputational risk impacts on the corporate group as a whole. The result of this assessment was a communication back to the subsidiary approving the transaction, rejecting the transaction or approving the transaction conditional on further risk mitigation.

At the corporate centre, the company developed an approach whereby several parties contributed to the referral assessment and final decision, including the risk function, communications function and ESG function. This approach ensured that multiple points of view, representing different professional backgrounds and areas of expertise, were always considered and reduced the likelihood that an important aspect might be overlooked or that personal bias could enter into the decision-making process.

In the event that the subsidiary did not agree with or wish to accept the decision of the corporate centre risk function, the final level of escalation was directly to the corporate centre risk committee, which comprised members of the management board. All reputational risk-management decisions taken by this committee were final.

Despite well-established processes and requirements, direct reputational risk management involved making difficult judgement calls. For example, how was the company supposed to view the provision of insurance within countries viewed critically due to political situations or instability when the insurance would ultimately help support the education or health of the population? Such circumstances highlighted the need to perform a case-by-case analysis of specific facts to arrive at a well-founded decision that both was transparent for senior management and enabled the communications function to proactively disclose the decision to the press and avoid any misunderstandings by stakeholders for publicly visible deals.

OUTLOOK

As insurance companies and banks were historically ranked at the very bottom of the Edelmann Trust Barometer, the management of reputational risk was constantly deemed a continuous area of potential improvement. Ultimately, the root cause was identified as being not only a result of the investments and insurance contracts of the industry, but also the behaviour, attitude and treatment of the company towards key stakeholders, in particular customers. As such, it was considered that, going forward, the focus for reputational risk should not be disproportionately skewed towards business relationships and transactions, but rather also proportionately consider all points where interactions with the various stakeholders occur.

Looking ahead, the reputational risk management should focus more on establishment of trust among the stakeholders, especially among customers. Trust is an asset that financial industry enterprises must understand and properly manage in order to be successful in today's complex operating environment. Fair treatment of customers, secure data protection and honest business behaviour are the key success factors for obtaining a good reputation based on trust, which is the basis for sustainable growth.

Any statements and opinions of the authors contained herein only represent the views of the authors themselves; no conclusions regarding the opinion of the employer nor of other third parties should be drawn from any statements contained in this chapter.

The view of the authors shall not be regarded as consulting services.

18

Reputational Consequence Management: The Future

Mike Finlay
RiskBusiness International Limited

"It takes 20 years to build a reputation and five minutes to ruin it. If you think about that, you'll do things differently."

Warren Buffet

The opening chapters of this book have dealt extensively with the reputation of the firm and the implications for the firm when that reputation is tarnished or damaged, irrespective of the cause behind the tarnishment or damage. In this chapter, building off these foundations, we will change focus to address how firms can make their reputational management strategies forward-looking and what challenges can be expected to be faced when managing reputation and the reputational consequences of, in particular, operational risk in the future. It is for this reason that, rather than use the much-disputed term "reputational risk" within this chapter, we shall rather refer to "reputational consequence management" as encompassing all aspects of risk identification, assessment, quantification, remediation and proactive management throughout this chapter.

WHEN THE UNACCEPTABLE BECOMES COMMONPLACE

When children are very young, most parents will warn them, particularly if they are female, that it takes only one silly or ill-conceived act to cause irreparable harm to their reputation. Yet, as children grow, they question the lessons taught by their parents, particularly when they leave the nest for university, in many cases doing things that, in later life, they may look back on and question their wisdom (or lack thereof) at the time.

The firm is, in some ways, similar: as it grows, expands, changes and matures, the risk appetite of its managers and stakeholders changes and behaviour, conduct and the culture of the firm in its earlier years may no longer be as appropriate as it once seemed. The terms "brash", "start-up", "cavalier" and "foolhardy" are often applied to firms for which the slogan "we can do it" aptly sums up management's approach to business. And, as these firms are in the "20 years to build a reputation" phase Warren Buffet refers to, there is often little or no real attention paid to the longer-term reputational consequences of the firm and its staff's current behaviour and activity. But, once they are more mature, reputation and trust become important, and management will pay an ever-increasing amount of attention to it.

However, the environment within which firms, especially financial services firms, exist and operate also changes. Cognitive behavioural theory teaches us that the longer and more frequently you are exposed to something, the more commonplace and acceptable it becomes. Following the global financial crisis of 2007 to 2010 – which was accompanied by misselling of packaged mortgages and collateralised debt obligations (CDOs) – as more and more firms were accused of involvement and subsequently fined, clients, customers, shareholders and employees became more or less accepting and the reputational consequence, typically measured through an impact on share price, became less and less. It was similar, then, with the personal-protection insurance missold to so many credit-card holders, mortgage borrowers and personal lenders: as the first firms set aside provisions in the billions of British pounds, the public was outraged, yet after a while it became just another case of "So what?"

Fast-forward to the cases of Libor-rate manipulation, foreign-exchange-rate manipulation and gold-price fixing of 2013 and 2014, and it seemed that those very stakeholders who should have been most adversely concerned about the reputational consequences of bankers gone bad seemed almost not to care. So, the question has to be asked: should we bother to manage reputation and reputational consequence in the future, or simply "go with the flow", take the good with the bad and assume that it will all even out over time?

The social-media era

With the advent of mobile or cellular phones, phone cameras and video, the short-message service (SMS) and the adoption by many of perpetual online personae, communication changed for ever. Historically, a firm could issue a press release that may have been picked up by a few wire services and may have made some local or regional news. Occasionally, a story may have been sensational enough to make national or even international news. Most firms had an idea of what was about to become public, and, through the use of public-relations staff or image service providers, could and frequently did manage to mitigate damage before it even happened.

In today's world, however, that has all changed. Someone uses their mobile phone to film something, uses their Internet connection to send the video clip from the phone to the press and, before you know it, the video has gone viral and a thousand blogs and tweets crisscross the globe in just a few minutes.

Not only do social media act as a distribution vehicle for information and detrimental stories, but are in many cases themselves the source of reputational harm. When a firm's systems crash, Twitter broadcasts the fact to the world; the firm tries to defend itself via the same medium and the defence becomes the subject of ridicule and scorn; "anonymous" insiders then leak "facts" and the story becomes sustained – "I read it on Twitter, it must be true" – and then inappropriately prepared management, usually of a generation or two above those employing the latest fad in technology, try to use that same technology to provide a balanced view.

With whistleblowers being paid in certain jurisdictions to "spill the beans", an increased regulatory scrutiny of behaviour linked to criminal sanctions, and revolutionary technology such as Google Glass, the very world within which firms exist and operate is changing and will continue to change. Values, ethics and individual behaviour are also changing and the concept of "acceptability" differs dramatically, depending on whose eyes you care to look through. With this background, how can a firm seek to manage its reputation looking forward? Should it even bother trying to do so?

REPUTATION, CULTURE, BRAND AND TRUST

> "Character is like a tree and reputation like a shadow. The shadow is what we think of it; the tree is the real thing."
>
> Abraham Lincoln

Within financial services, the concept of personal character is most closely associated to that of corporate culture. Depending on where you are standing, the time of day, the quality of light and the amount of sunlight, your corporate culture will cast a shadow, which is different from that of everyone who sees it. Thus, a firm's reputation is different to different spectators and differs from time to time. The firm's brand sits somewhere between culture and reputation; it has its roots in the firm's culture and strategy. Yet, from time to time, it is affected by reputational perception.

Consider the Japanese car maker Toyota, which went through a period of vehicle recalls around 2010. Culture had not changed; reputation, despite many recalls, did not materially change; yet, in certain sectors, the Toyota brand lost its association with quality. Then, in 2014, when it became known that Toyota had withheld fixes for economic reasons, trust was eroded. Similarly, despite obvious cultural issues and corporate-governance failings, and with many examples of cultural failure such as the Libor scandal, the foreign-exchange-rate manipulation and gold-price fixing causing reputational damage to Barclays Bank, the global Barclays brand remained relatively strong, a symbol, especially in developing markets, of dependency and infallibility. The reason for this lies in public trust: by senior Barclays management resigning when they did, the public retained its trust in the brand, thereby reducing the reputational consequences of an unsuitable culture.

Trust is an asset that firms must understand and properly manage in order to be successful in the ever-evolving and ever more complex environment of the future. The firm's culture, its current reputation and the overall perception of its brand are essentially an aggregate of the past, whereas trust is a forward-looking measure of stakeholder expectations. If we consider the 2014 Edelman Trust Barometer,[1] of all industries, financial services continues to rank the lowest, retaining the lowest position it has occupied since 2011, having been second last to the media before that in 2009 and 2010. To manage reputation in the future, today's financial services firm has to start by building – rebuilding – trust, not just in itself, but in the entire sector.

To develop trust in the financial services sector of the future, firms also have to understand the market for financial services. Consumers are changing, not just in their risk awareness facilitated by social media, but in their demand for specific services. Today's consumer wishes not only to be "treated fairly", but also to be engaged in a manner that conveys a deeper understanding of their personal goals, objectives and values, and it is important to them that their financial service providers deliver services that correspond to these goals, objectives and values. To win trust, firms need to demonstrate integrity, adaptability and a social consciousness. By winning trust, the firm will be accepted and have a good reputation and brand. To demonstrate integrity and social consciousness, the culture of the firm needs to change.

It is also crucial to recognise that reputation, image and trust are important barometers to many different stakeholders, particularly those outside of the firm itself. Institutional and private investors tend to migrate their investment monies towards firms that are considered trustworthy and portray an image commensurate with that desired by the investor. Ratings agencies are cognisant of image and reputation, and typically incorporate an assessment of trustworthiness into the ratings they issue on individual firms. Regulators and other authorities pay attention to a firm's reputation and image; any firm deemed to be losing the trust of its investors, staff and clients are soon subjected to closer regulatory scrutiny. Business partners and counterparties will quickly look to other business channels when a firm's reputation suffers adverse consequences and trust becomes questionable. Similarly, internal stakeholders in the form of staff and management may elect to terminate their relationship with the firm should its image and reputation suffer significant harm.

State of the nation

To manage reputation and reputational consequence in the future, the firm must first determine how it is currently perceived and whether that current perception is on par with its usual reputational status, in a period of negative reputational outlook or at a point of enhanced reputational outlook. In trying to determine this benchmark, it is crucial to remember that many different sources should be included in the assessment, as everyone is different and everyone views different things in different ways.

Once you have a view on where your reputation stands – independent of corrective actions to modify reputation – you need to monitor changes in your reputation over time. There are several traditional approaches to doing so, mostly focused on so-called "satisfaction surveys" and post-service delivery "exit polls" – did we do a good job? The problem with all of these approaches is that they are lagging in nature and cannot be used proactively to change things before reputational damage occurs, so the firm needs to augment, if not replace, these techniques, with more forward-focused approaches.

The next stage in reputational management thus incorporates the concept of emerging threats to the firm's reputation and seeks to add tools and techniques that try to influence culture and behaviour before they affect the firm's stakeholders. This may include establishing a social-media management team to be responsible for monitoring all forms of social media and in responding to, and where possible neutralising, adverse media mention as soon as it begins to emerge. Another technique is to employ reputational cleansing techniques that seek to remove adverse media and Internet references or, if they cannot be removed, to bury them so deep in search-engine responses that most casual browsers will fail to pick them up. A third technique includes introducing into every new-initiatives programme (new products, new services, new businesses, new marketing campaigns and so forth) an "RTB" assessment – an assessment of the possible positive and negative implications on the firm's reputation, brand and image of trust that may arise from or accrue to the new initiative.

The third stage in reputational management seeks to become even more proactive, seeking to collect a wide array of relevant data, integrate and aggregate the data into a reputational barometer and then trigger corrective action by management as and when negative changes in the barometer start to appear. This form of reputational management requires:

❏ deep searches of the Internet for any mention of the firm;
❏ constant monitoring of all media for either adverse or complimentary mentions of the firm;
❏ interpreting changes in lagging satisfaction surveys;
❏ analysing and incorporating social and environmental factors that potentially may affect the firm; and
❏ taking into account the national cultures, sociopolitical, economic and religious factors in each of the markets where the firm is active.

All of this data, coupled with more traditional data sources such as loss-data consortia, regulatory findings and industry statistics, is then combined to define a change in the reputational barometer.

However, the above is all based on the current understanding and approach towards managing reputation and, to become proactive and forward-looking, it is necessary to change the fundamental understanding of reputational consequences and to build reputation management into business-as-usual activities.

THE FUTURE OF REPUTATION MANAGEMENT

> "Regard your good name as the richest jewel you can possibly be possessed of – for credit is like fire: when once you have kindled it you may easily preserve it, but, if you once extinguish it, you will find it an arduous task to rekindle it again. The way to a good reputation is to endeavour to be what you desire to appear."
>
> Socrates

The future approaches to reputation management will focus more on what reputation the firm wishes to have, rather than being reactive to events that may have reputational consequence. It requires that the firm introduce into its core business strategy the concept of reputational state and seek for those tasked with designing, developing, implementing and achieving strategy to clearly articulate the desired reputational state that the firm wishes to achieve.

Strategy

In addition to defining the ultimate reputational state, the development, approval and implementation of strategy should incorporate risk assessments to identify what exposures may preclude the achievement of the desired state. Strategy should also be stress-tested for underachievement and overachievement implications on reputation, with proactive remedial actions implemented if and where necessary.

Without entering into the chicken-or-egg debate about which, of governance and strategy, comes first, it is imperative that tomorrow's enterprise ensure that its governance structures support strategic intentions, including the desired reputational state. This needs not only to encompass the behaviour of executives and their management skills, but also to go further, into the nomination and selection of individuals for senior executive and non-executive posts, taking into account each individual's previous and current associations and past track record.

On an ongoing basis, corporate governance protocols should incorporate a regular reassessment of each individual engaged in executive management and non-executive oversight to ensure that their ongoing business and personal activities remain appropriate for the firm and its desired image and to identify shifting circumstances that may indicate a need for change. Adverse or even indifferent comments via social media should be included in such an assessment.

With strategy having been determined, the various new-initiatives processes – which include processes for new-product approval, business-change management and process re-engineering – need to include an understanding of the implications on image, brand, reputation and trust that the new initiative will or may introduce. Whereas historically it may have been sufficient to focus on the legal, financial, regulatory, taxation, risk and system implications of new initiatives, if the firm wishes to proactively manage its image and reputation, then these aspects also need to be considered. Such considerations must also go beyond traditional risk assessments and need to understand the implications for reputation and trust under a wide range of outcomes – expected, adversely unexpected and positively unaffected – for the new initiative.

With each potential outcome, the implications for the firm's reputation and its image should be assessed and analysed, and the range of outcomes should be incorporated into the new-initiative decision making. As new initiatives are then implemented, ongoing reassessments should be undertaken to ensure that the implications for reputation remain within the accepted defined boundaries signed off in the new initiatives governance process.

Education

Any reputational management process focused on the future will by default incorporate educational components. While reputational management processes of today may seek to inform internal stakeholders of the potential dangers of inappropriate or undesirable action, in the future such education will be far more proactive and intrusive into everyday business activity. New business initiatives will need to deliver education on both the initiative itself and how to achieve the desirable reputational state, while all existing business activities will need to have retrospective educational programmes focused on reputation applied to them. New staff induction programmes will need to include comprehensive education on both the desired reputational state and the pitfalls that the firm has identified as obstacles to achieving such a desired state.

Education must also be applied to the firm's management and executives. Management needs to understand how its management skills, style and acts influence staff morale, attitude and culture, as well as client and customer perception. Many individuals placed into a management role do not have built-in management skills and need training to become good people and process managers.

In the future management environment, such training will need to incorporate how to manage reputation and image and how to manage situations where adverse implications on reputation and trust may or actually do occur. Similarly, specialised education will be required for the executives, to arm them with the tools needed to assist the firm in achieving its goals around reputation and image. History is littered with examples where senior executives have not been provided with such skills, ranging from the International Monetary Fund's chief executive's alleged activities in a New York hotel while on personal business to Ergo Insurance Group's sales management activities and reward processes of 2011 and 2012.

As a senior executive, the individual needs to understand that they are constantly "on duty" and that "personal time" is never quite as personal as they may think. Any dubious or questionable action, remark, non-action, facial reaction or body language will be interpreted by an audience far broader than ever known before according to each recipient's own agenda, terms of reference and strategic objectives. And, as the causes of adverse reputational consequence are numerous and constantly evolving, so should the education provided to those tasked with delivering corporate strategy be continuous and representative of current exposures and threats.

Assessment

Having determined strategy, established an appropriate governance approach and culture, assessed new initiatives and educated its people, the forward-looking, reputationally aware firm's next task may be compared to the "use test", that is, ongoing tests and assessments to ensure that staff, management and executives are actually assessing the implications of their actions, non-actions and attitudes against the desired reputational state that has been established as the overall objective for the firm. As and where appropriate, remedial action should be introduced to correct unsuitable behaviour, attitude and culture.

While the existing forms of reputation-consequence monitoring will also apply in the future, forward-thinking firms will seek to engage in peer-benchmarking exercises, where participating firms undertake a formalised and standardised assessment of the reputational consequence of various activities, then submit the assessment outputs using standardised scoring structures into a collective data pool and receive back industry benchmarks calibrated for their own firm. Firms can then use these benchmarks to reappraise and recalibrate their own assessments of new initiatives and threats.

Crisis management
Just as most firms have introduced the concept of crisis management teams to take control and manage the firm through a business-continuity crisis situation, firms focused on reputational consequence management will establish reputational crisis teams – specialist teams brought into play whenever an adverse or unexpected impact or threat to the firm's desired reputational state is detected. Such a team will include key executives capable of making executive decisions, image and communications specialists, social-media experts, legal advisers and, potentially, psychology specialists in the areas of human behaviour, human response and game theory.

Whether the reputational threat arises from an inappropriate tweet by a senior executive, unsuitable behaviour or dress by a recognised firm representative, an actual event leading to client dissatisfaction or a failed marketing campaign, the reputational crisis team should be convened to analyse the threat, quantify the potential damage and design, develop and implement an appropriate response plan, then monitor the effectiveness of the response plan through until the threat is extinguished.

As with business-continuity crisis management, for the duration of the crisis, the reputational crisis team has to have ultimate executive discretion to combat the threat with all means at its disposal. Post-crisis, just as with a business-continuity crisis, the actions, inactions and decisions of the reputational crisis team can then be reviewed and challenged, and, if necessary, lessons learned and incorporated into preparation for the next crisis.

However, despite a well-organised and well-considered threat-appraisal approach and reputational crisis management team, in the ever-changing world of modern communications, instantaneous information and evolving social-media tools, it remains a distinct possibility that even the best-prepared firms will still periodically suffer adverse consequences to their reputation. It is at this point that the firm should turn to specialist external support: to contracted firms or individuals specialising in the grey arts of reputation management or reputational cleansing. Reputational cleansing can involve:

❏ eradicating adverse content from the public domain;
❏ editing or altering adverse content; or
❏ manipulating adverse content so as to change public perception in a favourable manner of the previously threatened or damaged firm.

Tools employed by reputational cleaners include hacking, malware, phishing, redirection, blogs, blog impersonation and takeover, spam, denial-of-service attacks and many other "black arts" of the digital age, the objective being to change attitude and prevent adverse content reaching the broader public. Obviously, the firm needs to take care that by employing such techniques, it neither breaks the law nor commit acts which end up causing more harm than it initially attempted to remove or manage.

Stakeholder response

It is anticipated that, in the future, stakeholders will expect greater disclosure around both actual events causing adverse reputational consequences and management response to such events. Increasingly, investor groups are using the power of investment to change or direct corporate strategy to be more in line with their own ethical and image requirements, and it is expected that investor sentiment will become a factor in corporate governance and direct business management. The ratings agencies tend to monitor investor sentiment and, similarly, it is anticipated that these organisations will incorporate greater coverage of reputational consequence management, corporate image and investor and client trust in their ratings methodologies.

An interesting area of future development may also lie in the regulatory and supervisory communities: with the establishment in the UK of the Financial Conduct Authority (FCA) in 2013 and the Competition and Markets Authority (CMA) in 2014, the consequences of corporate culture, ethics, governance and action have been placed high on the regulatory agenda. Add to this the increased interest by various supervisors in individual firms' approaches to social media, and it takes no great leap of thought to see reputational consequence management and reputational crisis management being subjected to specialised regulatory oversight in the not-too-distant future. As a minimum starting point, regulators are likely to demand clear disclosure on preparation for adverse-consequence management, supported by detailed threat assessments.

GETTING IT RIGHT FIRST TIME

> "A reputation once broken may possibly be repaired, but the world will always keep their eyes on the spot where the crack was."
>
> Joseph Hall

While it is possible to reverse or minimise the reputational consequences of a multitude of threats, the old adage of there never being smoke without some form of fire will always hold true. Accordingly, the forward-looking firm will not rely on its defensive capabilities when it comes to reputational consequence management. Rather, the truly forward-thinking firm will focus on doing good things right the first time.

Flowing on from the global financial crisis of 2007 to 2010 and the era of market manipulation and treating customers unfairly that characterised 2010 to 2014, the overall public perception of the financial services sector could not sink much lower. It led regulatory authorities to question not just the conduct and ethics of the few but whether the very fabric of the financial services industry was fundamentally flawed.

However, at the very same time, a number of small, medium and even large, globally active banks seem to "dodge the bullet" and to go from strength to strength, rarely in the public eye, except for positive reasons. Why, we may ask ourselves, have some managed to achieve such "untouchable" status?

The answer is actually relatively simple: understand the reason for being (remember, banks were created as custodians for the public and as intermediaries to serve the public), set your objectives to deliver against this reason (grow, but grow by treating customers fairly), establish an appropriate and answerable governance structure and culture, and then, on an ongoing basis, link into your client sentiment and proactively respond when appropriate to deliver what your clients and customers actually want. This will establish trust, enhance and build your image and create a reputation for being the type of firm that the majority of individuals and businesses want to do business with. Reputation management is simple if you are in the right, it is incredibly hard if you are in the wrong.

1 See www.edelman.com.

Index

(page numbers in italic type refer to figures and tables)

A
Ackermann, Josef 205–6
Agencia Española de Protección de Datos (Spanish Data Protection Agency) (AEPD) 170–1
Aggarwal, Rajesh 52
AIG 85
Algo FIRST database 53
American Banker 31
American Crisis, The (Paine) 19
American Mercury 14
Andersen, Arthur 21
Ariovistus 15–16
Arthur Andersen 26–7
Association of German Public Banks (VÖB) 271–2
auto-suggest 169–72
AWD 173–4

B
Baghat, Sanjay 100
Banesto 23
Bank of America 85, 98
　consumer complaints against 99
Bank of England, obstinate refusal of, to support Northern Rock 7
Bank of New York Mellon 85, 90
Bank of Scotland 175
Bank Secrecy Act 46
Bank of Spain 23
Banking and Environment Initiative (BEI) 122
banks:
　reputation of, during global financial crisis xix
　reputation of, following global financial crisis 21–3
Baptist Foundation of Arizona 26
Barclays 302
　and data breach 98–9
　and Libor scandal 5, 98
　Salz review of 7–8
Barings Bank 6
Barnett, Michael L. 115, 116
Basel II 74, 75, 76, 117
　and definition of legal/compliance risk 45
Basel III 76
Basel Committee on Banking Supervision (BCBS) 4, 23, 33, 117–18
　Basel II framework issued by 75
　capital charge of, for reputational risk 74

313

compliance risk defined by 45
more detailed definition of
   reputational risk provided
   by 118
as most important global
   standard-setter 117
operational risk defined by 50,
   119
reputational risk defined by 23,
   75
reputational risk references in
   literature of 73
Risk Management Group of
   74
Bear Stearns 28, 85, 90
Beltatti, A. 100
Bitkom 177
blogs 173–5, 231, 301, 309
BNP Paribas 45
Bolton, Brian J. 100
Breuer, Rolf 6
Buffet, Warren 299, 300
Bundesgerichtshof (Federal High
   Court of Germany) 170
business continuity, management
   of:
   awareness 134
   d 133–4
   discussed 131–4
   programme management 132
   reputation as major factor in
      135–8
   and reputational risk
      management 129–44, *135*,
      136
   and reputational risk
      management:
      commonalities between
      140–1
and reputational risk
   management: difference
   between 138–40, *139*
and reputational risk
   management: key drivers
   and trends within financial
   industry 130
reputational risk versus *139*
strategy 133
test maintenance and monitoring
   134
understanding organisation 133
in UniCredit 132–5

C
Caesar, Julius 15–17
Caisse des Dépôts 271
Capone, Al 14
Carlson School of Management
   52
Carrefour 24
Cassa Depositi e Prestiti 271
Center for Research in Security
   Prices (CRSP) 56
Center for Strategic and
   International Studies 129
Citibank 13–15, 16
Citigroup 85, 98
   in Japan 24
City of Glasgow Bank, failure of
   12–13
Clausewitz, Karl von 17
Clean Water Act 113
coal-fired power plants 274
cognitive behavioural theory 300
Colgate-Palmolive 26
*Commercial Bank Examination
   Manual* (Fed) 38
Common Sense (Paine) 19

commonalities between business continuity management and reputational risk management 140–1
see also business continuity; reputational risk: and business continuity management
Competition and Markets Authority (CMA) 310
Consumer Goods Forum (CGF) 122
corporate governance and shareholder wealth 99–103
and executive compensation at TBTFs 100
corporate reputation 115–17
Corporate Social Responsibility (CSR) ranking score 90
corporate social responsibility (CSR) standards 178
Countrywide Financial 85, 90
Cox, Christopher 28
credit risk, and reputational risk 43–4
Credit Risk Committee 208
Credit Suisse 4–5
crises in reputational risk, recovery from 157–83
final checklist and dos and don'ts concerning 182–3
and illegitimate claims 163–5
dos and don'ts 165
and individual cases 165–78
AWD 173–4
Bank of Scotland 175
and blogs 173–5
and corporate social responsibility (CSR) standards 178

Deutsche Bank 166, 175
and employer assessment websites 176–8
and forums 167–8
Infinus 166
press 168–9
and review platforms 175–6
search engines – index and auto-suggest 169–72
Sparkasse Berlin 175
and tests and (private) institutes 172–3
legal perspective on 158–9
and legitimate claims 159–62
Dell case 161–2
dos and don'ts 162
Ing-Diba Bank case 159–61
and trials, hidden advantages of 179
and urgency 164
see also reputation; reputational damage; reputational risk
CRSP (Center for Research in Security Prices) 56

D

Darwin, Charles 18
Decline and Fall of the Roman Empire, The (Gibbon) 16
Dell 161–2
"Dell sucks" 161
Deutsche Bank 5–6, 166, 175, 205
and Libor scandal 98
tax-evasion investigation into 98
Diamond, Bob 5
difference between business continuity management and reputational risk management 138–40

see also business continuity; reputational risk: and business continuity management
Dimon, Jamie 9
Dougan, Brady 4–5
Dow Jones Sustainability Index 90

E

E&S risks, *see* environmental and social risks
Edelmann Trust Barometer 296, 302
EDGAR 56
employer assessment websites 176–8
"Enhancements to the Basel II framework" (BCBS) 75, 118
enterprise risk management (ERM) 106–7
  and TBTFs, poor social performance of 95
Environmental Protection Agency 113
environmental and social (E&S) risks 111–27
  and corporate reputation 115–17
  how banks manage 119–24
  introduced and discussed 112–15
  and reputational risk 117–19
environmental and social risks: managing, implementing framework for 122–4
  outlook 125–6
    external initiatives 126
    internal initiatives 125
    peer initiatives 125–6
Ergo Insurance Group 307

European Banking Authority xx, 74, 80
European Court of Human Rights 179
European Court of Justice (ECJ) 170–2, 179
European Data Protection Directive 170–2
European Investment Bank 269, 271
executive compensation at TBTFs 100
exit polls 304
explanatory panel, reputational risk for banks: soft-commodity trading 114

F

Federal High Court of Germany (Bundesgerichtshof) 170
Federal Swiss Banking Commission 8
figures:
  business continuity management system as cycle *135*
  business continuity management system as workflow *136*
  CEO turnover for two years ahead in US financial firms *60*
  chain of causality from primary risks to the RepRisk P&L effect *251*
  change in board meeting frequency for two years ahead in US financial firms *64*
  change in board size for two years ahead in US financial firms *63*

change-the-bank (CTB) process 257
classification matrix (traffic-light system) 261
core and other stakeholders 249
decision-making pyramid 214
inside-out, outside-in approach 234
non-binding opinion process 240
OpRisk/RepRisk matrix 216
reputation model 150
reputational risk:
　analysis 235
　building awareness of with employees, and establishing risk culture 191
　categorising, in context of risk inventory 189
　considering, in risk-bearing capacity concept 198
　defining 188
　and defining materiality limits 196
　direct versus indirect 283
　embedding, in stress testing 198
　embedding, into organisation 193
　embedding, into risk committee 193
　factors impacting on 40
　framework, structural elements of 213
　governance system 252
　identification 255
　identification and qualitative assessment 194
　implementing early-warning system for 197
　implementing, in risk strategy 190
　including, in risk management/mitigation 199
　including, in transaction/change processes (Global and German Studies) 201
　and key stakeholders 41
　management requirements 254
　measures, monitoring process for 202
　monitoring 241
　overview on impact and resulting losses 276
　prioritising stakeholders within management framework of 192
　registering losses due to 195
　reporting about, to senior management 201
　and reputation 248
　reputational issues management versus 283
　simple radar, example of 222
　survey, overview of 219
　within universe of risks 39
run-the-bank (RTB) classification tables 260
run-the-bank (RTB) process 258
run-the-bank (RTB) questionnaire 259
stakeholder reaction 236, 238
stock performance following corporate governance changes in US financial industry 65

TBTFs, environmental
    performance of: 2001–12 *91*
too-big-to-fail financial
    institutions:
  community performance of:
    2001–12 *92*
  corporate governance
    performance of: 2001–12 *97*
  diversity performance of:
    2001–12 *94*
  environmental performance
    of: 2001–12 *91*
  meeting-employee-
    expectations performance
    of: 2001–12 *93*
  product characteristics
    performance of: 2001–12 *95*
transactions reporting details *242*
turnovers of independent
    directors for two years
    ahead in US financial firms
    62
turnovers of non-CEO executive
    directors for two years ahead
    in US financial firms *61*
UniCredit reputation
    monitoring, overall
    coverage of *147*
Financial Conduct Authority
    (FCA) 310
Financial Services Agency (Japan)
    24
Financial Services Authority (FSA)
    6–7, 98
Financial Stability Board (FSB) 76,
    87
Fombrun, Charles 117, 149
  corporate reputation defined by
    116

Forbes 98
Fortune, annual ratings of 24
Forum on Reputational Risk
    Management in Banking,
    launch of 118
Four Oaks FinCorp (FOFC) 43
Freeman, Edward 88
Friedman, Milton 88
Fukushima 208, 273

G

G-SIBs (global systemically
    important banks) 191, 194,
    197, 200
General Accounting Office 54
General Motors 104
German financial institutions and
    global systemically
    important banks (G-SIBs),
    KPMG's survey into 185–203
  building employee awareness
    and establishing risk culture
    (German study) 190–1, *191*
  categorising RepRisk as material
    in context of risk inventory
    (German study) 188–9, *189*
  conducting risk identification
    and qualitative risk
    assessment? (Global and
    German Studies) 194–5, *194*
  considering RepRisk in concept
    of risk-bearing capacity
    (Global and German
    Studies) 197–8, *198*
  defining materiality limits
    (German study) 196, *196*
  defining reputational risk
    (Global and German
    Studies) 187–8, *188*

embedding RepRisk in stress testing (German study) 198–9, *198*
embedding RepRisk into risk committee (German study) 192–3, *193*
embedding RepRisk into risk organisation (Global and German Studies) 193–4, *193*
fundamentals 187–9, *188*, *189*
governance 189–94, *190*, *191*, *192*, *193*
identification and assessment 194–200, *194*, *195*, *196*, *197*, *198*, *199*
implementing early-warning system (German study) 196–7, *197*
implementing RepRisk in risk strategy (German study) 189–90, *190*
including RepRisk in risk management/mitigation 199–200, *199*
including RepRisk in transaction/change processes (Global and German Studies) 200, *201*
monitoring process for RepRisk measures (German study) 202, *202*
registering losses due to RepRisk (German study) 195, *195*
reporting and monitoring 200–2, *201*, *202*
reporting on RepRisk to senior management (German study) 200–2, *201*
stakeholder prioritisation in RepRisk-management framework (Global and German Studies) 191–2, *192*
Gibbon, Edward 16, 17
Gladiator 15
global financial crisis 14, 89
  banks' reputation during xix
  banks' reputation following 21–3
  and BCBS thinking on reputational risk 75
  roots of, and changing role of reputation 29–33
  stakeholder "disengagement" after 98
global systemically important banks (G-SIBs) and leading German financial institutions, KPMG's survey into 185–203
  building employee awareness and establishing risk culture (German study) 190–1, *191*
  categorising RepRisk as material in context of risk inventory (German study) 188–9, *189*
  conducting risk identification and qualitative risk assessment? (Global and German Studies) 194–5, *194*
  considering RepRisk in concept of risk-bearing capacity (Global and German Studies) 197–8, *198*
  defining materiality limits (German study) 196, *196*
  defining reputational risk (Global and German Studies) 187–8, *188*

319

embedding RepRisk in stress testing (German study) 198–9, *198*
embedding RepRisk into risk committee (German study) 192–3, *193*
embedding RepRisk into risk organisation (Global and German Studies) 193–4, *193*
fundamentals 187–9, *188, 189*
governance 189–94, *190, 191, 192, 193*
identification and assessment 194–200, *194, 195, 196, 197, 198, 199*
implementing early-warning system (German study) 196–7, *197*
implementing RepRisk in risk strategy (German study) 189–90, *190*
including RepRisk in risk management/mitigation 199–200, *199*
including RepRisk in transaction/change processes (Global and German Studies) 200, *201*
monitoring process for RepRisk measures (German study) 202, *202*
registering losses due to RepRisk (German study) 195, *195*
reporting and monitoring 200–2, *201, 202*
reporting on RepRisk to senior management (German study) 200–2, *201*
stakeholder prioritisation in RepRisk-management framework (Global and German Studies) 191–2, *192*
Goldman Sachs 22, 32, 85, 98
Google 161, 169–72
governance 49–68
  corporate, and reputational damage 49–68, *55, 56–7, 58, 60, 61, 62, 63, 64, 65*
  and bad-news announcements 50–3
  and empirical field, levelling 53–6
  and what data can impart 58–67, *58, 65*
corporate, reputational damage 49–68
and oversight of stakeholder issues 95–7; *see also* stakeholder expectations
and RepRisk management, starting point for process of 205–25, *213, 214, 216, 219, 222*
  actors and responsibilities 209–15
  database, categories and risk factors 217–18
  expert-based methods, identification by 218–22
  framework: setting-up of 212–15, *213*
  framework: who should be part of? 209–12
  instruments and processes 215–24
  and need for governance 205–6

outlook 224–5
and regulatory requirements versus stakeholder expectations 206–7
reporting 223–4
scaling/matrices 215–17, *216*
stages of 207–8
stakeholder analysis/dialogue 222–3
status quo, assessing 206–9
strategy 208–9
of reputational risk 285–8
reputational risk, and issues management *286*
reputational risk's need for 205–6
UniCredit's RepRisk system 252–3, *252*
Great Depression 13–14
Great Recession, *see* global financial crisis
Greenberg, Jeff 52–3

H
Hall, Joseph 310
Honey, Garry 25
Hong Kong Monetary Authority xx, 76
HSBC 45

I
IFC Environmental and Social Performance Standards 120–1
IFC Sustainability Framework 115
Infinus 165–6
ING 46
Ing-Diba Bank 159–61
Ingram, Paul 116

Institute of International Finance (IIF) 74
Institute of Operational Risk (IOR) xx
interdependencies between business continuity management and reputational risk management 141–3
see also business continuity; reputational risk: and business continuity management
Internal Capital Adequacy Assessment Process (ICAAP) 247, 251
interfaces to 264–5
International Finance Corporation (IFC) 120
International Organisation for Standardisation (ISO) 132
International Swaps and Derivatives Association (ISDA) 74
Investopedia 99

J
Jarvis, Jeff 161
Jensen, Michael 88–9
Jermier, J. 116
JPMorgan 15–18, 32, 85, 98, 120
and Bear Stearns 28
and "London Whale" 8–9, 22, 44–5, 98

K
Kerviel, Jerome 6
KfW 269, 271
on coal-fired power plants 274

321

King, Mervyn 7
Kirch, Leo 6
KLD 89–94 *passim*, 95–7
Kowalski, Michael J. 113
KPMG, survey of, into G-SIBs and leading German financial institutions 185–203
  building employee awareness and establishing risk culture (German study) 190–1, *191*
  categorising RepRisk as material in context of risk inventory (German study) 188–9, *189*
  conducting risk identification and qualitative risk assessment? (Global and German Studies) 194–5, *194*
  considering RepRisk in concept of risk-bearing capacity (Global and German Studies) 197–8, *198*
  defining materiality limits (German study) 196, *196*
  defining reputational risk (Global and German Studies) 187–8, *188*
  embedding RepRisk in stress testing (German study) 198–9, *198*
  embedding RepRisk into risk committee (German study) 192–3, *193*
  embedding RepRisk into risk organisation (Global and German Studies) 193–4, *193*
  fundamentals 187–9, *188*, *189*
  governance 189–94, *190*, *191*, *192*, *193*
  identification and assessment 194–200, *194*, *195*, *196*, *197*, *198*, *199*
  implementing early-warning system (German study) 196–7, *197*
  implementing RepRisk in risk strategy (German study) 189–90, *190*
  including RepRisk in risk management/mitigation 199–200, *199*
  including RepRisk in transaction/change processes (Global and German Studies) 200, *201*
  monitoring process for RepRisk measures (German study) 202, *202*
  registering losses due to RepRisk (German study) 195, *195*
  reporting and monitoring 200–2, *201*, *202*
  reporting on RepRisk to senior management (German study) 200–2, *201*
  stakeholder prioritisation in RepRisk-management framework (Global and German Studies) 191–2, *192*
"*kriminelle Energie*" 6

L
La Vanguardia 170–1
Lafferty, B. 116
leading German financial institutions and global systemically important

banks (G-SIBs), KPMG's survey into 185–203
building employee awareness and establishing risk culture (German study) 190–1, *191*
categorising RepRisk as material in context of risk inventory (German study) 188–9, *189*
conducting risk identification and qualitative risk assessment? (Global and German Studies) 194–5, *194*
considering RepRisk in concept of risk-bearing capacity (Global and German Studies) 197–8, *198*
defining materiality limits (German study) 196, *196*
defining reputational risk (Global and German Studies) 187–8, *188*
embedding RepRisk in stress testing (German study) 198–9, *198*
embedding RepRisk into risk committee (German study) 192–3, *193*
embedding RepRisk into risk organisation (Global and German Studies) 193–4, *193*
fundamentals 187–9, *188*, *189*
governance 189–94, *190*, *191*, *192*, *193*
identification and assessment 194–200, *194*, *195*, *196*, *197*, *198*, *199*
implementing early-warning system (German study) 196–7, *197*
implementing RepRisk in risk strategy (German study) 189–90, *190*
including RepRisk in risk management/mitigation 199–200, *199*
including RepRisk in transaction/change processes (Global and German Studies) 200, *201*
monitoring process for RepRisk measures (German study) 202, *202*
registering losses due to RepRisk (German study) 195, *195*
reporting and monitoring 200–2, *201*, *202*
reporting on RepRisk to senior management (German study) 200–2, *201*
stakeholder prioritisation in RepRisk-management framework (Global and German Studies) 191–2, *192*
Leeson, Nick 6
legal/compliance risk, and reputational risk 45–6
Lehman Brothers 47, 85
LexisNexis 54
Libor scandal 5, 98, 300, 302
Lincoln, Abraham 11, 19
"London Whale" 8–9, 22, 44–5

M

McGuire, William 52
Machiavelli, Niccolò 17–18
management of reputational risk: and business continuity 129–44, *135*, *136*

323

key drivers and trends within financial industry 130
and controlling processes 278–80
   compliance 279
   corporate governance 279–80
   marketing and communications 278–9
   sustainability 278
direct:
   assessment of 294–5
   and corporate centre, escalation to 295–6
   general strategy 291–2
   process of 291–6
   sensitive areas, establishment of 292
   tolerance for 285
   and triggers, embedding into business processes 293–4
and G-SIBs and leading German financial institutions, KPMG's survey into 185–203
   building employee awareness and establishing risk culture (German study) 190–1, *191*
   categorising RepRisk as material in context of risk inventory (German study) 188–9, *189*
   conducting risk identification and qualitative risk assessment? (Global and German Studies) 194–5, *194*
   considering RepRisk in concept of risk-bearing capacity (Global and German Studies) 197–8, *198*
   defining materiality limits (German study) 196, *196*
   defining reputational risk (Global and German Studies) 187–8, *188*
   embedding RepRisk in stress testing (German study) 198–9, *198*
   embedding RepRisk into risk committee (German study) 192–3, *193*
   embedding RepRisk into risk organisation (Global and German Studies) 193–4, *193*
   fundamentals 187–9, *188*, *189*
   governance 189–94, *190*, *191*, *192*, *193*
   identification and assessment 194–200, *194*, *195*, *196*, *197*, *198*, *199*
   implementing early-warning system (German study) 196–7, *197*
   implementing RepRisk in risk strategy (German study) 189–90, *190*
   including RepRisk in risk management/mitigation 199–200, *199*
   including RepRisk in transaction/change processes (Global and German Studies) 200, *201*
   monitoring process for RepRisk measures (German study) 202, *202*
   registering losses due to RepRisk (German study) 195, *195*

reporting and monitoring
  200–2, *201, 202*
reporting on RepRisk to senior
  management (German
  study) 200–2, *201*
stakeholder prioritisation in
  RepRisk-management
  framework (Global and
  German Studies) 191–2, *192*
in global insurance company
  281–97, *283*
  and context of business and
    risk strategy 284
  and governance 285–8
  outlook 296
  reputation and RepRisk
    defined in context of 282–4
  and reputational risk versus
    reputational issues
    management 283–4
governance as starting point for
  process of 205–25, *213, 214,
  216, 218, 222*
  actors and responsibilities
    209–15
  database, categories and risk
    factors 217–18
  expert-based methods,
    identification by 218–22
  framework: setting-up of
    212–15, *213*
  framework: who should be
    part of? 209–12
  instruments and processes
    215–24
  and management stages
    207–8
  need for 205–6
  outlook 224–5

and regulatory requirements
    versus stakeholder
    expectations 206–7; *see also*
    stakeholder expectations
  reporting 223–4
  scaling/matrices 215–17, *216*
  stakeholder analysis/dialogue
    222–3
  status quo, assessing 206–9
  strategy 208–9
in a group 229
impulse for 227–9
indirect 288–91
  evaluation 290
  monitoring 291
  operational risk control self-
    assessment process 289–90
  reporting 291
  roles and responsibilities for
    management of 286–8
  tolerance for 285
  top risk-assessment process
    288–9
in major European banking
  group (UniCredit), *see*
  UniCredit: reputational risk
  management in
and promotional banks 269–80,
  276
  and stakeholders' reaction
    275–7
reputational issues management
  versus 283–4, *283*
and reputational risk appetite
  and limits 285
and risk tolerance, for direct and
  indirect risk 285
stages of 207–8
strategy for 208–9

in UniCredit 227–43, 234, 235, 236, 238, 240, 241, 242
  assessment methodology 234–6
  holding committees, role of 238–41
  impulse for 227–9
  inside-out, outside-in approach 232–4, 234
  and RepRisk management in a group 229–34
  special policies for specific cases 236–8
  see also reputational risk
Mannesmann 205
market risk, and reputational risk 44–5
Markets in Financial Instruments Directive (MiFID) 114, 160
Marsh & McLennon 52
Mellon Financial 90
  see also Bank of New York Mellon
Merck 26
Merril Lynch 85, 90, 99
Miles, Samantha 88
Minnesota, University of 52
Mitchell, Charles E. 13–15, 16, 17
Morgan Stanley 32, 85, 98

N

National Australia Bank 24
National City Bank of New York (later Citibank) 13
NatWest Markets 3
"New Capital Adequacy Framework, A" (BCBS) 74
New Product Approval Committee 208

New York Times 88
Northern Rock 6–7
Nowitzki, Dirk 159

O

OECD Guidelines for Multinational Enterprises 115
online forums 167–8
operational risk:
  BCBS defines 50, 119
  and reputational risk 40–3

P

Paine, Thomas 19
panel, reputational risk for banks: soft-commodity trading 114
payment protection insurance (PPI) 7
Pebble Mine, Bristol Bay, Alaska 113
Pecora, Ferdinand 14
personal data, compromise of 98–9
Pollock, Timothy G. 115
Ponzi schemes 99
Prince, The (Machiavelli) 17–18
"Principles for Enhancing Corporate Governance" (BCBS) 118
Profumo, Alessandro *147–8*
promotional banks:
  Germany's special set of 271
  and reputational risk 269–80, 276
  stakeholders' reaction 275–7
prudential regulation and reputational risk 73–80
  and critical appraisal 77–9

R

Rentenbank 271
RepRisk radar 221–2, *222*
RepRisk survey (RRS) 212, 218–21, *219*
RepTrak 150–1, *152*
reputation:
  assessment of 149–52, *150*
    method of administration 151
    overall results 152
    questionnaire 152
    and questionnaire administration 151–2
    and Reputation Institute, methodology of 149–51
    target 151
    in UniCredit 146–8; *see also* UniCredit
  balance sheet of *26*
  in banking system, discussed 145–6
  of banks, asset–liability view of 21–34, *26*
    and global financial crisis 29–33
  of banks, during global financial crisis xix
  of banks, following global financial crisis 21–3, 227
  and business continuity management, major factor in 135–8
  changing role of, and roots of global financial crisis 29–33
  compartmentalisation of 5
  and culture, brand and trust 301–5
    and state of the nation 303–5
  fatal nature of loss of 3
  history's lessons to bankers on 11–19
    and Caesar 15–17
    and Darwin 18
    and Machiavelli 17–18
    and Paine 19
  as key asset xix
  long-term economic benefits of 27
  and management of perception at UniCredit 145–54, *147*
    assessment 146–8, 149–52
    organisational response 148–9
    and results, managing of, and action planning 152–4
  regulation influences relevance of 33
  and reputational risk, definition of 282–4
  trust intimately tied to 86
  UBS's cavalier attitude towards 8
  see also reputational crises; reputational risk
Reputation Institute 98, 146
  methodology of 149–51
  RepTrak model of 150–1
"reputational bankruptcy" 25
reputational consequence management 299–311
  future of 305–10
    assessment 307–8
    crisis management 308–9
    education 306–7
    stakeholder response 309–10
    strategy 305–6
  and getting it right first time 310–11
  reputation, culture, brand and trust 301–5

when unacceptable becomes
commonplace 299–301
and social-media era 301
reputational crises, recovery from
157–83
final checklist and dos and
don'ts concerning 182–3
and illegitimate claims 163–5
dos and don'ts 165
and individual cases 165–78
AWD 173–4
Bank of Scotland 175
and blogs 173–5
and corporate social
responsibility (CSR)
standards 178
Deutsche Bank 166, 175
and employer assessment
websites 176–8
and forums 167–8
Infinus 166
press 168–9
and review platforms
175–6
search engines – index and
auto-suggest 169–72
Sparkasse Berlin 175
and tests and (private)
institutes 172–3
legal perspective on 158–9
and legitimate claims 159–62
Dell case 161–2
dos and don'ts 162
Ing-Diba Bank case 159–61
and trials, hidden advantages of
179
and urgency 164
see also reputation; reputational
damage; reputational risk

reputational damage:
corporate-governance changes
following 49–68, *55, 56–7,
58, 60, 61, 62, 63, 64, 65*
and bad-news announcements
50–3
and empirical field, levelling
53–6
and what data can impart
58–67, *58, 65*
see also reputational crises,
recovery from
Reputational Risk Committee 208
reputational risk management:
and business continuity 129–44,
135, 136
key drivers and trends within
financial industry 130
and controlling processes 278–80
compliance 279
corporate governance 279–80
marketing and
communications 278–9
sustainability 278
direct:
assessment of 294–5
and corporate centre,
escalation to 295–6
general strategy 291–2
process of 291–6
sensitive areas, establishment
of 292
tolerance for 285
and triggers, embedding into
business processes 293–4
and G-SIBs and leading German
financial institutions,
KPMG's survey into
185–203

building employee awareness and establishing risk culture (German study) 190–1, *191*
categorising RepRisk as material in context of risk inventory (German study) 188–9, *189*
conducting risk identification and qualitative risk assessment? (Global and German Studies) 194–5, *194*
considering RepRisk in concept of risk-bearing capacity (Global and German Studies) 197–8, *198*
defining materiality limits (German study) 196, *196*
defining reputational risk (Global and German Studies) 187–8, *188*
embedding RepRisk in stress testing (German study) 198–9, *198*
embedding RepRisk into risk committee (German study) 192–3, *193*
embedding RepRisk into risk organisation (Global and German Studies) 193–4, *193*
fundamentals 187–9, *188*, *189*
governance 189–94, *190*, *191*, *192*, *193*
identification and assessment 194–200, *194*, *195*, *196*, *197*, *198*, *199*
implementing early-warning system (German study) 196–7, *197*
implementing RepRisk in risk strategy (German study) 189–90, *190*
including RepRisk in risk management/mitigation 199–200, *199*
including RepRisk in transaction/change processes (Global and German Studies) 200, *201*
monitoring process for RepRisk measures (German study) 202, *202*
registering losses due to RepRisk (German study) 195, *195*
reporting and monitoring 200–2, *201*, *202*
reporting on RepRisk to senior management (German study) 200–2, *201*
stakeholder prioritisation in RepRisk-management framework (Global and German Studies) 191–2, *192*
in global insurance company 281–97, *283*
and context of business and risk strategy 284
and governance 285–8
outlook 296
reputation and RepRisk defined in context of 282–4
and reputational risk versus reputational issues management 283–4
governance as starting point for process of 205–25, *213*, *214*, *216*, *218*, *222*

329

actors and responsibilities
209–15
database, categories and risk
factors 217–18
expert-based methods,
identification by 218–22
framework: setting-up of
212–15, *213*
framework: who should be
part of? 209–12
instruments and processes
215–24
and management stages
207–8
need for 205–6
outlook 224–5
and regulatory requirements
versus stakeholder
expectations 206–7; *see also*
stakeholder expectations
reporting 223–4
scaling/matrices 215–17, *216*
stakeholder analysis/dialogue
222–3
status quo, assessing 206–9
strategy 208–9
in a group 229
impulse for 227–9
indirect 288–91
evaluation 290
monitoring 291
operational risk control self-
assessment process 289–90
reporting 291
roles and responsibilities for
management of 286–8
tolerance for 285
top risk-assessment process
288–9

in major European banking
group (UniCredit), *see*
UniCredit: reputational risk
management in
and promotional banks 269–80,
276
and stakeholders' reaction
275–7
reputational issues management
versus 283–4, *283*
and reputational risk appetite
and limits 285
and risk tolerance, for direct and
indirect risk 285
stages of 207–8
strategy for 208–9
in UniCredit 227–43, *234*, *235*,
236, *238*, *240*, *241*, *242*
assessment methodology 234–6
holding committees, role of
238–41
impulse for 227–9
inside-out, outside-in
approach 232–4, *234*
and RepRisk management in a
group 229–34
special policies for specific
cases 236–8
see also reputational risk
reputational risk (RepRisk):
asset–liability view of:
and banks' reputation during
global financial crisis xix
and banks' reputation
following global financial
crisis 21–3
BCBS defines 23, 75
BCBS provides detailed
definition of 118

and business continuity
    management; *see also*
    business continuity:
    commonalities between 140–1
    difference between 138–40, *139*
*Commercial Bank Examination
    Manual* defines 38
in context of universe of risks
    37–48, *39*
    credit risk 43–4
    legal/compliance risk 45–6
    market risk 44–5
    operational risk 40–3
and corporate governance,
    changes to 49–68, *55*, *56–7*,
    58, *60*, *61*, *62*, *63*, *64*, *65*
    and bad-news announcements
    50–3
    and empirical field, levelling
    53–6
    what data can impart 58–67
and credit risk 43–4
as disputed term 299
as emerging topic xix
environmental and social (E&S)
    risks from perspective of
    111–27
    corporate reputation 115–17
    and how banks manage
    119–24
    implementing framework
    122–4
    introduced and discussed
    112–15
factors impacting on *40*
Fed defines 38
Goldman Sachs and SBC
    Warburg Dillon Read book
    defines 4

identification and assessment of,
    at UniCredit 254–62, *255*
    change-the-bank (CTB)
    approach 254–6, *257*
    evaluation 261–2
    and IT system 262–3
    mitigation and reporting 263–4
    run-the-bank questionnaire
    and assignment of
    stakeholders 258–61, *259*
    run-the-bank (RTB) approach
    254–62, *258*
impact of, evaluation 290
impact of, on other risks 46–7
introduced and discussed 3–10
key stakeholders *41*
and legal/compliance risk 45–6
lessons from history concerning
    11–19
    and Caesar 15–17
    and Darwin 18
    and Machiavelli 17–18
    and Paine 19
    Smith, and bankers'
        "contempt of risk" 11–14
and market risk 44–5
and need for governance 205–6
now seen as dedicated risk
    discipline xix
and operational risk 40–3
primary objective of
    management of xx
and prudential regulation 73–80
    critical appraisal 77–9
and reputation, definition of
    282–4
as "reputational consequence
    management" (*q.v.*) 299
and soft-commodity trading 114

stages of managing 207–8
UniCredit mitigation and reporting 263–4
  change the bank: embedded risk mitigation 263
  and Internal Capital Adequacy Assessment Process, interfaces to 264–5
  reporting 264
  run the bank: *ex post* risk mitigation 263
  second-level controls 263–4
UniCredit process, overview 250–1
UniCredit's definitions of 247–51
  and links to other risk types 249–50
  and profit-and-loss effect 247–8
  and stakeholders 248–9, *249*
  see also reputation; reputational crises; reputational risk management
review platforms 175–6
Rights of Man (Paine) 19
risk management, and governance and appetite 100–3
RiskMetrics 89
risks:
  reputation in context of 37–48, *39*
  universe of 37–40, *39*
Royal Bank of Scotland (RBS) 7
Ruggie, John 122

S

Salz review of Barclays 7–8
satisfaction surveys 304
Scientology 170
search engines – index and auto-suggest 169–72
Senate Banking Committee 14
Senate Commission of Manufactures 17
Senate Subcommittee on Investigations 5, 9
shareholder wealth and corporate governance 99–103
  and executive compensation at TBTFs 100
Smith, Adam 11–14
  "perfect liberty" concept of 12
Social Darwinism 18
Société Générale 6
Socrates 14, 305
Solvency II 284
Spanish Data Protection Agency (Agencia Española de Protección de Datos) (AEPD) 170–1
Sparkasse Berlin 175
Spencer, Herbert 18
stakeholder expectations 85–109, *91*, *92*, *93*, *94*, *95*, *97*, *101*, *102*
  and corporate governance and shareholder wealth 99–103
  and executive compensation at TBTFs 100
  and risk management, governance and appetite 100–3
  and corporate objective function 88–9
  and engagement, and financial institutions 88–99
  financial crisis points to failure in meeting 89

regulatory requirements versus 206–7
and reputation, going forward 103–7
  enterprise risk management 106–7
  governance remedies 104–6
  resolution 103–4
  and TBTFs; *see also* too-big-to-fail financial institutions:
  and governance and oversight 95–7
  and outcomes 90–5
Standard Chartered 46
  and E&S risk 120
State Police and Federal Financial Supervisory Authority 165–6
State Street 85
Stiftung Warentest 172
Stock Market Crash 1929, *see* Great Depression
Stulz, R. 100
Sunbeam 26

T
tables:
  bad-news announcements in US financial industry *55, 58*
  bad-news announcements, reputational damage and corporate governance changes in US financial industry: tested variables *56–7*
  business continuity management versus reputational risk *139*
  cashout by CEO 2000–8 *101*
  reputational balance sheet *26*
  reputational risk versus business continuity management *139*
  too-big-to-fail financial institutions, board characteristics of: 2014 *102*
TBTFs (too-big-to-fail financial institutions) 85
  bailouts of 89
  board characteristics of: 2014 *102*
  community performance of: 2001–12 *92*
  corporate governance performance of: 2001–12 *97*
  diversity performance of: 2001–12 *94*
  environmental performance of: 2001–12 *91*
  executive compensation at 100
  meeting-employee-expectations performance of: 2001–12 *93*
  pre-financial-crisis directors on boards of 105
  product characteristics performance of: 2001–12 *95*
  and stakeholder expectations and outcomes 90–5
  unwieldiness of 106
Ted Spread 87
"10 Most Shameful Bank Scandals of 2013" (*Investopedia*) 99
third-party payment processors (TPPPs) 42–3
Thun Group of Banks 122
Tiffany & Co. 113
tone-at-the-top corporate governance mechanisms 49, 50, 52

333

too-big-to-fail financial institutions (TBTFs) 85
  bailouts of 89
  board characteristics of: 2014 *102*
  community performance of: 2001–12 *92*
  corporate governance performance of: 2001–12 *97*
  diversity performance of: 2001–12 *94*
  environmental performance of: 2001–12 *91*
  executive compensation at 100
  meeting-employee-expectations performance of: 2001–12 *93*
  pre-financial-crisis directors on boards of 105
  product characteristics performance of: 2001–12 *95*
  and stakeholder expectations and outcomes 90–5
  unwieldiness of 106
Toyota 302
TPPPs (third-party payment processors) 42–3

U

UBS 269
  and E&S risk 120
  and Libor scandal 98
UN Food and Agricultural Organization 114
UN Global Compact, 10 principles of 115
UN Guiding Principles on Business and Human Rights 122
UniCredit:
  business continuity management system in 132–5
    awareness 134
    planning 133–4
    programme management 132
    strategy 133
    test maintenance and monitoring 134
    understanding organisation 133
  Corporate Sustainability and Media Relations Department of 233
  group approach, implementation of 245–67
    identification and assessment 254–62
    management process 250–1, *254*
    and RepRisk definitions 247–51
    and RepRisk governance system 252–3, *252*
  Group Operational & Reputational Risks Committee (GORRIC) in 238–9
  Group Risk Committee in 238–9, 241
  Group Stakeholder and Service Intelligence Department in 148–9, 153, 154
  Group Transactional Committee (GTC) in 239
  Human Resources Department in 233
  Investor Relations Department in 233
  Management Body of 229–30
  Management Identity and Communications Department in 148

RepRisk definitions of 247–51
  and links to other risk types 249–50
  and profit-and-loss effect 247–8
  and stakeholders 248–9, *249*
RepRisk identification and assessment 254–62, *255*
  change-the-bank (CTB) approach 254–6, *257*
  evaluation 261–2
  and IT system 262–3
  mitigation and reporting 263–4
  run-the-bank questionnaire and assignment of stakeholders 258–61, *259*
  run-the-bank (RTB) approach 254–62, *258*
RepRisk management process of, overview 250–1
RepRisk mitigation and reporting 263–4
  change the bank: embedded risk mitigation 263
  and Internal Capital Adequacy Assessment Process, interfaces to 264–5
  reporting 264
  run the bank: *ex post* risk mitigation 263
  second-level controls 263–4
reputational risk management in 227–43, *234, 235, 236, 238, 240, 241, 242*
  assessment methodology 234–6
  and group management 229–34
  holding committees, role of 238–41
  impulse for 227–9
  inside-out, outside-in approach 232–4, *234*
  special policies for specific cases 236–8
  Strategic Supervisory Body of 229–30
  tracking reputation and management of perception at 145–54, *147*
  assessment 146–8, 149–52
  organisational response 148–9
  and results, managing of, and action planning 152–4
Union Bank of Switzerland (UBS) 3, 8
UnitedHealth 52
US banking system, lack of trust in 87
use test 224, 307

V
VÖB (Association of German Public Banks) 271–2

W
Wachovia bank 42
Washington, George 19
Waste Management 26
"We Are Singular Incidents" ("*Wir sind Einzelfall*") 160–1
Wealth of Nations (Smith) 11–13
weblogs 173–5, 231, 301, 309
Weidner, David 28
Wells Fargo 42, 85
"*Wir sind Einzelfall*" ("We Are Singular Incidents") 160–1

Works of Julius Caesar, The (Julius Caesar) 15–16
World Bank Group 115, 120, 270
World Check 218
World Development Movement 114

Y

Yue, Lori Qingyuan 116